OUTSTANDING DISSERTATIONS IN

LINGUISTICS

I0883365

edited by

LAURENCE HORN
YALE UNIVERSITY

EVENT SEMANTICS OF VERB FRAME ALTERNATIONS

A Case Study of Dutch and Its Acquisition

ANGELIEK VAN HOUT

Routledge
Taylor & Francis Group
LONDON AND NEW YORK

First published 1998 by Garland Publishing, Inc.

2 Park Square, Milton Park, Abingdon, Oxon OX14 4RN
711 Third Avenue, New York, NY 10017, USA

Routledge is an imprint of the Taylor & Francis Group, an informa business

First issued in paperback 2016

Copyright © 1998 Angeliek van Hout

All rights reserved. No part of this book may be reprinted or reproduced or utilised in any form or by any electronic, mechanical, or other means, now known or hereafter invented, including photocopying and recording, or in any information storage or retrieval system, without permission in writing from the publishers.

Notice:
Product or corporate names may be trademarks or registered trademarks, and are used only for identification and explanation without intent to infringe.

Library of Congress Cataloging-in-Publication Data

Hout, Angeliek van.
Event semantics of verb frame alternations : a case study of Dutch and its acquisition / Angeliek van Hout.
p. cm. — (Outstanding dissertations in linguistics)
A slight revision of the author's thesis (doctoral)—Tilburg University, 1996.
Includes bibliographical references and index.
ISBN 0-8153-3128-2 (alk. paper)
1. Dutch language—Verb. 2. Dutch language—Acquisition. 3. Dutch language—Semantics. 4. Children—Language. I. Title. II. Series.
PF271.H68 1998
439.31'5—dc21

98-27009

ISBN 978-0-8153-3128-5 (hbk)
ISBN 978-1-138-96918-6 (pbk)

Contents

Preface

This book is a minimally updated version of my 1996 PhD thesis submitted to the Linguistics Department at Tilburg University (the Netherlands). Writing the preface to my dissertation for the second time now gives me an opportunity to thank a couple of crucial people in my linguistic life again. There are three people I would like to single out: Henk van Riemsdijk, my first teacher of linguistics and *promotor* (head of the dissertation committee), Jürgen Weissenborn, my first teacher of language acquisition and Marco Haverkort, my first adviser in linguistics who suggested I submit the manuscript to this Garland series. Martin Everaert and Joe Emonds followed the research leading to this dissertation with interest and sharp comments. Bart Hollebrandse, Janet Randall and Harald Baayen, as well as Jürgen Weissenborn, were collaborators in the two acquisition projects I report on here. Thanks again to all of them, as well as to my colleagues and friends at the three places where I was affiliated with while working on the research and its write-up: the Linguistics Department at Tilburg University, The Max-Planck Institute of Psycholinguistics in Nijmegen and the Linguistics Department at the University of Massachusetts at Amherst. I also thank my quick and careful proofreaders David Holton and Mike Dickey.

In addition I want to thank the Institute of Research in Cognitive Science at the University of Pennsylvania, its staff and my colleagues and friends here for their support during the reformatting, editing and printing of the present version.

Final and most important thanks go to my parents and my brother Hein for their love and care all along, and especially to Bart whose unconditional love, support and suffering at mental, intellectual and practical levels were essential for turning this dissertation project to a good end.

The book is organized as follows. After introducing the state of the art of research on the lexicon and its interface to syntax, I present a study of Dutch verbs and verb frame alternations on the basis of which the exact ingredients for the mapping model and its design will be distilled. I then discuss the consequences of this mapping model for acquisition applying the insights in two case studies of Dutch verb-learning.

Since the early eighties, various theories on the lexicon-syntax interface have been proposed that analyze and explain the links between a verb's lexical specification and its appearance in one or more verb frames. **Chapter 1** reviews several models and serves as the theoretical background for the research presented in the dissertation.

Almost every verb appears in several different verb frames; they figure in so-called *verb frame alternations*. **Chapter 2** presents an overview of the variety of different types of verb frame alternations in Dutch. In **Chapter 3**, I examine the phenomenon of verb frame alternations viewing a verb's arguments as participants in the event referred to by the verb. It turns out that the great variety of alternations can be reduced to only three kinds: one set of alternations involves an atelic-telic event type-shift, another involves causativization and the third kind are alternations in which the two alternants present different foci on the same event. Analyzing how event type properties determine onto which syntactic position a particular event participant is mapped, two mapping generalizations are then formulated: (i) a telic event type requires the projection of an argument in direct object position; (ii) a causative event type requires the projection of arguments in both subject and direct object position. A verb's flexibility is thus directly related to event types and event-type shifting: different event types define different mappings.

Standard theories of the lexicon-syntax interface define the mapping relation by associating a verb's arguments, which are lexically listed as θ-roles, lexical-conceptual variables or bare variables, with positions in the syntactic configuration projected by the verb. Chapter 3 concludes, however, that an interface theory must be framed in terms of a relation between event types and verb frames. In **Chapter 4**, I develop such a theory, embedding it in the framework of the Minimalist Program. After presenting several kinds of problems with the standard view on the mapping relation, I extensively discuss the nature of the lexical primitives. I conclude that the mapping system needs to "see" a verb's basic event type and the number of participants that are involved in the event; it does not need any further semantic specification of the participants, nor any other verb-specific information. Assuming that a verb's event structure must be syntactically identified, I define the mapping relation in the so-called CHESS model as follows: mapping involves checking event-semantic features in the syntactic configuration. Arguments in the specifier positions of AgrS and AgrO identify an event or subevent as they are interpreted as participants in the event or subevent. In particular, telicity features must checked off in object position via strong Case assignment in AgrOP. The CHESS model naturally accounts for the event-semantic mapping generalizations from Chapter 3, explaining the phenomenon of lexical-syntactic flexibility as a derivative of event type-shifting.

In the last two chapters, I address verbs and their verb frames from the point of view of the child who is in the process of acquiring her language. A child learning the verbs of her language must not only acquire their meanings, but also the event-semantic features that determine the range of verb frames each verb can appear in. One question to ask is how does a child learn the meanings and the lexical features of the new verbs she is learning? Another is how does she acquire the mapping system between lexicon and syntax? Discussing these questions against the background assumptions on the lexicon-syntax interface as defined by the CHESS model, I present two case studies of verb learning: one concerns so-called *light verbs*; the other concentrates on intransitive verbs.

Assuming that verbs are characterized in the lexicon with their event types, I argue in **Chapter 5** that light verbs (e.g., *geven* 'give' in a light verb construction such as *een kus geven* 'give a kiss') are easy verbs to acquire, because they are pure event type denoters. In a longitudinal study of four Dutch children, I find support for this prediction. From early on, these children produce a great variety of light verb constructions, including also some overgeneralized ones. Looking at their light verb usage and evaluating the nature of their overgeneralized constructions, I conclude that child Dutch presents evidence for a basic claim of the CHESS model, namely that verbs are lexically characterized in terms of their event types.

In **Chapter 6**, I discuss the acquisition of intransitive verbs. Although intransitive verbs all appear with a single argument in subject position, the class splits up into two distinct subclasses which differ from each other in their further syntactic behavior: so-called unergative versus unaccusative verbs. Intransitive verbs pose an intriguing acquisition problem: how can a child find out that there are two different subclasses when they look so similar at the surface? Moreover, how does she determine to which subclass a new verb belongs? The results of an experimental study that aimed at finding out if two semantic factors, *telicity* and *agentivity*, determine unaccusativity in Dutch show that subjects (4 and 5 year-olds, 7 and 8 year-olds and a control group of adults) are able to split up novel intransitive verbs in two subclasses. Even the youngest children distinguish two classes which is evidence in favor of the Strong Continuity hypothesis on language development. Furthermore, the split is defined by telicity alone; agentivity does not play a role. These results present evidence for another claim of the CHESS model, namely that mapping is defined on the event-semantic properties of verbs.

The main ideas of the CHESS model have been presented in earlier work, in particular, in van Hout (1991a,b, 1992a,b, 1993, 1994) and have been laid down in full detail in my dissertation (van Hout 1996). The acquisition research discussed in Chapters 5 and 6 is based on joint research. The study on the acquisition of light verbs is joint work with Bart Hollebrandse and has appeared as Hollebrandse & van Hout (1995, 1996, 1998). The research on the acquisition of intransitive verbs was carried out in a project at the Max-Planck Institute for Psycholinguistics, Nijmegen (1992-1994) and was sponsored by the Deutsche Forschungsgemeinschaft (grant #WE-1236-2-2) and the Max-Planck Forschungspreis to Jürgen Weissenborn. My colleagues in this project are Harald Baayen,

Janet Randall and Jürgen Weissenborn; the work has been presented in van Hout, Randall & Weissenborn (1993) and Randall, van Hout, Weissenborn & Baayen (1994). Since finishing the dissertation, I have applied the insights of the CHESS model to applicative constructions in collaboration with Marco Haverkort (see van Hout & Haverkort 1995) and to deverbal nominalizations in collaboration with Thomas Roeper (see van Hout & Roeper 1998).

Philadelphia, May 1998

Event Semantics of Verb Frame Alternations

CHAPTER 1

Lexicon Theories: State of the Art

This chapter reviews various models of the lexicon-syntax interface that have been proposed since the early eighties. Interface models analyze and explain the links between a verb's lexical specification and its appearance in verb frames. There are two major issues an interface model has to address: (i) Which features are relevant in the interface and how can they be formalized? (ii) How does the mapping algorithm associate these features with verb frames? On top of these basic issues comes the need to deal with a verb's flexible behavior, i.e., the phenomenon that it can appear in various frames. Several kinds of lexical specification have been proposed, ranging from subcategorization frames to θ-roles and from argument structures to lexical-conceptual and lexical-relational structures. Various kinds of mapping systems have been proposed as well, ranging from principles of projection and linking and procedures of θ-role assignment to mapping governed by aspectual considerations. Verbs' flexible behavior challenges lexicon-syntax models. Some models resolve this challenge by locating flexibility in the lexicon, i.e., via lexical rules; others deal with it as a syntactic phenomenon, i.e., the outcome of movement.

1.1 Goals of this chapter

In this chapter, I introduce the issues at play in the lexicon-syntax interface. Essentially, an interface theory defines how a verb's lexical specification determines the ways this verb appears in syntactic configurations. This is the so-called *mapping problem*; it is presented in section 1.2.

In the remainder of the chapter, I will discuss the main proponents of different views on the lexicon and the lexicon-syntax interface, thereby reviewing various concepts of lexical specification and various systems of mapping lexical information onto syntax (section 1.3). This review will serve as background for the research presented in this dissertation. It will be a point of departure for pointing out other lexical features that are relevant to mapping (see Chapter 3) and developing a new model of lexicon-syntax mapping (see Chapter 4). The empirical motivation of the new mapping system lies in the phenomenon of verbal flexibility. In section 1.4, I present various analyses of and approaches to this phenomenon.

Deviating from existing models and taking a different approach to flexibility, I will remodel the lexicon-syntax interface, using the Dutch data discussed in Chapters 2 and 3 as the empirical basis. The overview of the state of the art of the research on argument structure in this chapter will thus serve as a resonator against which my view on lexical specification and mapping can be evaluated.

1.2 The mapping problem

Basically, mapping is a relation between the verbal lexicon and a small set of syntactic configurations sentences can be made up of, (1).

(1) Mapping is a relation between the verbal lexicon and syntax:

		Mapping	
Verbal	$V_{1[..]}$	↔	**Syntax**
lexicon	$V_{2[..]}$		_ SU
	$V_{3[..]}$		_ SU OBL
	$V_{4[..]}$		_ SU DO
	$V_{5[..]}$		_ SU DO OBL
	...		_ DO
	$V_{y[..]}$		_ DO OBL
	$V_{z[..]}$		

If the verbal lexicon is viewed as a very large set of verbal meanings, each with its own specification, indicated with [..] in (1), then mapping relates each lexical specification to one or more verb frames. The set of verb frames is a small set of six or so different D-structure configurations, differing in the number and location of their argument positions. Six different types of verb frames are illustrated in (1) as various subcategorization frames; these must be seen as shorthand for different D-structure trees.

SU stands for subject position, typically the argument position outside of and predicated of by VP, or, alternatively, the specifier of V position in the VP internal Subject Hypothesis (see Koopman & Sportiche 1988). *DO* stands for direct object position, traditionally the argument position that is a sister of and directly governed by V, or, alternatively, the specifier position of the lower V in a VP-shell structure (see Larson 1988). *OBL* stands for the position for the oblique argument, i.e., the indirect object or PP complement. I use *OBL* as a neutral term to refer to the position the indirect internal argument is mapped onto in the syntatic configuration. There are many proposals as to where that position is situated: as a second sister of V in a ternary branching V' (Oehrle 1976), as a sister of V' (Chomsky 1981), within a small clause (SC) complement of V (Kayne 1984) or as sister of the lower V in a VP-shell structure (Larson 1988).[1]

The picture in (1) represents an abstract picture of the relation between lexicon and syntax. It is independent of how one formalizes lexical primitives and mapping, or of which syntactic configurations one chooses as the frames verbs can map onto. In fact, the picture is often more sophisticated, as several theories assume an intermediate level between lexicon and syntax: the level of argument structure. In these theories the mapping system splits up in a two-part algorithm (see (11) below): one part relates the lexical-semantic specifications and different argument structures, the so-called *linking rules*; the other part argument structures and syntactic configurations, the so-called *projection rules*.

A theory of mapping then links verbal specifications in the lexical domain to frames (or configurations) in the syntactic domain. In more prosaic terms, a verb's lexical specification goes through a mapping "transformer" and comes out with a syntactic configuration with a certain number of argument positions. The mapping relation is complicated by the fact that one and the same verb can appear in more than one frame; I will refer to this phenomenon as *lexical-syntactic flexibility*. Lexical-syntactic flexibility can be pictured in (1) as a one-to-many relation between verbal meanings and verb frames. The mapping problem is this: how does a verb's lexical specification transform into a set of syntactic configurations?

1.3 Lexical primitives and mapping theories

In many of the present-day theories, the mapping from lexical information onto syntax is exclusively and exhaustively determined by the lexical-semantic arguments of the verb. Projection of different syntactic configurations, i.e., the various frames, depends on the number and kinds of a verb's arguments. Each verb is lexically characterized with a certain number of various kinds of arguments. The mapping algorithm more or less directly "translates" the lexical-semantic structure to a syntactic structure. I will refer to such systems as *argument-centered* mapping approaches.

The argument-centered conception has been formalized in a number of different ways. Theories differ in their assumptions about what kind of information about the arguments must be specified in a lexical entry. Basically, there are three major semantic kinds of lexical primitives: θ-roles listed in a θ-grid, arguments ordered in an argument structure and variables in lexical conceptual structures. Furthermore, there is one syntactic kind of lexical primitive: subcategorization frames. I will discuss their properties and the mapping algorithms defined on them in subsection 1.3.1.

In recent years, however, there have been other views around. The basic motivation behind these alternatives is that an argument-centered perspective misses important mapping generalizations as it turns out that other semantic features play a role as well, in particular event type features. In subsection 1.3.2, I will discuss how aspectual considerations play a role in three of these alternative theories: Tenny's (1987, 1994) aspectual interface hypothesis, Grimshaw's (1990) theory of aspectual prominence and the associations between argument structure and event structure and Hale & Keyser's (1992, 1993) lexical-relational structures and their association with different event types.

1.3.1 Argument-centered mapping

Subcategorization frames

The traditional kind of formalization of a verb's arguments is of a completely syntactic nature. It specifies verbs for their subcategorization frames (see Chomsky 1965). A subcategorization frame specifies the number of complements a verb takes, the syntactic category of those complements and whether they are optional or obligatory. Additional selection restrictions further specify the semantics of the complements. Consider transitive *drink* in (2a) and ditransitive *put* in (2b) with subcategorization frames (adopting the notation used by Emonds 1991a).

(2)	a.	*drink*	V,	[_ (NP "liquid")]
	b.	*put*	V,	[_ NP "object" PP "location"]

The lines in (2) indicate the position of the verb, NP and PP indicate the category of the complements and the semantic notions in quotes indicate selection restrictions on these complements. The brackets around the NP complement in (2a) indicate optionality of the object of *drink*; the absence of such brackets in (2b) implies obligatoriness of both complements of *put*. Notice that subjects are not mentioned in subcategorization frames; they do not require subcategorization as the subject position always needs to be projected. A subcategorization frame contains purely syntactic information in a lexical shorthand notation; it translates directly to a syntactic projection. Hence, mapping is a trivial operation.

Throughout all of his research, Emonds explores in great depth the notion of subcategorization frame and shows applications of its use for a large number of affixes and syntactic constructions (cf. Emonds 1976, 1985, 1987, 1991a,b, 1992).

θ-roles

Gruber (1965) has introduced the concept of *thematic relations* to examine the semantic relations involved in interpreting the NP arguments of verbs. Gruber considers the theme of a sentence to be the central and fundamental semantic notion, hence, his term *thematic relations*. He claims that every sentence has a noun phrase that functions as a theme, defining a theme as the NP understood as undergoing motion (with verbs of physical and abstract location). He furthermore distinguishes the relations of *agent*, *location*, *goal* and *source* (among others). Various people have proposed variations on the set of semantic relations and the ways they are relevant for and play a role in syntax. The concept has developed via Fillmore's (1968) Case roles, Jackendoff's (1972) derivation of thematic relations from underlying, more elementary lexical predicates to Chomsky's (1981) θ-roles.

Chomsky (1981) assumes that verbs are specified with both a subcategorization frame and a list of θ-roles. Mapping is still trivial as it is lexically defined for each verb in its subcategorization frame(s). However, the addition of θ-roles to the lexical specification requires an additional interface system, as the θ-roles need to be associated with the verb's arguments in a syntactic configuration. The additional system is θ-assignment. θ-Assignment is governed by general syntactic principles, including the Projection Principle and the θ-Criterion. The Projection Principle ensures that a verb minimally θ-marks the complements it subcategorizes for, plus, possibly, the subject position; the θ-Criterion imposes a strict one-to-one association between θ-roles and argument positions. Consider *drink* and *put* again, (3).

(3)	a.	*drink*	V,	{Agent, Theme}
				[_ (NP "liquid")]
	b.	*put*	V,	{Agent, Theme, Goal}
				[_ NP "object" PP "location"]

Grimshaw (1979, 1981) brings up the issue of whether a verb needs to lexically specify both the syntactic and semantic information of its arguments, or, alternatively, whether one can be derived from the other. Opting for the latter, simpler and less redundant alternative, she claims that categorial information can be derived from semantic specification. The simpler, alternative is also attractive because it reduces the learning task for the child acquiring her verbal lexicon. The issue has come to be known as *c- versus s-selection*: c-selection stands for categorial selection, i.e., subcategorization, and s-selection for semantic selection, i.e., θ-roles. Following up on Grimshaw's (1981) and Pesetsky's (1982) ideas, Chomsky (1986) also takes the position that c-selection can be predicted from s-selection: verbs only need to be specified for a list of θ-roles. He thus reduces ". . . syntactic representations at D-structure to projections of semantic properties of lexical items" (Chomsky 1986:90), assuming that " . . . D-structure is a "pure" representation of theta structure, where all and only the θ-positions are filled by arguments . . . " (Chomsky 1986:98). Hence, the lexical representations of, for example, *drink* and *put* become simpler, (3a.b).

(4)	a.	*drink*	V,	{Agent, Theme}
	b.	*put*	V,	{Agent, Theme, Goal}

Even though most people these days opt for s-selection as their lexical basis, the choice between c- versus s-selection is still an issue for ongoing debate. Emonds (1991a, 1992) draws renewed attention to the c- versus s-selection debate. He argues forcefully against any form of s-selection as a useful form of lexical specification and opts for c-selection as the sole basis for lexical selection, i.e., subcategorization frames which he extends with a small set of features.[2] Advocating a purely syntactic approach to predicate-argument relations, formulated as the principle of Semantic Atomism, Emonds (1991a) then proposes a set of general principles of θ-role interpretation that are defined on syntactic configurations.[3] Jackendoff (1993) takes up Emonds' challenge and argues in favor of lexical specification in terms of lexical-conceptual structures (see below).

In an s-selection approach to the lexicon, mapping is no longer trivial: some algorithm is needed to associate θ-roles to certain positions of a certain categorial nature in the syntactic D-structure configuration. As for the transformation into categorial information, Chomsky (1986) employs the notion *canonical structural realization*: " . . . if a verb (or other head) s-selects a semantic category C, then it selects a syntactic category that is the "canonical structural realization of C" (CSR (C))" (Chomsky 1986:87). This realization may differ across languages.[4]

The other element the mapping algorithm needs to specify is how θ-roles are mapped onto specific structural positions, i.e., the issue of so-called *argument alignment*. If one adheres strictly to s-selection as the sole form of lexical specification, it cannot be stipulated along with a θ-grid in the lexicon. Rather, it must be generated from the θ-roles; at least, it should be in the unmarked case. There are two possible sets of alignment principles: alignment either follows a strict pattern of associations, or the patterns of associations are relativized.

Employing the basic insight of Perlmutter & Postal's (1984) Universal Alignment Hypothesis, Baker (1988) strictly maps an argument with a particular θ-role onto a particular syntactic position. The θ-role labels themselves, i.e., the actual thematic contents of the arguments, play a crucial role in the mapping system. Baker assumes that " . . . identical thematic relationships between items are represented by identical structural relationships between those items at the level of D-structure" (Baker 1988:46). This view is formulated in his Uniformity of Theta Assignment Hypothesis (UTAH). For example, if a verb selects an agent and a theme, the agent argument will always map onto subject position and the theme onto direct object position.

In a less strict view on argument alignment, a particular θ-role is not uniformly assigned to a canonical structural position; rather, the assignment of a certain θ-role to a certain position depends on the other θ-roles of the verb. A verb's θ-roles are ordered with respect to each other according to a thematic hierarchy in which all different θ-roles are arranged in a certain order. The concept of thematic hierarchy is proposed by Jackendoff (1972); his hierarchy is listed in (5).[5]

(5) Agent > Location / Source / Goal > Theme

(Jackendoff 1972:148)

The resulting order of the verb's θ-roles is preserved in mapping: the one ordered highest is mapped onto the highest structural position, i.e., subject position; the second one to the second-highest structural position, and so forth. This kind of mapping algorithm is called *hierarchical argument linking* by Jackendoff (1990). One of its consequences is that an argument of a certain thematic type can map onto different positions, depending on the other arguments that are being mapped, if there are any. Mapping theories with a relativized view on argument alignment based on a thematic hierarchy are presented, by, among others, Jackendoff (1983, 1990); Carrier-Duncan (1985); Belletti & Rizzi (1988); Bresnan & Kanerva (1989); Grimshaw (1990); Speas (1990); Kornfilt & Correa (1993).[6]

Argument structures

Whereas the mapping algorithms discussed above (i.e., UTAH and hierarchical argument linking) are based on the semantics of a verb's arguments as expressed by thematic relations or θ-roles, other theories have developed along different, less semantic lines. Williams (1981) differentiates a verb's arguments into internal versus external arguments. Internal arguments map onto an argument position close to the predicate, i.e., within VP, whereas external arguments map onto a position external to the domain of the predicate, i.e. outside of VP. Different ways of θ-assignment account for these different mappings: the verb θ-marks an internal argument under government, hence it must be a sister of V, i.e., the object position. An external argument is θ-marked by VP through predication after the external θ-role has percolated up to VP. Williams' binary distinction has been refined by Marantz (1984) who distinguishes two types of internal arguments: direct and indirect ones. Direct internal arguments map onto a direct object position, θ-marked directly by V; indirect internal arguments map onto an oblique position, θ-marked by V only indirectly, i.e., via P. Consider the internal and external arguments of *drink* and *put*, (6).

(6)	a.	*drink*	V,	{Ag, *Th*}
	b.	*put*	V,	{Ag, *Th*, Go}

Williams (1981) uses underlining to indicate external arguments; the agent is the external argument in (6). Marantz (1984) italizes the θ-roles that are assigned directly by the verb, i.e., the theme is the direct internal argument in (6). The goal in (6b) is an indirect internal argument.[7]

Lexical distinctions between internal versus external argumenthood thus parallel syntactic distinctions between direct and indirect object and subject positions. Hence, mapping is defined on different syntactic kinds of arguments, rather than different semantic kinds. In Williams' work, the arguments are specified for internal-external argumenthood, on top of their thematic labels. These thematic labels do not play any role in the mapping algorithm, though. The relevant feature of arguments for mapping is their structural status (internal versus external, direct versus indirect), not their thematic content.

In fact, with the introduction of the notions *internal* and *external argument*, there was no more need for a semantic differentiation of the arguments. As thematic labels are irrelevant for the mapping system, θ-roles can be done away with altogether. This step is suggested by Williams (1981, 1994a) and explicitly argued for by Higginbotham (1985), Zubizarreta (1987) and Rappaport & Levin (1988).[8] They formalize a verb's arguments in a simpler way, using abstract variables (e.g., *x*, *y*, ...) instead of θ-labels. They refer to the list of arguments as *predicate-argument structure* (*PAS*) or, simply, *argument structure*, instead of θ-grid. The arguments are ordered among each other in a syntactic way, rather than along a thematic hierarchy. Consider the argument structures of *drink* and *put* as proposed by Zubizarreta (1987), (7), and Rappaport & Levin, (8).

(7) a. *drink* V, <drink⁀y>, x
<drink⁀LIQUID>, x
b. *put* V, put⁀y,x; Loc P⁀z
(adapted from Zubizarreta 1987:9-10)

(8) a. *drink* V, x <($\underline{y}$)>
b. *put* V, x <$\underline{y}$, P_{loc}z>
(adapted from Rappaport & Levin 1988:15)

The arguments are represented by variables, i.e., *x*, *y* and *z* in (7) and (8); they show different notations of indicating external versus internal and direct versus indirect internal argumenthood. In both notations in (7) and (8), *x* is the external argument, *y* the direct internal one and *z* the indirect internal one. While Rappaport & Levin indicate optionality of an argument with familiar bracket notation (e.g., the internal argument of *drink* in (8a)), Zubizarreta lists *drink* with two separate representations, one for its transitive and the other for its intransitive appearance, the latter with a constant internal argument, i.e., LIQUID, (7a).

Notice that argument structures with bare variables are much closer to subcategorization frames than θ-grids. For mapping based on θ-grids, one needs to define an independent set of argument alignment principles. An ordered argument structure on the other hand inherently contains the mapping information. Argument structures are different from subcategorization frames, in that they contain no categorial or case-marking information, nor do they state any linearization restrictions on the verb and its complements.

An important issue is whether internal and external argumenthood are lexical primitives that need to be diacritically annotated on the argument variables in a lexical entry, or, alternatively, whether this is a derived notion. Whereas Williams (1981) and Zubizarreta (1987) take it as a primitive notion, Rappaport & Levin (1988) assume there is an underlying lexical-semantic level from which internal and external argumenthood can be derived: lexical-conceptual structure.

Lexical-conceptual structures

Semantic specification is crucial in the lexical primitives proposed by Jackendoff (1983, 1990), which are partly based on his earlier work (Jackendoff 1972). For Jackendoff, lexical-conceptual structures (LCS) are the primitive lexical notions from which a verb's verb frames can be derived. An LCS decomposes a verb's meaning into (sometimes complex) functor-argument structures containing meta-predicates such as CAUSE, GO, BE, STAY, AT and TO which predicate of states and events. The configuration of an LCS follows lexical-conceptual formation rules; Jackendoff (1990) refers to this as *X'-semantics*. The arguments of a predicate appear as typed variables in an LCS. For example, a semantic constituent of the category "Event" involves Event-functions such as CAUSE and GO, each of which takes two arguments: CAUSE takes a "Thing" and another, embedded "Event"; GO takes a "Thing" and the "Path" it traverses. Consider the lexical entries of *drink*, (9), and *put*, (10), each with their LCS's.

(9) *drink* (Jackendoff 1990:53)

$$
\begin{bmatrix}
\mathrm{V} \\
\_\langle \mathrm{NP}_j \rangle \\
[_{\mathrm{Event}}\ \mathrm{CAUSE}\ ([_{\mathrm{Thing}}\ ]_i,\ [_{\mathrm{Event}}\ \mathrm{GO}\ ([_{\mathrm{Thing}}\ \mathrm{LIQUID}]_j, \\
\qquad\qquad [_{\mathrm{Path}}\ \mathrm{TO}\ ([_{\mathrm{Place}}\ \mathrm{IN}\ ([_{\mathrm{Thing}}\ \mathrm{MOUTH\ OF}\ ([_{\mathrm{Thing}}\ ]_i)])])])])]
\end{bmatrix}
$$

(10) *put* (Jackendoff 1990:80)

$$\begin{bmatrix} \text{V} \\ \_\text{NP}_j\ \text{PP}_k \\ [_{\text{Event}}\ \text{CAUSE}\ ([_{\text{Thing}}\ ]_i,\ [_{\text{Event}}\ \text{GO}\ ([_{\text{Thing}}\ ]_j, \\ \qquad [_{\text{Path}}\ \text{TO}\ ([_{\text{Place}}\ ]_{\{k\}})]_{\{k\}})])] \end{bmatrix}$$

The indexed entities in the LCS's refer to variables of lexical-conceptual predicates, i.e., "Things" in (9) and (10) and a "Path" or "Place" in (10). Their indices are related to the indexed complements in the subcategorization frames. Moreover, the notation in (9) with two "Things" co-indexed by *i* refers to the semantic entailment that what is drunk typically ends up in the mouth of the drinker. The selectional restriction on the object of *drink* appears as the conceptual information LIQUID.

Jackendoff (1987, 1990) argues that θ-roles are not primitives. Instead, they can be defined on lexical-conceptual structures. A particular θ-role corresponds to a particular, structural position in LCS. For example, "theme" can be defined as the first argument of a GO-function. The notion θ-grid is thus a derivative concept; a θ-grid could be reconstructed by gathering the LCS variables into a set. However, one does not need θ-roles for mapping purposes. Jackendoff (1990) defines a mapping algorithm (his Correspondence Rules) right on LCS's as a form of hierarchical argument linking (see above). After ordering the LCS variables along a lexical-conceptual version of the thematic hierarchy (see (5)), mapping preserves this relative ordering of the arguments in the structural ordering of the syntactic positions they are mapped onto.

Jackendoff's view of specifying a verb's lexical information in terms of LCS's is followed, among others, by Hale & Keyser (1986); Rappaport & Levin (1988); Pinker (1989); Carrier & Randall (1992, 1993); Kornfilt & Correa (1993). As for mapping algorithms based on LCS's, views differ. Pinker (1989) spells out a set of hierarchically ordered linking rules, each of which explicitly relates a variable in a certain LCS position with a syntactic position. For example, " . . . link the first argument of BE or GO (the theme) to: the external argument position if it is not already linked or to the direct internal argument position otherwise" (Pinker 1989:74).

Rappaport & Levin (1988), Carrier & Randall (1992, 1993) and Kornfilt & Correa (1993) on the other hand assume an intermediate level of argument structure that mediates the mapping between LCS and D-structure, (11).

(11) Argument structure as an intermediate level of representation:

	Linking rules		*Projection rules*	
LCS	→	Argument Structure	→	D-structure

On this view, the mapping system is a two-step algorithm. Linking rules account for the first step, taking LCS-representations as their domain and argument structures as their range. Projection rules deal with the second step, taking argument structures as their input and mapping these onto syntactic configurations. Rappaport & Levin (1988), Carrier & Randall (1992, 1993) and Kornfilt & Correa (1993) assume the kind of argument structure that consists of variables without thematic content which are specified for internal/external and direct/indirect internal argumenthood. Linking rules relate LCS-variables to arguments in the argument structure and familiar projection rules relate the latter to syntactic positions at D-structure (Williams 1981; Marantz 1984; see above).

Whereas Rappaport & Levin (1988) do not explicitly spell out their linking rules, Kornfilt & Correa (1993) follow the thematic version of hierarchical argument linking, making use of a thematic hierarchy to establish the linking to argument structure. They spell out the linking rules and the subsequent projection rules in formal details. Carrier & Randall (1992, 1993) follow some form of hierarchical argument linking as well. Rather than basing it on thematic relations and a thematic hierarchy, Carrier & Randall define the linking rules on the geometry of LCS's in their Structural Preference Principle which states that " . . . semantic arguments in a higher CS clause take precedence over arguments in a lower CS clause in linking" (Carrier & Randall 1993:123).[9] Hence, they preserve the structural ordering of the LCS-variables in the ordering of the argument variables in argument structure. In fact, by relying on the structural ordering of variables in an LCS, Carrier & Randall integrate semantic notions other than purely the number and kinds of arguments (i.e., LCS variables) into their linking rules. Decomposing the meaning of a verb, an LCS represents it as an event with subevents embedded inside it. Hence, the structural ordering of LCS-variables also reflects an aspectual ordering of the arguments.[10]

In a similar vein, but without committing to an LCS format of lexical specification, Levin & Rappaport Hovav (1992, 1994, 1995) formulate a set of linking rules that are based on conceptual-semantic notions such as *immediate causation*, *directed change* and *existence*. These rules determine how a verb's lexical-semantically described arguments link to particular arguments in the argument structure. For example, their Immediate Cause Linking Rule states that " . . . the argument of a verb that denotes the immediate cause of the eventuality described by the verb is its external argument" (Levin & Rappaport Hovav 1995:135). The linking rules are hierarchically ordered.

Summary of argument-centered mapping

To summarize the overview of primitives and mapping systems so far, I have discussed semantic and syntactic kinds of lexical primitives. Subcategorization frames specify the lexical information about a verb's arguments in a purely syntactic way. Argument structures specify it in a similarly syntactic way as they are defined on the notions *internal* and *external argument* which directly relate to the distance from the verb in a syntactic configuration. θ-Roles present a purely semantic specification of the verb's arguments. Lexical-conceptual structures decompose the broad semantic notions of θ-roles into semantically finer-grained elements. The latter two, semantic forms of lexical specification require a non-trivial mapping algorithm to relate them to syntactic positions in D-structure. Some form of hierarchial argument linking, or, in a more rigid form, UTAH, performs this function. Other summaries and reviews of these issues are presented by: Rappaport & Levin (1988); Grimshaw (1990); Speas (1990); Atkinson (1992); Stowell (1992); Déchaine (1993).

I want to emphasize the argument-centered conception of lexicon-to-syntax mapping that is shared by the theories discussed above. The theories differ with respect to the definition of their lexical primitives, but they are similar in that every verb needs to be listed with information on the number and type of its arguments (in the form of complements, θ-roles, arguments or LCS variables). The projection of a certain verb frame depends exclusively on lexical information about the arguments. In the next section I will discuss less argument-centered views.

1.3.2 Mapping governed by aspectual features

In recent years much work on argument structure and mapping has made crucial use of aspectual considerations, implementing them in some way or other in the mapping system, alongside or instead of lexical information on a verb's arguments. These works include: Tenny (1987, 1989, 1992, 1994); Van Valin (1987, 1990); Pustejovsky (1988, 1991, 1995); van Voorst (1988, 1993); Abraham (1990, 1993); Grimshaw (1990); Dowty (1991); van Hout (1991b, 1992a,b, 1994); Hale & Keyser (1992, 1993); Hoekstra (1992); Mulder (1992); Levin & Rappaport Hovav (1992, 1994, 1995); Grimshaw & Vikner (1993); van Hout, Randall & Weissenborn (1993); McClure (1993); Borer (1994); Randall, van Hout, Weissenborn & Baayen (1994); Davis & Demirdache (1995); Hollebrandse & van Hout (1995, 1996, 1998); van Hout, Randall, Weissenborn & Baayen (in progress); Davis (1997a,b); Demirdache (1997).

Opinions about the exact role of aspect for mapping vary, as do the implementations of aspectual notions into mapping systems. In this section I will present three views on how aspect interferes in mapping, by discussing Tenny's, Grimshaw's and Hale & Keyser's mapping theories.

An aspectual interface

Tenny (1987, 1989, 1992, 1994) claims that much (if not most) of mapping is regulated by aspectual properties. She introduces the aspectual notion of *delimitedness* in mapping theory. Delimitedness " . . . refers to the property of an event's having a distinct, definite and inherent endpoint in time" (Tenny 1994:4). It deals with whether or not an event is terminative, and, if so, how this terminativity comes about. Delimitedness is the core notion in the set of linking generalizations between lexical semantics and syntactic configurations. She proposes that aspect mediates the mapping between argument structure and syntax as determined by her Aspectual Interface Hypothesis (AIH).[11] The AIH replaces thematic linking triggered by UTAH or hierarchical argument linking, as it restricts the associations between the arguments in the semantic representation and the argument positions in the syntactic configuration.

The AIH can be viewed as aspectual role assignment, substituting thematic role assignment. The aspectual roles at play are: "measure", "terminus" and "path". Tenny assumes that aspectual roles are part of the lexical information associated with a verb. These aspectual roles are mapped onto internal argument positions. Mapping is governed by the following rules: a "measure" must be a direct internal argument; a "terminus" must be an indirect internal argument; a "path" is either implicit or an internal argument.

The AIH also functions as an interpretational device. The linking rules are formulated in such a way that the internal arguments, but not the external one, play a role in the matter of delimitedness. The direct internal argument undergoes ". . . a motion or change which measures out the event over time (where measuring out entails that the direct argument plays a particular role in delimiting the event). . . . An indirect internal argument can only participate in aspectual structure by providing a terminus for the event described by the verb which causes the event to be delimited. . . . An external argument cannot participate in measuring out or delimiting the event described by a verb. It cannot be a measure, a path or a terminus" (Tenny 1994:114).

These mapping conventions imply that a direct object, if present, provides the measure along which the event develops over time. If there is no (underlying) object, the event cannot be measured out. Intransitive *drink*, for example, denotes an undelimited event of drinking. If the object is present, it is a "measure" (as it undergoes a change or motion). In some events the direct object itself delimits the event. The object of transitive *drink* (e.g., *drink a beer*) measures out the event by itself, since the drinking is over when the beer is finished. In other cases, an indirect internal argument delimits the event. Ditransitive *put* requires an indirect internal argument that provides the "terminus" of the event, while its direct object is the "measure". For example, an event of *putting the tuna on the grill* is a delimited event, terminated when the tuna is lying on the grill.

Thus, in Tenny's view, argument structure forms the intermediate level between lexical semantics and syntax (see (11)). The linking rules between lexicon and argument structure are defined on purely aspectual notions.

Aspectual prominence and argument and event structure associations

Grimshaw (1990) follows a multi-leveled mapping system (see (11)), proposing a fine-grained theory of argument structure. She assumes a verb has a lexical-conceptual structure at the lexical-semantic level. This level contains all necessary information to link to a level of argument structure at which a verb is specified with its argument structure which has a thematic and an aspectual dimension. Linking computes prominence relations among the arguments on both dimensions, so that a verb's argument structure is a structured representation of its arguments. As for the thematic dimension, the thematic hierarchy underlies these prominence relations.[12] In the derivation of the argument structure of a certain predicate from its lexical-semantic representation, θ-role labels are dispensed with after they have served to compute the prominence relations among them. Hence, at the level of argument structure, the arguments bear no θ-labels; the prominence relations indirectly reflect thematic information in that a more prominent argument is higher on the thematic hierarchy than a less prominent one.

Grimshaw's formalization of the aspectual dimension is based on Pustejovsky (1988). Pustejovsky (1988, 1991, 1995) analyzes events not as atomic entities, but as entities with subeventual structure. He distinguishes the Vendler/Dowty verb classes by assuming different subeventual structures for each of them. There are three different aspectual primitives: state, process and transition.[13] Information about the lexical aspect of a verb and about its causality properties are linked to the aspectual dimension. Grimshaw assumes that the arguments of a predicate all participate in one or more (sub)events of the event structure: they are all associated with one or more (sub)events. The relation between the thematic and aspectual dimensions is expressed via these association links. For the aspectual dimension, prominence relations among the arguments are computed upon the temporal ordering of the subevents: an argument who participates in the first subevent is more prominent than those who participate in subsequent subevents.

The notion of *maximal prominence* plays a crucial role in the mapping system from argument structure to D-structure. Mapping to D-structure is defined on the aspectual dimension: the aspectually most prominent argument maps as the subject; the other arguments map onto internal argument positions.[14] If there is no such argument (that is aspectually most prominent), no argument is mapped onto subject position: the case of unaccusatives. Prominence relations on both levels define whether an argument is internal or external. External argumenthood is defined as maximal prominence on both dimensions. Internal or external argumenthood is not related to syntactic configurations, however. These concepts are relevant for lexical operations (e.g., passivization, nominalization, reflexivization, causativization). Hence, the notion *external argument* is not equivalent with the notion *D-structure subject* (as it is in the view of Williams (1981) and followers of his notion).

Grimshaw crucially employs event structure in two cases, with aspectual prominence determining whether or not an argument is mapped onto subject position. Presence or lack of an aspectually prominent argument accounts for the different mappings of the two famous kinds of psych predicates, i.e., the *fear* and *frighten* classes, and for those of unergative versus unaccusative predicates. The experiencer or the theme of *frighten* verbs is an aspectually prominent argument, hence these verbs map as unaccusatives with two internal arguments; the experiencer of *fear* verbs on the other hand is aspectually prominent and maps as a subject (i.e., onto a transitive frame). Unergatives and unaccusatives both have a single argument on the thematic dimension of argument structure. Grimshaw assumes that unergatives denote activities, whereas unaccusatives denote states or changes of state (i.e., transitions), following Tenny (1987), Zaenen (1988, 1993) and Van Valin (1990). Since these verbs have different event structures, their single argument is associated with event structure in different ways. The argument that participates in an activity is aspectually prominent, but one that is involved in a change of state is not. Hence, unergatives map their argument as a subject, but unaccusatives do not.

Thus, for Grimshaw, mapping is basically determined by the associations between a verb's arguments and its event structure. These associations determine prominence relations among the arguments which, in turn, are preserved in the mapping onto different syntactic positions.

Lexical-relational structures and event types

Hale & Keyser (1992, 1993) propose a syntactic kind of lexical primitive which they call a *lexical-relational structure* (*LRS*). An LRS is a representation of argument structure in the form of a lexical head that projects its category to a phrasal level and determines within that projection structural relations between the head and its arguments (its complement and, if present, its specifier). Hence, the notion *argument structure* by which verbs are lexically characterized is a syntactic entity, represented by syntactic structures projected by lexical heads. A difference with subcategorization frames is that an LRS has more structure.

Hale & Keyser furthermore assume that LRS's are the lexical-syntactic correlates of semantic entities, to wit different event-semantic relations. Each type of LRS is related to a different event-semantic relation. Hence, a verb's lexical specification includes an LRS and an associated event-semantic relation. Given that there is a limited number of lexical categories, i.e., verb, preposition, adjective and noun, Hale & Keyser assume there is an equally limited number of different LRS types, (12)-(15). They distinguish the following relations: causal, change of location, change of state and creation. These event-semantic relations are associated with the different LRS's in the following ways, (12)-(15).

(12) Causative event LRS:

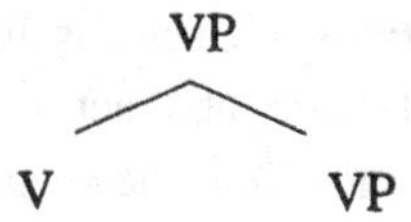

(13) Change of Location LRS:

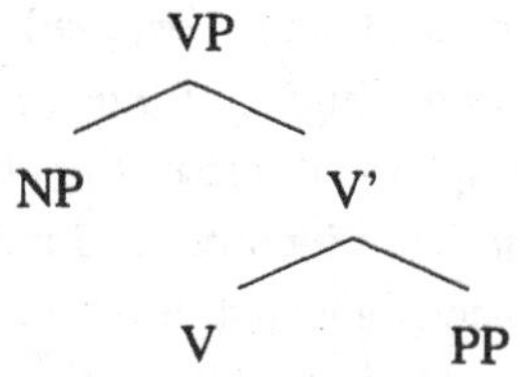

(14) Change of State LRS:

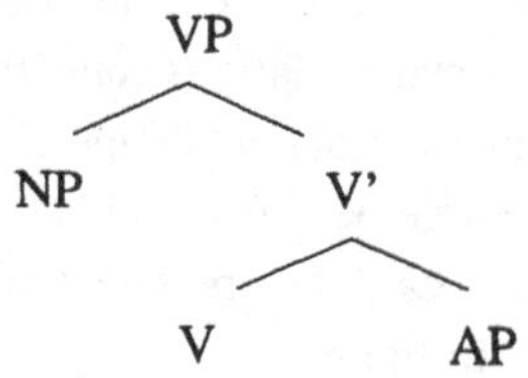

(15) Creation event LRS:

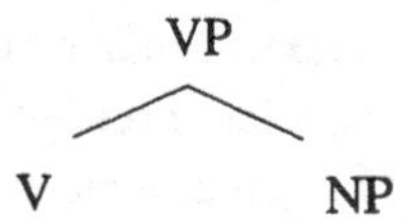

At a lexical level (Hale & Keyser's *l-syntax*), operations can apply on and in LRS's (e.g., lexical incorporation). These are governed and restricted by principles and conditions familiar from s-syntax (e.g., the ECP for head movement). Hale & Keyser derive denominal and deadjectival verbs (such as *shelve*, *open* and *laugh*) via head movement inside an LRS. For example, *shelve* denotes a causative event which is represented by a verb that takes a VP complement which, in turn, represents another, embedded event (e.g., (12)). The embedded event is a change of location; the final state can be identified as a relation between an entity and a location (e.g., (13)). In order to derive *shelve the books* from *put the books on the shelf*, they incorporate the noun complement of the preposition via the lower V into the higher V; this yields a denominal, transitive verb: *shelve*. The direct object (i.e., *the books*) is the NP in the specifier position of a locative PP (abstract *on the shelf*) (e.g., (13)).

Intransitive *open* is an example of a change of state LRS, (14); it is derived from abstract *become open*, when the adjective *open* has incorporated into the verb position. Transitive *open* is represented by a double VP structure with a causal LRS on top of the change of state LRS (i.e., abstract *make open*). Here the adjective incorporates via the lower V to the higher V. *Laugh* is represented by a creation LRS with an NP complement, (15); it is derived from abstract *do a laugh*, as the noun *laugh* has incorporated into the verb. Notice that all incorporations take place at a lexical level, i.e., before the verbs are inserted into syntax.

Notice that thematic relations play no role whatsoever in the mapping system; as in LCS theories, the notion θ-role is not a lexical primitive. Thematic relations could be defined on the argument positions in an LRS. For example, a "theme" is the specifier of an LRS with a PP or an AP complement (e.g., (13) and (14)). A mapping theory based on LRS's implies that there is a restricted set of θ-roles and allows for unambiguous definitions.

Hale & Keyser put forward some empirical evidence to support their theory on lexical-relational structures. They refer to the fact that in many languages, a large set of the verbal lexical items are overtly phrasal. In others, the verbal lexicon contains many entries whose morphological make-up is overtly the result of incorporation. And, yet other languages, among them Dutch and English, have an inventory of so-called *light verb* constructions that represent a class of overtly phrasal lexical entries.[15]

Thus, if LRS's are the lexical primitives, mapping is trivial, as the lexical projection of an LRS projects further into a functional projection. Aspectual properties of verbs and the frames they map onto are integrated via the inherent association of LRS's with event-semantic relations.

Summary of mapping governed by aspectual features

This concludes the presentation of interface theories that are based on aspectual notions as well as a list of arguments. I have discussed in detail three views with different ideas as to how aspect plays a role in the mapping system: Tenny's mapping theory (1987, 1994) is defined on the aspectual roles borne by the arguments; Grimshaw's (1990) system is defined on the aspectual prominence of the arguments in the event structure; in Hale & Keyser's (1993) mapping system, different event types are associated with different lexical-relational structures.

1.4 A challenge for mapping systems: lexical-syntactic flexibility

The mapping systems discussed in the previous section associate a particular lexical specification with one particular verb frame. Most verbs, however, appear in several different verb frames. Verbs are flexible as to how many syntactic argument positions they project, which positions they project and how they map their arguments onto these positions. They figure in so-called *argument alternations* (also referred to as *diathesis patterns*). Such flexible mapping behavior complicates the notion of a verb's lexical specification, since it must be associated with more than one verb frame. I will refer to the phenomenon of flexible mapping behavior with the neutral term *lexical-syntactic flexibility.*[16]

Lexical-syntactic flexibility has long been a topic of research in different frameworks. Levin (1993) presents a fairly exhaustive range of different types of (what she calls) diathesis alternations in English; she includes many references to various kinds of analyses of certain alternations. I recommend her book as a work of reference. Chapter 2 presents a (more modest) overview of different types of alternations in Dutch. In this section, I will briefly present the different kinds of approaches to the phenomenon (subsection 1.4.1), illustrating them with some typical analyses of a few actual cases of flexibility (subsection 1.4.2).

1.4.1 Different approaches to lexical-syntactic flexibility

Considering lexical-syntactic flexibility with respect to the lexicon-syntax interface, one can in principle conceive of three possible ways to analyze the phenomenon. These three different approaches to dealing with lexical-syntactic flexibility are schematically pictured in (16) for a verb *V* with its lexical specification [..] that can appear in three different frames, F_a, F_b and F_c.

(16) Three approaches to lexical-syntactic flexibility:

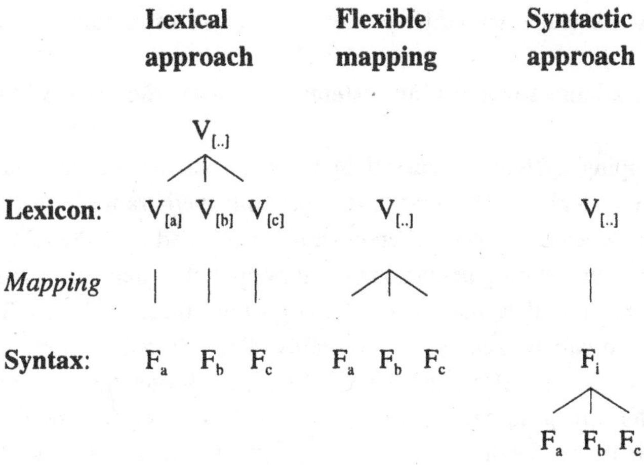

First, there is the lexical approach. There are two different views within this type of approach. The first is to incorporate a verb's flexibility into its lexical representation, i.e., the verb is lexically represented with more than one representation, each of which is linked to a certain verb frame. This is the view behind the use of various kinds of diacritics in subcategorization frames (cf. Chomsky 1965; Emonds 1991a). Diacritics allow for collapsing various subcategorization frames into one. On the other lexical view, different lexical representations are related to each other via lexical rules, i.e., operations on lexical specifications. A lexical rule affects the basic specification of a verb and yields a derived representation which in turn maps onto syntax. Lexical rules are thus indirectly frame-relating rules. The latter lexical approach is taken in mapping theories defined on various kinds of lexical primitives; the rules are defined in equally various ways. Lexical-syntactic flexibility creating rules have been defined on argument structures (e.g., Williams 1981; Zubizarreta 1987; Grimshaw 1990), on lexical-conceptual structures (e.g., Hale & Keyser 1986; Rappaport & Levin 1988; Pinker 1989; Jackendoff 1990; Carrier & Randall 1993), on aspectual roles (e.g., Tenny 1987, 1994), on event structures (e.g., Parsons 1990; Pustejovsky 1991, 1995) and on lexical-relational structures (e.g., Hale & Keyser 1992, 1993).

Another way to approach the phenomenon of lexical-syntactic flexibility is by means of a flexible mapping system (see (16)): the mapping algorithm itself creates flexibility by mapping one verb with its basic lexical specification onto more than one verb frame (e.g., van Hout 1991b, 1992a,b, 1994; see also Chapter 4; Borer 1994). Finally, there is the syntactic approach: a verb has one lexical representation that maps onto one particular verb frame; syntactic operations, i.e., movement of an argument, create flexibility. This approach is inevitable in mapping systems based on UTAH (e.g., Baker 1988); it has also been employed by, among others, Larson (1988) and den Dikken (1992).

Each of these views raises its own specific research issues. If, in a lexical approach, a verb is represented with a set of lexical specifications and the lexicon-syntax mapping is one-to-one, one must deal with the issue of how to keep the lexicon as parsimonious as possible, since multiple listings of the same verb create lexical redundancy. On the other hand, if, in a lexical approach, alternative lexical specifications are derived from one basic lexical specification, one must carefully choose a verb's basic representation and formulate the lexical operations in such a way so as not to derive too many or too few alternative specifications. If, in a flexible mapping approach, a verb is lexically specified with sufficiently general information that allows for a one-to-many mapping, one must deal with the issue of how exactly to define the mapping system so as to associate each verb with the appropriate set of possible verb frames. Finally, if, in a syntactic approach, a verb is lexically specified only once, maps onto syntax in an unambiguous way, after which syntactic operations shuffle the arguments around, one must figure out which restrictions apply to these syntactic operations, so that each verb ends up in the right set of possible verb frames.

1.4.2 An illustration of different approaches to lexical-syntactic flexibility

In order to illustrate the workings of the different approaches to lexical-syntactic flexibility, I will present some typical analyses.

Subcategorization frames and lexical-syntactic flexibility

If mapping is defined in terms of subcategorization frames, lexical-syntactic flexibility is incorporated in the lexical specification of the verb. It is dealt with via special diacritics in the subcategorization frame. The bracket notation is an (almost trivial) example of such a diacritic; it is used to indicate an optional argument and collapses two frames into one (e.g., pseudo-transitive *eat* is specified as [_ (NP)]).

Emonds (1991a) introduces more kinds of diacritics for the purpose of analyzing other kinds of frame alternations; they are defined as lexical features on the verb: ± LOCATIONAL (L) and ± ACTIVITY. Frame alternations arise in the case of predicates for which one of these features is optional; the verb frame is projected either with or without the feature. Incorporating Talmy's (1985) insights on locational and motion verbs, Emonds furthermore formulates a set of interpretational principles that are defined on these lexical features: Figure, Ground and Agent.[17] These principles assign an interpretation to a phrase in a certain argument position.

Emonds analyzes the locative alternation with a verb such as *smear* (e.g., *smear paint on the wall, smear the wall with paint*) in terms of an optional feature LOCATIONAL (L) on the verb. *Smear* is lexically specified as in (17); this specification gives rise to the two deep structures in (18).

(17) *smear* V, +ACTIVITY, (+L), __ NP (PP)

(Emonds 1991a:397)

(18)

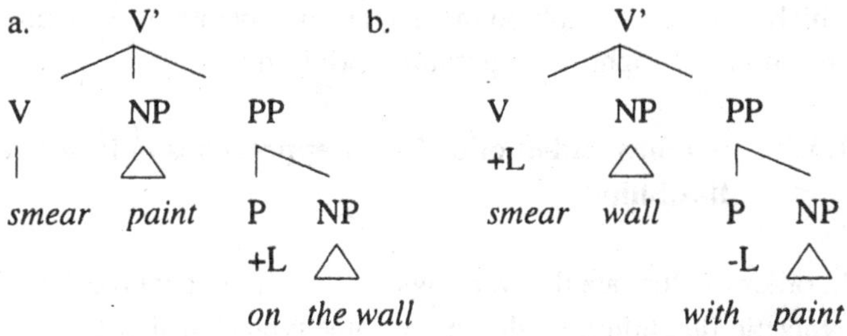

(Emonds 1991a:397)

The interpretation of the arguments in object and oblique positions depends on the presence of the feature L on the verb. By defining the specifications for "figure" and "ground" on this feature (see endnote 17), Emonds derives two different interpretations for the objects in (18): the object in (18a) is interpreted as the "figure" and the object in (18b) is the "ground".

Syntactic movement derives lexical-syntactic flexibility

Lexically listing the possible frames in a verb's subcategorization frame is impossible in a mapping approach based on UTAH in which a verb always maps its arguments onto syntax in the same ways as determined by their θ-roles. An alternative approach to dealing with lexical-syntactic flexibility is by analyzing it as a purely syntactic phenomenon. There is no need for exhaustive specifications in the lexicon, nor for lexical rules that derive one specification from the other. Instead, a verb always maps onto D-structure in the same way, i.e., onto one particular frame; subsequent syntactic operations create alternative frames.

This approach is strongly advocated by Baker (1988). Baker claims that all phenomena that look as if grammatical function changing operations have been applied such as passivization, causativization and the applicative construction can be reduced to syntactic incorporation processes. Incorporation refers to processes by which one semantically independent word comes to be inside another; they are the result of standard syntactic movement operations. Incorporation yields grammatical function changing effects as a side effect.

Baker analyzes applicative alternations as preposition incorporation, following a proposal by Marantz (1984). An applicative alternation can be descriptively characterized as follows: the indirect object becomes an object while the original object remains an object. Baker illustrates the alternation with an example from Kimenyi (1980) in Kinyarwanda, (19).

(19) a. Umwaana y-a-taa-ye igitabo mu maazi.
child throw book in water
'The child has thrown the book into the water.'

b. Umwaana y-a-taa-ye-mo amaazi igitabo.
child throw-APP water book
'The child has thrown the book into the water.'
(Baker 1988:238-239; from Kimenyi 1980)

Applying UTAH, Baker claims that the verb in (19) maps its arguments onto D-structure in the same way in both alternants: the "theme" is mapped onto object position and the "goal" is mapped onto oblique object position. No further operations apply in (19a). In order to derive (19b), Baker argues that the preposition incorporates into the verb which is marked by the applicative morpheme. The complement of the preposition is left behind and becomes the so-called applied object. In this way, syntactic incorporation derives a frame-alternating effect.

Operations on argument structure derive lexical-syntactic flexibility

Assuming that internal versus external argumenthood are the basic distinctions among a verb's arguments, Williams (1981) claims that there are two possible operations on argument structure: Externalize and Internalize. The effect of particular morphological affixes is to internalize or externalize a particular argument in the argument structure. Williams employs the operation of Externalize for "theme" arguments in his analysis of *-able* affixation and adjectival passivization. Verbal passivization also reflects a form of Externalize; it " . . . erases the underlining in the argument structure giving an argument structure with no external argument" (Williams 1981:94). Internalize is applied in nominalization and causativization. Under causativization (e.g., causative suffixes *-en*, *-ize*), the original external argument of a verb internalizes and a new external argument is added; intransitive-causative pairs (e.g., *melt*) are analyzed in the same way. As Williams' perspective on argument structure naturally leads to these two argument-changing operations, it presents a restrictive theory of possible lexical rules.

The distinction between the notions *internal* and *external argument* has been very useful in the study of lexical-syntactic flexibility. Following Williams (1981), many analyses of passivization are phrased in terms of suppressing the external argument or blocking it from being projected; middle formation is often analyzed as the deletion of the external argument (cf. Keyser & Roeper 1984; Hale & Keyser 1987; Jaeggli 1986; Di Sciullo & Williams 1987; Roberts 1987; Roeper 1987; Zubizarreta 1987; Baker 1988; Baker, Johnson & Roberts 1989; Grimshaw 1990; Woolford 1993; Hoekstra & Roberts 1993). The operation of suppressing or blocking an argument has been formalized in a number of different ways. For example, Grimshaw (1990) analyzes both passivization and nominalization as operations that suppress the external argument in an argument structure which yields a different, derived argument structure. Zubizarreta (1987) derives argument structure changes in a more indirect way. She argues for specifying argument structures with additional features: CAUSE and STATE. Lexical operations may add or delete these features which immediately affects the argument variables in the argument structure. Causativization (e.g., *modern-modernize*) adds a CAUSE feature and, consequently, an external argument. Anti-causativization (e.g., transitive-intransitive *sink*) deletes a CAUSE feature and the external argument disappears with it. Zubizarreta analyzes adjectival passivization as the addition of the feature STATE.[18] Passivization on the other hand does not actually affect the argument structure or its features; rather, it blocks the external argument from being mapped.

Operations on LCS's derive lexical-syntactic flexibility

In mapping systems that are defined on a verb's lexical semantics, lexical-syntactic flexibility is analyzed as operations on a verb's basic lexical-semantic specification. Lexical operations are meaningful operations; they affect the basic semantic specification. Subsequently, the derived verb is mapped onto syntax as determined by the derived specification.

Several analyses of various alternations have been proposed within the framework of lexical-conceptual structures (to mention a few, Rappaport & Levin 1988; Pinker 1989; Jackendoff 1990; Carrier & Randall 1993). Picking out one analysis for illustration, Rappaport & Levin (1988) analyze the locative alternation (e.g., *load cartons onto the truck, load the truck with cartons*) as follows. Decomposing the semantics of the verb *load* into fine-grained conceptual notions, Rappaport & Levin propose that there are two variants of *load* which differ slightly in their LCS's, (20).

(20) a. *load* [*x* cause [*y* to come to be at *z*] /LOAD]
b. *load* [*x* cause [*z* to come to be in STATE]
BY MEANS OF [*x* cause [*y* to come to be at *z*] /LOAD]
(Rappaport & Levin 1988:26)

The representation in (20a) indicates that *load* names an event which involves a change of location "by loading", whereas the representation in (20b) indicates that *load* names an event in which a change of state is brought about by means of a change of location. The former is mapped as the locative variant (e.g., *load cartons onto the truck*), while the latter is mapped as the *with* variant (e.g., *load the truck with cartons*). The alternation is not the result of an alternation in the syntactic expression of the arguments of a verb with one single lexical-semantic representation. Rather, it reflects the existence of two distinct but related LCS's which each realize their arguments in accordance with the general set of linking rules. The two LCS's are related via a rule that operates on an LCS such as the one in (20a), deriving the one in (20b).

The aspectual interface hypothesis and lexical-syntactic flexibility

Tenny (1987, 1994) claims that there is no absolute mapping from verb meanings to syntactic structure; rather, aspectual interpretation principles act as a filter on verb meanings. Therefore, focusing on the event in different ways may lead to different mappings. Tenny analyzes the locative alternation (e.g., *spray paint onto the wall, spray the wall with paint*) in terms of two different perspectives on the same event. In her terminology, a spraying event can be measured out in two different ways: by focusing either on the "theme" (i.e., how much of the paint got sprayed) or on the "goal" (i.e., how much of the wall got sprayed). Hence, the aspectual role "measure" can be assigned to either of these arguments.

Given her Measuring-Out constraint which requires that the argument that is undergoing a change is mapped as a direct internal argument, the two different assignments of "measure" lead to two different mappings. If the "theme" is the "measure", it appears as direct object (e.g., *spray paint onto the wall*); if the "goal" is the "measure", it appears as direct object (e.g., *spray the wall with paint*).

This concludes a brief discussion and illustration of different kinds of approaches to the phenomenon of lexical-syntactic flexibility.

1.5 Summary: the state of the art of lexicon and mapping theories

After introducing the mapping problem as the issue of how a verb's lexical specification leads to the set of verb frames this verb appears in (section 1.2), I have reviewed different models of the lexicon-syntax interface that define the links between a verb's lexical specification and its appearance in verb frames. The two major issues every interface theory must address are: (i) which features are relevant in the interface? (ii) how does the mapping system associate these features with verb frames? In section 1.3, I have discussed different proposals for the lexical specification of verbs: subcategorization frames, θ-roles, argument structures, lexical-conceptual structures and lexical-relational structures. Furthermore, I have discussed different proposals for mapping systems: projection and linking principles, θ-role assignment, UTAH, hierarchical argument linking (based on the thematic hierarchy) and mapping governed by aspectual considerations.

Next, I pointed out that mapping theories must also deal with a verb's flexible behavior, i.e., the phenomenon that it can appear in various frames (section 1.4). Theories of the lexicon and the interface are challenged by this phenomenon. Different approaches have been pursued in dealing with verbal flexibility: some models resolve this challenge by locating flexibility in the lexicon (via lexical rules), whereas others analyze it as a syntactic phenomenon (as the end result of movement).

Having introduced the mapping problem and having presented the state of the art of research in this field, I have prepared the ground for developing an alternative theory on the lexicon and the lexicon-syntax interface in which I will analyze lexical-syntactic flexibility in terms of a flexible mapping relation.

Notes

1. If indirect objects map onto different positions than PP complements, the set of syntactic frames in (1) contains three more elements.
2. Emonds'(1991a) subcategorization frames are slightly more sophisticated than the ones in (2), as he adds the feature ± LOCATION and some more diacritic devices that express syntactic and semantic optional/obligatory presence of complements. See section 1.4.2.
3. Emonds (1991a) formulates a set of three interpretational linking rules: "agent", "figure" and "ground". These are defined on a verb's lexical features and its subcategorization frame. See subsection 1.4.2.
4. English, for example, has: CSR (agent) = CSR (patient) = CSR (goal) = NP and CSR (proposition) = NP or clause (Chomsky 1986:87).
5. Other orders of the θ-roles in the hierarchy have been proposed since Jackendoff (1972), among others, by Carrier-Duncan (1985); Larson (1988); Baker (1988); Bresnan & Kanerva (1989).
6. Jackendoff's (1990) and Grimshaw's (1990) mapping systems are discussed below.
7. Various kinds of notations have been employed to indicate these distinctions. See (7) and (8) below.
8. Zubizarreta explicitly states that she "... does not share the view that the level of representation that encodes the grammatically relevant aspects of lexical meaning consists of a list of substantive thematic roles (known as the "theta-grid" in much current work in GB)... substantive notions like *theme*, *patient*, *goal*, *experiencer* have no grammatical import" (Zubizarreta 1987:11-12).
9. Carrier & Randall (1993) add that structural linking rules must be seen as redundancy rules that account "cost free" for predictable linkings. Given that there exist verbs with arbitrary linkings (e.g., certain psych verbs), they assume that linkings cannot be eliminated from lexical entries all together.
10. See the discussion of Grimshaw (1990) in the next subsection who assumes aspectual prominence is the determining factor in mapping.
11. The Aspectual Interface Hypothesis states that "... the universal principles of mapping between thematic structure and syntactic structure are governed by aspectual properties. Constraints on the aspectual properties associated with direct internal arguments, indirect internal arguments, and external arguments in syntactic structure constrain the kinds of event participants that can occupy these positions. Only the aspectual part of thematic structure is visible to the universal linking principles" (Tenny 1994:2).

12. Grimshaw (1990), following Grimshaw & Mester (1988), assumes the thematic hierarchy in (i) which is an extension of Jackendoff's (1972) original hierarchy in (5).
    (i) (Agent (Experiencer (Goal/Source/Location (Theme))))
    Grimshaw (1990:24)
13. See Chapter 3, section 3.3 for a detailed description of Pustejovsky's (1988, 1991) event structures.
14. Pustejovsky's (1991) mapping theory is very similar to Grimshaw's theory; he defines his linking rules on arguments associated with subevents in an event structure as well.
15. Chapter 5 discusses Dutch light verb constructions and their acquisition. See also Hollebrandse & van Hout (1995, 1996, 1998).
16. The term *argument alternation* suggests that the phenomenon is caused by arguments alternating their positions in an argument structure. However, as will be discussed below, this represents only one way of dealing with lexical-syntactic flexibility; several other solutions have been proposed as well.
17. The Ground specification states that " . . . a direct object NP of a transitive Y^0 is a Ground if and only if Y^0 is + LOCATION" (Emonds 1991a:397). A Ground is defined as " . . . a reference object . . . with respect to which the figure's site, path, or orientation is characterized (Emonds 1991a:394). The Figure specification states that " . . . exactly one Figure NP, distinct from the Ground must be present among the deep structure arguments of X^{0}" (Emonds 1991a:395). Figure (Jackendoff's 1972 and Gruber's 1965 term *theme*) is defined as " . . . the moving or conceptually movable object whose site, path, or orientation is conceived as variable" (Emonds 1991a:394).
18. Notice that the addition of features such as CAUSE and STATE in an argument structure makes the lexical representation less syntactic and more semantic.

CHAPTER 2

Verb Frame Alternations in Dutch

Almost any verb appears in several different verb frames. Verbs are flexible as to how many syntactic argument positions they project, and which positions they project. They figure in *verb frame* or *argument alternations*. Such flexible verb behavior complicates the intuitively clear notion of a verb's lexical argument structure. What is its lexical specification if a verb sometimes projects one argument position and sometimes two or even three positions? In this chapter I demonstrate the dimensions of the phenomenon of this lexical-syntactic flexibility by presenting a survey of many different forms of frame alternations in Dutch. The data set includes verbs and their prefixed and particle variants. Describing these alternations in terms of the links between a verb's lexical-semantic arguments and the syntactic argument positions they appear in, I distinguish three kinds of flexibility: (i) the same set of lexical-semantic arguments map onto syntax in both alternants, but they appear in different syntactic positions; (ii) the two alternants have different numbers of lexical-semantic arguments; hence, the verb projects different numbers of syntactic argument positions; (iii) the two alternants have the same number of lexical-semantic arguments, but not all of them appear in argument positions in each alternant.

2.1 Goals of this chapter

It is not an accidental property of only a few verbs that they appear in more than one verb frame. On the contrary, it is a wide-spread phenomenon: Most verbs can appear in several different frames, figuring in so-called *verb frame* or *argument alternations* or patterns of *diathesis*.

The phenomenon is systematic: subsets of verbs, also including pairs of verb and related particle or prefixed verb, appear in the same set of frames, i.e., they figure in the same alternations.

In this chapter I illustrate the variety of frame alternations. I will demonstrate the systematic character of the phenomenon by pointing out how a verb's meaning remains constant and how it differs across the various frames it appears in. By including prefixed and particle verbs in the data set, the systematic properties of lexical-syntactic flexibility become even clearer. A verb or its prefixed or particle variant crystallizes in each different frame with a slightly different focus on or an extension of its basic meaning.

Another aim in listing and describing many different frame alternations is to prepare the ground for raising fundamental questions about standard notions of lexical specification of verbs and standard assumptions on the mapping from lexicon to syntax. I first present a preview of these issues before diving into the data in the next sections, in order to focus the attention on elementary issues. In Chapters 3 and 4, I will take up these elementary issues, taking a verb's systematic flexibility as a starting point for developing a theory of the lexicon-syntax interface.

The concept *verb type* has been defined and formalized in many different ways. Views differ on whether they focus more on a verb's syntactic or semantic properties. To mention four different present-day kinds of lexical specification, verb types have been defined in terms of primitives such as subcategorization frames, argument structures, theta-grids and lexical-conceptual structures. What does verbal flexibility mean for the concept of verb type? What are its implications for the syntactic-semantic specification of verbs in the lexicon? What does it suggest with respect to the lexicon-syntax interface?

Seeing that a verb appears in more than one verb frame, the conclusion is that it belongs to more than one verb type and, hence, that it must be listed with multiple lexical specifications rather than just one; however, given that a verb keeps the same meaning across different frames, the conclusion is that there is one basic lexical entry underlying each of the verb frames a verb maps onto. Integrating the two, the phenomenon of frame alternations shows that the relation between verbs as lexical items and verbs figuring in syntactic configurations is one-to-many. I will refer to the phenomenon of frame alternations as *lexical-syntactic flexibility*.

The present chapter aims to show the dimensions of the phenomenon of lexical-syntactic flexibility in Dutch, dimensions that must be accounted for in any view on lexicon and mapping. I present the alternations without any pretension of completeness, neither as far as different kinds of alternations are concerned, nor as to listing the verbs that participate in them. Also, I am not concerned in the present chapter with productivity of alternations, i.e., the issue of which verbs can and cannot participate in a certain alternation. The set of data as presented by the phenomenon of lexical-syntactic flexibility forms the empirical domain with which theories on lexicon and the lexicon-interface are confronted. In Chapter 3, I will show how this domain can be characterized in terms of event semantics, all alternations falling into one of three kinds of event type-shifting. Interpreting the mapping generalizations that fall out from these event-semantic characterizations in Chapter 4, I will develop a proposal for a new lexicon-syntax theory. After discussing the pro's and con's of the other views on lexical-syntactic flexibility, I will conclude that the phenomenon of lexical-syntactic flexibility must be viewed as flexible mapping, i.e., one lexical representation maps onto many syntactic representations.

Before presenting Dutch flexibility data in the present chapter, I first introduce some terminology I will use for describing syntactic and semantic argument-taking properties and introduce the classification of frame alternations on which the chapter is organized.

2.2 Terminology and types of verb frame alternations

2.2.1 Terminology

In the discussion of frame alternations below, I use theory- and analysis-neutral terminology where possible. I refer to the two clauses of an alternation as its two *alternants* without making any assumptions about how to relate one to the other or derive one from the other.

In order to properly describe frame alternations, one needs to distinguish between a semantic and a syntactic characterization of the alternants. Semantically, a verb is a predicate which is characterized by a certain adicity or valency (its number of semantic arguments). A verb denotes a monadic, dyadic or triadic relation, taking one, two or three arguments, respectively. The notion *semantic argument* can be loosely defined as a participant in an event (see Chapters 3 and 4 for further definitions). Syntactically, a verb is characterized by the kind of frame it projects; a verb appears in an intransitive, transitive or ditransitive frame.

Often, linguistic usage of these terms is confusing. Sometimes people use the latter, syntactic terms (intransitive, transitive, etc.) to refer to a verb's lexical-semantic specification when talking about verbs with different numbers of variables in their subcategorization frame, argument structure, theta-grid or LCS. Traditionally, however, these terms refer to different syntactic configurations. I will use the terms here in the traditional way, i.e., to refer to a verb in an actual syntactic configuration, and employ the terms *valency* and *n-adic predicate* to refer to its lexical-semantic argument taking properties. Thus, an intransitive verb is a verb that projects only one syntactic argument position, a transitive projects two and a ditransitive three positions. I use the term *intransitive* to generalize over the two kinds of verb frames a monadic verb can appear in: an unergative or an unaccusative frame. An unergative verb projects a D-structure subject position for its single argument; an unaccusative projects a D-structure object position for its argument from where it NP-moves to subject position at S-structure.

The semantic and syntactic notions *argument* are integrated in terminology using *internal* and *external argument*; these terms refer to semantic arguments that map onto certain syntactic positions. The external argument is the semantic argument that is mapped onto subject position; internal arguments are mapped onto positions within the VP. Internal arguments are divided into direct and indirect ones. A direct internal argument is an argument in direct object position; an indirect internal argument is an argument in an oblique position.

Notice the tension between semantic and syntactic valency. Whereas two verbs can have the same number of arguments in terms of semantic valency and the same number of argument positions in their verb frames, they may still project two different verb frames. A monadic predicate maps its single argument either as external in an unergative frame or as internal in an unaccusative frame. A dyadic predicate maps its two arguments either as subject and object in a transitive frame, as subject and PP complement, or as direct object and PP complement. Surprisingly, there are no traditional names for the latter two verb frames. In order to distinguish the three different kinds of frames a dyadic predicate can appear in, I call a frame with a subject and a PP complement (and no direct object) an *oblique unergative* frame, and a frame with a direct object and a PP complement (and no subject) an *oblique unaccusative*. A triadic predicate maps its three arguments either as subject, object and PP complement, or as subject and two objects. I refer to the former frame as an *oblique transitive* frame, and to the latter as a *double object construction*. Generalizing over these two kinds of frames I use the term *ditransitive frame*.

I can now define more precisely the term *lexical-syntactic flexibility* introduced above: it refers to the phenomenon that a verb with a certain semantic valency can map its arguments onto several verb frames.

A final terminological issue concerns my usage of thematic labels. When discussing where a certain semantic argument ends up syntactically, it is sometimes convenient to use thematic labels such as "agent", "theme", "goal", "source", to ease reference to the appearances of a certain event participant in each alternant. I will not attempt to define these labels, but will simply use them as heuristics. To emphasize that usage of these labels does not imply any theoretical stand and is purely assumed for expository reasons, I will consistently put quotes around them.

2.2.2 Types of verb frame alternations

In pointing out verbs' flexibility by showing how they occur in different verb frames, one can take two different perspectives for grouping different kinds of alternations, i.e., from one side or the other of the mapping between semantic valency and verb frame. Looking at it from a syntactic perspective, flexibility can be described in terms of transitivity alternations involving a change in a verb's transitivity. Levin (1993) presents verb frame alternations in English from this perspective. On the other hand, looking from the semantic side of the mapping, flexibility can be described in terms of variations of the projection of semantic arguments onto syntax, variations both in the number of projected arguments and the positions onto which they are projected. Under both perspectives one will describe the same alternations, the only difference being the way they are grouped.

Here I choose the latter, semantic perspective. On a view of grammar in which projection of the syntactic argument positions is triggered by a verb's lexical-semantic specification, it is insightful for the study of the lexicon-syntax mapping to focus on the semantic arguments and see where they end up syntactically. Taking this perspective means that alternations with a certain syntactic form may show up under several semantic headings, since variation in transitivity can have various causes. It may be caused by adding an argument, by optionality of an argument, by suppressing an argument or by an argument's mapping onto different syntactic positions.[1]

Organizing the set of frame alternations from a lexical-semantic perspective then, I essentially distinguish three different kinds of flexibility. A first kind of flexibility is alternations in which the same set of arguments is mapped in both alternants, but in which the arguments appear in different syntactic positions. The number of semantic arguments and the number of syntactic positions is the same across both alternants, but the arguments vary the position they map onto (see (1a)). Typical examples are the locative (e.g., *load hay on the wagon-load the wagon with hay*) and the dative alternation (e.g., *send a letter to Mary-send Mary a letter*).

In other kinds of alternations, the two alternants do not project the same number of semantic arguments, i.e., one alternant projects one argument more than the other. There are two reasons why different numbers of arguments show up in each alternant. First, one alternant semantically has one argument more than the other. In the "longer" alternant there is an additional argument as compared to the "shorter" alternant, hence the number of syntactic argument positions differs (see (1b)). A typical example is the causative-inchoative alternation (e.g., *Mary breaks the vase-the vase breaks*). Second, the number of semantic arguments is the same, but not all arguments are syntactically projected, i.e., there is a discrepancy between the set of semantic arguments and the set of actually projected arguments. The alternant with one argument less has a so-called *understood* argument: an unprojected argument which is semantically present, but which does not surface syntactically. Along with the term *understood argument*, many other terms circulate, including *null*, *zero*, *optional*, *absorbed*, *suppressed* and *implicit argument*. They all refer to the same concept of a semantically present but unprojected argument. I use the term *understood argument*, which is the most neutral and general among them (see the beginning of section 2.5 for further discussion of terminology).

Alternations with an understood argument split up again: alternations in which not projecting the understood argument does not affect the syntactic positions of the other arguments and alternations in which the syntactic positions of the other arguments are affected (see (1c)). I refer to the understood argument of the former type as an *optional argument* (e.g., the object of pseudo-transitive verbs such as *eat*). The understood argument of the latter type is referred to as a *suppressed argument*. The active-passive alternation is a typical example of this kind (e.g., *Mary kisses John, John is kissed by Mary*). If the external argument is not projected in one alternant, another argument must NP-move and appear in subject position in order to satisfy the Extended Projection Principle or, alternatively, requirements on Predication (clauses need a subject). Thus, not projecting the external argument affects the surface syntactic position of another argument. At the beginning of section 2.6, I further discuss this issue.

(1) Different kinds of lexical-syntactic flexibility:

a. The set of projected arguments is the same in both alternants.
   - An argument varies the position it maps onto.

b. A different number of arguments is projected in each alternant, because the set of semantic arguments differs across the alternants
   - There is an additional argument in one alternant.

c. The set of semantic arguments is the same, but the number of projected arguments is different in each alternant: one argument is not projected.
- The unprojected argument is an optional argument;
- The unprojected argument is a suppressed argument.

The notions *additional*, *optional* and *suppressed argument* will be defined more precisely in the sections in which alternations with such arguments are illustrated. Of course, several kinds of flexibility can conflate in a particular alternation (e.g., the locative alternation is a conflation of arguments varying their syntactic position and being optional). The data are taken from Dutch. For each kind of flexibility, several frame alternations will be discussed. Each alternation is illustrated with one or two verbs. More verbs that participate in a certain alternation are listed alongside. I will not discuss restrictions on flexibility, i.e., which verbs can appear in which alternations and which cannot.

In many cases, Dutch marks an alternation pattern overtly with its morphology; it does so much more often than English. In one alternant, the verb is morphologically simplex, i.e., a root, and in the other alternant, it is a prefixed or particle variant of the simplex verb. Thus, the verbs in the two alternants of a frame alternation are often morphologically related pairs of verbs; the morphology overtly marks the alternation. Of course, there are smaller or bigger meaning differences between a root verb and its morphologically complex variants which are due to the additional prefix or particle. I will use the term *variant* to refer to root, prefixed and particle verbs when they denote similar kinds of events. In all cases to be discussed in this chapter, the meanings of the root verb and its variants are more or less transparently related.

There exist different kinds of meaning relations between two variants of one verbal meaning. Sometimes the semantic relation is one of entailment: the event as denoted by one variant entails a subevent which is the event as denoted by another or the root variant (e.g., an event of *uitlachen* 'laughing at somebody' entails a *lachen* 'laughing' event). In other cases, the two verbs are hyponyms (e.g., the event denoted by *inschrijven* 'register' is a more specific writing event than the one denoted by *schrijven* 'write'). Often, the slight meaning differences across two variants of one verbal meaning cause verbs to impose different selectional restrictions on their arguments.

Even though I do not take over Levin's (1993) classification of verb classes nor all her names for alternations, I used her detailed description of English verb classes and alternations for systematically singling out many different kinds of flexibility in Dutch and compiling the alternations I am about to present. Levin provides a rather exhaustive set of very up to date references to work on various frame alternations. I therefore refrain from listing many references in this chapter and refer to her work.

In sections 2.3 through 2.6, I illustrate the different kinds of lexical-syntactic flexibility distinguished in (1).

2.3 Position-varying arguments

A first kind of lexical-syntactic flexibility is alternations in which an argument (or arguments) varies with respect to which syntactic position it maps onto. All semantic arguments are projected; flexibility lies in the ways they map onto syntax. There are two different types: (i) the flexible argument is mapped either as direct or indirect internal argument, i.e., as direct object or PP complement (subsection 2.3.1); (ii) the flexible argument is mapped either as internal or external argument, i.e., as object or subject (subsection 2.3.2). Several alternations of each type will be discussed. Finally, I discuss an alternation in which an argument is projected either as a head or as a maximal projection (subsection 2.3.3).

2.3.1 An argument maps onto direct or indirect internal argument position

First, I discuss some alternations with triadic predicates in which the two internal arguments change their position. Consider the dative alternation illustrated with *geven* 'give' in (2).

Dative alternation

(2) a. Claire geeft een tekening aan Henriëtte.
'C. gives a drawing to H.'
b. Claire geeft Henriëtte een tekening.
'C. gives H. a drawing.'

The two internal arguments of *geven* 'give' are mapped onto syntax in one of two ways. In the dative construction (2a), the "theme" is mapped as direct object and the "goal" in a dative PP complement. In the double object construction (2b), both "theme" and "goal" are mapped as objects. Many triadic verbs selecting a "goal" argument participate in this alternation, including *vragen* 'ask', *verkopen* 'sell', *sturen* 'send', *uitlenen* 'lend', *verhuren* 'rent', *uitleggen* 'explain', *beloven* 'promise', *toestaan* 'allow'.

Oehrle (1976) points out that there is a slight meaning difference between the two alternants of the dative alternation.[2] The meaning implications are different: in the double object construction the "goal" actually receives the "theme"; in the dative construction this is not necessarily the case. The difference is rather subtle. Compare *sturen* 'send' in (3a) and (3b).

(3) a. Elly heeft een overlevingspakket aan haar broer in Amerika gestuurd.
E. has a survival package to her brother in America sent
'E. sent a survival package to her brother in America.'
b. Elly heeft haar broer in Amerika een overlevingspakket gestuurd.
E. has her brother in America a survival package sent
'E. sent her brother in America a survival package.'

The dative construction in (3a) may be followed by: ... *but it never reached him.* The double object construction in (3b), however, implies that the package is actually received.

Benefactive alternation

A similar alternation is the benefactive alternation. While the "theme" maps as direct object, the benefactive argument is mapped in one of two ways: in one alternant it appears in a PP complement headed by *voor* 'for'; in the other it shows up as a second object. Consider *inschenken* 'pour' in (4).

(4) a. Mieke schenkt een glas port in voor Moniek.
'M. pours a glass of porto for M.'
b. Mieke schenkt Moniek een glas port in.
'M. pours M. a glass of porto.'

Other examples include: *opscheppen* 'dish up' and *voordoen* 'demonstrate'. Only very few verbs that take a benefactive *voor* 'for' complement undergo the benefactive alternation in standard Dutch. In certain Dutch dialects (e.g., Limburgian), the benefactive alternation is much more productive, as it is in English.

Notice that although many verbs can combine with a benefactive phrase, it is not always a complement of the verb, as Henk van Riemsdijk (personal communication) points out. A benefactive phrase can also be an adjunct. The interpretation of *inschenken* 'pour' intended in (4) is the one in which the person whom the wine is poured for will also drink the wine. An adjunct interpretation of the benefactive phrase is also possible in (4a), i.e., that the pourer is helping the other person pouring drinks for others. This interpretation is not available in the double object alternant, (4b).

Locative alternation

In the locative alternation another kind of position-varying effect appears: the two internal arguments seem to take over each other's syntactic positions. Consider *sproeien* 'spray' in (5).

(5) a. Kees sproeit het regenwater op de fuchsia's.
'K. sprays the rainwater on the fuchsia's.'

b. Kees besproeit de fuchsia's (met regenwater).
K. PFX-sprays the fuchsia's (with rainwater)
'K. sprays the fuchsia's (with rainwater).'

In one alternant (5a), *sproeien* 'spray' projects its "theme" as an object and its "goal" in a PP complement. In the other alternant (5b), *besproeien* 'spray' (literally, PFX-spray) maps its "goal" as an object and its "theme" in a PP. The locative alternation is well known for the meaning difference between the two alternants. The argument mapped as direct object receives a so-called holistic interpretation (S. Anderson 1971). In (5a) the interpretation focuses on the rainwater (all of it gets sprayed), while in (5b) its focus is on the fuchsia's (all of them get sprayed). Or, as Tenny (1987, 1994) puts it, in (5a) the rainwater measures out the spraying event, while in (5b) the fuchsia's measure it out. Notice that in the second alternant (5b), the PP is optional. When the PP is absent, the "theme" argument is an understood argument, i.e., it is underlyingly present. Thus, the locative alternation in fact conflates two kinds of flexibility: two arguments vary their syntactic position and one of them is optional (see section 2.5 on optional arguments).

The locative alternation is typically marked with *be*-prefixation in Dutch, but it also occurs with particle verbs when the root verb combines with a resultative particle (e.g., *vol* 'full'; *leeg* 'empty') or with a prepositional particle (e.g., *in* 'in'; *op* 'on(to)'). *Smeren* 'smear' in the locative alternation can appear in four different forms, (6).

(6) a. Ingrid smeert henna op / in / door haar haar.
'I. smears henna on / in / through her hair.'

b. Ingrid besmeert haar haar (met henna).
I. PFX-smears her hair (with henna)
'I. covers her hair (with henna).'

c. Ingrid smeert haar haar vol (met henna).
'I. smears her hair full (with henna).'

d. Ingrid smeert haar haar in (met henna).
I. smears her hair in (with henna)
'I. greases her hair (with henna).'

Although all these different variants of *smeren* 'smear' refer to smearing events, there are slight meaning differences. *Besmeren* 'PFX-smear' in (6b) implies that the henna gets smeared onto the outer part of the hair; *volsmeren* 'smear full' in (6c) implies that all of the hair becomes full of henna; *insmeren* 'grease' (literally, 'smear in') in (6d) implies that the hair also absorbs the henna.

As they express different meanings, various prefixes and particles put different selectional restrictions on the "goal" object.[3] These meaning differences and their associated selectional restrictions are the reason why certain verbs only combine with prefix *be-*, others only with particle *vol* 'full' or prepositional particles, and yet others with all types. Some verbs that only take *be-* are: *sprenkelen-besprenkelen* 'sprinkle'; *stelen-bestelen* 'rob'; *roven-beroven* 'rob'. Some verbs only take *vol*, including: *proppen-volproppen* 'stuff-stuff full'; *gooien-volgooien* 'throw-throw full; *stoppen-volstoppen* 'stuff-stuff full'; *schenken-volschenken* 'pour-pour full'. Most verbs can combine with a *be*-prefix and particles in the locative alternation. Some examples are: *sproeien-besproeien, volsproeien, afsproeien* 'spray-spray, spray full, spray off' (see (5)); *spuiten-bespuiten, volspuiten* 'squirt-squirt, squirt full '; *laden-beladen, opladen, inladen, uitladen* 'load-load, load, load, unload'; *gieten-begieten, volgieten* 'pour-pour, pour full'; *drukken-bedrukken, voldrukken* 'print-print, print full'; *planten-beplanten, volplanten* 'plant-plant, plant full'; *hangen-behangen, volhangen* 'hang-hang, hang full'; *strooien-bestrooien, volstrooien* 'strew-strew, strew full'; *zaaien-inzaaien, volzaaien* 'plant-sew, plant full'.

Alternatively, the position changes in the locative alternation can be looked upon in a different way. In view of the fact that the *met* 'with'-PP is optional in the second alternant in (5b) and (6b-d) and is interpreted as an "instrument" rather than a "theme", one can view it as an adjunct rather than an argument (e.g., Jackendoff 1990; Booij 1992). Hence, the verb is triadic in the first alternant (*sproeien* in (5a), *smeren* in (6a)), whereas it is dyadic in the second alternant (*besproeien* in (5b), *besmeren, volsmeren, insmeren* in (6b-d)). In this alternative view, the locative alternation is a conflation of two kinds: an argument varies its syntactic position and the verb has an extra argument in one of the alternants.

Similar to the locative alternation is the *strijken* 'iron'-alternation (the Dutch variant of Levin's 1993 *wipe*-alternation). This alternation conflates variable syntactic positions with an extra argument. In one alternant the verb takes two internal arguments and in the other it takes only one of them which is in a different syntactic position. Consider *strijken* 'iron' in (7).

(7) a. Mai strijkt de plooien in de rok.
'M. irons the pleats into the skirt.'
b. Mai strijkt de rok (*met plooien).
'M. irons the skirt (*with pleats).'
c. Mai strijkt de rok glad.
'M. irons the skirt smooth.'

In one alternant the two arguments of *strijken* 'iron' are a "theme" as direct object and a "goal" in a PP complement headed by *in* 'into' in (7a). In the other alternant, only the "goal" argument appears, but now as a direct object and with a "theme" interpretation, (7b). The other argument cannot be mapped, not even in an adjunct PP, (7b). A resultative particle can be added, e.g., *glad* 'smooth' in (7c).

Some verbs in the *strijken* 'iron'-alternation take a PP complement headed by *in* 'into' while others take a PP with *van (af)* 'off' or *uit* 'of'. Some examples include: *prikken* 'pin'; *steken* 'sting'; *wassen* 'wash'; *scheren* 'shave'; *schuren* 'sandpaper'; *schrobben* 'scrub'; *boenen* 'brush'; *borstelen* 'brush'; *stofzuigen* 'vacuum'. Another set of verbs in this alternation strongly prefer or even require a particle in the second alternant. Some examples include: *vegen-uitvegen, afvegen, schoonvegen* 'wipe-wipe out, wipe off, wipe clean'; *stoffen-afstoffen* 'dust-dust off'; *schrapen-afschrapen, uitschrapen, schoonschrapen, leegschrapen* 'scrape-scrape off, scrape out, scrape clean, scrape empty'; *krabben-afkrabben, schoonkrabben, leegkrabben* 'scratch-scratch off, scratch clean, scratch empty'; *spuiten-afspuiten, schoonspuiten, leegspuiten, volspuiten* 'spray-spray off, spray clean, spray empty, spray full'; *spoelen-afspoelen, uitspoelen, schoonspoelen* 'rinse-rinse off, rinse down, rinse clean'; *likken-aflikken, uitlikken* 'lick-lick off, lick out';

wrijven-uitwrijven, inwrijven, schoonwrijven 'rub-rub out, rub in, rub clean'; *sproeien-afsproeien* 'spray-spray off'.

Material-Product alternation

Another set of triadic verbs that participate in an alternation in which the internal arguments are shuffled around are verbs of "creation", i.e., some product is created out of some material. In one alternant, the argument denoting the product is the direct object and the material is a "source" PP complement; in the other alternant, the material is the direct object and the created product is a "goal" PP complement. Levin (1993) dubs this alternation the *material-product alternation*. Consider *naaien* 'sew' in (8).

(8) a. Ilse naait de kostuums (van zelfbedrukte stof).
'I. sews the costumes (from hand-printed cloth).'
b. Ilse (ver)naait de zelfbedrukte stof tot kostuums.
I. (PFX)-sews the hand-printed cloth into costumes.
'I. sews the hand-printed cloth into costumes.'
c. Ilse naait de gordijnen om tot kostuums.
I. sews the curtains around into costumes.
'I. changes the curtains into costumes by sewing.'

In the first alternant, the material PP complement is optional, (8a). In the second alternant, *naaien* 'sew' prefers a prefix *ver-* or a particle *om* 'around' which changes the meaning slightly. Prefixed *vernaaien* 'sew' in (8b) suggests that all of the cloth is getting sewn and transformed into costumes; particle verb *omnaaien* 'sew' in (8c) implies that the material argument, *gordijnen* 'curtains', once was a product itself and is transformed into a new product.

The material-product alternation applies to many "creation" verbs. Verbs that do not take a prefix or particle include: *bakken* 'bake'; *kneden* 'knead'; *houwen* 'chop'; *kleien* 'clay'; *vouwen* 'fold'; *blazen* 'blow'; *draaien* 'roll'; *rollen* 'roll'; *ontwikkelen* 'develop'; *snijden* 'carve'; *weven* 'weave'; *spinnen* 'spin'; *persen* 'press'; *rijgen* 'thread'. Other verbs need a prefix or particle in the second alternant. Verbs combining only with *ver-* include: *snijden-versnijden* 'cut-cut (into something else)'; *maken-vermaken* 'make-change'; *timmeren-vertimmeren* 'build (out of wood)-build (into something else)'; *knippen-verknippen* 'cut-cut (into something else)'. A verb that combines with both *ver-* and *om* is *vormen-vervormen, omvormen* 'form-form (into something else)'.

Having discussed some position-changing alternations which involve triadic predicates, I now turn to alternations with dyadic predicates.

Transitive-conative alternation

In the transitive-conative alternation the single internal argument varies its status between direct and indirect internal arguments. The name *conative frame* applies to a subset of the verbs with a subject and PP complement, namely verbs that ". . . describe an 'attempted' action without specifying whether the action was actually carried out (Levin 1993:42)".[4] In the transitive-conative alternation, dyadic verbs map their "theme" argument either as direct or oblique object. Different verbs select a different preposition in the conative alternant. Consider *duwen* 'push' in (9) and *schieten* 'shoot' in (10).

(9) a. Paola duwt de auto.
'P. pushes the car.'
b. Paola duwt tegen de auto.
'P. pushes against the car.'

(10) a. Theo schiet een konijn.
'T. shoots a rabbit.'
b. Theo schiet op een konijn.
'T. shoots at a rabbit.'

The events in both frames are the same kinds of events. While the focus in the conative frame is on the activities of the "agent", the transitive frame focuses not only on the action but also on its effect. In (9a) the car gets into motion when it is being pushed; in (9b) it does not, at least not necessarily. In (10a) the rabbit is hit by the shooting; in (10b) it is not (or not necessarily). Some other examples include: *bijten-bijten naar* 'bite-bite at'; *trappen-trappen naar* 'kick-kick at'; *schoppen-schoppen naar, tegen* 'kick-kick at, against'; *slaan-slaan naar* 'hit-hit at'; *trekken-trekken aan* 'pull-pull at'.

Transitive-oblique alternation

The transitive-conative alternation can be subsumed under a more general alternation which I call the transitive-oblique alternation. Many dyadic predicates can map their internal argument either as direct or indirect object.[5] The alternation is very productive. All transitive verbs with a so-called incremental theme also have an alternant in which the theme occurs as PP in an oblique intransitive frame. Consider *schilderen* 'paint' in (11).

(11) a. Toos schilderde het huis.
'T. painted the house.'
b. Toos schilderde aan het huis.
T. painted at the house
'T. was painting the house.'

The meaning effect is the same as in the transitive-conative alternation, but the oblique frame does not have an attempt-interpretation. In the oblique frame (11b) the focus is on the process of painting a house without being specific about its outcome; in the transitive frame (11a) the focus is not only on the painting process but also on its outcome: the house gets completely painted.[6] Some other verbs with *aan* 'on' in the oblique alternant include: *schrijven* 'write' (see (45) below); *draaien* 'turn'; *bouwen* 'build'; *naaien* 'sew'; *breien* 'knit'; *voelen* 'feel'; *ruiken* 'smell'. Another set of verbs selects other prepositions in the oblique alternant, depending on the meaning of the verb, for example, *eten-eten van* 'eat-eat of' (see (46) below); *nemen-nemen van* 'take-take of'; *lezen-lezen in* 'read-read in'. The same transitive-oblique alternation also applies to stative verbs, e.g., *vertrouwen-vertrouwen op* 'trust-trust on'.

Also pairs of verb/prefixed verb appear in the transitive-oblique alternation. Consider *luisteren-beluisteren* in (12) and *reizen-bereizen* in (13).

(12) a. Hein luistert naar zijn nieuwe CD van Rodney Kendrick.
'H. listens to his new CD of Rodney Kendrick.'
b. Hein beluistert zijn nieuwe CD van Rodney Kendrick.
H. PFX-listens his new CD of Rodney Kendrick
'H. listens to his new CD of Rodney Kendrick.'

(13) a. Kirstin reist door Zuid-Amerika.
'K. travels through South-America.'
b. Kirstin bereist Zuid-Amerika.
K. PFX-travels South-America
'K. travels through South-America.'

In the oblique alternant, the verb is a simplex verb and the internal argument occurs as PP complement, (12a) and (13a). In the transitive alternant, the verb is prefixed with *be-* and the internal argument occurs as direct object, (12b) and (13b). Notice that prefixation with *be-* has the same syntactic position-changing effect here as in the locative alternation: the argument that appears as PP complement of the simplex verb, appears as direct object of the *be-*verb. The meaning effects are the same as in the unprefixed form of the transitive-oblique alternation: the oblique frames focus on listening and traveling as ongoing processes; the transitive frames highlight both processes and some sort of effects. In (12b) the new CD is completely listened to, while in (12a) he may have listened to parts of it only. The travels in (13b) suggest a complete span of the continent, while the (single) trip in (13a) may have been to just one part of it.

The transitive-oblique alternation encoded with *be-*prefixation is very productive. Other examples with transitive *be-*verbs are: oblique *praten over* 'talk about' and transitive *bepraten* 'discuss'; *spreken over-bespreken* 'speak about-discuss'; *denken over-bedenken* 'think about-think up'; *kijken naar-bekijken* 'look at-examine'; *gluren naar-*

begluren 'peek at-peek'; *voelen aan-bevoelen* 'feel at-feel'; *liegen tegen-beliegen* 'lie to-belie'; *spotten met-bespotten* 'ridicule-ridicule'; *klimmen op-beklimmen* 'climb up-climb'; *varen over-bevaren* 'navigate over-navigate'; *zeilen over-bezeilen* 'sail over-sail'; *sluipen naar-besluipen* 'steal-steal'. For another set of verb pairs, the alternation is encoded with other prefixes and particles. Some examples include: *werken aan-bewerken, verwerken* 'work on-work, work into'; *luisteren naar-afluisteren* 'listen to-overhear'; *kijken naar-afkijken* 'look at-copy'; *vluchten uit-ontvluchten* 'flee from-flee'; *zorgen voor-verzorgen* 'look after-take care of'; *binden aan-verbinden* 'bind to-connect'; *lachen om-uitlachen* 'laugh at'; *rijden op-berijden, inrijden* 'ride on-ride, run in'; *springen op-bespringen, naspringen* 'jump onto-jump, jump after'; *studeren op-bestuderen, instuderen* 'study at-study, learn'; *rekenen met-berekenen, verrekenen, uitrekenen* 'calculate with-calculate, deduct, figure out'; *schieten op-beschieten, afschieten* 'shoot at-shoot, fire'; *jagen op-verjagen, opjagen* 'chase-chase away, rout'.

This concludes the discussion of position-changing alternations involving the syntactic position of internal arguments, i.e., whether they are mapped as direct or oblique object. The next subsection discusses a second kind involving arguments that are mapped either as internal or external argument.

2.3.2 An argument maps onto internal or external argument position

Unergative-unaccusative alternation

Many intransitives map their single argument either as internal or as external argument, displaying what I call the unergative-unaccusative alternation. In most cases, this alternation is morphologically marked: the unaccusative variant is a prefixed or particle variant of a simplex, unergative verb. This alternation can be tracked down in Dutch by comparing the auxiliaries the two variants select. Unergatives select HAVE and unaccusatives select BE.[7] Compare *drogen-uitdrogen* 'dry-dry out' in (14) and *reizen-afreizen* 'travel-set off to travel' in (15).

(14) a. De klei heeft in de zon gedroogd.
the clay has in the sun dried
'The clay dried in the sun.'
b. De klei is in de felle zon helemaal uitgedroogd.
the clay is in the blazing sun out-dried
'The clay dried out in the blazing sun.'

(15) a. Farook heeft voor zijn werk veel gereisd.
F. has for his job much travelled
'F. travelled a lot for his job.'
b. Farook is naar Kiev afgereisd.
F. is to Kiev off-travelled
'F. set off to travel to Kiev.'

In one alternant, (14a), the "theme" is an external argument of simplex *drogen* 'dry'; in the other, (14b), the same argument is an internal argument of *uitdrogen* 'dry out'. Similarly, the "agent" is an external argument of *reizen* 'travel' in (15a), and an internal argument of *afreizen* 'set off to travel' in (15b). The events in both alternants are the same kinds of events. The verbs in the unergative alternants focus on the processes of drying and travelling. The particle verbs in the unaccusative alternants denote the same processes, plus some transition moment in the events: the result of the drying clay in (14b) is that it dried out; *afreizen* 'set off to travel' in (15b) marks the inchoative moment of travelling.

All verbs of manner of motion participate in the unergative-unaccusative alternation. The alternation is independent of the kind of subject, i.e., whether it is an "agent" or a "theme". The root verb appears in an unergative frame. In the unaccusative alternant, the verb is extended with a particle that denotes a "goal". All verbs can combine with the general "goal" particle *weg* 'away', e.g., *weglopen* 'walk away'; *wegzwemmen* 'swim away'. Many verbs also combine with other particles, e.g., *aflopen* 'expire'; *inlopen* 'warm up for walking'; *afgaan* 'go off'; *uitgaan* 'go out'; *omdraaien* 'turn around'; *uitrijden* 'ride out'; *uitvaren* 'sail out'; *uitzeilen* 'sail out; *uitzwermen* 'swarm out'; *afzwemmen* 'take a swimming exam'.

Even without a prefix or particle, but with a clear meaning difference, certain motion verbs undergo the alternation. For example, unergative *springen* 'jump' denotes an ongoing jumping event (it takes HAVE as its auxiliary), whereas unaccusative *springen* 'jump' implies that the jump(ing) finished at a certain endpoint (it takes BE as its auxiliary). Motion verbs in the unergative-unaccusative alternation will be discussed again in section 2.4 where the unaccusativity trigger is a "goal" PP complement (see (33) and (34)).

More in general, many intransitive verbs have a particle or prefix variant with which they appear in the unergative-unaccusative alternation. These include: unergative *slapen* 'sleep' and unaccusative *inslapen* 'fall asleep'; *drogen-verdrogen, opdrogen* 'dry-dry, dry up'; *bloeien-opbloeien* 'flower-revive'; *gloeien-opgloeien* 'glow-glow up'; *groeien-opgroeien, vergroeien* 'grow-grow up, become deformed'; *stromen-wegstromen* 'stream-stream away'; *dwalen-afdwalen, verdwalen* 'roam-stray, get lost'; *koken-inkoken, overkoken* 'boil-boil in, boil over'; *hongeren-verhongeren* 'starve'; *branden-verbranden, ontbranden, opbranden, uitbranden* 'burn-burn (away), burn up, ignite burn out'; *rotten-verrotten* 'rot-rot (away)'; *slijten-verslijten* 'wear out'; *dampen-verdampen* 'steam-evaporate'. Sometimes the unergative-unaccusative alternation is marked morpho-syntactically: the verb in the unaccusative alternant is a reflexive variant of the verb in the unergative alternant, e.g., *werken-zich inwerken* 'work-get adjusted to new work'; *bewegen-zich bewegen* 'move'.[8]

Reciprocal alternation

Another kind of alternation that varies the syntactic status of the internal and external argument is the reciprocal alternation. The alternation applies to transitives like *ontmoeten* 'meet', (16).

(16) a. Lidy ontmoette Maarten op een boot.
'L. met M. on a boat.'
b. Lidy en Maarten ontmoetten elkaar op een boot.
'L. and M. met each other on a boat.'

In one alternant, (16a), the arguments are distributed over subject and object positions; in the other, (16b), they form a plural subject, and there is an obligatory reciprocal object. There is a slight meaning difference between the two alternants: the singular subject alternant is an "asymmetric" event of meeting, whereas the plural subject alternant denotes a "symmetric" event with both participants equally involved. Other examples include: *aantreffen* 'find'; *treffen* 'meet'; *zoeken* 'look for'; *vinden* 'find'; *tegenkomen* 'meet'; *aaien* 'pet'; *strelen* 'stroke'; *kussen* 'kiss'.

The reciprocal alternation also applies to dyadic predicates in an oblique intransitive frame, for example *trouwen* 'marry', (17).

(17) a. Paul is vorige zomer met Anastasia getrouwd.
P. is last summer with A. married
'P. married A. last summer.'

b. Paul en Anastasia zijn vorige zomer (met elkaar) getrouwd.
P. and A. are last summer (with each other) married
'P. and A. married (each other) last summer.'

In one alternant, (17a), the two arguments are distributed, one in subject and the other in the complement of a *met* 'with' PP. In the other alternant, (17b), both arguments are conjoined, creating a plural subject, and there is an optional PP complement with the reciprocal pronoun *elkaar* 'each other'. When the PP is absent, there is an understood reciprocal argument.[9]

Other dyadic predicates that figure in the reciprocal alternation with oblique intransitive alternants with a *met* 'with PP include: *vrijen* 'make love to'; *zich verloven* 'get engaged to'; *zich vergelijken* 'compare oneself to'; *afspreken* 'have an appointment with'; *praten* 'talk'; *konverseren* 'converse'; *diskussiëren* 'discuss'; *debatteren* 'debate'. Another set of dyadic predicates in this alternation take an obligatory PP complement, i.e., the reciprocal PP cannot remain unprojected. The PP complements of these verbs are headed by other prepositions; they include: *lijken op* 'resemble to'; *kijken naar* 'look at', *luisteren naar* 'listen to', *voelen aan* 'feel at'.

2.3.3 An argument projects as head or maximal projection

Finally I present one more alternation which is of a different kind than the previous position-varying ones. Verbs that take a "goal" argument either map it as a PP complement or combine with a "goal" word, i.e., a particle. Looking at this paradigm from the lexical side of the lexicon-syntax mapping, it seems that the projection of the "goal" argument alternates between a head and a maximal projection. I call this alternation the particle-PP alternation.

Particle-PP alternation

The alternation is very productive and essentially applies to all verbs that take a "goal" argument. A "goal" can appear as a particle, as a prepositional, postpositional or circumpositional PP, or as a PP headed by an intransitive preposition.[10] For ease of exposition, I will group together the different kinds of one-word "goals" and call them all particles.

Examples include both triadic and dyadic verbs taking different kinds of "goal" phrases: *sturen* 'mail' with a dative "goal", (18); *fietsen* 'bike' with a directional "goal", (19); *kijken* 'look' with a "goal" indicating a direction, (20); *zetten* 'put' with a locative "goal", (21).

(18) a. Moon stuurt een CD naar Bart.
'M. mails a CD to B.'
b. Moon stuurt een CD op.
M. mails a CD up
'M. mails a CD.'

(19) a. Daniel fietst naar school toe.
D. bikes to school to
'D. bikes to school.'

b. Daniel fietst weg.
'D. bikes away.'

(20) a. Lia kijkt naar de sterren.
'L. looks at the stars.'
b. Lia kijkt op.
'L. looks up.'

(21) a. Philip zet de kliko in de schuur.
'P. puts the trash can in the shed.'
b. Philip zet de kliko binnen.
'P. puts the trash can inside.'

The two alternants refer to the same events; the sentence in which a full PP is projected describes the event in more detail than the one with only a particle. A verb selects a particle of a certain semantic kind, e.g., a locative one such as *weg* 'away' in (19b) and *binnen* 'inside' in (21b), or it selects a particular particle idiosyncratically, e.g., *opsturen* 'mail (out)' in (18b) and *opkijken* 'look up' in (20b).

Often, the lexically selected particle has the same form as the preposition that heads the PP in the other alternant. Consider *stapelen-opstapelen* 'stack-stack up', (22).

(22) a. Juliëtte stapelt de blokken op elkaar.
'J. stacks the blocks on each other.'
b. Juliëtte stapelt de blokken op.
'J. stacks up the blocks.'

Some more verbs of the latter kind include: *gieten-opgieten* 'pour'; *spuiten-inspuiten* 'inject'; *schenken-inschenken* 'pour-pour out'; *wrijven-inwrijven* 'rub-rub in'; *smeren-uitsmeren* 'smear-smear out'; *stoppen-instoppen* 'put-tuck in'; *breken-afbreken* 'break-break off'; *scheuren-uitscheuren* 'tear-tear out'; *trekken-uittrekken* 'pull-pull out; *trekken-aantrekken* 'put-put on'; *zetten-opzetten* 'put-put on'; *zetten-afzetten* 'put-

put off'; *doen-omdoen* 'put-put around'; *doen-aandoen* 'put on'; *doen-indoen* 'put-put in'.

By discussing the particle-PP alternation in this section, I have chosen to classify it as an alternation in which arguments vary their syntactic status, taking the fact that the "goal" occurs as a PP complement or as particle as its determining characteristic. In his system of thematic relations, Gruber (1965) also collapses phrasal and word "goals" as expressions of the thematic relation "goal".

This classification may seem questionable; it is very uncommon to consider a particle an argument of the verb. Consider some alternatives. One might classify the alternation as a ditransitive-transitive or a transitive-intransitive alternation in which the "goal" argument remains unprojected in one alternant, for example because it is an optional argument. In particular, the example in (22) seems to suggest that the internal argument of the preposition *op* 'on' is optionally projected. This cannot be right, however. An unprojected argument (whether it is optional or suppressed) must be semantically present as an understood argument (see the definitions in sections 2.5 and 2.6). This is not the case in the b-alternants of (18)-(22). Semantically, the particle saturates the role of "goal", and there is no other, understood "goal". Moreover, the head of the PP and the particle are not the same in (18)-(21), which excludes the possibility of analyzing the internal argument of the preposition as an optional argument in the first place.

Another alternative would be to consider it as a transitive-ditransitive alternation in which the PP complement is an additional argument. However, an additional argument involves a meaning extension between the two alternants, the second alternant taking one more argument because the verb's meaning is extended (see definition in section 2.4). This is not the case in the PP-particle alternation: there is no such meaning difference between the two alternants.

In order to see that the particle really is a "goal" argument, notice what happens when both particle and PP are present (23)-(27).

(23) Moon stuurt een CD op naar Bart.
'M. mails a CD to B.'

(24) Daniel fietst weg naar school.
'D. bikes away to school.'

(25) Lia kijkt op naar de sterren.
'L. looks up to the stars.'

(26) Philip zet de kliko binnen in de schuur.
'P. puts the garbage container inside in the shed.'

(27) Juliëtte stapelt de blokken op op de tafel.
'J. stacks up the blocks on the table.'

All of these sentences are grammatical. Notice, however, their exact meanings. In (23)-(26), the "goal" seems to be doubled: the combination of verb, particle and PP is only grammatical on an interpretation in which the PP modifies the particle, rather than the verb. For example, in (24): he bikes away, namely to school. In (27), interpreting both particle and PP as "goal" is equally impossible; it would be one "goal" too many. The sentence is grammatical with a modifier interpretation of the PP, i.e., if the stacking event takes place on the table, the PP is a modifier of the event rather than of the verb.

The fact that the PPs in (23)-(27) can only be interpreted as modifiers (and not as arguments), both semantically as well as syntactically, and the fact that the interpretation of both particle and PP as "goals" in (27) feels like a Theta Criterion violation, suggest that the particles must indeed be considered as "goal" arguments in these examples. Therefore, classifying the particle-PP alternation with alternations involving an argument varying its syntactic status is not as outrageous as it may have seemed.

2.3.4 Summarizing position-varying alternations

The particle-PP alternation concludes the first set of alternations which involve arguments mapping onto various syntactic positions or having a different status (head or maximal projection). The alternations in subsection 2.3.1 present arguments varying between direct and indirect internal argument position: the dative, benefactive, locative, *strijken* 'iron', material-product, transitive-conative and transitive-oblique alternations. Internal arguments such as "themes" and "goals" can map either as direct object or as PP complement. In subsection 2.3.2 the alternations involve an argument varying between internal and external argument position: the unergative-unaccusative and reciprocal alternations. Examples of the latter show how "agents" and "themes" map either as subject or as direct object (at D-structure). In the final subsection 2.3.3 I discussed an alternation involving variable syntactic projections rather than positions: the particle-PP alternation.

In the alternations discussed so far, the number of arguments is the same across the two alternants. In the rest of this chapter, I discuss several kinds of lexical-syntactic flexibility in which the number of arguments is different.

2.4 Additional arguments

Verbs can be flexible in the sense that they project different numbers of argument positions (one or two, two or three). These alternations divide into two different types. In one set of alternations, one alternant has one argument more than the other, syntactically as well semantically. In another set of alternations, the number of semantic arguments is the same in both alternants, but the number of syntactic argument positions is not. Alternations of the first kind can be thought of as having an additional argument in the "longer" alternant, as compared to the "shorter" alternant. An additional semantic argument triggers the projection of an extra syntactic position. Alternations of the latter kind have a syntactically unprojeced argument which is semantically "present" as an understood argument. This section presents alternations with additional arguments.

A verb can vary its meaning, usually by extending it; this may trigger an extra argument. Extra arguments are different from understood arguments: when an extra argument is not mapped, there is no semantic "understanding" of it. I discuss four kinds of causativization alternations, followed by several other alternations with additional arguments.

Causative-inchoative alternation

The most well known addition alternation is the causative-inchoative alternation. In the inchoative alternant, the verb selects one argument; in the causative alternant, it selects two arguments. Consider *breken* 'break', (28).

(28) a. Het ei is gebroken.
the egg is broken
'The egg broke.'
b. Inge breekt het ei.
'I. breaks the egg.'

In the inchoative alternant (28a), the verb is unaccusative (BE-selection); the single argument is mapped onto direct object position. In the causative alternant (28b), the verb is transitive. The semantic relation between the two alternants is an entailment relation. The transitive alternant entails the intransitive one: when Inge breaks the egg, the egg breaks.

More verbs that appear in the causative-inchoative alternation are: *afbreken* 'break off'; *omdraaien* 'turn around'; *smelten* 'melt'; *splitsen* 'split'; *oplossen* 'dissolve'; *verdampen* 'evaporate'; *doven* 'extinguish'; *sluiten* 'close'; *trouwen* 'marry'; *verdrinken* 'drown'; *scheuren* 'tear'; *inscheuren* 'tear in'; *veranderen* 'change'; *opvrolijken* 'cheer up'; *opknappen* 'recover/patch up'.[11] The intransitive variant of all these verbs is unaccusative.

Causative-process alternation

The entailed subevent in a causative event can be one of various aspectual types: an inchoative event (i.e., an achievement) as in (28), a process, an accomplishment or a state (see section 3.3 for a discussion of these aspectual notions). In what I will call the causative-process alternation, the intransitive alternant denotes a process and the transitive denotes a caused process. Consider *koken* 'boil', (29).

(29) a. De aardappels hebben te lang gekookt.
the potatoes have too long boiled
'The potatoes boiled for too long.'
b. Bart heeft de aardappels precies lang genoeg gekookt.
B. has the potatoes exactly long enough boiled
'B. boiled the potatoes exactly long enough.'

Some more examples are: *bakken* 'bake'; *braden* 'saute'; *fruiten* 'fry'; *stomen* 'steam'; *bewegen* 'move'; *rijden* 'drive'; *varen* 'navigate'; *zeilen* 'sail'; *vliegen* 'fly'; *rollen* 'roll'; *(rond)draaien* 'turn (around)'. The intransitive variants of all these verbs are unergative.

Causative-accomplishment alternation

In the causative-accomplishment alternation the intransitive alternant denotes an accomplishment, the verb is unaccusative, and the transitive alternant denotes a causative event. Consider *inkoken* 'boil down', (30).

(30) a. De saus is langzaam ingekookt.
the sauce is slowly in-boiled
'The sauce slowly boiled down.'
b. Henk heeft de saus langzaam ingekookt.
H. has the sauce slowly in-boiled
'H. slowly boiled down the sauce.'

Some more examples are: *gaarstomen* 'steam cooked'; *drogen* 'dry'; *buigen* 'bend'; *uitrekken* 'stretch'; *verbeteren* 'improve'; *verzachten* 'soften'; *verbranden* 'burn'; *verslijten* 'wear out'; *vertragen* 'slow down'; *versnellen* 'speed up'; *verzwakken* 'weaken'. The intransitive variant of all these verbs is unaccusative.

Also, some manner of motion verbs appear in the causative-accomplishment alternation when they are accompanied by a "goal" phrase or particle. Consider *rollen* 'roll', (31).

(31) a. De bal is naar de andere baan gerold.
the ball is to the other court rolled
'The ball rolled to the other court.'

b. Ilona heeft de bal naar de andere baan gerold.
I. has the ball to the other court rolled
'I. rolled the ball to the other court.'

Only a few of the motion verbs can appear in this alternation: *schuiven* 'shove'; *zwaaien* 'swing'; *draaien* 'turn'; *rijden* 'ride'; *varen* 'navigate'; *zeilen* 'sail'. Some other verbs that take a "goal" complement and appear in this alternation include: *verschuiven* 'move'; *spuiten* 'squirt'; *spetteren* 'spatter'; *spoelen* 'rinse'; *druipen* 'drip'; *druppelen* 'trickle'.[12]

Causative-state alternation

One last kind of causativization alternation is the causative-state alternation: the intransitive variant denotes a state and the transitive variant denotes a causative event. Consider *hangen* 'hang', (32).[13]

(32) a. De foto hangt aan de muur.
'The picture hangs on the wall.'

b. Joep hangt de foto aan de muur.
'J. hangs the picture on the wall.'

Some other examples are: *uithangen* 'air'; *afdekken* 'cover'; *bedekken* 'cover'.

Causativization alternations are sometimes morphologically marked. Compare unaccusative *verbleken* 'bleach' denoting an accomplishment and transitive *bleken* 'bleach' denoting a causative accomplishment; *verkleuren-kleuren* 'color'; *opdrogen-afdrogen* 'dry'; *bevriezen-invriezen* 'freeze'. Compare unergative *kreukelen* 'crinkle' denoting a process and transitive *verkreukelen* 'crinkle' denoting a causative accomplishment; *schuiven-verschuiven* 'shove'; *hongeren-uithongeren* 'starve'. Compare stative *hangen* 'hang' and transitive *ophangen* 'hang up'. Sometimes the alternation is morpho-syntactically marked: the verb in the intransitive alternant is a reflexive variant of the verb in the transitive alternant. These include: *zich (uit)strekken-(uit)strekken* 'stretch (out)'; *zich (uit)rekken-(uit)rekken* 'stretch (out)'; *zich (uit)vouwen-(uit)vouwen* 'fold (out)'; *zich stabiliseren-stabiliseren* 'stabilize'; *zich (om)draaien-(om)draaien* 'turn (around)'; *zich herstellen-herstellen* 'recover'; *zich uitspreiden-uitspreiden* 'spread'; *zich verspreiden-verspreiden* 'spread'; *zich bewegen-bewegen* 'move'; *zich vormen-vormen* 'form'.

Causativization alternations are classified here as alternations with an additional argument. Alternatively, they could be viewed as alternations with an optional subject argument. For example, in the causative-transitive alternant, both a subject and a direct object position are projected, but in the inchoative-unaccusative alternant, only an object position is projected (following the Unaccusative Hypothesis as formulated by Perlmutter 1978). My definition of optional argumenthood requires the presence of an understood argument as its determining characteristic. Applying this criterion to causativization alternations, the question is whether the causer is semantically present in the intransitive alternant or not. Some underlying sense of causation seems to be present in all intransitive examples in (28)-(32). However, is it our general knowledge of the laws of causality that tell us that every change of state or location requires an external force, or is this driven by lexical-conceptual knowledge of individual verb meanings? For example, when an egg breaks, is there an underlying cause involved for general reasons or is it part of the lexical-semantic specification of the meaning of *break*? The notions *optional* versus *additional argument* seem almost indistinguishable here. I opt for the view that the "causer" is not an understood argument in the intransitive alternant, but rather, an additional argument in the causative alternant. One first needs to expand the meaning of the verb in the intransitive alternant by adding an extra, causer participant to the event in order to map the extra argument in the transitive alternant. On this view, then, verbs displaying one of the causativization alternations are flexible, in the sense that they select different numbers of arguments.

Unergative-unaccusative alternation

Verbs of manner of motion take an "agent" or a "theme", i.e., the moving entity; they can take an extra, "goal" complement toward which the motion is directed. Absence or presence of a "goal" triggers the unergative-unaccusative alternation (which was also discussed in the context of (14) and (15) above where it was triggered by "goal" prefixes or particles). Consider *dansen* 'dance', (33), and *rollen* 'roll', (34).

(33) a. Anneke heeft in een opera gedanst.
A. has in an opera danced
'A. danced in an opera.'
b. Anneke is van het podium af gedanst.
A. is of the stage off danced
'A. danced off the stage.'

(34) a. De tennisbal heeft over de baan gerold.
the tennis-ball has over the court rolled
'The tennis ball rolled over the court.'
b. De tennisbal is de baan op gerold.
the tennis-ball is the court onto rolled
'The tennis ball rolled onto the court.'

Dansen 'dance' has an "agent" argument which is mapped as external argument in (33a). In (33b) *dansen* 'dance' also takes a "goal" argument; now the "agent" is mapped as internal argument. Similarly for the "theme" argument of *rollen* 'roll': it is mapped as external argument in (34a) and as internal argument in (34b). The "goal" argument is an additional argument in (33) and (34), rather than an optional argument. In its absence, there is no implication that the motion is directed toward some goal; there is no understood "goal". Notice that projection of an additional argument position induces a change in the mapping of the other argument. This paradigm applies to all manner of motion verbs.

Transitive-oblique transitive alternation

Transitive motion verbs can also take an additional "goal" argument. The transitive-oblique transitive alternation has a transitive verb in one alternant and an oblique transitive verb in the other. Consider *duwen* 'push', (35).

(35) a. Judy duwde de kinderwagen.
'J. pushed the baby carriage.'
b. Judy duwde de kinderwagen naar het park.
'J. pushed the baby carriage to the park.'

Duwen 'push' basically takes an "agent" and a "theme", (35a). As it is a verb of motion, it can also take an additional "goal" complement, (35b). Some more examples in the transitive-oblique transitive alternation: *trekken* 'pull'; *dragen* 'carry'; *slepen* 'drag'; *rijden* 'drive'; *varen* 'navigate'; *zeilen* 'sail'; *draaien* 'turn'; *manoeuvreren* 'maneuver'; *gooien* 'throw'; *slaan* 'hit'; *schoppen* 'kick'.

Cognate object alternation

In the cognate object alternation the verb is intransitive in one alternant and transitive in the other alternant; a cognate object shows up as an additional argument. Consider *lachen* 'laugh', (36).

(36) a. Susan lacht.
'S. laughs.'
b. Susan lacht een *(schaterende) lach.
'S. laughs a *(roaring) laugh.'

A cognate object is not a real argument in the sense that it denotes another participant in the event. A typical characteristic of cognate objects is the obligatory modifier (an adjective, a PP, a relative clause), which modifies the verb rather than the object: (36b) is interpreted as *schaterend lachen* 'laugh roaringly, roar with laughter'. The modifier is obligatory to avoid semantic redundancy. Some more verbs in this unergative-transitive alternation include: *(een rustig leven) leven* 'live (a quiet life)'; *(een enge droom) dromen* 'dream (an scary dream); *(een gevecht op leven en dood) vechten* 'fight (a fight on life or death'). Some examples with unaccusative verbs include: *(een vredige dood) sterven* 'die (a peaceful death)'; *(een meterslange val) vallen* 'fall (a meters-long fall)'.

Summarizing alternations with additional arguments

Summarizing this section, several alternations have been discussed in which the verb in one alternant has one additional argument as compared to the other alternant. Alternations in which the alternant with the lowest number of arguments is intransitive are: the causative-inchoative, causative-process, causative-accomplishment, causative-state, unergative-unaccusative and cognate object alternation. The transitive-oblique transitive alternation illustrates an addition alternation in which the alternant with the lowest number of arguments is transitive.

2.5 Optional arguments

The second type of alternations with different numbers of arguments is the kind of alternation in which the number of semantic arguments is the same for both alternants, but not all of them are projected. There is a discrepancy between the set of semantic arguments and the set of actually projected arguments. In the alternant with one argument less, there is one semantically present, but syntactically unprojected argument. There are many different terms that indicate such an argument: *understood*, *null*, *zero*, *optional*, *absorbed*, *suppressed* and *implicit argument*. I will use the term *understood argument*, as it is the most neutral among them.

This type of alternation splits up again: alternations in which not mapping the understood argument does not affect the (surface) syntactic positions of the other arguments and alternations in which it does affect them. I will call the unprojected argument of the former type an *optional* argument and that of the latter a *suppressed* argument.

In this section different kinds of optional arguments will be discussed: optional direct objects, optional oblique objects and optional complements of a preposition. Suppressed arguments are presented in section 2.6. When an optional argument remains unprojected, it is nevertheless semantically present. The sentence is interpreted with a generic constant for this argument (cf. Gruber 1965).

Optional direct object

Verbs with an optional direct object map onto a transitive or an intransitive frame. In the intransitive frame, there is an understood "theme" argument. This phenomenon has also been called *pseudo-transitivity.* Consider *schrijven* 'write', (37), and *eten* 'eat', (38), with optional direct objects.

(37) a. Elena schreef haar proefschrift.
'E. wrote her thesis.'
b. Elena schreef.
'E. wrote.'

(38) a. Dave at de haring.
'D. ate the herring'.
b. Dave at.
'D. ate.'

Intransitive *schrijven* 'write', (37b), and *eten* 'eat', (38b), are interpreted as dyadic predicates, i.e., some food is being eaten and some text is getting written. Transitively, the direct object spells out this argument. The set of pseudo-transitive verbs includes: *drinken* 'drink', *lezen* 'read', *roken* 'smoke', *spelen* 'play', *zingen* 'sing', *tekenen* 'draw', *graven* 'dig', *verven* 'paint'.

The unprojected argument is to some extent syntactically available, or rather, discourse available, as an understood argument. Consider (39) and (40).

(39) Na maanden TEXT$_i$ schrijven heeft ze *er*$_i$ uiteindelijk niets van ingeleverd.
after months write has she there$_i$ finally nothing of handed-in
'After months of writing TEXT$_i$, she finally did not hand in anything of *it*$_i$.'

(40) Nadat hij uren FOOD$_i$ had zitten eten, heeft hij *het*$_i$ daarna weer allemaal overgegeven.
after-that he hours has sit eat, has he it afterwards again all thrown-up
'After he had been eating FOOD$_i$ for hours, he threw *it*$_i$ all up again.'

The pronouns *er* 'there', (39), and *het* 'it', (40), can be interpreted as referring to the text she has been writing and to the food he has been eating, respectively. Thus, an unprojected argument can serve as antecedent for pronouns. In this sense, it plays a syntactic role, although it is not projected.

Interestingly, certain prefixed and particle variants of these pseudo-transitive verbs are obligatorily transitive; their object is not an optional argument. Pseudo-transitives *schrijven* 'write' and *eten* 'eat' with an optional object form a minimal pair with two particle variants: *afschrijven* 'finish writing', (41), and *opeten* 'eat up', (42), take obligatory objects.

(41) a. Elena schreef haar proefschrift af.
E. wrote her thesis off
'E. finished writing her thesis.'

b. *Elena schreef af.
E. wrote off

(42) a. Dave at de haring op.
D. ate the herring up
'D. ate up the herring.'

b. *Dave at op.
D. ate up

There are many verb pairs of which the morphologically simplex verb is optionally transitive and the prefixed or particle verb is obligatorily transitive. Some examples include: *roken-oproken, uitroken, beroken* 'smoke-finish smoking, smoke out, (blacken with) smoke'; *lezen-uitlezen, overlezen, doorlezen, herlezen* 'read-finish reading, gloss over, read over, reread'; *zingen-inzingen, nazingen, bezingen* 'sing-warm up for singing, copy by singing, celebrate (in song)'; *spelen-uitspelen, overspelen, bespelen* 'play-finish playing, play again, play'; *graven-opgraven, uitgraven, afgraven, begraven* 'dig-dig up, dig out, dig off, bury'; *tekenen-uittekenen, natekenen, intekenen* 'draw-work out by drawing, copy by drawing, register'; *verven-opverven, oververven, afverven* 'paint-paint up, repaint, finish painting'; *bakken-uitbakken* 'fry-fry'; *knippen-verknippen, uitknippen, inknippen* 'cut-cut wrongly, cut out, cut in'; *snijden-insnijden, afsnijden* 'cut-cut in, cut off'; *scheuren-verscheuren, afscheuren, uitscheuren* 'tear-tear up, tear off, tear out'; *slurpen-opslurpen* 'slurp-slurp up'; *wisselen-omwisselen* 'change-exchange'; *bouwen-verbouwen, ombouwen* 'build-restaurate'; *smelten-versmelten, omsmelten* 'melt-melt (into something else)'.

Not all particles have the same effect. While the ones discussed so far turn the verb into an obligatorily transitive verb, the effect of other particles is that the particle verb becomes obligatorily intransitive. Consider *doorschrijven* 'write on', (43), and *meeëten* 'eat along', (44).

(43) a. Elena schreef door.
'E. wrote on.'
b. *Elena schreef haar proefschrift door.
E. wrote her thesis on

(44) a. Dave at mee.
'D. ate along.'
b. *Dave at de haringen mee.
D. ate the herrings along

The "theme" argument cannot be mapped as object. It can be mapped, however, in a PP complement in an oblique intransitive frame. Consider *doorschrijven* 'write on', (45), and *meeëten* 'eat along', (46), again.

(45) Elena schreef door aan haar proefschrift.
'E. wrote on at her thesis.'

(46) Dave at mee van de haringen.
'D. ate along of the herrings.'

The verb pairs *schrijven-doorschrijven* 'write-write on' and *eten-meeëten* 'eat-eat along' thus participate in the transitive-oblique alternation (see also (11) in section 2.3.1). In Chapter 3, I extensively discuss the frame alternating effects of different particles.

Optional oblique object

The oblique argument of many triadic verbs is optional, while their "theme" argument is obligatory. These verbs participate in a transitive-ditransitive alternation. Optionality of the oblique argument and obligatoriness of the direct object is shown with *krijgen* 'get', (47), and *geven* 'give', (48).

(47) a. Angela kreeg een pastamachine van Joop.
'A. got a pasta machine from J.'
b. Angela kreeg een pastamachine.
'A. got a pasta machine.'
c. *Angela kreeg (van Joop).
A. got (from J.)

(48) a. Joop gaf een pastamachine aan Angela.
'J. gave a pasta machine to A.'
b. Joop gaf een pastamachine.
'J. gave a pasta machine.'

c. *Joop gaf (aan Angela).
J. gave (to A.)

In the transitive frames in (47b) and (48b), the unprojected oblique argument is an understood argument. It is a constant "source" and "goal", respectively, i.e., every getting-event implies a "source" argument and every giving-event a "goal". Again, the unprojected argument is to some extent discourse available. Consider (49) and (50).

(49) Angela zou eerst een jojo krijgen FROM SOURCE$_i$, maar Joop$_i$ gaf haar een pastamachine.
A. would first a yoyo get, but J. gave her a pasta machine
'A. was going to get a yoyo FROM SOURCE$_i$, but then J.$_i$ gave her a pasta machine.'

(50) Joop wilde TO GOAL$_i$ een jojo geven, maar Angela$_i$ nam hem niet aan.
J. wanted a yoyo give, but A. took it not on
'J. wanted to give a yoyo TO GOAL$_i$, but A.$_i$ did not accept it.'

In (49) and (50) there are possible coreference relations between the unprojected arguments of *krijgen* 'get' and *geven* 'give' and the coindexed NPs in the subsequent clauses.

Notice that an often cited variant of (48c) is grammatical: *John gave to the church*. However, the unprojected object can only be understood as money, not more generally, as anything giveable. I think this example is idiomatic, and therefore exceptional; it only works in a very special context of giving (namely money donations). In all other giving-events, the object cannot be left out.

Other triadic predicates that take an optional oblique argument include verbs with a "source" goal headed by *van* 'from': *kopen* 'buy'; *ontvangen* 'receive'; *lenen* 'borrow'; *huren* 'rent'; verbs with a dative "goal" headed by *aan* 'to': *teruggeven* 'give back'; *verkopen* 'sell';

uitlenen 'lend'; *verhuren* 'rent (out)'; *uitleggen* 'explain', *beloven* 'promise'; *toestaan* 'allow'; verbs with an locational "goal" headed by *naar* 'to': *sturen* 'send'; *brengen* 'bring'.

There are also dyadic verbs with an optional oblique complement. They figure in an oblique intransitive-intransitive alternation. In one alternant, the PP complement is present in an oblique intransitive frame; in the other alternant, it is not projected, but present as an understood argument. Consider *luisteren* 'listen', (51).

(51) a. Alette luisterde naar cajun muziek.
'A. listened to cajun music.'
b. Alette luisterde.
'A. listened.'

Every listening-event implies a "theme" argument, i.e., something listenable. When it is not projected, the "theme" argument is semantically present and available in the discourse. In (52) there can be a coreference relation between the unprojected argument of *luisteren* 'listen' and the pronoun *het* 'it' in the subsequent clause.

(52) Alette luisterde TO LISTENABLE$_i$, maar ze hoorde het$_i$ niet.
A. listened, but she heard it not
'A. listened TO LISTENABLE$_i$, but she did not hear it$_i$.'

Some more verbs include: *kijken (naar)* 'look (at)'; *werken (aan)* 'work (at)'; *dromen (over)* 'dream (about)'; *preken (over)* 'preach'; *opscheppen (over)* 'boast (about)'; *mopperen (over)* 'grumble (about)'.

For a subset of the intransitives with an optional PP complement, the understood argument is a very specific object. Consider *kwispelen* 'wag', (53).

(53) a. Bruno kwispelt met zijn staart.
'B. wags with his tail.'

b. Bruno kwispelt.
'B. wags.'

The optional PP complement in (53b) necessarily refers to a specific body part, i.e., *een staart* 'a tail'. Similar verbs are: *(in je handen) klappen* 'clap (in your hands)'; *(met je ogen) knipperen* 'blink (with your eyes)'; *(met een vinger) wijzen* 'point (with a finger)'; *(met je hoofd) knikken* 'nod (with your head)'.[14] For each of these verbs, the understood argument involves a certain body part.[15]

Optional complement of a preposition

A last case of optional arguments involves the complement of a preposition. Some oblique transitive verbs with a "goal" PP complement optionally project the NP complement of the preposition heading the PP complement. When the prepositional complement is not projected, the "goal" is an intransitive PP. One such case is *slaan-omslaan* 'put-put on', (54).

(54) a. Luus sloeg een sjaal om haar hals.
'L. put a scarf around her neck.'
b. Luus sloeg een sjaal om.
'L. put a scarf on.'

This alternation has the form of a particle-PP alternation (see section 2.3.3). It applies to verbs that deal with putting on clothes. When the prepositional complement is absent, the preposition takes an understood argument, i.e., some constant body part.[16] In fact, the interpretation of the understood prepositional complement is a very specific body part; it can only be a neck or shoulders in (54b). Moreover, there is no doubt about whose body is involved, i.e., there is an obligatory coreference relation with the subject. Similarly, other verbs are associated with specific understood body parts: *een hoed opzetten* 'put on a hat'; *een bril opzetten* 'put on glasses'; *een sok aantrekken* 'put on a sock'; *een broek aantrekken* 'put on pants'; *een jas aandoen* 'put on a coat'; *oorbellen indoen* 'put in earrings'; *een ketting omdoen* 'put on a necklace'.

Summarizing alternations with optional arguments

Summarizing this section, in alternations with an optional argument there is no one-to-one mapping from semantic arguments to syntactic positions. Rather, one of the semantic arguments remains unprojected, but is semantically present, and to some extent also syntactically active. Three types of optional argumenthood have been discussed in this section. Dyadic predicates map onto either a transitive or an intransitive frame (i.e., pseudo-transitives). Triadic predicates appear in a ditransitive, a transitive or an intransitive frame. Some triadic verbs optionally project the prepositional complement of their PP complement, i.e., the oblique object is mapped as transitive or intransitive PP. The optional arguments discussed in this section are all internal arguments. There is one more type of alternation with an optional argument that has not been discussed yet: optional external arguments. These will be discussed in the next section.

2.6 Suppressed arguments

Whereas many verbs project their direct or indirect object optionally, optional subjects do not seem to be attested. What happens when an external argument is not projected? The Extended Projection Principle and/or Predication Theory require that a subject position be projected. Thus, when no external argument is mapped onto it, one of the other, internal arguments must NP-move into subject position. Thus, in alternations with an optional external argument, not projecting the external argument has the side-effect that the surface position of another argument is changed.

In this section I discuss two kinds of such alternations: passivization and middle formation. As with unprojected internal arguments, an unprojected external argument is an understood argument; it is semantically present in some way and in certain ways also syntactically. Usually, the unprojected external argument in passives and middles is analyzed as (some sort of) a suppressed argument (among others, Williams 1981; Keyser & Roeper 1984; Hale & Keyser 1987; Di Sciullo & Williams 1987; Roberts 1987; Roeper 1987; Zubizarreta 1987; Baker 1988; Baker, Johnson & Roberts 1989; Grimshaw 1990; Woolford 1993; Hoekstra & Roberts 1993).

2.6.1 Passivization

Personal passivization

One of the best known and most thoroughly studied alternations is passivization. The passive voice defocuses the active going-on of the event and zooms in on the effect of the event. In the active alternant an external argument and, possibly, other internal arguments are mapped onto argument positions; in the passive alternant the external argument is not mapped onto subject position. Consider dyadic *vertalen* 'translate', (55), and triadic *laden* 'load', (56).

(55) a. Andrew vertaalde "Hercules".
'A. translated "Hercules".'
b. "Hercules" werd vertaald.
'"Hercules" got translated.'

(56) a. Rob laadt de surfplank op de kar.
'R. loads the surfboard onto the cart.'
b. De surfplank wordt op de kar geladen.
the surfboard gets onto the cart loaded
'The surfboard gets loaded onto the cart.'

In the active alternant, the arguments are mapped in the "standard" way. An "agent" is mapped onto subject position and the other arguments onto internal argument positions: a "theme" in object position, (55a), and a "goal" argument in a PP complement, (56a). In the passive alternants (55b) and (56b), the "theme" appears in subject position at the surface. In standard analyses of passivization, the "theme" is mapped onto object position at D-structure and NP-moves on to subject position. Passivization has thus affected its surface position.

Even though, the "agent" cannot be mapped onto subject position in the passive alternant, i.e., it is "suppressed", it is not deleted altogether. On the contrary, the "agent" can still appear in a *door* 'by'-phrase, (57) and (58).

(57) "Hercules" werd vertaald door Andrew.
'"Hercules" got translated by Andrew.'

(58) De surfplank wordt door Rob op de kar geladen.
the surfboard gets by R. onto the cart loaded
'The surfboard is loaded onto the cart by R.'

Comparing (55a) and (56a) on the one hand and (57) and (58) on the other, passivization also affects the syntactic position of the "agent" argument.

In passive alternants without a *door* 'by'-phrase, (55b) and (56b), the unprojected "agent" is an understood argument. It also plays a syntactic role which can be shown with purpose clauses in control structures. Consider (59) and (60).

(59) a. "Hercules" werd vertaald om PRO de zomer door te komen.
"Hercules" got translated to the summer through to get
'"Hercules" got translated to PRO get through the summer.'

b. "Hercules" werd vertaald door Andrew$_i$ om PRO$_i$ de zomer door te komen.
"Hercules" got translated by A. to the summer through to get
'"Hercules" got translated by A.$_i$ to PRO$_i$ get through the summer.'

(60) a. De surfplank wordt op de kar geladen om PRO te gaan surfen.
the surf-board gets onto the cart loaded to go surfing
'The surf board is loaded onto the cart to PRO go surfing.'

b. De surfplank wordt door Rob_i op de kar geladen om PRO_i te gaan surfen.
the surf-board gets by R. onto the cart loaded to go surfing
'The surf board is loaded onto the cart by $R._i$ to PRO_i go surfing.'

The only interpretation of the purpose phrases in (59a) and (60a) is that the understood "agents", i.e., the translator of the translation and the loader of the loading events, respectively, control the PRO subjects of the purpose clauses. Similarly, PRO in (59b) and (60b) is coreferent with the arguments in the *door* 'by'-phrase.

Another way to notice the syntactic presence of an unprojected, yet understood "agent" is through agent-oriented, depictive predicates (cf. Chomsky 1986; Roberts 1987). Consider the interpretation of the depictives in (61) and (62).

(61) Wanhopig werd "Hercules" vertaald.
desperately is "Hercules" translated
'"Hercules" got translated desperately.'

(62) Enthousiast wordt de surfplank op de kar geladen.
enthousiastically gets the surf-board onto the cart loaded
'The surf-board gets loaded onto the cart enthusiastically.'

The predicates *wanhopig* 'desperately' and *enthousiast* 'enthusiastically' must be predicated of people. The most natural interpretation of the depictives in (61) and (62) is that they describe properties of the suppressed "agents", i.e., the translator in (61) and the loader in (62).

Impersonal passivization

Passivization is often analyzed as an operation affecting the external argument (possibly "suppressing" it in some way or another). Its strong association with external arguments is reinforced by the fact that it applies differently to the two different types of intransitives. Consider *lachen* 'laugh', (63) and *verdwijnen* 'disappear', (64).

(63) a. De leerlingen lachten hardop.
'The pupils laughed aloud.'
b. Er werd hardop gelachen.
there was aloud laughed
'There was laughing aloud.'

(64) a. De leerlingen verdwenen stiekem.
'The pupils disappeared sneakily.'
b. *Er werd stiekem verdwenen.
there was sneakily disappeared

Passivization does apply to unergatives which have an external argument, (63b), but not to unaccusatives which do not have an external argument, (64b). In the passive alternant of an unergative verb there is no argument in object position that can NP-move to subject position. Hence, an expletive subject appears, *er* 'there', (63b). Since an expletive subject is not a "personal" argument, passivization applied to monadic verbs is called impersonal passivization. The unprojected "agent" is syntactically present, as can be shown when interpretating the purpose clause in (65).

(65) Er werd hardop gelachen om de leraar in verwarring te brengen.
there was aloud laughed to the teacher in confusion to bring
'There was laughing aloud to confuse the teacher.'

The only interpretation of (65) is that the laughers are the confusers; the understood "agent" in the impersonal passive clause controls the PRO subject of the purpose clause.

Prepositional passivization

Unlike English, Dutch does not have a prepositional passive. In English, the oblique "goal" argument of triadic or dyadic verbs moves to subject position after passivization (see the glosses of (66b) and (67b)). In Dutch, the "goal" argument of a triadic verb cannot NP-move in this way. Consider *beloven* 'promise', (66).

(66) a. Joop beloofde haar een pastamachine.
'J. promised her a pasta machine.'
b. Haar / *Zij werd een pastamachine beloofd.
her / she was a pasta machine promised
'She was promised a pasta machine.'

The "goal" remains a dative object under passivization; only the original object can become subject.[17] A prepositional passive of the English kind in which the prepositional complement NP-moves to become subject is impossible. Consider *slapen* 'sleep', (67).

(67) a. De koningin sliep in dit bed.
'The queen slept in this bed.'
b. *Dit bed werd geslapen (in) (door de koningin).
'This bed was slept in (by the queen).'

There is a deeper reason behind the ungrammaticality of the passive construction in (67b), as an impersonal passive of *slapen* 'sleep' is fine, (68).

(68) Er werd in geslapen.
there was in slept
'It was slept in.'

The ungrammaticality of (67b) cannot be due to the operation of passivization itself as (68) shows. Rather, it has to do with P-stranding. P-stranding is much more restricted in Dutch than in English; in Dutch only so-called *R-pronouns* can strand a preposition (cf. van Riemsdijk 1978). In (68) the prepositional complement is an R-pronoun, *er* 'there'; hence, it can move out of the PP (thereby stranding the preposition).[18] The impossibility of prepositional passivization such as (67b) can thus be related to the general impossibility of extracting NPs out of PPs in Dutch.

For some verbs, however, there is a way out. The intransitive verb first needs to transitivize with a prefix or particle. The now transitive verb can then passivize in a regular way. Consider prefixed variant of *slapen* 'sleep', *beslapen* 'sleep', (69).

(69) a. De koningin heeft dit bed beslapen.
the queen has this bed PFX-slept
'The queen slept in this bed.'

b. Dit bed werd beslapen (door de koningin).
this bed was PFX-slept (by the queen)
'The bed was slept in (by the queen).'

Having classified different versions of passivization as alternations with a suppressed argument, I will briefly consider an alternative. Another option is to view the active-passive alternation as an alternation with an optional subject argument. In the active alternant, it is mapped onto the subject position, but in the passive it is not. In this way, the case seems to be similar to other alternations with optional arguments discussed in section 2.5 where an understood argument is semantically present, but unprojected. However, the "agent" argument in the passive alternant is not an understood argument in the same sense. It is possible to project it in the passive alternant, i.e., not as a subject, but in a *door* 'by'-phrase. Projecting the "agent" does not mean "flipping back" to the fully projected active alternant, as is the case with the other optional arguments which do not have an alternative way of projecting their optional argument.

Summarizing this subsection, in the active-passive alternation the "agent" argument figures as a suppressed argument in the passive alternant. When it is not projected, it is still present as an understood argument. It is also syntactically present, since it can bind a PRO argument of a purpose clause. Middle formation presents another case in which the "agent" is a suppressed argument.

2.6.2 Middle formation

The middle voice " . . . is characterized by a lack of specific time reference and by an understood, but unexpressed agent" (Levin 1993:26). A middle expresses a stative predicate, often a generic truth. Typically, in the middle alternant, the "agent" is suppressed, and another argument occurs in subject position. Middle formation applies to many different kinds of verbs. Consider dyadic *snijden* 'cut' with a "theme", (70).

(70) a. Jeanne snijdt het sesamzaadbrood.
'J. cuts the sesame seed bread.'
b. Sesamzaadbrood snijdt gemakkelijk.
'Sesame seed bread cuts easily.'

Whereas in passive alternants only "theme" objects can NP-move to subject position, in middle alternants all kinds of different elements can appear in subject position. They include instrumental phrases, (71); locative phrases, (72); directional phrases, (73); temporal phrases, (74) and manner phrases, (75).

(71) a. Marco schrijft met een nieuwe vulpen.
'M. writes with a new fountain pen.'
b. Zijn oude vulpennen schrijven niet meer.
his old fountain pens write not more
'His old fountain pens do not write any more.'
c. Het schrijft niet erg prettig met een nieuwe vulpen.
it writes not very pleasant with a new fountain pen
'Writing with a new fountain pen is not very pleasant.'

(72) a. Annemarie slaapt onder een klamboe.
'A. sleeps under a mosquito net.'
b. Deze klamboe slaapt niet prettig.
this mosquito net sleeps not comfortable
'This mosquito net does not sleep comfortably.'
c. Het slaapt prima onder een klamboe.
it sleeps perfectly under a mosquito net
'Sleeping under a mosquito net is perfect.'

(73) a. Kay fietst de berg op.
K. bikes the mountain up
'K. bikes up the mountain.'
b. ?Deze berg fietst gemakkelijk.
'This mountain bikes easily.'
c. Het fietst makkelijker de berg af dan de berg op.
it bikes easier the mountain down than the mountain up
'Biking down the mountain is easier than biking up the mountain.'

(74) a. Astrid schrijft het liefst in de middag.
A. writes the dearest in the afternoon
'A. prefers writing in the afternoon.'
b. De middag schrijft het prettigst.
'The afternoon writes best.'
c. Het schrijft prettiger in de middag.
it writes better in the afternoon
'Writing in the afternoon is better.'

(75) a. Peter belt in snel tempo een serie klanten af.
P. calls in a quick tempo a series customers off
'P. quickly calls a series of customer.'
b. Een snel tempo belt prettiger.
'A quick tempo calls better.'

c. Het belt prettiger in een snel tempo.
it calls better in a quick tempo
'Calling in a quick tempo is nicer.'

Each case of middle formation in this series of examples shows the same pattern: the active alternant projects a subject and a PP adjunct, (71a)-(75a).[19] In the middle alternant, either the prepositional complement appears in subject position, (71b)-(75b), or there is an expletive subject, (71c)-(75c). Notice that number agreement with the verb shows that the prepositional complements are really in subject position, (71b)-(75b).

In standard views on middle formation, the "theme" argument of a transitive verb is mapped onto object position at D-structure while the "agent" argument is suppressed; the "theme" NP-moves to subject position. Thus, in middle formation, the surface position of another argument changes, in which sense it is similar to passivization. Another similarity is that the unprojected external argument is an understood argument. In a middle alternant, however, unlike a passive alternant, there is no way to overtly express the "agent". Another difference is that in passives only the original object can appear in subject position, whereas in middles, all kinds of other phrases can appear there.

Although there is a semantic understanding of an "agent" argument in middles, it is difficult to prove its syntactic presence. As sentences in the middle voice denote states, they cannot combine with purpose clauses and so one cannot use this as a diagnostic to determine whether the suppressed agent in middle controls the PRO subject of the purpose clause. Manowsky (1995) shows how German middles have a syntactically active "agent". Some of his tests apply to Dutch middles as well. Consider the interpretation of agentive depictive predicates, (76).

(76) a. Ziek slaapt het niet erg prettig onder een klamboe.
sick sleeps it not very nice under a mosquito net
'It does not sleep very nice under a mosquito net when one is sick.'

b. Met bier in je benen fietst het erg zwaar de berg op.
with beer in your legs bikes it very heavy the mountain up
'With beer in one's legs, it bikes very difficult up the mountain.'

The depictive *ziek* 'sick' can only refer to persons; the preferred interpretation in (76a) is that the sick one is the understood "agent", i.e., the sleeper. Similarly for the depictive predicate in (76b): it is predicated of the understood biker. So, the understood "agent" is syntactically tractable in middles as well as in passives.

Summarizing alternations with suppressed arguments

I have discussed two types of alternations with an optional external argument: alternations triggered by passivization and alternations triggered by middle formation. In their analyses of these alternations, several people have claimed that what is involved is some sort of suppression of the external argument. The effect is that no argument is mapped onto subject position. This triggers NP-movement of another argument or phrase to subject position, which causes the argument alternating effects.

2.7 Summary: lexical-syntactic flexibility in Dutch

Most verbs appear in several different frames; they do so systematically. I have dubbed this *lexical-syntactic flexibility*. The term refers to the phenomenon that a verb (or pairs of verbs, including its prefixed and particle variants) with a certain number of semantic arguments can map these arguments onto several verb frames. Looking at the phenomenon from the lexical-semantic side of the mapping system, I have classified different kinds of flexibility in terms of variations in the ways semantic arguments are mapped onto syntax, variations both in the number and the type of projected positions. In Chapter 3, I will introduce another perspective on lexical-syntactic flexibility; I will classify the various alternations in terms of flexibility of event type.

Concluding the discussion of lexical-syntactic flexibility in Dutch, I summarize the different types of alternations discussed. A first kind of flexibility is alternations in which the same set of arguments is mapped in both alternants, but in which the arguments appear in different syntactic positions. All semantic arguments are projected; flexibility lies in the ways they map onto syntax. There are three different types: the flexible argument is mapped as direct or indirect internal argument (i.e., as direct object or PP complement, subsection 2.3.1); it is mapped as internal or external argument (i.e., as object or subject, subsection 2.3.2); the "goal" argument is the flexible one, as it is projected as PP complement or head (subsection 2.3.3).

In other kinds of flexibility the two alternants do not project the same number of semantic arguments, i.e., one alternant projects one more argument position than the other. I distinguish two reasons for the discrepancy. First, the "longer" alternant has syntactically, as well as semantically, one argument more than the "shorter" one, i.e., there is an additional argument (section 2.4).

Second, the number of semantic arguments is the same, but not all arguments are syntactically projected; there is a discrepancy between the set of semantic arguments and the set of actually projected arguments. The alternant with one argument less has a so-called understood argument, i.e., an unprojected argument that is semantically present, but does not surface syntactically. Additional arguments are different from understood arguments, because, if the additional argument is not present, there is also no semantic "understanding" of it. I have again split up alternations with an understood argument: alternations with an optional argument in which not projecting the understood argument does not affect the syntactic positions of the other arguments (section 2.5), and alternations with a suppressed argument in which the syntactic positions of the other arguments are affected (section 2.6).

The data described in this chapter show what a pervasive and varied phenomenon lexical-syntactic flexibility is. A theory of the lexicon and its interface with syntax must account for the multiple and systematic mapping possibilities of verbs.

Notes

1. In Chapter 3, I will generalize over the various relations between semantic valency and syntactic frame by discussing the second-order meaning. properties of lexical-syntactic flexibility. Taking the perspective from event semantics, I will show that the relation between the two alternants of an alternation is one of three kinds: (i) atelic-telic event type shifting; (ii) causativization; (iii) event view or event focus shifting.
2. Not everybody feels this difference, however.
3. *Haar* 'hair' happens to be a proper object for all three verbs of smearing in (6), i.e., *besmeren, volsmeren* and *insmeren.*
4. Cf. Latin *conare* 'attempt'.
5. The transitive-oblique alternation is similar to the applicative alternation where an argument alternates between oblique object and direct object (e.g., Baker 1988; see (19) in Chapter 1). See van Hout & Haverkort (1995).
6. Some languages express a similar meaning alternation with two different Cases on the "theme" argument. For example, Finnish and Russian use partitive Case for the action without effect and the *attempt* meanings and accusative Case for the *action-plus-effect* meaning (cf. Tenny 1987, 1994; de Hoop 1992).
7. It is generally assumed that BE selection is an indication of unaccusativity in Dutch (e.g., Perlmutter 1978; Hoekstra 1984; Burzio 1986; Zaenen 1988, 1993; Levin & Rappaport Hovav 1995). In Chapter 6, I discuss unaccusativity in full detail.
8. Everaert (1986) discusses a class of unaccusative reflexive verbs. One property of this class is that the reflexive may precede the subject in embedded clauses; the reflexive object of a regular transitive verb cannot. According to this criterion, the *zich*-verbs listed above are unaccusative. Consider for example, *zich inwerken* 'get adjusted to new work' in (i).

   (i) . . . dat zich Martin snel ingewerkt heeft.
   . . . that himself M. quickly in-worked has
   '. . . that M. quickly got adjusted to the new work.'
9. Notice that *trouwen* 'marry' is an unaccusative verb (given auxiliary BE). So, the alternation actually involves two internal argument positions and belongs to the alternations discussed in the previous section. I have listed it here, because it involves a reciprocal argument.
10. Superficially, intransitive prepositions and prepositional particles look alike, i.e., the two sets overlap very much. Van Riemsdijk (1978) employs the following criteria to distinguish the two classes in Dutch: a particle can go along with the verb in verb clusters; an intransitive preposition cannot. A

particle cannot topicalize; an intransitive preposition can. An extra, confusing factor is presented by the fact that postpositions can incorporate into the verb, in which case they, too, look like particles and intransitive prepositions.

11. In Dutch there are considerably fewer verbs that appear in causativization alternations than in English (cf. the long list in Levin 1993). Instead, Dutch uses more often periphrastic causatives with *laten* 'let'. Van Voorst (1993) discusses the causative-inchoative alternation with respect to the differences between Dutch, English and French, and offers an analysis for these crosslinguistic differences.
12. Levin (1993) calls the causative-accomplishment alternation applied to motion verbs the *induced action alternation.*
13. Whether the intransitive verb in (32a) is unergative or unaccusative is not clear. The auxiliary is HAVE which suggests that the verb is unergative. Mulder & Wehrmann (1989), however, claim that positional verbs including *hangen* 'hang' are nevertheless unaccusative.
14. Interestingly, the optional argument in the English translations is a direct object, not a PP complement, e.g., *wag his tail* (cf. Levin 1993).
15. When these verbs take an inanimate subject, there is, of course, no understood body part argument, (i)-(ii).

    (i) Het richtingsbord wijst naar het westen.
    'The sign points toward the west.'

    (ii) Het stoplicht knippert.
    'The traffic light blinks.'
16. This example represents a more general picture about the interpretation of intransitive prepositions. They always imply an understood internal argument. For example, a locative intransitive preposition involves some constant LOCATION, (i). As Henk van Riemsdijk points out (personal communication), there is no such transparent semantics for particles; they do not imply an understood argument, (ii).

    (i) De auto staat voor LOCATION.
    'The car sits in front LOCATION.'

    (ii) Willem II staat voor.
    'Willem II is winning.'
17. Henk van Riemsdijk (personal communication) points out that the dative object of certain triadic verbs can become a subject after passivization, (i), which may suggest that Dutch is changing in this respect.

    (i) De toeschouwers worden verzocht het terrein te verlaten.
    the spectators are requested the terrain to leave
    'The spectators are requested to leave the grounds.'

18. In fact, *er* 'there' in (68) is both an existential *er* 'there' and a prepositional *er* 'there'; in this case the two R-pronouns have conflated (cf. van Riemsdijk 1978).
19. With the exception of the directional PP in (73) which is a complement.

CHAPTER 3

Event Type-Shifting

Viewing semantic arguments as participants in an event and focusing on the event type properties of the alternants, lexical-syntactic flexibility becomes a phenomenon of easily grasped dimensions. The many different kinds and forms of alternations fall in one of only three classes: alternations with an atelic-telic event type-shift, alternations characterized by causativization and alternations in which the alternants present different foci on the same event. Moreover, how many arguments are mapped and onto which syntactic positions depends to a great extent on event type. There are two correlations between event type on the one hand, and verb frame on the other. A telic event type requires the projection of an argument in direct object position; a causative event type requires the projection of arguments in both subject and direct object position. The question why a verb appears in more than one frame is thus related to the fact that it can present the same event from various event-semantic angles. The question why it appears in a particular set of frames reduces to the mapping requirements of particular event-semantic perspectives as expressed by these two generalizations. The conclusion that frame alternations must be analyzed in terms of the relations between event types and verb frames implies that a theory of the lexicon-syntax interface must be framed in those terms as well (see Chapter 4).

3.1 Goals of this chapter

The data presented by the different types of lexical-syntactic flexibility in Dutch in Chapter 2 show that while a verb's basic meaning remains constant across the set of frames it appears in, it takes a different focus on or extends its basic meaning in each different frame. In the present chapter I discuss in detail which kinds of meaning elements remain the same and which differ across alternants.

As I will demonstrate in this chapter, these meaning elements will be revealed when one reviews the phenomenon of lexical-syntactic flexibility from the perspective of event semantics. What remains constant across frames is the kind of event the verb denotes and, usually, one of the verb's event participants that is mapped onto an argument position. What differs across frames is the aspectual event type a verb refers to, the selection of event participants that are mapped onto syntax and the selection of syntactic argument positions they are mapped onto.

Before one can develop a theory on lexicon and mapping that is to account for flexibility, it must be clear which are the relevant lexical-semantic properties the mapping system needs to "see" and which are the associated syntactic consequences. The aim of this chapter is to discover generalizations over lexical-syntactic flexibility, both on the lexical-semantic as well as on the syntactic side of the mapping system. Drawing generalizations will prepare the ground for developing a theory on lexicon and mapping. I will thereto review the alternation patterns from Chapter 2 in event-semantic terms, in order to precisely characterize the empirical domain over which lexical-syntactic flexibility stretches. The implications of the phenomenon of lexical-syntactic flexibility for the specification of a verb's lexical-syntactic properties in the lexicon and for mapping verbal predicates onto syntax will be the topic of Chapter 4.

Frame alternations can be classified in different ways. In Chapter 2, I organized the alternations according to what happened with the semantic arguments when they map onto syntax: arguments mapped onto different syntactic positions, additional arguments and unprojected arguments. I dubbed most of these alternations in terms of their syntactic form (e.g., transitive-intransitive or unergative-unaccusative alternation). In the present chapter I discuss the same alternations in an event-semantic classification. The event-semantic perspective on the phenomenon of lexical-syntactic flexibility reduces the variety back to just three different kinds while offering insightful generalizations over the systematic differences between two alternants.

After raising the relevant questions that need to be answered in order to derive generalizations over frame alternations (subsection 3.2.1), I will introduce my research methodology by discussing the intransitive-transitive and the unergative-unaccusative alternations (subsection 3.2.2). Before continuing with an event-semantic presentation of Dutch alternations, I will introduce event-semantic terminology and notation in section 3.3. The first set of alternations to be investigated are characterized by an atelic-telic event type-shift (section 3.4). The next set involve those characterized by a shift from a non-causative to a causative event type (section 3.5). The remaining alternations do not involve an event type-shift. Still, there is an event-semantic difference as the two alternants present different foci on the same event (section 3.6). At the end of each section I will derive correlations between event type, event participants and verb frames. It will be shown that a verb's flexibility with respect to the verb frames it appears in and its ability to express different event types are intricately related.

3.2 Lexical-syntactic flexibility: different views of the same event

3.2.1 Empirical questions about lexical-syntactic flexibility

The phenomenon of lexical-syntactic flexibility forms the empirical domain that a theory on lexicon and projection must capture. Are there lexical-syntactic generalizations across the many different alternations? If so, what do these imply about the nature of a verb's lexical features that provide the mapping algorithm with the necessary input to map verbs onto the right verb frame or frames? Viewing the mapping system as a relation between the verbal lexicon and the small set of verb frames, these questions lie at the heart of the mapping problem as formulated in Chapter 1, depicted again in (1).

(1) Mapping is a relation between the verbal lexicon and syntax:

		Mapping	
Verbal	$V_{1[..]}$	↔	**Syntax**
lexicon	$V_{2[..]}$		_ SU
	$V_{3[..]}$		_ SU OBL
	$V_{4[..]}$		_ SU DO
	$V_{5[..]}$		_ SU DO OBL
	...		_ DO
	$V_{y[..]}$		_ DO OBL
	$V_{z[..]}$		

In the previous chapter the classification of lexical-syntactic flexibility the behavior of the semantic arguments as its point of departure. I distinguished three different kinds of alternations: (i) alternations in which the number of semantic arguments is the same in both alternants, but the positions they map onto vary; (ii) alternations in which the set of semantic arguments differs across the alternants and so does the set of syntactically projected argument positions; (iii) alternations in which the set of semantic arguments is the same, but the number of actually surfacing arguments is different, i.e., in the shorter alternant there is an understood argument. This classification describes what happens with the semantic arguments in mapping. The next step is to ask why these things happen.

As for the alternations of type (i), why does a certain semantic argument vary the position it maps onto? As for the alternations of type (ii), why do certain verbs take different numbers of semantic arguments? As for the alternations of type (iii), why do semantic arguments not always need to map onto syntax? One must find answers to these questions if one hopes to generalize over these different kinds of flexibility. The answers will point toward the deeper causes of lexical-syntactic flexibility. They will also uncover the kind of lexical-syntactic features by which verbs are characterized and how these feed the mapping system.

In order to find the common denominator that characterizes lexical-syntactic flexibility, I assume the following methodology. First, I will determine what remains constant and what is variable in all these different kinds of alternations, i.e., which part of the meaning of a verbal predicate is specific to the verb in each of its occurrences and which to the verb in a particular frame. In this way, for each verb, one can determine its constant meaning element and the meaning differences across frames. Then, generalizing over many different verbs and over many different kinds of alternations, one can determine the nature of the meaning element that stays the same for all verbs across different frames and the nature of the meaning differences. A lexicon-syntax theory must be based on these notions.

In the next subsection I will suggest some preliminary answers to the questions raised above. In the rest of this chapter, I then discuss the issues in a systematic way.

3.2.2 Toward the answers: event type-shifting

To see some intuitive answers to the questions of constant and variable meaning elements of verbs across alternations, reconsider two different kinds of alternations from Chapter 2: *dansen* 'dance' in the unergative-unaccusative alternation, (2), and optionally transitive *schrijven* 'write', (3).

(2) a. Anneke heeft in een opera gedanst.
A. has in an opera danced
'A. danced in an opera.'
b. Anneke is van het podium af gedanst.
A. is of the stage off danced
'A. danced off the stage.'

(3) a. Elena schreef.
E. wrote
'E. was writing.'
b. Elena schreef haar proefschrift.
'E. wrote her thesis.'

In each alternant, both verbs refer to the same kinds of events, i.e., dancing and writing events, respectively. Moreover, there is one event participant that is projected in both alternants, i.e., the dancer and the writer. Thus, the constant meaning aspects of these two verbs across their frames are the kinds of events they refer to plus the presence of one of their event participants in an argument position. This generalization about (2) and (3) holds across the board for other verbs that participate in the unergative-unaccusative alternation and for other transitive verbs with an optional direct object.

What about the differences? While both alternants in (2) and (3) refer to the same kinds of events, they present different views on these events. On the one hand, *dansen* 'dance' in an unergative frame and intransitive *schrijven* 'write' refer to events that denote atelic (ongoing, durative) processes. On the other hand, *dansen* 'dance' in an unaccusative frame and transitive *schrijven* 'write' refer to telic (resultative, terminative) events. Different temporal modifiers illustrate the different event type properties (cf. Dowty 1979). An atelic event only combines with durative adverbials such as *jarenlang* 'for years', (4a) and (5a); a telic event only combines with frame adverbials such as *binnen een minuut* 'within one minute' or *binnen een jaar* 'within a year', (4b) and (5b).

(4) a. Anneke heeft jarenlang / *binnen een week bij de opera gedanst.
A. has years-long / within a week with the opera danced
'A. danced with the opera for years / *within a week.'

b. Anneke was binnen een minuut / *urenlang van het podium af gedanst.
A. was within one minute / hours-long of the stage off danced
'A. danced off the stage within one minute / *for hours.'

(5) a. Elena schreef jarenlang / *binnen een jaar.
E. wrote years-long / within a year
'E. was writing for years / *within a year.'

b. Elena schreef binnen een jaar / *jarenlang haar proefschrift.
E. wrote within a year / years-long her thesis
'E. wrote her thesis within a year / *for years.'

Van het podium af dansen 'dance off the stage' in (4b) is a telic event involving a dancing process and a final state that is reached when the dancer is off the stage. Likewise, *een proefschrift schrijven* 'write a thesis' in (5b) involves a writing process and a culminating, final state when the thesis has reached its completion, i.e., the writer is writing "at" the thesis until she finishes it by having written it completely. The dancer and the writer participants appear in both alternants. In the telic alternants an additional "goal" or "theme" participant surface, respectively. Whereas telic dancing involves an explicit "goal", (4b), no "goal" is implicit in atelic dancing events, (4a). However, in both telic as well as atelic writing events, there is always a second, "theme" participant involved, even though it is not always projected, (5a). Furthermore, the dancer is mapped onto subject position in the atelic alternant, (4a), but onto object position in the telic one, (4b). The unergative-unaccusative alternation in (4) is an additional argument alternation, i.e., the two alternants have different numbers of semantic arguments (see section 2.4). The transitive-intransitive alternation in (5) illustrates the type of alternation in which the alternants have semantically the same, but syntactically different numbers of arguments; the unprojected argument is an understood argument (see section 2.5).

The meaning effects in the unergative-unaccusative and the transitive-intransitive alternation can be characterized as follows. Whereas a verb refers to the same kinds of events in both alternants, what differs across frames are the event types, and, moreover, the exact selection of event participants projected syntactically as arguments. Similar meaning differences hold for other verbs that participate in the unergative-unaccusative alternation and for other transitive verbs with an optional direct object.[1]

In the remainder of this chapter, I will demonstrate more generally that two alternants of a frame alternation denote different views of the same event. The atelic-telic event type-shift exemplified in (4) and (5) illustrates one particular way of taking different views. I will call this relation between the two alternants *event type-shifting* (cf. Verkuyl 1972, 1993; Bach 1986; Pustejovsky 1991, 1995; see also section 3.3 and Chapter 4).

Having briefly shown the importance of event semantics in characterizing the two different kinds of alternations above, I will review the frame alternations from the previous chapter. I will discuss the empirical issue of which arguments surface in which position in terms of event types and shifts of event type across two alternants, viewing the arguments as participants in the event (cf. Davidson 1967).[2] Specifically, I will explore the following two-part hypothesis on the semantic characterization of frame alternations, (6).

(6) Hypothesis on the semantic characterization of frame alternations:
The kind of event a verb refers to remains constant across frames. Often, one (or more) of the event participants is mapped onto an argument position of the verb in each frame.
The aspectual event type a verb refers to differs across frames. Often, the exact selection of event participants that are mapped onto argument positions of the verb and the selection of these positions differ as well.

It has been observed by several people that there are strong associations between argument structure and event type. To mention a few among them: Tenny (1987, 1994); Van Valin (1987, 1990); van Voorst (1988); Grimshaw (1990); Levin & Rappaport Hovav(1992, 1994, 1995); van Hout (1991a,b, 1992a,b, 1994); Pustejovsky (1991); Hoekstra (1992); Mulder (1992); Grimshaw & Vikner (1993); Hale & Keyser (1993); van Hout et al. (1993, in progress); McClure (1993); Verkuyl (1993); Borer

(1994); Randall et al. (1994); Davis & Demirdache (1995); Davis (1997a,b); Demirdache (1997).

In order to facilitate the discussion of frame alternations in terms of event type-shifting, I introduce some event-semantic terms and notation.

3.3 Event structure preliminaries

To some extent or another, much actual work in event semantics draws on or departs from Vendler's (1957) classification of events. Inspired by the old Aristotelian tripartition of situational types, Vendler distinguishes four verb classes denoting different kinds of events, i.e., the so-called *Vendler-classes*: states, activities, accomplishments and achievements. Vendler uses two parameters in his definitions: the temporal unit, i.e., an instant or a stretch, and the definiteness or indefiniteness of the temporal unit: a *state* is an indefinite instant (e.g., *love somebody*); an *activity* is an indefinite stretch (e.g., *running*); an *accomplishment* is a definite stretch (e.g., *drawing a circle*); an *achievement* is a definite instant (e.g., *win a race*).

Presenting a battery of linguistic tests to distinguish the different classes, Dowty (1979) also reaches Vendler's original four-way classification of aspectual types. He advocates a reductionist analysis of the aspectual classes characterizing them in terms of aspectual operators, i.e., DO, BECOME and CAUSE. The notion of stative predicate is primitive. Activities are defined with a DO operator; accomplishments with both CAUSE and BECOME operators; achievements with a BECOME operator.

While for Vendler the classification is basically a verb classification, Verkuyl (1972) shows that aspect is not a verbal property, nor even a VP property, but, rather, that it is determined by the entire sentence. This can be seen when comparing one verb, e.g., *play,* in different sentences, (7).

(7)	a.	She played that sonata.	*terminative*
	b.	She played sonatas.	*durative*
	c.	Soldiers played that sonata.	*durative*

(from Verkuyl 1972)

The paradigm in (7) illustrates a case where the same event of playing a sonata is viewed in two different ways, i.e., as a durative or as a terminative event. The fact that the same verb can denote both a durative as well as a terminative event type indicates that it is not just a verb's aspectual properties that determine the aspectual type of the sentence. The arguments matter as well, in particular, their quantificational properties. Verkuyl therefore rejects the idea of fixed verbal aspectual classes and appeals instead to a principle of aspectual composition. Verkuyl (1972) lays the basis for a theory of aspect construction based on properties of the verb and its arguments. He further develops this theory in his later work (Verkuyl 1989, 1993), grounding it firmly in model-theoretic semantics. He defines an aspectual calculus in his so-called *Plus Principle*. It is defined on the quantificational properties of a verb's arguments, i.e., whether or not they denote a specified quantity of A, [±SQA], and on the aspectual features of the verb, [±ADD TO].[3] Mass terms and bare plurals are non-quantified NPs, [-SQA]; quantified NPs are [+SQA]. Stative verbs are [-ADD TO]; non-stative verbs, i.e. processes and events, are [+ADD TO]. The Plus Principle counts up the values of these features: only a "plus-plus-plus" configuration derives a bounded, i.e., terminative, sentential aspect: the event is telic only if a [+ADD TO] verb combines with a [+SQA] subject and [+SQA] object.

Whereas Verkuyl accepts Vendler's notions of state and process, he dismantles the criteria for distinguishing between accomplishments and achievements (Verkuyl 1989). He collapses these two classes as terminative events and opposes this class to states and processes which are both durative eventualities, thereby ending up with a tripartite classification. As Verkuyl points out, following up on Vendler's introduction of verb classes, various people have distinguished various numbers of aspectual classes with equally various definitions. While for Vendler there are four classes that are on equal footing, the number of classes has been extended by other people. Moreover, the classes have been partially ordered in terms of more than two features. For example, Bach (1986) distinguishes six different aspectual classes, (8).

(8) Bach's (1986) scheme of aspectual distinctions:

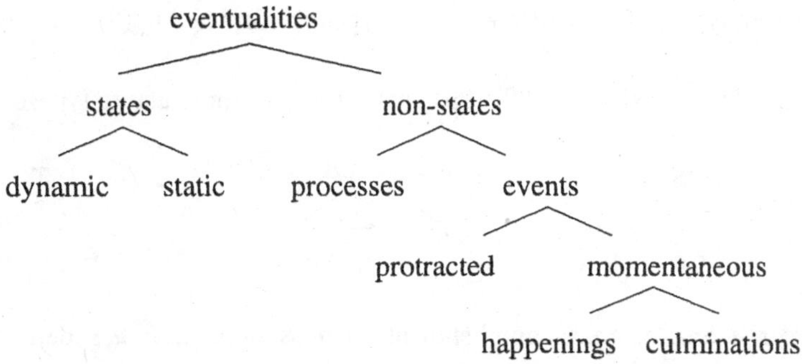

Bach subdivides states in two separate classes: dynamic states (e.g., *sit*) and static states (e.g., *love*). Processes are characterized as non-stative and non-eventive (e.g., *push a cart*). Vendler's class of accomplishments is Bach's class of protracted events (e.g., *build a house*). Achievements are momentaneous events, subdivided again into happenings (e.g., *recognize*) and culminations (e.g., *reach the top*). Bach points out that many verbs can switch their event type from process to event. Drawing parallels with the phenomenon that nouns can shift between a count and a mass denotation, he proposes analyzing this process-event shift along the same lines as Link (1987) analyzes type-shifting in the nominal domain, that is, in Boolean algebraic terms. In a similar approach, Krifka (1989a,b, 1992) not only parallels type-shifting effects in the nominal and verbal domains, but also connects the two (via a homomorphism) in order to account for event type-shifts caused by different quantificational properties of the nouns (e.g., (7)).

Pustejovsky (1988, 1991, 1995) proposes yet another formalization of event types. While he essentially follows the Vendler classification, Pustejovsky assumes that the different event types are not atomic entities, but rather, entities with subeventual structure. He distinguishes three aspectual primitives: states, processes and transitions. He defines a *state* (S) as a single event, which is evaluated relative to no other event, a *process* (P) as a sequence of events identifying the same semantic expression, and a *transition* (T) as an event identifying a semantic expression, which is evaluated relative to its opposition (E ranges over all event types). These different event types are depicted in (9).

(9) Pustejovsky's (1988, 1991) basic set of event structure types:

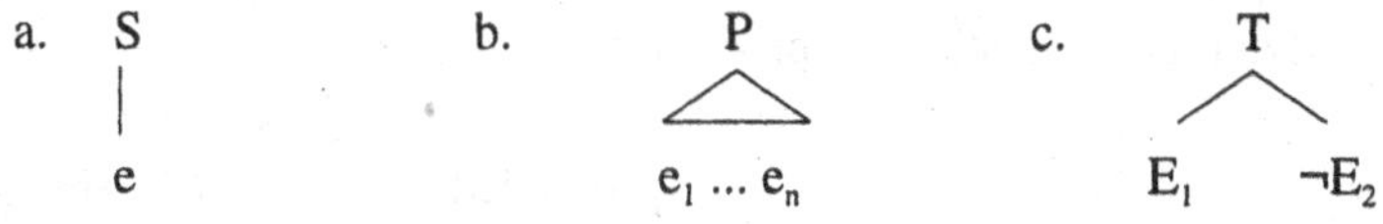

For example, an accomplishment such as *build a house* denotes a transition with a process as first subevent, i.e., building at the house, and a state as final subevent, i.e., when the house is finished. In the case of *build* the transitional event structure is lexically given. In other cases, the complex event type of a transition is constructed compositionally on the basis of the event types of the verb and prepositional complements. For example, *run* basically denotes a process. When it occurs with a directional PP such as *to the store* (which is a function from a process to a transition), the event type of the VP *run to the store* is a transition from a running process to a state of being at the store (see (10c) below). Pustejovsky refers to this process as *event composition.*

As Pustejovsky points out, an advantage of having subeventual structure in the event is that the ambiguous interpretation of adverbial modifiers can easily be described in terms of different scopes over the event structure or parts of it. For example, a manner adverb like *rudely* in a VP like *depart rudely* can either take scope over the process subevent of the transition (i.e., the manner of departing was rude) or over the transition as a whole (i.e., it was rude to depart). In similar ways, the ambiguity of *almost* and the effect of temporal modifiers get straightforward explanations.

In my discussion of the event semantics of frame alternations in this chapter, I will make use of a Pustejovskian notation, because it presents an intuitively perspicuous formalism for indicating the kinds of event type-shifts that are involved in various alternations. The same observations could be made in terms of other event-semantic formalisms, though. Furthermore, the Pustejovskian notation offers an intuitively straightforward way of relating arguments to events, namely by associating them as event participants to events and subevents (cf. Grimshaw 1990; Pustejovsky 1991; Grimshaw & Vikner 1993).[4]

While Pustejovsky only illustrates transitions between a process and a state, his definition of transitions allows for other kinds of transitions as well. As it will prove useful to have more kinds of transitions in the discussion below, I extend Pustejovsky's definition to range over four different types of transitions. If the E-variables in the subevents of the transition in (9) are taken as meta-variables, i.e., if they can be any one of the basic types, then a transition is a recursive event type. Hence, if *alpha* and *beta* are event types, then a *transition* between [*alpha*, *beta*] is also an event type. This definition of transition as a complex and recursive event type means that with the two basic event types *state* and *process* there are four different ways to form a complex event type of the type transition. These four types are indeed attested. Consider the four possibilities and some examples in Dutch, (10).

(10) Different types of transitions:

a.
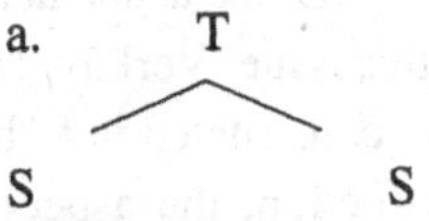

breken 'break'

b.
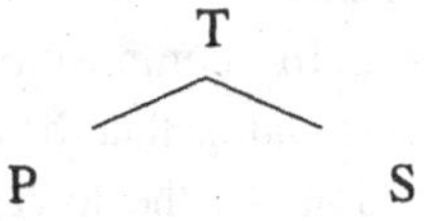

naar de winkel rennen 'run to the store'

c.
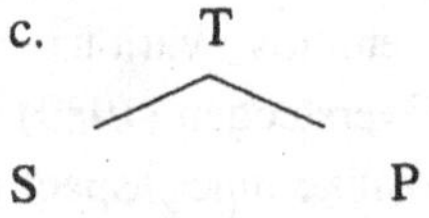

afreizen 'set off travelling'

d.
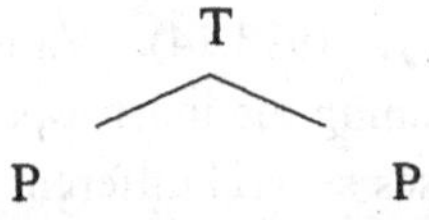

langs het huis fietsen 'bike past the house'

Given that a transition is a recursive event type, a transition can itself be embedded as a subevent in another transition.[5] Such a complex event type characterizes one kind of causative event, i.e., a transition with a causing event as first subevent and any other event type as the second subevent (see subsection 3.5.2 on causative event type-shifting). Dutch periphrastic causative constructions denote events of this event type. For example, *laten breaken* 'let break' can be depicted as in (11).

(11) Causative event type for Dutch periphrastic causatives:

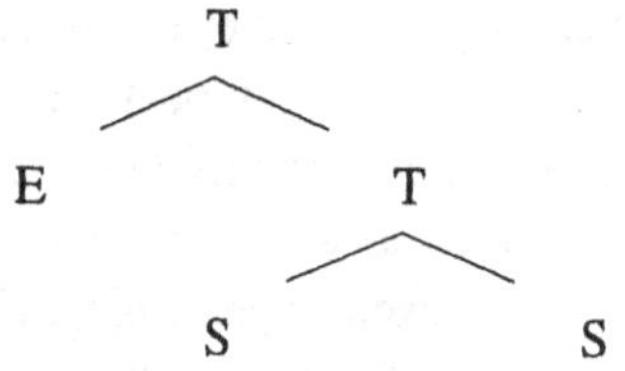

laten breken 'let break'

The aspectual value of a sentence is determined by a number of different elements and effects, only one of which is the verb's basic event type. The major goal of research on aspect is to find out what is involved in event type-shifting and which elements determine the aspectual value of a sentence. In a compositional approach to this issue, Verkuyl (1972 and later work) claims that the aspectual value is constructed in a "bottom to top" fashion. At the lower levels of construction, the aspect may be different from the final outcome at the sentential level. Verkuyl makes a distinction between what he calls *inner* and *outer aspect* (Verkuyl 1987): "*Inner aspect* concerns the relationship between a verb and its arguments" (Verkuyl 1993:14). Various languages employ various ways of determining the inner aspect. For Dutch, Oversteegen (1989) lists and discusses several different factors that determine inner aspect in Dutch (thematic roles, directional PPs, scope, the lexical properties of the verb, bare plural and mass NPs, the unicity of reference of NPs, the closedness/openness of the denotation of set NPs).

On top of these determiners of inner aspect, other operators such as tense, temporal adverbs and adverbial phrases determine the final aspectual outcome of a sentence; the latter set of elements determines the outer aspect of a clause. With the proper choice of adverbial phrases, an event that is unbounded in its inner aspect can be given temporal boundaries, (12a). Similarly, in a proper context a bounded event can be perceived as durative, or, more precisely, iterative, (12b).

(12) a. Judith at boterhammen van 1 tot 3.
'J. ate sandwiches from 1 to 3.'
b. Judith at de hele dag door een boterham.
J. ate the whole day through a sandwich
'During the whole day J. ate a sandwich.'
(adapted from Verkuyl 1993)

Verkuyls' terms *inner* and *outer aspect* refer to similar notions as Smith's (1991) terms *situation type* and *viewpoint*, respectively. According to Smith, *situation type* refers to the temporal structure of situations; different situation types vary in the temporal properties dynamism, durativity and telicity. Defining different situation types on these properties, Smith distinguishes the four Vendler classes (state, activity, accomplishment and achievement) plus a fifth class: *semelfactives*. A semelfactive is a dynamic, atelic and instantaneous event (e.g., *tap*, *knock*). The viewpoint of a sentence on the other hand characterizes an event with a particular extent and focus; it can present a full or partial view of a situation. Smith distinguishes three types: perfective, imperfective and neutral viewpoints.

As my concern is the verb and its arguments, I will only be dealing with inner aspect issues (or situation type), leaving out the effects of outer aspect (or viewpoint).

Touching upon only a few of the issues in the research domain involved with aspect, I have discussed above some formal ways of looking at events and event types. The notion *event type* is also referred to in the literature as *Aktionsart*, *inner aspect*, *situation aspect* and *temporal constitution* of the event. There is a lot of confusing terminology in the vast literature on aspect, so in finishing this section, I will dwell a little on the terms *aspect* and *event type*. As Comrie (1976) puts it, "aspects are different ways of viewing the internal temporal constituency of a situation . . . it is not concerned with relating the time of the situation to any other time-point" (Comrie 1976:3, 5). Event types are "perspectives on events. Perspectives that differ with respect to involvedness in the event, proximity to the event and the presentation of the beginning and/or ending as being part of the event. . . . But although events are not in themselves of a certain Aktionsart type, usually there are restrictions with respect to the types of Aktionsart that can be used to express them. Not every event can be represented by means of just any Aktionsart" (Oversteegen 1989:38, 40).

Finally, I want to mention my usage of certain terms. I use the term *event* in the same sense as Bach (1986) uses *eventuality* (see (8)), i.e., to refer to states, activities, accomplishments and achievements alike. I use the term *atelic event type* to refer to states and processes and *telic event type* to refer to transitions. Note that I use the term *telic* in a broad sense, i.e., to refer to all event types with a moment of temporal transition, including resultative but also inchoative and causative events. For lack of a term that covers these different kinds of transition events, I use the term *telic*, even though the traditional usage is restricted to terminative events.[6] When I talk about a verb's *event participants*, I refer to its semantic arguments; each event participant plays a certain role in the event.

3.4 Atelic-telic event type-shifting

The type-shift between an atelic and a telic event not only characterizes the unergative-unaccusative and the transitive-intransitive alternations in (2)-(5), but many other alternations as well. In this section I will discuss in more detail the Dutch alternations that exemplify this event type-shift: first, different kinds of transitivity alternations in which the alternants involve verbs in intransitive, transitive, conative and oblique frames (subsection 3.4.1); then, two forms of resultative formation applied to intransitive and transitive verbs (subsection 3.4.2).

In most cases of atelic-telic event type-shifting, the atelic event is a process and the telic event is a complex, transitional event type. It denotes a transition from an atelic process to an end state (i.e., a resultative event), or from a beginning state to an atelic process (i.e., an inchoative event). The process is the constant element in this event type-shift, (13).

(13) Atelic-telic event type-shifting:

P type-shifts into

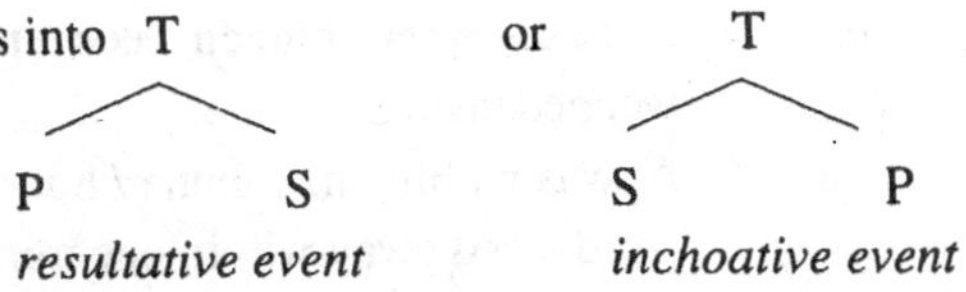

For all alternations that will be discussed in this section, the meaning shift from atelic to telic event type characterizes all verbs that participate in a certain alternation; it is not an idiosyncratic property of the particular verb with which it is going to be illustrated.

3.4.1 Transitivity alternations and atelic-telic event type-shifting

In order to show that the atelic-telic event type-shift is not dependent on the number of projected arguments, but, rather, on the syntactic positions in which the arguments are projected, I first discuss in more detail different versions of the unergative-unaccusative and the transitive-intransitive alternation. I continue with the other kinds of atelic-telic transitivity alternations.

Unergative-unaccusative alternation

Compare unergative and unaccusative *dansen* 'dance' (repeated from (4) above) with the unaccusative particle verb *wegdansen* 'dance away', (14c).

(14) a. Anneke heeft jarenlang / *binnen een week bij Raz gedanst.
A. has years-long / within a week with Raz danced
'A. danced with Raz for years / *within a week.'

b. Anneke was binnen een minuut / *urenlang van het podium af gedanst.
A. was within one minute / hours-long of the stage off danced
'A. danced off the stage within one minute / *for hours.'

c. Anneke was binnen een minuut / *urenlang weggedanst.
A. was within one minute / hours-long away-danced
'A. danced away within one minute / *for hours.'

Comparing the auxiliary choice HAVE in (14a) versus BE in (14b) and (14c) shows that *dansen* 'dance' is unergative when it refers to an atelic event and unaccusative when it refers to a telic event. The telicity of the predicate is due to an additional "goal" argument that makes the event telic or to a telic "goal" particle such as *weg* 'away'. The verb appears in an oblique unaccusative frame, (14b), or in a simple unaccusative frame, (14c), respectively.

Notice that which intransitive frame *dansen* 'dance' maps onto (unergative on the one hand or simple or oblique unaccusative on the other) is not dependent on the number of event participants it selects. While both *dansen* 'dance' in (14a) and *wegdansen* 'dance away' in (14c) are monadic predicates and project only one participant, i.e., the dancer, the former is unergative and the latter is unaccusative. While *dansen* 'dance' in (14b) is dyadic and projects two participants and *wegdansen* 'dance away' in (14c) projects only one, both verbs map onto an unaccusative frame. Thus, which frame *dansen* 'dance' maps onto depends on the event type properties of the verbal predicate, including complement PPs or particles: when the event is atelic, the verb maps onto an unergative frame; when it is telic, the verb maps onto an unaccusative frame. The same holds for a verb such as *rollen* 'roll', which takes a "theme" participant, (15).

(15) a. De tennisbal heeft minutenlang over de baan gerold.
the tennis-ball has minutes-long over the court rolled
'The tennis ball rolled over the court for minutes.'
b. De tennisbal is in 2 tellen de baan op gerold.
the tennis-ball is in 2 counts the court onto rolled
'The tennis ball rolled onto the court in 2 seconds.'

Atelic *rollen* 'roll' maps the "theme" onto an unergative frame, (15a); telic *rollen* 'roll' maps it onto an unaccusative frame, (15b). This shows that only event type, not number, nor kind of participants, matters for the selection of an intransitive frame. Both "agent" and "theme" single participants undergo the unergative-unaccusative alternation, triggered by an atelic-telic event type-shift.

The telic events in (14b), (14c) and (15b) are resultative events that consist of a process part plus a final state. Another verb pair in the unergative-unaccusative alternation, *reizen-afreizen* 'travel-start travelling', also displays the atelic-telic event type-shift, but now the telic event is inchoative, (16).

(16) a. Farook heeft jarenlang / *binnen een jaar veel gereisd voor zijn werk.
F. has years-long / within a year much travelled for his job
'F. travelled a lot for his job for years / *within a year.'
b. Farook is binnen een uur / *urenlang naar Kirgistan afgereisd.
F. is within an hour / hours-long to Kirgistan off-travelled
'F. set off to travel to Kirgistan within an hour / *for hours.'

The telic event in (16b) denotes an inchoative event: a transition between a state, i.e., not having left yet, and a process, i.e., travelling. Like resultative telic events, a telic event with an inchoative transition moment also maps onto an unaccusative frame.

Transitive-intransitive and transitive-conative alternation

Consider the different verb frames *schrijven* 'write' can appear in: an intransitive, a conative and a transitive frame, (17). ((17a) and (17c) are repeated from (5a) and (5b) above.)

(17) a. Elena schreef jarenlang / *binnen een jaar.
E. wrote years-long / within a year
'E. was writing for years / *within a year.'

b. Elena schreef jarenlang / *binnen een jaar aan haar proefschrift.
E. wrote years-long / within a year at her thesis
'E. was writing (at) her thesis for years / *within a year.'

c. Elena schreef haar proefschrift binnen een jaar / *jarenlang.
E. wrote her thesis within a year / years-long
'E. wrote her thesis within a year / *for years.'

Comparing the three different frames in (17) one sees that *schrijven* 'write' refers to an atelic event in two cases: when it projects only one event participant in an intransitive frame, (17a), or when it projects two participants in a conative frame, (17b). When it projects two event participants in a transitive frame, (17c), it refers to a telic event. Hence, which verb frame *schrijven* 'write' maps onto does not depend exclusively on the number of event participants that are selected by the verb. Rather, it depends on which view one presents of the writing event; the verb frame correlates with the event type properties of the verbal predicate. When the event is atelic, the verb maps onto an intransitive or conative (i.e., oblique intransitive) frame; when it is telic, the verb maps onto a transitive frame.[7]

The same correlations between telicity-atelicity of the event and particular verb frames show up with two particle variants of *schrijven* 'write': *afschrijven* 'finish writing', (18), and *doorschrijven* 'write on', (19).

(18) a. Elena heeft binnen een jaar / *jarenlang haar proefschrift afgeschreven.
E. has within a year / years-long her thesis off-written
'E. finished writing her thesis within a year / *for years.'

b. *Elena heeft binnen een jaar / jarenlang afgeschreven.
E. has within a year / years-long off-written

(19) a. Elena heeft jarenlang / *binnen een jaar doorgeschreven.
E. has years-long / within a year through-written
'E. wrote on for years / *within a year.'

b. Elena heeft jarenlang / *binnen een jaar doorgeschreven aan haar proefschrift.
E. has years-long / within a year through-written at her thesis
'E. wrote on at her thesis for years / *within a year.'

c. *Elena heeft jarenlang / binnen een jaar haar proefschrift doorgeschreven.
E. wrote years-long / within a year her thesis through-written

Afschrijven 'finish writing' inherently refers to a telic event; the meaning of the complex verb can be derived from the meanings of verb and particle *af* 'off' in a transparent way. This verb can only be projected in a transitive frame, (18). *Doorschrijven* 'write on' on the other hand inherently refers to an atelic event; the particle *door* 'on' (meaning 'continue to') productively combines with atelic process verbs. This particle variant can be projected in an intransitive or a conative frame, but not in a transitive frame, (19).

These observations reflect a more general picture. In van Hout (1991b, 1992a,b, 1994), I show for many Dutch transparent pairs consisting of a verb and a particle verb that the event-semantic properties of the particle determine whether there is an event type-shift from atelic to telic, as in (18), or whether the event type is fixed onto an atelic event type, as in (19). The event type properties of the complex verb correlate with the kinds of syntactic positions the verb's event participants are projected onto. When the event is atelic, the verb maps onto an intransitive or conative frame; when it is telic, the verb maps onto a transitive one.[8]

Some other verb pairs for which the particle brings about the same atelic-telic effect and "makes" the particle verb obligatorily transitive are: *eten-opeten* 'eat-eat up'; *lezen-uitlezen* 'read-finish reading'; *roken-oproken* 'smoke-smoke up'; *spelen-naspelen* 'play-copy by playing'; *knippen-afknippen* 'cut-cut off'; *graven-uitgraven* 'dig-dig out'; *duwen-afduwen* 'push-push off' (more examples in section 2.5). There are two productive atelic particles in Dutch: *door* 'on' and *mee* 'along'; some examples include: *dooreten* 'continue eating'; *meeëten* 'eat along'; *doorroken* 'continue smoking'; *meeroken* 'smoke along'; *doorspelen* 'continue playing'; *meespelen* 'play along'; *doorlezen* 'continue reading'; *meelezen* 'read along'; *doorzoeken* 'continue looking for'; *meezoeken* 'look along for'. *Door*- and *mee*-verbs cannot appear in a transitive frame (see (19c)).[9]

As *door* 'on' and *mee* 'along' are atelic particles, they select an atelic root verb to combine with. This implies that they cannot combine with inherently telic verbs such as *doden* 'kill', *vinden* 'find', *breken* 'break'. In fact, **doordoden*, **meedoden*, **doorvinden*, **meevinden*, **doorbreken* and **meebreken* do not exist.[10] One cannot continue on with an event that has an inherent transition moment; the event types of verb and particle clash.

Transitive-conative alternation

Consider another example of the transitive-conative alternation with *schieten* 'shoot' in (20).

(20) a. Theo schoot de hele dag / *binnen 5 minuten op konijnen.
'T. shot during the whole day / *within 5 minutes at rabbits.'

b. Theo schoot binnen 5 minuten / *de hele dag een konijn.
'T. shot a rabbit within 5 minutes / *during the whole day.'

When the verb is mapped onto a conative frame, (20a), it denotes an atelic event, i.e., a process of shooting at rabbits, whereas when it is mapped onto a transitive frame, (20b), it denotes a telic event, i.e., a shooting that results in an end state of a rabbit being hit.[11] Notice that the same event participants surface in both alternants; the "theme" appears in different positions, depending on the telic or atelic perspective on the event. Some particle variants of *schieten* 'shoot' also denote telic events; they are obligatorily transitive: *afschieten* 'shoot off'; *neerschieten* 'shoot down'; *doodschieten* 'shoot dead'.

Transitive-oblique alternation

Consider *schilderen* 'paint' in the transitive-oblique alternation, (21).

(21) a. Toos schilderde de hele dag / *binnen 5 uur (aan het huis).
T. painted the whole day / within 5 hours (at the house)
'T. was painting (the house) during the whole day / *within 5 hours.'

b. Toos schilderde het huis binnen 5 uur / *de hele dag.
'T. painted the house within 5 hours / *the whole day.'

When projected in an oblique or intransitive frame, (21a), *schilderen* 'paint' denotes an atelic event, i.e., a process of painting. When projected in a transitive frame, (21b), it denotes a telic event, i.e., an accomplishment of the house getting painted. Here, too, the "theme" event participant appears in both alternants, but in different positions, which yields different perspectives on the event. Telic particle and prefixed variants only appear in a transitive frame: *opschilderen* 'paint up'; *afschilderen* 'finish painting'; *beschilderen* 'paint'.

Also, some verb pairs in the transitive-oblique alternation, where the transitive verb is a prefixed form (with *be-*) of the oblique verb, exemplify an atelic-telic event type-shift. Consider *luisteren-beluisteren* 'listen', (22).

(22) a. Hein luisterde urenlang / *in een half uur naar de CD van Thomas Chapin.
H. listened hours-long / in a half hour to the CD of Thomas Chapin
'H. was listening to the CD of Thomas Chapin for hours / *within half an hour.'

b. Hein heeft in een half uur / *urenlang de CD van Thomas Chapin beluisterd.
H. has in a half hour / hours-long the CD of Thomas Chapin PFX-listened
'H. finished listening to the CD of Thomas Chapin within half an hour / *for hours.'

The simplex verb in an oblique frame, (22a), denotes an atelic event; the *be-*verb in a transitive frame, (22b), denotes a telic event.[12]

Not all verb pairs with a transitive prefix or particle variant demonstrate the same atelic-telic shift. Some *be-*verbs are ambiguous: they denote a telic or atelic event, e.g., *bespreken* 'discuss', *bekijken* 'examine', *beschrijven* 'describe', *bezingen* 'sing about' and *bebouwen* 'build'. Other *be*-variants of transitive-oblique verb pairs denote an atelic event: *bewerken* 'work on', *berijden* 'ride', *beschieten* 'shoot', *bedreigen* 'threaten'. Still, for all pairs of a verb plus *be*-verb there is a meaning difference across the two alternants. The event does not (necessarily) affect the "theme" participant when it is projected in a PP complement in the oblique alternant, but it does affect it when it is mapped as an object in the transitive alternant. This meaning effect in the transitive-conative alternation is further discussed in section 3.6.

Transitive-oblique transitive alternation

Again other dyadic verbs undergo an atelic-telic event type-shift when they take an additional "goal". Consider *duwen* 'push', (23).

(23) a. Judy duwde de kinderwagen urenlang / *binnen een uur.
'J. pushed the baby carriage for hours / *within an hour.'
b. Judy duwde de kinderwagen binnen een uur / *urenlang naar het park.
'J. pushed the baby carriage within an hour / *for hours to the park.'

As with monadic motion verbs in the unergative-unaccusative alternation (see (14) and (15)), the telicity of the telic predicate is due to an additional "goal" argument. The atelic verb appears in a transitive frame, (23a), and the telic verb in an oblique transitive frame, (23b).

Some more verbs that appear in this form of an atelic-telic event type-shift: *trekken* 'pull'; *dragen* 'carry'; *slepen* 'drag'; *rijden* 'drive'; *varen* 'navigate'; *zeilen* 'sail'; *draaien* 'turn'; *manoeuvreren* 'maneuver'; *gooien* 'throw'; *slaan* 'hit'; *schoppen* 'kick'. Alternatively, the "goal" can also be expressed by a particle such as *weg* 'away', or by a telic particle variant of the verb, e.g., *afduwen* 'push off'; *optrekken* 'pull up; *intrekken* 'pull in'; *opgooien* 'throw up'; *opslepen* 'drag up'; *opslaan* 'serve (in tennis)'; *inslaan* 'stock'.

Cognate object alternation

Consider *lachen* 'laugh' in the cognate object alternation, (24).

(24) a. Susan heeft urenlang / *in een uur gelachen.
S. has hours-long / in an hour laughed
'S. laughed for hours / *within an hour.'

b. Susan lachte *in een uur / *urenlang een schaterende lach.
S. laughed in an hour / hours-long a roaring laugh
'S. laughed *within an hour / *for hours a roaring laugh.'

The verb in the intransitive variant (24a) clearly denotes an atelic laughing event. It is not so clear, however, which event type the transitive variant with a cognate object denotes; both kinds of temporal modifiers give ungrammatical results, (24b). Whatever the exact event semantics of verbal predicates with a cognate object are, the event types of the two alternants in (24) are clearly different. Hence, the cognate object alternation presents different views on the same event (cf. Macfarland 1994, 1995).

State - telic event shift

All atelic-telic event type-shifts discussed so far involve an atelic event that is a process, i.e., a non-stative durative event. There is one alternation that denotes a state in the atelic alternant and a transition between two states in the transitive alternant, as depicted in (25). Consider the verb pair *staan-opstaan* 'stand-stand up', (26).

(25) State-transition event type-shift:

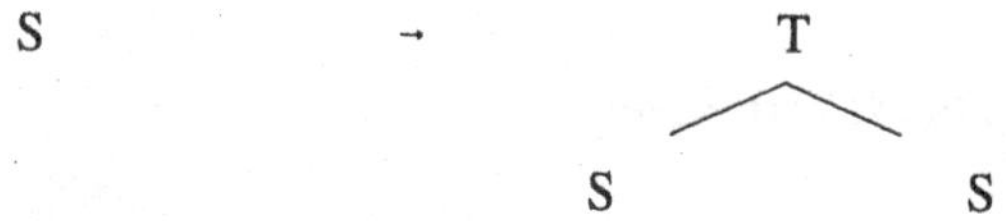

(26) a. Annemarie heeft een kwartier / *binnen een kwartier op haar hoofd gestaan.
A. has a quarter / within a quarter on her head stood
'A. stood on her head for a quarter of an hour /*within a quarter of an hour.'

b. Annemarie is binnen een kwartier / *urenlang opgestaan.
A. is within a quarter / hours-long up-stood
'A. stood up within a quarter of an hour / *for hours.'

Staan-opstaan 'stand-stand up' displays the unergative-unaccusative alternation: unergative *staan* 'staan' denotes an atelic state, (26a); telic *opstaan* 'stand up' denotes a telic event, (26b).[13] The telic event in (26b) is a transition from a state of not standing into one of standing. The event participant who is involved in standing is projected in both alternants.

With other positional verbs, this atelic-telic event type-shift is expressed with an aspectual auxiliary, i.e., *gaan* 'go', e.g., *zitten-gaan zitten* 'sit-sit down'. More in general, the state-telic event type-shift is not very productive.[14] There are only few other verb-pairs or frame alternations that exemplify it, e.g., *kennen-herkennen* 'know-recognize'.

3.4.2 Resultative formation and atelic-telic event type-shifting

Resultative formation by its very nature exemplifies an event type-shift from an atelic event to a resultative, i.e., telic event. The semantics of resultative formation involves the notion "to the extent of": a resulting state is reached when a process has gone on long enough that some transition takes place. It applies to monadic and dyadic verbs, yielding so-called *intransitive* and *transitive resultative formation.*

Intransitive resultative formation

First, consider an instance of intransitive resultative formation with *zwemmen* 'swim', (27).

(27) a. Claartje zwom de hele zomer / *binnen één zomer in zee.[15]
C. swam the whole summer / within one summer in sea
'C. swam in the sea during the whole summer / *within one summer.'

b. Claartje zwom haar badpak binnen één zomer / *maandenlang aan flarden.
C. swam her bathing suit within one summer / months-long to tatters
'C. s wam her bathing suit to tatters within one summer / *for months.'

Monadic *zwemmen* 'swim' by itself denotes an atelic event, (27a). When it is accompanied by a resultative clause, (27b), the event becomes telic. The verb varies between an intransitive and a transitive frame, which correlates with an atelic and telic event type, respectively. Many different analyses have been proposed for the syntactic structure of resultative sentences such as (27b), among others by Rothstein (1983); Simpson (1983); Kayne (1985); Hoekstra (1988, 1992); Carrier & Randall (1992); Déchaine (1993); Neeleman (1994). Without committing myself to any of these analyses, I will refer to the resultative alternant as a transitive frame and to the "subject" of the resultative predicate as a direct object.

The event type-shift in resultative formation is an atelic-telic one, as in all alternations discussed so far. However, the event-semantic make-up of the telic event as denoted by monadic *zwemmen* 'swim' plus resultative clause in (27b) differs from the telic events discussed so far. In (2)-(22) the two parts of the telic event are necessarily related, i.e., it is one integrated event. For example, in (2b) the dancer got off the stage by way of dancing; in (3b) the thesis came into existence in a writing process. The telic event in (27b), however, consists of two independent parts: one part is an atelic swimming process with a swimmer and the other part is the resultative state of a bathing suit gone to tatters. The two subevents are also related, but only through inferencing on the basis of world knowledge (for example, the knowledge that salty sea water affects bathing suits and that a lot of swimming can wear away a bathing suit).

Moreover, considering the roles of the event participants in the resultative event also shows that the two parts are independent. The subject is the "agent" of the swimming event, i.e., the swimmer; the direct object *badpak* 'bathing suit' is the "theme" of the state of being *aan flarden* 'to tatters'. The swimmer does not participate in the resultative state, nor is the bathing suit involved in the swimming process. In the telic events discussed above there is always one argument that figures as an event participant in both parts of the event. For example, the single participant in (2b) is the dancer of the dancing as well as the "theme" in being off the stage. The direct object in (3b) is the "theme" of writing as well as the "theme" of having come into existence.

The minimal pair in (28), adapted from German examples given by Seibert (1993), clearly illustrates these different kinds of telic events.

(28) a. De gevangene zwom urenlang.
the prisoner swam hours-long
'The prisoner was swimming for hours.'

b. De gevangene is in 5 minuten de gevangenis uitgezwommen.
the prisoner is in 5 minutes the prison out-swam
'The prisoner swam out of the prison within 5 minutes.'

c. De gevangene heeft zich binnen 5 maanden uit de gevangenis gezwommen.
the prisoner has himself within 5 months out the prison swam
'The prisoner swam himself out of prison within 5 months.'

The pair (28a) and (28b) is an instance of the unergative-unaccusative alternation; the pair (28a) and (28c) is an instance of an intransitive-transitive alternation. Both (28b) and (28c) are telic events, related to an atelic swimming event, (28a). In (28b) the prisoner got out of the prison by way of swimming; in (28c) he did not get out of prison by swimming (at least, most probably he did not), but rather, as a reward for winning the prison swimming competitions, for example. The swimming event and the resulting state of both types of telic events and their participants are the same, but the involvement of the event participants in the two subevents differs. Both types of telic events can be formalized as a transition. Associating the event participants in different ways with the subevents expresses the difference between the two kinds, as depicted in (29).

(29) Different types of telic events:

a. Subevents have independent participants:

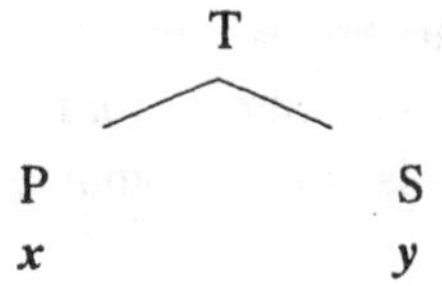

b. Subevents have the same participant:

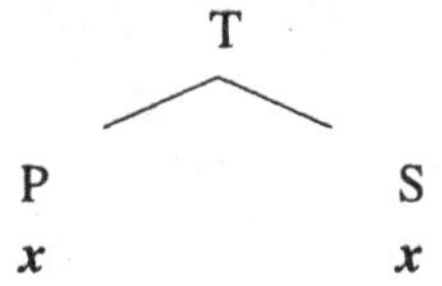

In (29b), *x* represents an event participant who is engaged both in a process (i.e., swimming) and in a certain state (i.e., being out of the prison). In (29a), *x* represents an event participant who is involved in a process (i.e., the swimmer) and y represents another participant involved in a certain state (i.e., somebody got out of prison). Accidentally, the two participants are coreferential in (28c).

Consider another example of intransitive resultative formation with *regenen* 'rain', (30).

(30) a. Het heeft dagenlang geregend.
it has days-long rained
'It rained for days.'

b. Claartje en Maarten waren in 2 uur de kamping afgeregend.
C. and M. were in 2 hours the campground off-rained
'C. and M. were swept away from the campground by the rain within 2 hours.'

Regenen 'rain' in (30) presents another instance of the unergative-unaccusative alternation, given the different auxiliaries HAVE and BE. It is a special version of this alternation. Like the previous unergative-unaccusative alternations in (14)-(16) and (28), the kind of event remains the same (i.e., a raining event). However, unlike the previous examples, there is no event participant that appears in both alternants. *Regenen* 'rain' in the unergative alternant (30a) denotes an atelic raining event that does not take any event participants.[16] The event in the unaccusative alternant (30b) is telic and there is an event participant, i.e., a "theme". The "theme" is not involved in the raining event. The two parts of the telic event are independent events: there is a raining event without any event participants and a change of location event of campers getting off a campground. Hence, (30) is a similar instance of intransitive resultative formation to (27b) and (28c) of the type depicted in (29a).

Transitive resultative formation

The atelic events in (27a), (28a) and (30a) are associated with monadic predicates in an intransitive frame that involve one or no event participants. In another version of resultative formation, the atelic event is denoted by a dyadic predicate in a transitive frame with two participants. This is transitive resultative formation. Consider *martelen* 'torture', (31).

(31) a. De diktator heeft de gevangene urenlang / *binnen een uur gemarteld.
the dictator has the prisoner hours-long / within an hour tortured
'The dictator tortured the prisoner for hours / *within an hour.'

b. De diktator heeft de gevangene binnen een uur / *urenlang doodgemarteld.
the dictator has the prisoner within an hour / hours-long dead-tortured
'The dictator tortured the prisoner to death in an hour / *for hours.'

Transitive resultative formation in (31) shows a shift from an atelic to a telic event of torturing. A torturing event takes an "agent" and a "theme" argument. Shifting to a telic event type requires the addition of a resultative predicate. Unlike the examples of intransitive resultative formation in (27), (28c) and (30), there is one participant, i.e., *the prisoner*, involved in both subevents in (31b). After being tortured for a while, the prisoner ends up in a resulting state: he is dead. Note that this event type-shift does not trigger a verb frame alternation: both alternants are transitive.

In all versions of resultative formation, the shift from atelic to telic triggers the projection of a direct object in the telic alternant (i.e., a transitive or an unaccusative frame). Thus, depending on how many event participants the verb selects, resultative formation involves different types of frame alternations. When the verb selects no participants, the event type-shift to a telic event type triggers an unergative-unaccusative alternation (see *regenen* 'rain' in (30)). When the atelic verb selects one participant, resultative formation triggers an intransitive-transitive (e.g., *zwemmen* 'swim' in (27) and (28)). When the atelic verb selects two participants, the telic alternant must be transitive (e.g., *martelen* 'torture' in (31)).

3.4.3 Generalizing over atelic-telic alternations

To summarize this section, the following alternations have been characterized by an event type-shift from an atelic to a telic event type: the unergative-unaccusative, transitive-intransitive, transitive-conative, transitive-oblique and the cognate object alternations and transitive and intransitive resultative formation. In all of these atelic-telic alternations, the verb or verb phrase denotes an atelic process or state in one alternant and a telic event, i.e., a transition, in the other. The atelic subevent of the telic event is the same one as the atelic event denoted by the other alternant.

Given that various telic event types are made up semantically in different ways, the event type-shift from atelic to telic comes about in different ways. In some cases, a telic event falls apart into a process followed by a final state (i.e., a resultative event). In other cases, it splits up into a beginning state followed by an atelic part (i.e., an inchoative event). Finally, there is one example where the telic event is a transition between two states. In addition, in most alternations at least one and sometimes two of the event participants are projected in both alternants, although some appear in different positions across alternants. Looking at which event participant is involved in which event or subevent, in almost all cases there is one participant involved in both subevents. Only intransitive resultative formation sometimes involves two independent subevents with no common participant.

Given that the different forms of alternations as discussed in (2)-(26) are all characterized by the same event type-shift, are there any generalizations between event type and verb frame? Verbs that denote an atelic event type appear in one of the following frames: unergative, conative, oblique intransitive or transitive. Verbs that denote a telic event type appear in an unaccusative, transitive or oblique transitive frame. What is the generalization? There is no common feature to the different frames of atelic verbs. The common feature of verbs denoting a telic event type, on the other hand, is that in all of these frames at least the direct object position is projected. Thus, the overall generalization is that a telic event requires the projection of a direct object.

Exploring further this generalization between event type (i.e., telicity) and verb frame (i.e., projection of a direct object position), notice that the relation is uni-directional: if the event is telic, there must be an (underlying) direct object position. The opposite is not necessarily true: it is not the case that all transitive clauses denote telic events. Compare (32) and (33), repeated from above.

(32) Elena schreef binnen een jaar / *jarenlang haar proefschrift.
E. wrote within a year / years-long her thesis
'E. wrote her thesis within a year / *for years.'

(33) De diktator heeft de gevangene urenlang / *binnen een uur gemarteld.
the dictator has the prisoner hours-long / within one hour tortured
'The dictator tortured the prisoner for hours / *within one hour.'

Even though both verbs appear in a transitive frame, *schrijven* 'write' denotes a telic event, (32), and *martelen* 'torture' denotes an atelic event, (33). Other verbs that pattern with *schrijven* 'write' and denote a telic event when they are transitive include: *schieten* 'shoot'; *schilderen* 'paint'; *bouwen* 'build'; *eten* 'eat'; *drinken* 'drink'; *naaien* 'sew'. Other verbs that pattern with *martelen* 'torture' and denote an atelic event when they are transitive include: *duwen* 'push'; *trekken* 'pull'; *dragen* 'carry';

slepen 'drag'; *aaien* 'pet'; *liefkozen* 'fondle'; *strelen* 'caress'; *masseren* 'massage'. Thus, a transitive frame by itself does not "guarantee" a telic event; the lexical-semantic properties of the verb play a role as well.[17] I will discuss these properties in Chapter 4.

To conclude this section, the generalization for Dutch alternations characterized by an atelic-telic event type-shift can now be formulated as in (34).

(34) Empirical generalization over atelic-telic alternations: If a verb denotes a telic event, it projects an argument in direct object position.

This generalization seems to be universal, holding across many different languages, as reported by Tenny (1987, 1994); Van Valin (1990); van Hout (1991b, 1992a,b, 1994); Pustejovsky (1991).

Having discussed the alternations that are characterized by an event type-shift from an atelic to a telic event, I now turn to a set of alternations that will be characterized by another kind of event shift: causativization.

3.5 Causativizing the event

Causativization extends an event with a causative meaning element. As I will show in this section, the causative extension means that another, additional event participant becomes involved as the initiator of the original event. Causativization may, but does not necessarily, involve an event type-shift. Comparing the event types of the events denoted by a non-causative and a causative alternant, they will turn out to be the same in certain causative alternations, i.e., there is no event type-shift. In this case, the new participant is simply added to the existing event, in particular to its first subevent. In other causative alternations, causativization not only adds a participant, it also triggers an event type-shift. In these alternations, the extra participant is associated with the added subevent. Both in type-shifting and non type-shifting alternations, the two alternants have different numbers of event participants, the causative has one more than the non-causative.

The alternations that will be discussed in this section illustrate causativization as applied to different types of events (i.e., achievements, accomplishments, processes and states). I will first discuss the alternations in which the event type remains the same across both alternants (subsection 3.5.1) and then those with an event type-shift (subsection 3.5.2). Whereas the verbs in causative alternations without an event type-shift are lexical causatives, causative alternations with an event type-shift split up into: (i) simple frame alternations with a lexical causative and (ii) alternations with a periphrastic causative construction.

3.5.1 Causative alternations without event type-shifting

Causativizing an achievement

The often discussed causative-inchoative alternation is a causative alternation in which both alternants denote a transition: the intransitive alternant denotes an achievement and the transitive a caused achievement. Consider *breken* 'break', (35).

(35) a. Het ei breekt.
'The egg breaks.'
b. Inge breekt het ei.
'I. breaks the egg.'

Both breaking events in (35) denote a transition between two different states of the egg: first the egg is a whole, then it is broken. The breaking event expressed in the intransitive alternant involves only one participant, i.e., the "theme" which is changing state, (35a). The breaking event in the transitive alternant is a transition with two participants: the same "theme" and an "agent" who initiates the change of state, (35b). The subeventual make-up of both kinds of breaking events is the same (i.e., a transition between two states); what differs is the number of event participants involved. This is pictured in (36).

(36) Causativizing an achievement:

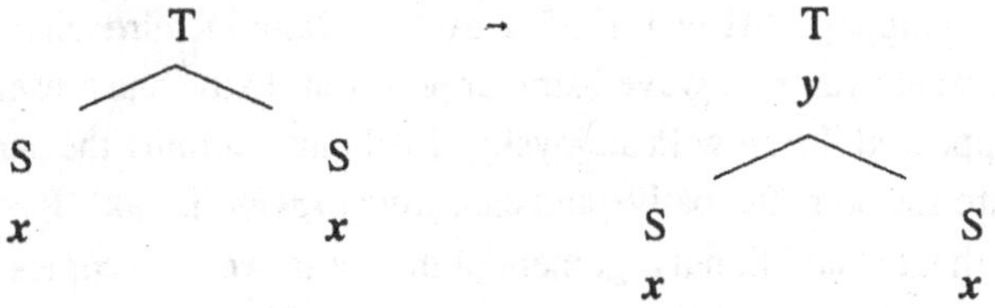

In the non-causative as well as in the caused achievement there is an event participant variable, *x*, involved in the change of state (i.e., the egg in (35)). In the causative alternant there is an additional event participant variable, *y*, involved as the initiator of this change of state (i.e., the breaker in (35)). The latter participant identifies the causative character of the transition. The additional participant *y* is associated with the top node of the transition in (36); this reflects the fact that this participant does not identify one of the subevents, but, rather, initiates the transition.

Other verbs that exemplify this type of causative event shift in the causative-inchoative alternation include: *splitsen* 'split'; *oplossen* 'dissolve'; *verdampen* 'evaporate'; *doven* 'extinguish'; *sluiten* 'close'; *trouwen* 'marry'; *verdrinken* 'drown'; *scheuren* 'rip'; *inscheuren* 'rip in'; *veranderen* 'change'; *opvrolijken* 'cheer up'; *opknappen* 'recover, patch up'.

Notice that even though the causative event in (36) has a complex event type, i.e., a transition, it still is one integrated event, rather than two independent events, one a causing subevent, the other the caused. The latter is the event structure I will propose for Dutch periphrastic causatives, e.g., *laten breken* 'make break' (see (45) in subsection 3.5.2).

Many analyses of the causative-inchoative alternation reflect a different view which has its origins in generative semantics (cf. Lakoff 1971; McCawley 1971). These alternatives all assume a bi-eventual analysis of the causative alternant. The causative alternant is associated with a more complex event type than the inchoative event; it is a complex event type that subdivides in a causative part plus an inchoative event. They follow some version of the formula: '*y* CAUSES *x* to BECOME *P*' (cf.

Dowty 1979; Hale & Keyser 1986; Pinker 1989; Jackendoff 1990; Parsons 1990; Brousseau & Ritter 1991; Davis & Demirdache 1995; Levin & Rappaport Hovav 1995; Davis 1997a,b; Demirdache 1997).

In recent years, however, similar proposals to the one presented here have appeared. I follow Pustejovsky (1991) in assuming the same event structure for both inchoative and causative *breken* 'break'. Pustejovsky claims that the additional argument of the causative verb comes from the agentivity of the predicate, and not from a change in event structure. Comparing resultative constructions and lexical causatives in Dutch, Hoekstra (1992) claims that causatives (like resultatives) involve an integration of an embedded predication into the event structure of the governing verb. According to Hoekstra, this is precisely how lexical causatives differ from non-lexical causatives which involve reference to a causing and a caused event. Interpreting how various kinds of modifiers modify the event, van Voorst (1993) concludes that causative events such as transitive *breken* 'break' are not composite events, but, instead, one whole. Ritter & Rosen (1993a,b), comparing lexical and periphrastic causatives in English, argue that lexical causativization only involves the addition of an argument and not the addition of a CAUSE predicate in the LCS. Finally, Fodor (1970) gives three reasons why causative *kill* does not mean the same as *cause to die*. (His discussion is embedded in a slightly different discourse, as he is arguing against generative semanticists.)

Causativizing an accomplishment

In one alternant, the verb, or rather, the verbal predicate, denotes an accomplishment; in the other, it denotes a caused accomplishment. This type of causative alternation characterizes a subset of the verbs of motion: when they appear with a "goal" phrase. Consider *rollen* 'roll' in the unaccusative-transitive, (37), and in the oblique unaccusative-oblique transitive alternation, (38).

(37) a. De bal is weggerold.
the ball is away-rolled
'The ball rolled away'.
b. Ilona heeft de bal weggerold.
I. has the ball away-rolled
'I. rolled the ball away.'

(38) a. De bal is naar de andere baan gerold.
the ball is to the other court rolled
'The ball rolled to the other court.'
b. Ilona heeft de bal naar de andere baan gerold.
I. has the ball to the other court rolled
'I. rolled the ball to the other court.'

As in the causative-inchoative alternation, the difference between the two alternants in (37) and (38) does not reflect an event type-shift, i.e., both alternants denote a single transition between a process part and a final state. The difference is the number of event participants involved. This causative shift is pictured in (39).

(39) Causativizing an accomplishment:

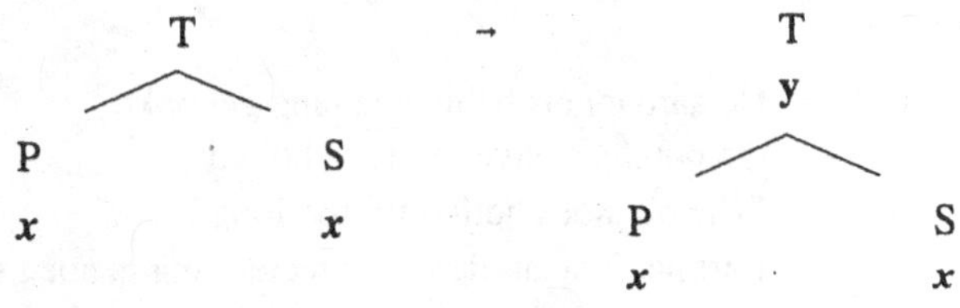

In both alternants in (37) and (38), the "theme" participant, x, is involved in both the rolling processes (i.e., the ball is the rolling entity) and the final state which is reached when the ball is *weg* 'away', (37), or *op de andere baan* 'on the other court', (38). In the causative alternants, there is an additional event participant, y, who initiates the rolling processes and thereby identifies the causative character of the transition.

Other verbs in the unaccusative-transitive alternation with the same shift of causativizing an accomplishment include: *smelten* 'melt'; *uitrekken* 'stretch'; *verbeteren* 'improve'; *verzachten* 'soften'; *verbranden* 'burn'; *afbranden* 'burn down'; *verslijten* 'wear out'; *vertragen* 'slow down'; *versnellen* 'speed up'; *verzwakken* 'weaken'; *inkoken* 'boil-boil down'; *gaarstomen* 'steam until cooked'; *drogen* 'dry'; *buigen* 'bend'. Also, some morphologically related verb pairs in the unaccusative-transitive alternation can be characterized as causativization of an accomplishment. These include: unaccusative *verbleken* 'bleach' and transitive *bleken* 'bleach'; *verkleuren-kleuren* 'color'; *opdrogen-afdrogen* 'dry'; *bevriezen-invriezen* 'freeze'; *zich (uit)strekken-(uit)strekken* 'stretch (out)'; *zich uitvouwen-uitvouwen* 'fold out'; *zich stabiliseren-stabiliseren* 'stabilize (itself)'; *zich verspreiden-verspreiden* 'spread (itself)'; *zich verbeteren-verbeteren* 'improve'.

Causativizing a process

In one alternant, the verb denotes a process; in the other, it denotes a causative process. This type of causativization characterizes a set of verbs in the unergative-transitive alternation: the unergative variant denotes a process and the transitive variant denotes a causativized process. Consider *koken* 'boil' in (40).

(40) a. De aardappels hebben te lang gekookt.
the potatoes have too long boiled
'The potatoes boiled for too long.'

b. Bart heeft de aardappels precies lang genoeg gekookt.
B. has the potatoes exactly long enough boiled
'B. boiled the potatoes exactly long enough.'

Both alternants in this type of causative alternation denote a process; the difference is the number of event participants involved in these processes. In both the non-causative and the causative alternant in (40), the "theme", i.e., the potatoes, is involved in the boiling process. In the causative alternant, there is an additional "agent" participant, involved as the initiator of the boiling process.[18] This causative shift is pictured in (41).

(41) Process type-shifts into a caused process:

P	→	P
x		*x, y*

Other examples in the unergative-transitive alternation denoting the same shift of causativizing a process include: *bakken* 'bake'; *braden* 'fry'; *fruiten* 'fry'; *bewegen* 'move'; *rijden* 'drive'; *varen* 'navigate'; *zeilen* 'sail'; *vliegen* 'fly'; *rollen* 'roll'; *(rond)draaien* 'turn (around)'. Some morpho-syntactically marked verb pairs include: *zich draaien-draaien* 'turn'; *zich strekken-strekken* 'stretch'.

Summarizing causativization without an event type-shift

Three different types of causative alternations without an event type-shift have been illustrated in this subsection: causativization of achievements, accomplishments and processes. These various causative types are similar because the causing and the caused parts of the event cannot be separated from each other into two subevents. The causative event is one composite whole. Causativization only involves the addition of another, "agent" argument which is the initiator in the event. These causative alternations take on different forms: the unaccusative-transitive, unergative-transitive and the oblique unaccusative-oblique transitive alternation.

There are interesting differences across languages in causative alternations. Van Voorst (1993; also 1994, 1995) shows that there are different restrictions on how the "agent" participant must be involved in the causative event. In Dutch, the subject in a transitive frame that denotes a causative event must be what van Voorst calls "the energy source of the action chain". Dutch patterns with French, but differs from English where the "agent" participant of a causative event may also be what he calls "the responsible entity for the coming about of the event" (e.g., the boiling water in (42)). Compare causative *break* with two different subjects in these three languages, (42).

(42) a. Inge / *Het kokende water brak het ei.
b. Inge / *L'eau bouillant a cassé l'oeuf.
c. Inge / The boiling water broke the egg.

In Dutch and French, a "responsible entity" cannot be the subject of a lexical causative. An event caused by such a "responsible entity" can be expressed in a periphrastic causative construction in Dutch (see (48)).

In the next set of causative alternations, causativization not only involves the addition of a participant, but also event type-shifting.

3.5.2 Causative alternations with event type-shifting

All causative alternations, both with and without an event type-shift, involve the addition of an extra event participant. The crucial difference between them lies in the subeventual make-up of the causative events and, consequently, the ways in which the event participants are distributed over the subevents. I will discuss event type-shifting causativizations applied to states, achievements, accomplishments and processes. The causatives discussed in the previous section all involved lexical causatives; the examples in the present section are expressed in a periphrastic causative construction (except for the first one, causativization of a state, which is a lexical causative).

Causativizing a state

Certain stative verbs can causativize with a lexical causative. This characterizes a set of verbs in the intransitive-transitive alternation. The intransitive variant denotes a state and the transitive variant denotes the causative event of bringing about this state.[19] Consider *hangen* 'hang', (43).

(43) a. De foto hangt aan de muur.
'The picture hangs on the wall.'
b. Joep hangt de foto aan de muur.
'J. hangs the picture on the wall.'

The additional participant in (43b) is involved as an "agent" who manipulates the "theme", so that it ends up hanging on the wall. This event type-shift is pictured in (44).

(44) State type-shifts into a caused state:

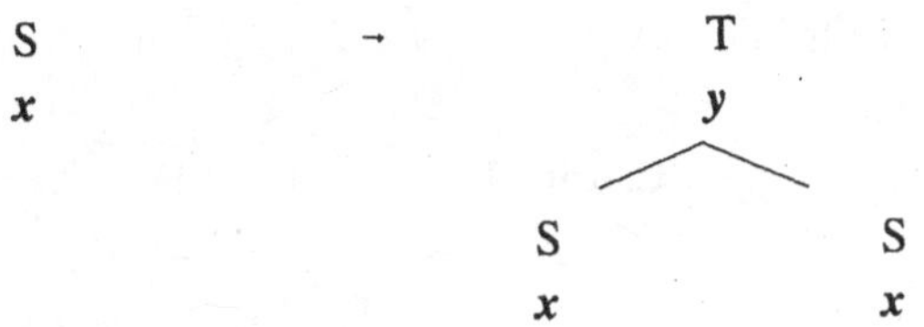

More verbs in the intransitive-transitive alternation with this event type-shift include: *leunen* 'lean'; *uithangen* 'air', *afdekken* 'cover' and *bedekken* 'cover', and verb pairs such as: *hangen-ophangen* 'hang (up)'; *liggen-leggen* 'lie-lay'; *zitten-zetten* 'sit-put'; *zich uitspreiden-uitspreiden* 'spread'; *zich verspreiden-verspreiden* 'spread'.

Bi-eventual causativization

All causative alternations discussed in the previous subsection plus (44) are frame alternations. The additional "agent" is directly involved in the causative event; it is mapped onto subject position. Other forms of causativization trigger an alternation in which the causative alternant has a complex syntactic structure, i.e., a periphrastic causative construction with auxiliary verbs *laten* 'make' (literally, 'let') or *doen* 'make' (literally, 'do'). The additional participant in such causative events does not directly interfere in the event. This form of causativization can apply to all different event types; it is independent of the number and kinds of participants in the caused event.

Bi-eventual causativization involves a particular type of event type-shift. The event turns into a more complex event type in which the original event becomes a subevent. In the event-semantic make-up of a bi-eventual causative event, there are separate causing and caused subevents: the complex event denotes a transition from a causing subevent to the caused (original) event, (45).

(45) Causative event type-shifting:

E type-shifts into
x, ...

T
Causing E — E
c — *x*, ...

The causing subevent can cause any type of event (i.e., meta-variable *E* in (45)). The event participants are distributed over the two subevents: the causing subevent has its own "causer" participant, *c*; the caused event has its own set of participants, *x*, ..., which is the same in both alternants.

The difference between single-event versus bi-eventual causative event types is that in the latter the causing event is an independent subevent of the complex event type, whereas in single-event causatives, the causative event is one whole. Consequently, the additional participants are involved in different ways. In single-event causatives, the additional "agent" is involved throughout the event, influencing the "theme" participant in some direct way. In bi-eventual causativizations, the influence of the additional participant is restricted to the causing subevent which is separate from the caused event and its participants.

Comparing atelic-telic and causative event type-shifting, the similarity between the two is that an event type is extended with an additional part and becomes a complex, transitional event type. The difference between the two types lies in the kind of extension: in an atelic-telic event type-shift, a transition plus a final or beginning state is added. In a causative event type-shift a transition plus a causing event is added as first subevent.

In all kinds of causativization, the projection of an additional participant affects the positions of the other participants, as the additional participant is projected onto subject position. Different languages employ different ways to "find" a new position for the so-called *demoted argument(s)*. In a crosslinguistic study, Comrie (1976) observes that there is a paradigm case of what happens to the original arguments in causativization. All languages more or less conform to the paradigm, deviating from it in small details. Essentially, the demoted subject ends up in a lower position of a hierarchy characterized by Keenan & Comrie (1977) as: subject < direct object < indirect object < oblique object. In which position it ends up depends on which other arguments are present and, hence, which other position is available. Hence, the demoted subject of an intransitive appears as direct object in the causative variant; the demoted subject of a transitive appears as indirect object; the demoted subject of a ditransitive appears as oblique object.

Pairs of non-causative and periphrastic causative alternants are not exactly like the simple frame alternations above, since these only involve verbs, rather than pairs of verb and verb cluster.[20] However, the fact that these causatives involve a periphrastic construction rather than a simple frame seems to be specific for Dutch. English, for example, employs lexical causatives in many instances where Dutch uses a periphrastic construction (cf. van Voorst 1993). Moreover, in morphologically richer languages, the additional participant of a morphologically causative verb is mapped as a subject of a simple frame (e.g., Turkish, Inuit, Japanese and Lillooet Salish).

In the remainder of this subsection, I will illustrate different kinds of causative alternations with a periphrastic construction in which the caused subevent is an achievement, an accomplishment, a process or a state. Typically, a bi-eventual causative does not specify the event type of the causing subevent, i.e., the first subevent of the transition. In order to distinguish the two kinds of additional participants, I will call that of bi-eventual causatives a *"causer"*, as opposed to the *"agent"* in the previous single-event causativizations. A "causer" is indirectly involved in initiating the event, whereas an "agent" is directly involved. Moreover, a "causer" participates in a separate causing subevent, whereas an "agent" is involved in the event as a whole (for definitions in terms of event structure configurations of notions such as *"agent"* and *"causer"*, see Davis & Demirdache 1995; Davis 1997a,b; Demirdache 1997).

Causativizing an achievement

First, consider a causativized achievement, (46). In one alternant the verb denotes an achievement; in the other, it denotes a transition from a causing event to an achievement. This shift is illustrated with intransitive and transitive *breken* 'break', (47).

(46) Achievement type-shifts into a caused achievement:

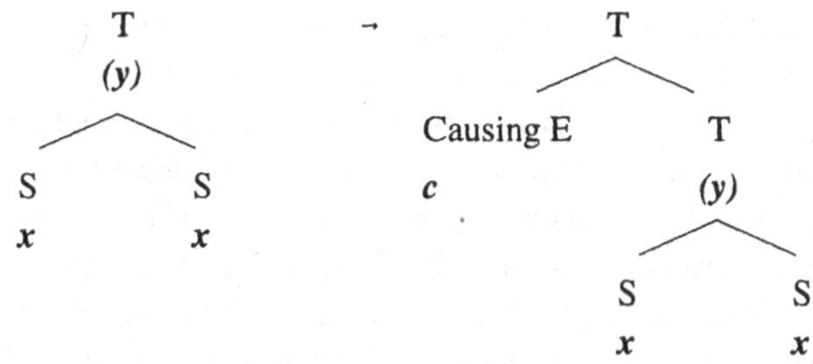

(47) a. Het ei breekt.
'The egg breaks.'
b. Inge breekt het ei.
'I. breaks the egg.'
c. Dave liet het ei breken.
'D. made the egg break.'
d. Dave liet Inge het ei breken.
'D. made I. break the egg.'

Both monadic and dyadic *breken* 'break' denote achievements. *Bi*-eventual causativization applies to monadic *breken* 'break' with only a "theme" participant, *x*, yielding the pair (47a) and (47c). It applies to dyadic *breken* 'break' which has already causativized and has a "theme" and an "agent", *x* and *y*, yielding the pair (47b) and (47d). Hence, in order to derive (47d), monadic *breken* 'break' first causativizes with an additional "agent", but without an event type-shift. Next, bi-eventual causativization changes the event type and adds a "causer". Note that the "agent" and a "causer" are involved in different ways: (47c) can describe a situation in which the "causer" refrains from any action, thereby causing the egg to break, whereas (47b) can only describe a breaking event in which the "agent" is in some way or other directly involved in the event (i.e., the distinction between direct and indirect causativization, cf. Shibatani 1976)

If the participant in the causing subevent is not a person purposely acting upon the other event participant(s) (i.e., a "causer"), but, rather, some natural force or certain circumstances, one cannot employ auxiliary *laten* 'make' (literally 'let'). Instead, the auxiliary in the periphrastic causative is *doen* 'make' (literally 'do'). Consider *breken* 'break', (48).

(48) Het kokende water deed het ei breken.
the boiling water did the egg break
'The boiling water made the egg break.'

Notice that one can, in principle, causativize all verbs with a bi-eventual causative. This includes those which cannot appear in a single-event causative, because the "theme" participant is involved in the transition "all by itself" (e.g., transitive *verdwijnen* 'disappear' or *sterven* 'die' are ungrammatical, but *laten verdwijnen* 'make disappear' and *laten sterven* 'make die' are perfect).

Causativizing an accomplishment

Next, consider causative event type-shifting of an accomplishment. In one alternant, the verb denotes an accomplishment; in the other, it denotes a transition from a causing event to an accomplishment. This event type-shift is pictured in (49); it is illustrated with *wegrollen* 'roll away', (50).

(49) Accomplishment type-shifts into a caused accomplishment:

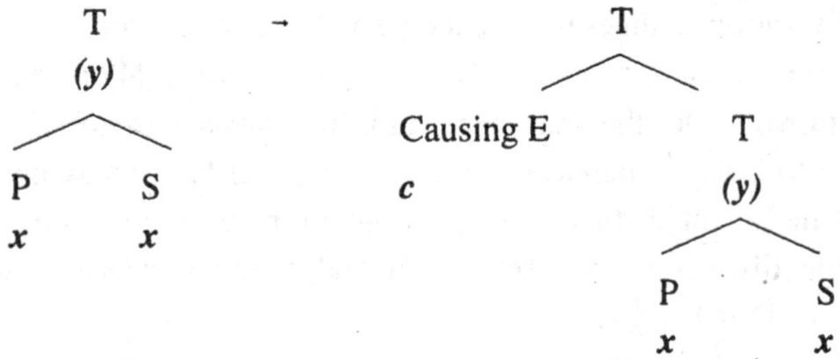

(50) a. De bal rolt weg.
'The ball rolls away.'
b. Ilona rolt de bal weg.
'I. rolls the ball away.'
c. Piet laat de bal wegrollen.
P. lets the ball away-roll
'P. makes the ball roll away.'
d. Piet laat Ilona de bal wegrollen.
P. lets I. the ball away-roll
'P. makes I. roll the ball away.'

The pair (50a) and (50c) is a periphrastic causative of monadic *wegrollen* 'roll away' with just a "theme", *x*, and (50b) and (50d) is the causative of the causativized monadic verb which has an "agent" and a "theme", *x* and *y*. Like (47d), (50d) has been causativized twice, first with an additional "agent", then with an additional "causer"; the latter operation also involves event type-shifting.

Causativizing a process

Third, consider causative event type-shifting of a process. In one alternant the verb denotes a process; in the other, it denotes a transition from a causing event into a process. This event type-shift is pictured in (51); it is illustrated with *koken* 'cook', (52).

(51) Process type-shifts into a caused process:

P → T
(y,) x

Causing E P
c *(y,) x*

(52) a. De aardappels koken te lang.
'The potatoes cook too long .'
b. Bart kookt de aardappels.
'B. cooks the potatoes.'
c. Francis laat de aardappels koken.
F. lets the potatoes cook
'F. makes the potatoes cook.'
d. Francis laat Bart de aardappels koken.
F. lets B. the potatoes cook
'F. lets B. cook the potatoes.'

Bi-eventual causativization applies to monadic *koken* 'boil', (52a) and (52c), and to its lexical causative, (52b) and (52d). The latter causative in (52d) involves double causativization.

Causativizing a state

Finally, there is causative event type-shifting of a state. In one alternant the verb denotes a state; in the other, it denotes a transition from a causing event to a state. This event type-shift is pictured in (53a). Alternatively, the state causativizes twice, in two steps, as pictured in (53b). These shifts are illustrated with *hangen* 'hang', (54).

(53) State type-shifts into a caused state:

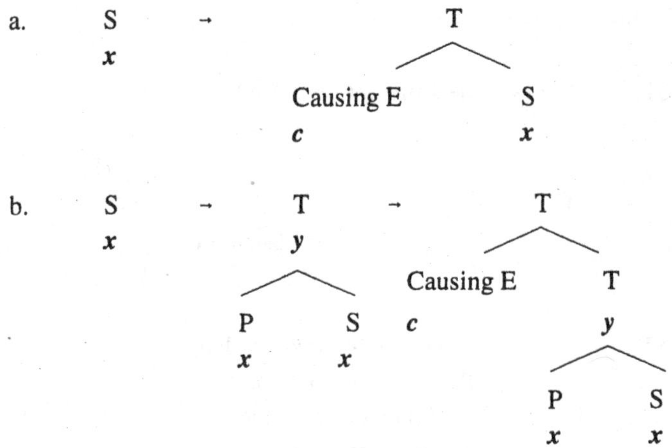

(54) a. De foto hangt aan de muur.
'The picture hangs on the wall.'

b. Joep hangt de foto aan de muur.
'J. hangs the picture on the wall.'

c. Moniek laat de foto aan de muur hangen.
M. lets the picture on the wall hang
'M. lets the picture hang on the wall.'

d. Moniek laat Joep de foto aan de muur hangen.
M. lets J. the picture on the wall hang
'M. makes J. hang the picture on the wall.'

Causativization of a stative verb necessarily triggers an event type-shift from a state to a transition (in which the original state is the final subevent), because a causative is an eventive eventuality. There are two different ways to expand the original state, depending on how much the additional participant is involved in causing this state to come about. One way leads to a lexical causative verb, (54b) (= (43) above), the other to a periphrastic causative, (54c). There is a meaning difference between the two causatives, *hangen* 'hang' in (54b) versus *laten hangen* 'let hang' in (54c). The "agent" in the lexical causative *hangen* 'hang', (54b), directly manipulates the picture and initiates the change of state so that the picture ends up hanging (it was not hanging before). The "causer" in a periphrastic causative *laten hangen* 'let hang', (54c), does not directly manipulate the "theme" and is only involved in the causing subevent (in this case the picture is already hanging on the wall and is not touched). In (54d), there are two steps of causativization, each involving an event type-shift, first, from a state to a transition between a process and the state (see (44)); next, from this transition to a second transition with a causing first subevent and the transition as the caused subevent (see (49)).

3.5.3 Generalizing over causative alternations

The operation of causativization extends an event with a causative meaning element. In all cases, this means that an additional event participant who is involved as the initiator of the event, is projected in the causative alternant. In some cases, causativization also involves an event type-shift: the event type of the original event is extended with another, causative subevent. I have distinguished these two kinds of causative alternations in the two subsections above. Causativization without an event type-shift triggers the projection of a transitive or oblique transitive frame in which the additional participant is mapped onto subject position and the original participant onto object position. They include the intransitive-transitive alternation (both the unaccusative-transitive and the unergative-transitive alternation) and the oblique unaccusative-oblique transitive alternation (subsection 3.5.1). The other kind of causativization involves an event type-shift from the non-causative to the causative alternant. In one case, the causative verb was a lexical causative and causativization triggered a frame alternation, i.e., the intransitive-transitive alternation. In all other cases, event type-shifting causativization triggers a periphrastic causative construction with auxiliary, *laten* 'let, make' or *doen* 'do, make' (subsection 3.5.2).

With respect to the number and kinds of participants that are projected in each alternant, there is always one more participant in the causative alternant which is projected in subject position (of the verb or the verb cluster), whatever the position(s) of the participant(s) in the non-causative alternant is (are). In most cases projection of an additional participant affects the position(s) of the non-causative event participant(s). As the additional argument is mapped onto subject position, the original subject is demoted to object position (e.g., the unergative-transitive and periphrastic causative constructions).

Comparing lexical and periphrastic causatives, I have characterized the difference in terms of how the additional participant is involved in the causation. Lexical causatives denote a single causative event. The additional participant initiates this event and is itself involved in it via manipulating the "theme" participant in a direct way; I have called this additional participant a (regular) *"agent"*. Periphrastic causatives denote a bi-eventual causative event that falls apart in two separate and independent subevents. The additional participant is only involved in the causing subevent and does not manipulate the "theme" participant in a direct way; I have called this additional participant a *"causer"*. Thus, which causative form is chosen in Dutch (a lexical or a periphrastic causative construction) depends on how the additional participant is involved in the causative event.

What are the correlations between event type and verb frame? As for simple frame-alternating causativizations (i.e., lexical causatives that denote a single causative event), the verb in the non-causative alternant is mapped onto one of the intransitive frames (unergative, unaccusative, oblique unaccusative); the verb that denotes a single-event causative event is mapped onto a transitive or an oblique transitive frame. The common factor of the non-causative alternants is that they are all intransitive. The causative alternants, on the other hand, involve verbs in an (oblique) transitive frame with a causing "agent" in subject position. Thus, a single-event causative event type requires the projection of an argument in subject position and one in object position. This generalization holds across all causative frame alternations, (55).

(55) Empirical generalization over causative alternations:
If a verb denotes a single-event causative event, it projects an argument in subject position and one in direct object position.

This generalization seems to be universal, holding across many different languages, as reported in several crosslinguistic studies (cf. the collection of studies in Shibatani 1976).

As for causative alternations with a periphrastic causative, the verb in the non-causative alternant is mapped onto any kind of frame (intransitive, transitive, etc.); the causative clause involves a verb cluster in which the "causer" is mapped onto subject position and the caused event is an embedded infinitive clause. Generalizing over both kinds of causativizations then, every verb that denotes a causative event always maps an event participant onto subject position, i.e., the additional "agent" or "causer". Which positions the other event participants are mapped onto depends on the kind of causativization, i.e., with or without a separate causing subevent, and, hence, whether it is a lexical or periphrastic causative.

3.6 Different foci on the event

Briefly considering the remaining alternations in Dutch that have been discussed in Chapter 2, one notices that the event type remains the same, but the two alternants present different foci on the same event. There are several possible ways in which one can zoom in on a particular aspect of the event. In the case of telic events, one may employ different scales of how the event develops toward its transition point. Another way is that different foci may have different implications for one of the event participants or that one may present different foci on a certain event participant. Without going into much detail, I briefly discuss the remaining alternations in order to complete the event-semantic overview of frame alternations.

3.6.1 Alternations with different foci on the event

Different measures of a telic event

For many verbs in the locative alternation (e.g., *smeren* 'smear'), the *strijken* 'iron' alternation and the material-product alternation (e.g., *naaien* 'sew'), the verb denotes a telic event in both alternants. One can take different foci on these events by following two different scales along which the event develops toward its transition point. Alternatively formulated in Tenny's (1987, 1994) terminology, the event can be "measured out" in different ways depending on which argument is the so-called "measure" of the event. Consider *smeren* 'smear' in the locative alternation, (56).

(56) a. Ingrid smeerde de henna in een uur / *urenlang in haar haar.
I. smeared the henna in an hour / *hours-long in her hair
'I. smeared the henna in her hair within an hour / *for hours.'

b. Ingrid besmeerde haar haar in een uur / urenlang (met de henna).
I. PFX-smeared her hair in an hour / hours-long (with the henna)
'I. covered her hair (with the henna) within an hour / for hours.'

Both alternants of *smeren* 'smear' in (56) (can) denote telic events of smearing in which an "agent" and a "theme" are involved and develop toward a certain "goal". Both the material smeared, i.e., the henna, and the surface it is smeared on, i.e., the hair, can be taken as the "theme" participant and mapped onto object position, (56a) vs. (56b). The focus on the smearing event is different, though. Either one focuses on the material to reach the final state when all of it is smeared, (56a), or, one focuses on the surface to reach the final state when it is smeared all over, (56b). A smearing event is thus measured along two different scales: one provided by the amount of henna and the other provided by the amount of hair. Hence, a telic smearing event can therefore be "measured out" in two different ways, depending on which scale is chosen. In both cases, the object position is crucial to express these different foci: the participant that measures the aspectual scale must be mapped as direct object. In similar ways, the telic events denoted by verbs in the *strijken* 'iron' and the material-product alternation can be measured along two different scales.

Several people present analyses of the locative alternation in which they express these semantic effects (including, among others, Tenny 1987, 1994; Wunderlich 1987; Levin & Rappaport 1988; Pinker 1989; Jackendoff 1990; Gropen et al. 1991a,b; Brinkmann 1995).

Different implications for an event participant

Many verbs and verb pairs in the transitive-oblique alternation are characterized by an atelic-telic event type-shift (see section 3.2.3). There is, however, another set of verb pairs in this alternation for which the meaning effect across the two alternants does not involve event type-shifting, as both alternants denote atelic events. Still, the event participants in these pairs of verbs are focused on differently. Consider *schieten op-beschieten* 'shoot at-shoot', (57).

(57) a. De Bosnische Serviërs hebben urenlang op Sarajevo geschoten.
the Bosnian Serbs have hours-long at Sarajevo shot
'The Bosnian Serbs were shooting at Sarajevo for hours.'

b. De Bosnische Serviërs hebben urenlang Sarajevo beschoten.
the Bosnian Serbs have hours-long Sarajevo PFX-shot
'The Bosnian Serbs were shooting at Sarajevo for hours.'

Both alternants of *schieten-beschieten* ' shoot' in (57) denote atelic events of shooting in which an "agent" and a "theme" participant are involved. However, the meaning implications for the "theme" participant differ, depending on whether it appears in a PP complement of the (simplex) verb in the oblique alternant, (57a), or as an object of the *be*-variant in the transitive alternant, (57b). The shooting does not (necessarily) affect the town in the oblique alternant, for instance, because the grenades do not reach it. In the transitive alternant with the *be*-variant, on the other hand, the town is necessarily hit, (57b). In (57a), but not in (57b), one can add: . . . *maar zij konden de stad niet raken* ' . . . but they were not able to hit the town'. Hence, if the "theme" participant is affected in some way or another by the shooting, it must be projected as direct object; if it is not affected or if one chooses not to focus on the effects of the shooting, it is projected in a PP complement.[21] The two alternants in the transitive-oblique alternation thus present different views by focusing different implications of the same event.

Similarly, for other verbs in the transitive-oblique alternation, different meaning implications are associated with different alternants. For example, *spreken over-bespreken* 'speak about-discuss': the "theme" argument is/is not thoroughly and exhaustively discussed; *kijken naar-bekijken* 'look at-examine': the "agent" argument does/does not take a precise and serious look at the "theme"; *werken aan-bewerken* 'work at-edit': the "theme" argument does/does not undergo extensive revision; *rijden op-berijden* 'ride on-ride': the "theme" argument is/is not ridden on a regular basis.

In similar ways, mapping the "theme" participant as object or as PP complement triggers different meaning implications for verbs that participate in the dative (e.g., *geven* 'give', *sturen* 'send') and benefactive alternation (e.g., *inschenken* 'pour') and for verbs in the locative alternation with two atelic alternants (e.g., *besproeien* 'spray', *bespuiten* 'spray', *begieten* 'water'). In all cases, the object position is crucial for these different foci: if the "theme" participant is affected in some way or another, it is mapped onto object position.

Several people discuss and incorporate these meaning effects in their analyses of one of these alternations. For example, Oehrle (1976) discusses them for the dative alternation; Tenny (1987, 1994) for the transitive-oblique alternation; Tenny (1987, 1994) and Brinkmann (1995) for the locative alternation.

Different foci on the event and its participants

Both alternants of the active-passive alternation denote the same event; choosing an active or passive voice does not affect the event type. Rather, different foci on the event and its participant(s) require an active or passive voice. The active voice presents a view that focuses on the active involvement of an "agent". The passive voice presents a view that focuses on the passive involvement of the "theme" participant, independent of whether or not the event also involves some action by another participant. In the passive, the active character of the event and the "agent" participant are defocused, while its passive character and the "theme" participant are brought into focus. Consider *vertalen* 'translate', (58).

(58) a. Andrew vertaalde "Hercules".
'A. translated "Hercules".'
b. "Hercules" werd vertaald.
'"Hercules" was translated.'

One and the same translating event can be seen from an active viewpoint, i.e., somebody is doing the job, (58a), or from the viewpoint of the effect of the event, i.e., something is getting translated, (58b).

More precisely, as impersonal passivization shows, the passive voice abstracts away over the agentive participant of the event and focuses purely on the kind of event that is going on, not necessarily on its effect.

No event participant needs to be projected. Passivization merely defocuses the agentive character of the event and the "agent" participant; it does not necessarily focus on another event participant. Consider monadic *lachen* 'laugh' in impersonal passivization, (59).

(59) a. Susan heeft urenlang / *in een uur gelachen.
S. has hours-long / in an hour laughed
'S. laughed for hours / *within an hour.'
b. Er werd urenlang / *in een uur hardop gelachen.
there was hours-long / in an hour loud laughed
'There was loud laughing for hours / *within an hour.'

The active, unergative alternant denotes an atelic event of laughing with an "agent", (59a). In the passive alternant the verbal predicate refers to the same event, i.e., laughing, of the same event type, i.e., an atelic process, but without mentioning its participant, (59b).

Notice that if the operation of passivization involves defocusing the agentive character of an event, the event must be agentive to start out with. This creates restrictions on which verbs can passivize: only those with an agentive participant can passivize.[22] In fact, passivization is impossible with a verb such as *krijgen* 'get' because none of the event participants are agentive, (60). It is equally impossible with verbs such as *weten* 'know' because it denotes a stative eventuality, and, by definition, states do not involve an agentive participant, (61).

(60) a. Angela krijgt een pastamachine.
'A. gets a pasta machine.'
b. *De pastamachine werd gekregen.
The pasta machine is gotten by A.

(61) a. De hele klas weet het antwoord.
'The whole class knows the answer.'
b. *Het antwoord werd door de hele klas geweten.
'The answer was known by the whole class.'

Defocusing the "agent" participant in passivization has been typically analyzed as suppression of the external argument by, among others, Hale & Keyser (1986); Di Sciullo & Williams (1987); Roberts (1987); Roeper (1987); Zubizarreta (1987); Baker (1988); Baker, Johnson & Roberts (1989); Grimshaw (1990); Woolford (1993).

Middle formation, like passivization, defocuses the agentive character of the event and the "agent". However, while passivization preserves the event type of the active verb, the middle voice completely takes off the eventive character. Thus, middle formation affects the event type: independent of the event type of the active alternant it operates on, a middle denotes a state. Middle formation abstracts over the kind of event denoted by the verb in the active voice and turns it thereby into a stative predicate. Furthermore, since it involves event type-shifting from an eventive to a non-eventive event type, i.e., a state, the verb in the middle alternant cannot project the "agent", because states do not have "agents".

In analyses of middle formation, the external argument is either suppressed or deleted altogether (cf. Hale & Keyser 1987; Roberts 1987; Roeper 1987; Hoekstra & Roberts 1993; Ackema & Schoorlemmer 1994, 1995; Manowsky 1995).

3.6.2 Generalizing over alternations with different foci on the event

In this section, the event-semantic properties of alternations that do not involve event type-shifting have been very globally touched upon. In a broad and general way, I have characterized them in terms of taking different foci on the same event. In many cases, the direct object position is the crucial position for putting some special focus on one of the event participants.

In fact, the different foci characterization holds for all alternations that have been discussed throughout this chapter. Atelic-telic event type-shifting and causativization are two more specific operations of what different foci on an event may involve. Further research of the non-type-shifting alternations from the viewpoint of the event semantics is needed for a more complete picture. In the next chapter I will exclusively deal with event type-shifting alternations.

3.7 Summary: the empirical domain of lexical-syntactic flexibility

Before one can develop a theory on the lexicon-syntax interface, one first needs to mark out the empirical dimensions of the phenomenon of lexical-syntactic flexibility. What are the lexical-syntactic generalizations across different kinds of flexibility? What do they suggest with respect to the nature of lexical specification relevant to mapping? While Chapter 2 has laid out the empirical groundwork by showing the magnitude of the phenomenon, the present chapter has cut back the enormous variety, bringing down to seizable dimensions the domain that the interface theory must capture. Viewing semantic arguments as participants in an event and focusing on the event type properties of the alternants, the syntactically diverse forms of lexical-syntactic flexibility can be reduced to just three different event-semantic kinds. Event-semantic mapping requirements underlie the correlations between particular event type-shifts and particular verb frame shifts. Rather than setting up analyses for each separate kind of alternation, a lexicon-syntax theory should be based on generalizations across many different alternations. As these generalizations turn out to be of an event-semantic nature, an interface theory must be developed along event-semantic lines.

Frame alternations fall into one of three kinds: alternations with an atelic-telic event type-shift (section 3.4), alternations characterized by causativization (section 3.5) and alternations that do not involve an event type-shift but present different foci on the same event (section 3.6). How many arguments are mapped and onto which syntactic positions depends on the event type. Two correlations between event type on the one hand and verb frame on the other have emerged. A telic event type requires the projection of an argument in direct object position. A causative event type requires the projection of arguments in both subject and direct object position. The answer as to why a verb appears in more than one frame is thus related to presenting the same event from various event-semantic angles. The question why it appears in a particular set of frames is related to the mapping requirements of particular event-semantic perspectives as expressed by the generalizations on telic and causative event types. Hence, an event-semantic analysis of the phenomenon of lexical-syntactic flexibility not only reduces its dimensions to just three different kinds, it also allows for insightful generalizations over systematic frame differences between two alternants. The interface theory must express these intricate relations between different event types and different verb frames.

The conclusion that frame alternations must be analyzed in terms of the relations between event types and verb frames implies that a theory of the lexicon-syntax interface must be framed in those terms as well. Developing such a theory is the goal of the next chapter.

Notes

1. Not all optionally transitive verbs denote a telic event when they appear in a transitive frame, though. This issue will be touched upon in subsection 3.4.3 and discussed in detail in Chapter 4.
2. Davidson (1967) has introduced the notion of *event* as a separate ontological entity. Higginbotham (1985) points out its relevance for linguistic theory. The introduction of the notion of *event participant* is equally attributed to Davidson (1967), although he himself does not employ the term in his paper. Typically, the predicates *Davidsonian* and *neo-davidsonian* refers to event-semantic views in which a verb denotes an event to which its arguments and adjuncts are related as event participants (e.g., Parsons 1990).
3. SQA is Verkuyl's abbreviation of Gruber's (1965) notion *specified quantity of A*. Verkuyl interprets Gruber's notion as a feature of NPs.
4. By choosing a Pustejovskian notation to describe event types, I do not commit myself to his theory on mapping (although my theory will converge with his to a certain extent; see Chapter 4).
5. My goal here is not to explore the complete range of possibilities of complex event types, but, rather, to introduce the types that will reappear in the discussion of frame alternations below.
6. Cf. Greek *telos* 'goal'.
7. In Chapter 4 this last statement will be discussed in more detail in light of the atelic effect non-quantized objects have, e.g., *brieven schrijven* 'write letters' is an atelic writing event. I will argue there that non-quantized objects are not interpreted as true objects, but, rather, as part of predicate following de Hoop (1992) and van Geenhoven (1996).
8. These observations are more general: In Russian and Hungarian, pairs of verb-prefixed verb display similar correlations between the event-semantic properties of the complex verb and the frame it appears in (cf. van Hout 1991b, 1992a,b, 1994).
9. Note that *door* is ambiguous: next to its atelic, 'continue to'-meaning, it sometimes has a telic interpretation. In such cases it does appear in a transitive frame. The telic meaning effect shows up in verbs such as *doorknippen* 'cut through'; *doorprikken* 'pierce through'; *doorzoeken* 'search' (notice the stress difference: *dóorzoeken* 'continue looking for' versus *doorzoéken* 'search').
10. In fact, *doorbreken* exists but not with a 'continue to'-meaning of *door*; it means 'break through'.

11. I am interested here in the frame adverbial interpretation of *binnen 5 minuten* 'within 5 minutes', which is ungrammatical. (20a) is ok in an inchoative interpretation in which he started shooting within 5 minutes.
12. The durative adverbial *urenlang* 'for hours' in (22b) is ok under a different interpretation, i.e., as a repetition of listening again and again to the same CD. The fact that the adverbial triggers this meaning shift is actually an indication of the telicity of the single event (cf. Verkuyl 1993).
13. The verb pair in (26) displays the HAVE-BE shift which I have taken as an indication for the unergative-unaccusative alternation. Mulder & Wehrmann (1989), however, claim that verbs of position are nevertheless unaccusative.
14. In this respect, Dutch is unlike English, where the static atelic-telic shift is grammaticalized in verb pairs for all positional verbs, e.g., *stand-stand up*. German also employs particle verbs, e.g., *stehen-aufstehen*, alongside with reflexive verbs, e.g., *setzen-sich setzen* 'sit-sit down'.
15. An interpretation of *binnen één zomer* 'within one summer' in (27a) as frame adverbial is ungrammatical. The sentence is ok under an interpretation that she was able to swim within one summer.
16. In general, no event participants surface in the unergative alternants of weather verbs (*regenen* 'rain' in (30a), *sneeuwen* 'snow', *waaien* 'blow', *vriezen* 'freeze', etc.). Notice at this point the careful formulation in hypothesis (6) of what remains constant across alternants, ". . . often, one (or more) of the event participants that the verb takes as argument surfaces in both frames". (30) presents a case where there is no participant that appears in both.
17. Moreover, telicity of the transitive clause also depends on the quantificational properties of the direct object, see (7b). This issue will be discussed in detail in Chapter 4.
18. In fact, transitive *koken* 'boil' is ambiguous between a process and an accomplishment reading. The latter one includes a resulting state, reached when the potatoes are done. In (40b), however, it is an atelic process.
19. Whether the intransitive verb in (43a) is unergative or unaccusative is an issue of discussion.
20. Notice that passivization also involves a cluster with an auxiliary in the passive alternant. Still, passivization is considered to be a "real" argument alternation.
21. M. Anderson (1978) introduces the notion of *affectedness* as a restriction on prenominal objects in nominalizations, i.e., they need to be affected by the verb. Affectedness is an intuitively clear notion but it has proven hard to define precisely (cf. Zubizarreta 1987; Tenny 1987, 1994; Rozwadowska

1988; Grimshaw 1990).

22. The agentivity restriction on Dutch passivization will be discussed extensively in Chapter 4, section 4.6.

CHAPTER 4

The Lexicon and the Lexicon-Syntax Interface: the CHESS Model

In this chapter I model the lexicon-syntax interface by defining it on event-semantic lexical primitives: the number of participants that are involved in the event denoted by a verb and the verb's basic event type. The mapping system only needs to "see" these lexical properties in order to relate a verb's lexical specification and the syntactic configuration it appears in. I will argue that the need to identify event structure defines the mapping relation: mapping involves checking of event-semantic features in the syntactic configuration, rather than the association of lexical arguments with syntactic positions. I call this approach the *CHESS model* (*ch*ecking *e*vent-*s*emantic *s*tructure). Arguments in the specifier positions of AgrS and AgrO identify an event or subevent by being associated with participants in the event structure. Telicity features must be checked off in object position via strong Case assignment in AgrO. As telicity is determined by the event-structural properties of the VP predicate to which a verb's lexical event structure contributes compositionally, the event feature checking approach to mapping accounts for the aspectual nature of the mapping generalizations in a natural way. Furthermore, this approach explains the phenomenon of lexical-syntactic flexibility as a derivative of event type-shifting. Argument-centered views on mapping (i.e., theories based on θ-roles, argument structures or lexical-conceptual structures), on the other hand, cannot account for the effects of event type-shifts that determine lexical-syntactic flexibility, since they define mapping solely on a verb's lexical arguments.

4.1 Goals of this chapter

I have presented different kinds of lexical-syntactic flexibility in Chapter 2 in Dutch and given an event-semantic characterization analyzing the phenomenon in terms of event type-shifting in Chapter 3. I have stressed that certain meaning elements remain constant across the set of frames a verb appears in: it denotes the same kind of event and one or more of its event participants appear in both frames. Each different frame, however, presents a different focus on the verb's basic meaning: each frame expresses a different perspective on the event, or, more specifically, a different event type. Moreover, the selection of overtly present event participants differs, as does the selection of syntactic positions they are mapped onto. From this event-semantic perspective, three different types of lexical-syntactic flexibility have been distinguished: atelic-telic alternations, causativization alternations and alternations without event type-shifting, but whose alternants express different foci on the event. The following empirical generalizations hold about verbs, their frames and the event-semantic associations in Dutch: (i) If a verb phrase denotes a telic event, it maps an argument onto direct object position. (ii) If a verb phrase denotes a causative event, it maps one argument onto subject position and another one onto direct object position.

The general goal of the present chapter is to derive the implications of the phenomenon of lexical-syntactic flexibility for determining what the lexical-syntactic primitives are for mapping verbal predicates onto syntax. The specific goal I will pursue is: how can one model lexical-syntactic flexibility in a theory on the lexicon-syntax interface in an explanatory and maximally general way? Assuming as a null hypothesis that the projection of a verb plus its arguments onto syntax is determined by its lexical specification (see Chomsky 1986), this question has two main components.[1] One, what is the nature of the lexical primitives that are involved in determining which verb frames a verb can map onto? Two, how does the mapping system derive the complete set of possible frames a verb can occur in from these lexical-syntactic features?

The chapter is organized into three parts. In the first part, I will lay out my first considerations on the lexicon and mapping. I establish my standpoint with respect to the lexicon as a separate and generative module (section 4.2) and with respect to the evaluation criteria for a parsimonious lexicon and maximally general mapping system (section 4.3). Furthermore, I will discuss a set of problems for argument-centered mapping theories which lead to the conclusion that they cannot adequately deal with lexical-syntactic flexibility (section 4.4).

These evaluation criteria and the ways in which argument-centered theories fail set a baseline for the subsequent development of a new approach to the lexicon and mapping. The next two parts will form the core of this chapter. In order to determine the lexical primitives of the new mapping theory, I discuss in Part II which lexical properties are involved in the lexicon-syntax interface and must therefore be considered as lexical-syntactic features. I will conclude that these include a verb's set of event participants (sections 4.5-4.6) and its basic event type (section 4.7).

In Part III, I define the new mapping system. Reviewing the mapping generalizations over lexical-syntactic flexibility from the previous chapter, I discuss the nature of the mapping system (section 4.8). I base the mapping system on event-semantic primitives and define it as a set of mapping conditions that *ch*eck *e*vent *s*emantic *s*tructure: the CHESS model. Mapping onto syntax depends on the perspective that is taken of the event; various event types present different perspectives, each of which is associated with a different syntactic configuration. Hence, lexical-syntactic flexibility is a function of different perspectives on the event. Having modeled the systematic part of the lexicon-syntax interface, I briefly return to the lexicon as a reservoir of unpredictable and unsystematic properties (section 4.9). To conclude, I position the CHESS model among other lexicon-syntax theories by reviewing some standard notions and discussing how these come back or are derived in the new model (section 4.10). The CHESS model differs crucially from argument-centered mapping systems (theories defined on subcategorization, θ-role, argument structure or LCS's), as they depend exclusively on the number and kinds of event participants. A summary of the properties and advantages of the CHESS model concludes this chapter.

Part I: Initial considerations on the lexicon and the lexicon-syntax interface

In order to prepare the ground for the discussions on the nature of lexical primitives and the mapping system, I first present some general considerations on the lexicon as a generative module of the grammar (section 4.2). Next, I list what I believe to be evaluative criteria for comparing theories on lexicon and mapping (section 4.3). Concluding these initial considerations, I discuss to what extent argument-centered mapping theories can deal with lexical-syntactic flexibility in an insightful way (section 4.4).

4.2 A generative lexicon or an unpredictable dictionary?

If parsimony were not a relevant criterion, the phenomenon of verbs mapping onto different frames could be dealt with by simply taking the lexicon as a storehouse for unpredictable information (cf. Chomsky 1965) or as the repository of all that is not fully predictable in grammar (cf. Chomsky 1970; Wasow 1977). One could list each verb with a set of lexical specifications, each associated with its own argument alignments, e.g., a set of subcategorization frames, θ-grids or argument structures. One could say that for each verb there is an exhaustive list of independent lexical entries, each with a different specification corresponding to a different verb frame. Alternatively, given that a verb has a constant meaning element in each of its occurrences, one might reduce the redundancy somewhat by listing each verb in just one entry, which in turn exhaustively lists all of its potential subcategorization frames, θ-grids or argument structures.

In fact, Jackendoff (1975) proposes such an approach with respect to the lexical representation of derived nominals. While he claims that a verb and "its" derived nominal each have their independent entries, he proposes lexical redundancy rules to account for their shared subcategorization and argument structure properties. Lexical redundancy rules relate lexical entries to each other, simplifying the individual entries by means of abbreviatory devices. Hence, they only simplify lexical entries, but do not create new ones and, therefore, they have limited productivity and allow for idiosyncratic exceptions.

With respect to verbs and their lexical properties, Gross (1973) advocates an exhaustive listing approach. Comparing some 3000 French verbs for 110 different distributional and transformational properties (among which their subcategorization possibilities), Gross concludes that there are no two verbs in French that have exactly the same syntactic properties.[2] Therefore, generalizing over verbs and classifying them into verb classes is not the right kind of methodology. Each verb needs to be uniquely and exhaustively specified in the lexicon.

In such non-systematic approaches, the lexicon is either redundantly large or completely unsystematic, or both. Systematic meaning similarities and differences across the frames a verb appears in are not explained, nor are the systematic regularities across different verbs in the same frames. Moreover, such a lexicon could only be learned in a completely unsystematic way, namely by conservatively listing every new frame a verb is heard in, independent of its meaning or the frames it or other verbs have been heard in before.

Research of the past decade on the lexicon and on its acquisition suggests that lexical specification is organized in systematic ways and that the lexicon represents a dynamic module of the grammar. Lexicon research shows that not only are there systematic regularities across the different verb frames a particular verb appears in, but there are also meaning regularities across verbs for each type of verb frame (see among others, Zubizarreta 1987; Rappaport & Levin 1988; Pinker 1989; Jackendoff 1990; Grimshaw 1990; Levin 1993; Levin & Rappaport Hovav 1992, 1994, 1995; for more details on these works, see Chapter 1, section 1.4).

Along with these theoretical results, language acquisition data show that children do not learn their lexicon in a conservative way: children use verbs in verb frames in which they have never heard them (because these are ungrammatical for adults), and creatively form verbal predicates (which do not exist in the adult lexicon). Overgeneralizations such as these have been noted and discussed in relation to their implications for the lexicon by Bowerman (1974, 1982a,b, 1978a,b, 1983, 1988a,b); *Pinker* (1989); Randall (1990, 1992); Clark (1993), among others.

Further proof of the systematic properties of the lexicon comes from new verbs in the language: adults have no difficulties coining and understanding new verbs and subsequently using them in several frames. In English, relatively new verbs such as *fax* and *e-mail* appear in the dative alternation. In Dutch, verbal prefixes such as *ver-* may productively attach to new verbs without creating any comprehension problems. For example, *ver-emailen* 'PFX-e-mail' can be used in a sentence such as: *Ik heb de hele middag veremaild* 'I wasted the whole afternoon e-mailing'. In addition to this, one can stretch the borders of one's language by using verbs in unconventional frames (e.g., in poetry or other forms of creative language). These facts suggest that there is some form of productive lexical operations.

Furthermore, psycholinguistic experiments show that, when taught new (nonsense) verbs, adults as well as children are able to understand and use these verbs immediately. Subjects can use syntactic information, i.e., a transitive or intransitive frame, to disambiguate the meaning of a scene which is interpretable as either one (e.g., Gleitman 1990; Fisher et al. 1994). Moreover, semantic information (e.g., whether or not an object in a scene has been affected, whether or not a scene is telic) is used by subjects when they select a syntactic form for a verb describing that scene (e.g., Pinker 1989; Gropen et al. 1989, 1991; van Hout et al. 1993, in progress; Randall et al. 1994).

What are the implications for lexical theory of the systematic correlations between a predicate's syntactic flexibility and its variable semantics, between the different frames and the different meaning foci in each alternant? What are the implications suggested by overgeneralizations of argument alternations, creative composition of verbal predicates, and new or nonsense verb usages?

In order to explain regularities in alternation patterns, various kinds of lexical theories have emerged to propose that the verbal lexicon is a generative system, its generative power defined by equally various kinds of lexical rules (see Chapter 1, section 1.4). Williams (1981), who assumes that verbs are characterized by their argument structures, proposes lexical rules that are formalized as argument structure affecting operations (i.e., "internalize" or "externalize" an argument). Jackendoff (1983, 1990), who assumes that verbs are characterized by their lexical-conceptual structures (LCS's), proposes lexical rules that operate on LCS's (see also Rappaport & Levin 1988; Pinker 1989; Pustejovsky 1995).

The common idea behind these different approaches is that of a generative lexicon. The common goal of theories with a generative lexicon is to keep the lexicon small: each verb has just one basic specification from which the other ones are derived. A small lexicon is not only theoretically attractive, it also makes the acquisition task of learning a lexicon less hard. On top of this, by capturing regularities across frames in terms of lexical rules, one can explain why children and adults can come up with their creative usage of verbs in the first place, and, more importantly, why they make certain kinds of creations and not other kinds (cf. Pinker 1989; see also, Hollebrandse & van Hout 1995, 1996, 1998 and Chapter 5). Assuming a lexicon with lexical rules opens up the possibility that these rules can be over-applied, thereby creating systematic overgeneralizations (i.e., a particular lexical rule operates on verbs with specific lexical features, but not on others). Therefore, in a generative view of the lexicon, creative verb usage is actually expected.

Integrating lexical rules as part of their theory, most of these lexical theories thus adopt a view in which the lexicon is organized as some sort of a "syntax" which manipulates the lexical primitives. It is clear from current lexical theories (see Chapter 1) that a view of the lexicon as a generative system is widely accepted; it is preferred above a view in which the lexicon simply lists verbs with unstructured, hence idiosyncratic, lexical specifications.

On the other hand, the verbal lexicon is not exclusively rule-governed, given the existence of all kinds of idiosyncratic exceptions and lexical accidents. For every lexical rule, there exist exceptions: even though certain verbs seem to have all the necessary lexical-semantic properties for a certain rule to apply, this rule may "happen" not to apply to them. A standard example is *donate* that does not undergo the dative alternation, although it has similar lexical-semantic properties to *give*. Furthermore, even though certain lexical operations trigger certain meaning effects, for a specific verb that undergoes the operation they may "happen" to have a different, or even unpredictable, meaning effect. For example, the Dutch prefix *ver-* in general turns the event into a telic event (e.g., *branden-verbranden* 'burn', *draaien-verdraaien* 'turn', *knippen-verknippen* 'cut'; see also Chapter 3, section 3.4); *verlichten* 'light', however, denotes an atelic event. Furthermore, certain *ver*-variants are not transparently related to the root verb at all, e.g., *raden-verraden* 'guess-betray' (for further discussion, see section 4.9).

Finally, a more subtle case of lexical exceptions shows up when one considers the effects of lexical rules on selection restrictions. Even though certain lexical operations do not affect a verb's selection restriction properties, certain verbs that undergo these operations "happen" to have idiosyncratic selection restrictions afterwards. For example, Dutch particle verbs with the particle *op* 'up' differ from their simplex variants in that the *op*-verb denotes a telic event, but both variants can take the same objects (e.g., *opeten* 'eat up', *opdrinken* 'drink up', *oproken* 'smoke up'; see also Chapter 3, section 3.4). The pair *schrijven-opschrijven* 'write-write down' is slightly different. *Opschrijven* 'write down' is a telic variant of *schrijven* 'write'. Whereas *schrijven* 'write' can take an object such as *proefschrift* 'thesis', *opschrijven* 'write down' cannot combine with it: **een proefschrift opschrijven* 'write down a thesis'. It seems that one can only write down things that already exist, whereas one writes things that come into existence (for further discussion, see section 4.9).

So, in the end, the lexicon is to a certain extent a repository of unpredictable information. Clearly, there is tension between productive rules and lexical exceptions. This property sets the lexical module apart from other, exceptionless and completely rule- or principle based modules of the grammar (i.e., syntax and phonology). It also causes lexical judgments to be far more variable and idiolect-sensitive than syntactic and phonological ones. This tension is an intrinsic characteristic of the lexical module.

The goals of this chapter are to lay out and develop an economic theory on lexicon and projection that accounts for a verb's flexibility in a systematic way and at the same time for lexical gaps, accidents and idiosyncracies. In this theory, the lexicon must be organized in such a way that it lists as little as possible item-particular specification (a truly parsimonious lexicon), while deriving as much as possible flexibility in mapping from general conditions on the interface between lexicon and syntax. Yet, item-particular lexical specification must at the same time be sufficiently detailed and fine-grained to account for idiosyncracies. I focus on the systematic lexicon, searching for what it systematic and what this implies.

4.3 Evaluation criteria for lexicon and mapping theories

In order to evaluate a theory of the lexicon, one must first mark out the empirical domain the theory must be able to cover, and set the evaluation criteria by which it is to be measured. In this section, I define in an abstract way the empirical domain of lexical-syntactic knowledge and formulate the evaluation measures for a theory that models this domain.

What does lexical-syntactic knowledge of verbs involve? By its very nature, the lexicon is the place where associations between words, meanings and lexical specifications are stored. I will refer to this property as the *item-particular character* of the (verbal) lexicon. Lexical knowledge of verbs is constituted as a list of the verbs of a language with their specifications. On the one hand, item-particular knowledge characterizes verbs in terms of general lexical-syntactic features every verb is specified for. On the other hand, it must also list unpredictable lexical details, such as lexical accidents, exceptions to rules, etc. The latter type of lexical features is idiosyncratic.

Along with this item-particular lexical knowledge, the verbal lexicon has general properties. The discussion of the data in Chapter 3 has shown that lexical-syntactic flexibility is to a large extent systematic and predictable which suggests that lexical knowledge of verbs is to the same extent rule- or pattern-based. Also, the phenomenon of children overgeneralizing when they are learning their verbal lexicon suggests a rule- or pattern-based lexical system. These facts point to the systematic and generative character of lexical knowledge. At an abstract level, then, the verbal lexicon has the following properties, (1).

(1) Properties of lexical-syntactic verbal knowledge:
  a. Item-particular properties that systematically characterize individual verbs in terms of their lexical-syntactic features.
  b. Item-particular properties that store a verb's unpredictable idiosyncratic features.
  c. A generative system that derives predictable lexical-syntactic behavior of verbs on the basis of a verb's item-particular features.

The mapping theory must be able to cover the empirical domain over which lexical-syntactic flexibility stretches. How should such a theory be set up? Assuming criteria such as maximum generality, economy and parsimony, I formulate the following evaluation measures, (2).

(2) Evaluation criteria for the verbal lexicon:
  a. Verbs are listed with the least amount of item-particular specification.
  b. Conditions on the lexicon-syntax interface derive lexical-syntactic flexibility defined on a verb's item-particular lexical specification. They compute the set of all verb frames a certain verb can occur in, capturing the meaning similarities and differences across these different verb frames.

The criteria in (2) ensure that item-particular lexical specification is kept to a minimum and that the lexical generative system is assigned a maximally large function. Not only general science theoretic considerations drive the search for a theory that incorporates these requirements. Learnability considerations also strongly motivate a lexicon that lists only a minimum amount of lexical specification per verb, in order to keep the learner's assignment of learning her verbal lexicon as light as possible. Assuming that the systematic and generative part of lexical knowledge, (1c), is part of Universal Grammar, the task of learning a verbal lexicon boils down to filling in for each individual, new verb its lexical-syntactic features, (1a), and finding out about its idiosyncratic features, (1b).

In order to evaluate different lexical theories, one must compare how they make the division of labor in their organization of lexical knowledge of verbs. How much and what kinds of lexical specification does a theory list for each individual verb? How does the lexical generative system deal with systematic lexical knowledge and what does it do with idiosyncratic lexical knowledge? And, above all, how do item-particular knowledge and the mapping system interact to account for lexical-syntactic flexibility? Thus, for every theory, one must determine how it defines its lexical primitives and its generative power. Moreover, one must determine how the lexicon-syntax interface is set up and in what way the model deals with lexical-syntactic flexibility. Finally, one must determine how idiosyncratic features interact with systematic ones.

Having determined at an abstract level the different kinds of properties of verbal lexical knowledge in (1), I will now review how various lexicon theories implement them. Given the evaluation criteria for the verbal lexicon in (2), I will show how argument-centered mapping theories fail to adequately deal with lexical-syntactic flexibility.

4.4 A critique of argument-centered mapping theories

In this section I argue that mapping theories that define the mapping system exclusively based on a verb's semantic arguments cannot deal with lexical-syntactic flexibility in a satisfactory way. Pointing out first how these theories are similar, in that the mapping links onto syntax are exhaustively determined by the set of arguments (subsection 4.4.1), I will discuss various kinds of problems that arise in these argument-centered views on mapping. The first type are methodological problems with the lexical primitives: for argument-centered theories, there is no independent way of validating their formalization of lexical primitives (subsection 4.4.2). Moreover, the dichotomy between arguments and non-arguments which is an inherent and crucial distinction in argument-centered mapping theories is problematic; the distinction is too rigid and should be relaxed (subsection 4.4.3). Next, there are problems with their account of the phenomenon of lexical-syntactic flexibility. These include some descriptive problems (subsection 4.4.4) and also explanatory problems with the rules dealing with it (subsection 4.4.5). Finally, given the way they are designed, argument-centered mapping theories cannot draw the event-semantic generalizations across alternations (subsection 4.4.6). I conclude that a mapping system fed by lexical-syntactic primitives including only the number and kinds of arguments cannot provide a good model of the lexicon-syntax interface (subsection 4.4.7).

4.4.1 Argument-centered mapping theories

Semantically, a verb expresses a relation between its arguments. As I discussed in Chapter 1, many present-day theories of the lexicon-syntax interface define mapping on the number and types of semantic arguments the verb is lexically specified for (i.e., its arguments, θ-roles, LCS-variables). Thus, the number of syntactically projected argument positions depends on the number of arguments, θ-roles or LCS-variables in a verb's lexical entry. The selection of which syntactic positions they are mapped onto (i.e., subject, object or oblique complement) depends on the kind of argument, θ-role or LCS variable, either rigidly, as in UTAH, or relativized, as in hierarchical argument linking. Different theories define their lexical-semantic argument primitives in different ways. I briefly review different lexical primitives and mapping systems. Extensive discussion has been presented in Chapter 1, section 1.3.1.

In Chomsky's (1981, 1986) θ-theory, grounded on Gruber's (1965) work on thematic relations, θ-roles are the lexical primitives. The mapping system is formulated in the θ-Criterion that requires that a verb assigns all of its θ-roles to phrases in syntactic argument positions, and, conversely, each phrase in a syntactic argument position is assigned a θ-role. In Baker's (1988) version of θ-theory, the mapping system crucially relies on lexical differentiation of a verb's arguments in terms of θ-role labels. θ-Roles are ordered along a thematic hierarchy and each type of θ-role is assigned in a particular syntactic position, as defined by his *Universal Theta Assignment Hypothesis (UTAH)*.

In his theory of argument structure, Williams (1981) makes reference to the semantic type of the arguments by labeling them with θ-roles, but the labels have no linguistically relevant content; they are only used to distinguish the arguments from each other. What is relevant for mapping is a structural distinction: an argument's external versus internal argumenthood. External and internal arguments are linked to VP-external (i.e., subject) and VP-internal (i.e., object and oblique) argument positions, respectively. Marantz (1984) adds another distinction, dividing the internal arguments into two kinds: direct and indirect (mapping onto direct and oblique object positions, respectively). The mapping system only "sees" a verb's lexical-syntactic specification, i.e., a set of semantically unspecified arguments that are lexically annotated as external versus internal arguments. Zubizarreta (1987), Rappaport & Levin (1988) and Carrier & Randall (1993), in effect, leave out semantic labeling from their argument structures altogether.

Jackendoff's (1990) mapping system is defined as hierarchical argument linking based on lexical-conceptual structures (LCS's). The variables in an LCS are ordered thematically, whereby thematic relations are defined in terms of specific positions in particular LCS predicates. The same relative ordering of the LCS-variables is preserved in their mapping onto syntactic positions. Combining hierarchical argument linking with a Williams-style intermediate argument structure, Rappaport & Levin (1988) and Carrier & Randall (1993) propose a two-step mapping algorithm. Linking rules relate LCS-variables to an intermediate level of argument structure, defined on the relative hierarchical ordering of LCS-variables, while projection rules map argument structures onto syntax, defined on the internal versus external argument status of the arguments.

The common view across all of these different theories is that the phrases that appear in syntactic argument positions (subject, object, oblique) are mapped as they are because they are listed as particular kinds of θ-roles, arguments or LCS-variables in a verb's lexical specification. The mapping systems yield a one-to-one relation between this lexical set of arguments and the syntactic set of argument positions.

The arguments that I will raise in the rest of this section plead against argument-centered views on mapping. They do not apply to alternative views on mapping that take aspectual considerations into account (e.g., Tenny 1987, 1992, 1994; Grimshaw 1990; Pustejovsky 1991; Hale & Keyser 1992, 1993; Levin & Rappaport Hovav 1995; see Chapter 1, section 1.3.2). First, I will discuss some problems concerning the lexical-syntactic primitives of argument-centered mapping theories (subsections 4.4.2-4.4.3). Next, I discuss their adequacy in dealing with lexical-syntactic flexibility (subsections 4.4.4-4.4.6).

4.4.2 Methodological problems with the lexical primitives

In order to closely scrutinize the various lexical notions *argument*, one must check a methodological issue: how can one determine how many different kinds there are? The answers range widely. For theories based on thematic relations and LCS predicates, the domain of different kinds of lexical-semantic arguments is determined by some form of semantics; for theories based on semantically unspecified arguments in an argument structure, on the other hand, the domain is determined by the variety of syntactic argument positions. Ever since argument structure theories have been introduced into syntactic theory, this issue has been raised. I will review the methodological issue for the three different lexical notions of argument: θ-roles, arguments and LCS-variables.

For a number of reasons, several researchers doubt the validity of lexically formalizing the notion *argument* in terms of thematic relations or θ-roles. First, if thematic relations are defined in Gruberian terms, then phrases in syntactic argument positions often bear more than one thematic relation, as discussed extensively by Jackendoff (1972, 1987, 1990).[3] Consider the ambiguity in (3).

(3) Max rolled down the hill. (Jackendoff 1972:34)

On one reading, the subject, Max, is only a "theme", rolling down the hill, not in control of the action going on; on the other reading, the subject is both a "theme" and an "agent", volitionally and actively rolling down the hill. Jackendoff gives more examples of arguments having multiple thematic relations. Consider for example a verb pair such as *buy-sell*, (4).

(4) a. Fred bought some hashish from Reuben.
b. Reuben sold some hashish to Fred.
(Jackendoff 1972:34)

Obviously, there is some similarity in the events in (4a) and (4b): the "theme" *hashish* is passing from a "source", *Reuben*, to a "goal", *Fred*. On the other hand, there are differences with respect to who is taking the initiative. In (4a) the subject *Fred* is the "agent", as well as the "goal"; in (4b) the subject *Reuben* is the "agent", as well as the "source".

The fact that arguments can bear more than one thematic role is devastating for a θ-theory based on the θ-Criterion which requires that precisely one θ-role be assigned to each argument position, as Jackendoff (1990) and Dowty (1991) point out. Moreover, it ruins the concept of *θ-role* as the formalization of the notion *semantic argument*, since in (3) there is only one semantic argument, not two, and in (4) there are only two semantic arguments, not three.

Another problem is the issue of how many different θ-roles there are. Various theories use different subsets from a set including "agent", "patient", "theme", "goal", source", "experiencer", "instrumental", etc. Nobody dares to make explicit claims as to how many there are. Moreover, definitions of θ-roles are vague and vary from θ-theory to θ-theory. There is disagreement even on the definition of the most familiar roles. Many people address the problem that there is no consensus on how many different θ-roles there are and discuss the vagueness of θ-role labels, concluding that θ-roles should be dispensed with as lexical primitives (e.g., Jackendoff 1972, 1987, 1990; Zubizarreta 1987; Rappaport & Levin 1988; Dowty 1989, 1991; Hoekstra & Mulder 1990; Emonds 1991a; Mulder 1992; Déchaine 1993; Hale & Keyser 1993).

Two different approaches have come up to circumvent the problems with θ-roles. As the problems arise from difficulties in specifying precisely the thematic content of an argument, Williams (1981) introduces another view on arguments. He argues that syntax does not need to "see" the thematic content of a verb's arguments; it only needs to see how many arguments a verb has and of what "syntactic" kind they are (internal versus external), rather than what thematic kind. Argument structures do not have a methodological problem with their primitives, since the lexical differentiation of kinds of arguments is defined by the set of syntactically different argument positions.

Jackendoff (1972, 1987, 1990) approaches the methodological problems by arguing that θ-role is a derived notion, defined within the structure provided by an LCS. For him and his theory on LCS's, the methodological question becomes how to determine how many different kinds of LCS-variables there are. Jackendoff (1983, 1990) seeks the answer in conceptual semantics, laid down in his *X'-semantics*, a meaning decomposition system in which semantic meta-predicates restrict and define the numbers and kinds of variables. However, the same methodological problem still arises when considering how meta-predicates are used in the definition of X'-semantic rules. The set of meta-predicates is arbitrary to a similar extent as the set of θ-roles is. It determines which different kinds of LCS-variables exist; employing one meta-predicate more or less creates a different number. Jackendoff deals with this issue by claiming that conceptual semantics "... is concerned most directly with the form of internal mental representations that constitute conceptual structure and with the formal relations between this level and other levels of representation" (Jackendoff 1990:15). He concedes that his view may be called the *Syntax of Thought* hypothesis. This answer shifts the problem to a philosophical domain. The methodological question becomes: how can one know what the elements of thought are? This problem has been pointed out by Emonds (1991a) and responded to by Jackendoff (1993).

4.4.3 Arguments versus non-arguments: Too strong a dichotomy

The basis for argument-centered theories is the distinction between arguments and non-arguments: only arguments are represented in the lexical specification. Integrating the typical properties on which arguments and non-arguments are distinct, Grimshaw (1990) characterizes the distinction as follows: "A generally acknowledged and fairly clear distinction has been made between argument and adjuncts. Arguments can be selected and subcategorized, in the sense that their presence and the form they take are under the control of individual predicates. Arguments must be licensed: they can occur only if they are theta-marked by a predicate as a function of the predicate's argument structure. Adjuncts are not theta-marked and do not need to be licensed by a relationship to an a-structure; their licensing conditions pertain to other domains (McConnell-Ginet (1982)). They are not subcategorized. Hence, their form is free, and they are never required by a-structure" (Grimshaw 1990:108).

However, the argument-adjunct distinction is not always clear-cut, especially not in the case of PPs. Which PPs count as an oblique complement of the verb and are thus in a verb's lexical specification (θ-grid, argument structure, LCS) and which are not? For verbs such *geloven* 'believe' and *steunen* 'rely' that take an obligatory PP with an idiosyncratically selected preposition (*geloven in* 'believe in', *steunen op* 'rely on'), it seems indisputable that the PP is an argument. The same holds for verbs such as *zetten* 'put' that take an obligatory locative PP and for verbs such as *geven* 'give' (even though the "goal" PP it selects is optional). It is less clear, however, how to classify the obligatory phrases that must occur with verbs such as *wonen* 'live', *zich gedragen* 'behave' and *wegen* 'weigh'. Since they are obligatory, one would reckon them among the arguments. But since they typically express adjunct meanings and can be expressed as adverbs (rather than DPs or PPs), they would fall under non-arguments. Even if one decides that these so-called obligatory adjuncts must be listed in the verb's lexical specification, it is unclear how they must be formalized in a θ-grid or in an argument structure. There are no θ-roles "manner" (for *zich gedragen* 'behave') or "measure" (for *wegen* 'weigh'). Similarly, elements in an argument structure, by definition, cannot be "syntactically" annotated to link to an adjunct position.[4]

It is clear from research on the argument-adjunct distinction that this issue is far from settled (cf. Jackendoff 1975, 1990; McConnell-Ginet 1982; Zubizarreta 1987; Grimshaw 1990; Grimshaw & Vikner 1993; and in particular for PPs, see van Riemsdijk 1978, 1992; Hornstein & Weinberg 1981). In many cases, the distinction is clear-cut, but in many other cases it is not. What is even more bothersome is that there are no clear criteria that could resolve the issue. To some extent, then, the argument-adjunct distinction seems to be a matter of theory and definition, rather than a linguistic reality. A mapping theory that is defined on some notion of *argument* as its lexical primitive must assume, however, a strict dichotomy between arguments and non-arguments at the lexical level. As definitions of syntactic as well as semantic argument- versus adjuncthood are far from trivial, grounding the mapping system exactly on this distinction is problematic.

A final problem for the dichotomous argument-adjunct view in θ-role and argument structure theories is the fact that arguments can be mapped onto non-argument positions in syntax as well. They appear in adjunct phrases; for example, the *by*-phrase in passive alternants, the *with*-phrase in the locative alternation and the possessive phrase in nominalizations (e.g., *the Serbs' destruction of Sarajevo*). They can be modifying adjectives; for example, in nominalizations (e.g., *the Serbian destruction of Sarajevo*). They can even be part of morphologically complex words; for example, in deverbal nouns (e.g., Dutch *taartjes-eter* 'pie-eater'). In a similar vein, compare the following three expressions denoting the same event: (i) *een taart eten* 'eat a pie', (ii) *van de taart eten* 'eat of the pie' and (iii) *taart eten* 'pie-eating'. Semantically, *taart* 'pie' is the same (lexical) argument in all three occurrences. Syntactically, however, it is not clear what the status of a conative PP is, (ii). Moreover, the noun in a noun-incorporated verb is definitely not in a syntactic argument position, (iii).

There have been some attempts to resolve these problems, specifically via the introduction of a new syntactic concept with an intermediate status between argument and adjunct. Zubizarreta's (1987) notion *adjunct-argument* and Grimshaw's (1990) notion *argument-adjunct* represent such (very similar) concepts; these refer to semantic arguments that appear in a non-argument position (e.g., the *by*-phrase in passives and nominalizations, adjectival possessives in nominalizations). Still, even though the mapping of a lexical argument to a syntactic non-argument position is taken care of by using these notions, the strict lexical dichotomy between arguments and non-arguments remains problematic.

Having discussed some problems with the lexical primitives of argument-centered mapping theories, I now turn to how they deal with lexical-syntactic flexibility.

4.4.4 Descriptive problems

In order to evaluate argument-centered theories, one must first ask if they are able to deal with the complete domain of data (i.e., if they are empirically adequate), and, next, if they do so in an explanatory and theoretically interesting way. The phenomenon of lexical-syntactic flexibility, as described in Chapter 3, suggests that other, aspectual notions also play a role. In a frame alternation there are two meaning elements that remain constant across the different alternants, and two that vary. One constant element is the kind of event a verb refers to; what varies across frames is the event type or the perspective on the event (i.e., atelic-telic event type-shifting, causativization, different foci). The other constant element is one or two event participants that are present in both frames; what varies is the exact selection of event participants and/or the selection of positions (argument or non-argument positions) they are mapped onto. How well do argument-centered mapping theories deal with these empirical observations?

θ-Role theories have problems describing or even distinguishing certain alternation patterns. Consider the position-varying alternations (e.g., the oblique intransitive-transitive alternation, the unergative-unaccusative alternation, the locative alternation). In these alternations, the number and thematic kinds of arguments are constant across alternants; the only difference is the position an argument with a certain θ-role ends up in (i.e., in direct or indirect internal argument position, in internal versus external argument position). In a hierarchical argument linking mapping system one cannot derive this difference, however, as there is no difference in the number nor the kinds of arguments. The θ-roles are thematically ordered in the same ways and should map in the same ways in both alternants. Hence, there is no way to account for position-varying alternations.

Alternatively, in a mapping system based on UTAH (see Baker 1988), one is forced to analyze these position-varying alternations as syntactic transformations, since UTAH requires that an argument with a particular θ-role always be mapped onto the same syntactic position. Flexibility can be derived by manipulating the syntactic structure the arguments are mapped onto (e.g., Baker's 1988 analysis of applicative constructions; see Chapter 1, subsection 1.4.2). One can account for the oblique intransitive-transitive alternation and the locative alternation in this way. Consider, however, the unergative-unaccusative alternation from a UTAH perspective. What is crucial in alternations of this form is the variable D-structure position of the single argument; it is mapped either onto subject or onto object position. By definition, post-D-structure operations cannot create such flexibility. Hence, there is no way to express the unergative-unaccusative alternation as such in a UTAH-based mapping system.

A different kind of descriptive problem arises in θ-role theories: the impossibility to express specific semantic restrictions on the productivity of frame alternations in θ-theoretic notions. Many authors, among them Hale & Keyser (1986), Levin & Rappaport (1988), Pinker (1989) and Levin & Rappaport Hovav (1994, 1995), point out that most frame alternations apply only to a subset of the verbs with a particular θ-grid. These subsets are characterized by finer-grained semantic notions than θ-roles. For example, Pinker's (1989) holism constraint on the object in the locative alternation correctly allows *slather* (e.g., *slather paint on the wall, slather the wall with paint*), but rules out *throw* (e.g., *throw confetti in the air, *throw the air with confetti*). However, the θ-grid of both verbs is the same and cannot distinguish between the two: {Ag, Th, Go}. Hence, in θ-theoretic terms, one cannot not express this difference. The problem is even worse if frame alternations are analyzed at a syntactic level (in UTAH-based theories). By their very nature, the power of syntactic operations cannot be restricted in any semantic way.

Another problem for a syntactic approach to lexical-syntactic flexibility is alternations that are expressed by verb pairs. Henk van Riemsdijk (personal communication) argues that if one analyzes, for example, the locative and dative alternation as resulting from syntactic incorporation of the preposition of the "goal" complement (cf. Baker 1988), one cannot explain why the verb does not have the form P-V, but a different one in the derived structure, i.e., prefixed with *be-* (e.g., *sproeien-besproeien* 'spry') or *ver-* (e.g., *sturen-versturen* 'send') in Dutch. Such effects point to the need for a lexical analysis of these alternations.

Finally, there is a more subtle descriptive problem. θ-Role theories cannot explain the effect of "θ-role shift": the phenomenon that one and the same event participant seems to bear various θ-roles across alternants. Consider the locative alternation (e.g., *load the hay onto the cart* versus *load the cart with hay*). The location (*the cart*) is a "goal" in one alternant, but a "theme" in the other (see Rappaport & Levin 1988; Pinker 1989). Consider also motion verbs in the unergative-unaccusative alternation (e.g., *John runs* versus *John runs to the store*). The runner (*John*) is an "agent" in both alternants, but also a "theme" in the unaccusative alternant. One cannot keep track of the position-varying arguments in θ-theoretic terms, precisely because they are changing or shifting their θ-roles.

4.4.5 Arbitrariness of lexical rules

For argument structure and LCS theories, the problems do not lie at the level of describing frame alternations, but rather at the level of the lexical rules that describe them.

Frame-relating rules that are formulated as rules that relate argument structures (e.g., Williams' 1981 "internalize" and "externalize" an argument) are of a rather arbitrary nature. They do the job of creating lexical-syntactic flexibility, but do not give any insight or explanation as to why an argument is manipulated the way it is, i.e., why an argument changes its status in the argument structure from internal to external, or vice versa. While rules that add or delete an argument are, to a certain extent, semantically meaningful and, hence, explanatory, rules that would change a certain argument's status from indirect internal to direct internal (e.g., for the locative and oblique intransitive-transitive alternation), or from external to internal (e.g., for the unergative-unaccusative alternation), are completely arbitrary from a semantic point of view.[5] They could just as well have operated the other way around. Hence, more generally, operations on argument structure do not provide, let alone, explain, any meaning similarities and differences of a certain verb across different frames.

From an explanatory point of view, it is more insightful to analyze frame-relating rules as a side-effect of rules that relate LCS's (see Levin & Rappaport 1988; Pinker 1989; Jackendoff 1990). Since LCS's express certain meanings, operations on LCS's by definition affect the meaning of a verb. After a certain operation at the level of LCS, the argument structure of the derived verb is computed on the derived LCS. Hence, argument structure effects are derived, rather than primary effects.

In order to (indirectly) relate the two alternants of a frame alternation via operations on LCS, one must choose one lexical representation as the basic one, and derive the other one(s) from it. This is not trivial, however. The problem is a methodological one: how can one tell which is the basic representation? This is easy to determine for frame alternations that are accompanied by morphological operations; the morphologically simpler variant is the basic one. However, it is not clear what the criteria are for distinguishing basic lexical representations from derived ones when there are no such effects. For example, how does one determine which is more basic, the lexical specification of a dative or that of the double object construction? Or, which of the two is more basic in the causative-inchoative alternation (e.g., *melt*), the causative or the inchoative alternant? In other words, does this alternation express an operation of causativization or, alternatively, anti-causativization?

4.4.6 Failure to generalize across alternations

Finally, there is the issue of how to generalize across various kinds of alternations in an argument-centered perspective. How do the generalizations that crosscut the heterogeneous set of frame alternations come out in such theories?

Consider the oblique intransitive-transitive and the unergative-unaccusative alternations again. In the oblique intransitive-transitive alternation (e.g., *schieten op-schieten* 'shoot at-shoot'), the "theme" participant is mapped once as direct internal argument and once as indirect internal argument. In the unergative-unaccusative alternation (e.g., *reizen-afreizen* 'travel-start traveling'), the "agent" participant is mapped once as external argument and once as direct internal argument. The former involves a verb with two arguments, the latter only one. Even though they have very different forms, both alternations express an atelic-telic event type-shift. One can generalize across these alternations in terms of mapping: the participant that is involved in the transition maps onto direct object position in the telic alternant in both cases.

One can account for these alternations in terms of operations on argument structure or LCS, but there is no way to generalize over both alternations. In order to do so, one would need to refer to event types and event type-shifting as the common effect. This is impossible in argument structure terminology. In LCS terminology it could be done. However, although an atelic-telic event type-shift might be expressed in LCS-style lexical operations, one cannot draw the generalization that telic event types always require an argument in direct object position, since linking rules only refer to event participants (i.e., LCS-variables), not to event types. It would, at best, be accidental if the derived argument structures both have a direct internal argument. Hence, unless the linking rules would actually be formulated in terms of mapping an LCS-variable involved in a transition onto the direct internal argument position, one cannot express the right generalizations.

In general, in approaches with lexical rules, one needs to spell out the effects of each separate frame alternation in a separate operation. There is no obvious sense in which one can generalize across rules. Even in an LCS framework with meaningful operations on LCS's, the effects of these operations with respect to their consequences for mapping are not directly expressible.

A final issue is a failure to draw the most maximal generalizations. As mapping theories define the mapping system on the lexical properties of a verb, they are not able to draw generalizations over simplex verbs, complex verbs and complex predicates. However, the discussion of atelic-telic alternations in Chapter 3 revealed that in the case of the unergative-unaccusative alternation, mapping depends on whether or not the whole predicate (not just the verb) is telic. This generalization cannot be expressed in argument-centered mapping theories, since they define mapping in a purely lexicalistic way: D-structure is projected on the properties of individual lexical entries (for the same conclusion, see Borer

1994).[6] Instead, these theories must list those verbs (e.g., motion verbs) for which this generalization applies twice: once with an unergative and once with an unaccusative argument structure (e.g., Levin & Rappaport Hovav 1992, 1995). So, the very basic starting-point for argument-centered theories (that mapping is fully determined by the lexical properties of the verb) prevents them from drawing larger generalizations.

4.4.7 Summary: problems for argument-centered mapping theories

I have discussed some descriptive and some methodological problems for argument-centered mapping theories with respect to their lexical primitives as well as their lexical rules that account for lexical-syntactic flexibility. I have furthermore pointed out that argument-centered theories cannot adequately generalize across alternations.

To conclude, the crucial empirical generalization about lexical-syntactic flexibility is that the event type or event perspective determines how a certain event participant is mapped onto a particular syntactic position, if it must be present in the first place. This implies that, in order to account for this generalization, the mapping system cannot be defined exclusively on some notion of event participant as lexical primitive (i.e., arguments, θ-roles, LCS-variables). Hence, argument-centered mapping theories fail to generalize over lexical-syntactic flexibility in an insightful way. The strong correlations between event types and the positions event participants are mapped onto (see Chapter 3) should be incorporated in the mapping system. Not defining the mapping algorithm in terms of different event types means that the theory is not maximally strong.

Developing an event-semantic approach to mapping in the rest of this chapter, I will resolve some of the problematic issues of argument-centered mapping approaches. With respect to the methodological issue of defining the lexical primitives, I will discuss how much, or rather, how little lexical information a verb needs to be listed with. This is the main goal of Part II. I conclude that a verb only needs to specify the number of event participants (the lexical arguments), but not their kinds (in terms of θ-labels or LCS-labels). It also does not need to syntactically annotate them in terms of external and internal (sections 4.5 and 4.6). A verb further needs to specify its basic event type (section 4.7). The event-semantic feature checking approach that I define in section 4.8 in Part III resolves the problematic argument-adjunct dichotomy, as it distinguishes between the lexical notion of event participant and the syntactic notion of argument position. An event participant can, but need not appear in a syntactic argument position: it does not always need to be mapped onto syntax or, if it is, it can remain part of the predicate. Finally, the way the new approach to mapping is designed derives the phenomenon of lexical-syntactic flexibility in a natural way and accounts for the event-semantic generalizations across various alternation patterns. Hence, since one does not need to define a separate set of lexical rules to deal with it, there is no problem with arbitrary rules.

Part II: The nature of the lexical primitives

Before designing a model of the lexicon-syntax interface, the nature of the lexical features that feed mapping onto syntax needs to be discussed. Mapping does not depend on what particular kind of event is going on, e.g., whether it is dancing or walking, or writing or pushing; the mapping rules do not need to "see" a verb's content. Rather, the projection of argument positions correlates with certain second-order properties of the event. By determining what exactly the mapping algorithm needs to "see" in a verb's lexical semantics, I will uncover the nature of the lexical primitives that are involved in the lexicon-syntax interface. I will call these properties *lexical-syntactic features*, as they form the link between lexicon and syntax. The conclusion will be that mapping depends on a verb's specification with respect to its event participants in interaction with its event type features (as was already suggested by the generalizations from Chapter 3). The detailed discussion of event participants and event types that will be presented in this part thus serves to set the preliminaries for a model of the lexicon and its interface to syntax which will be developed in Part III.

In order to get a clear picture of how mapping onto syntax depends on which lexical features, I restrict the domain of investigation to eventive verbs. I leave stative and psychological verbs for further research.

Following up on the review on lexical-semantic arguments above, I first consider their role in mapping, after redefining them as event participants (section 4.5). Keeping in mind the problems of argument-centered mapping, I will unravel how much of the mapping system is indeed determined by event participant features and how much cannot be attributed to them (section 4.6). The determining semantic factor in mapping is the event structure of the sentence. I will determine which of a verb's event type features co-determine the event structure of the sentence by discussing in detail how different kinds of verbs manifest atelic-telic event type-shifting and causativization (section 4.7). I will conclude that the lexical primitives of a verb consist of the number of event participants involved in the event and the basic event type.

4.5 Event participants

In the spirit of Davidson (1967), I view the semantic function of a verb as follows: a verb denotes a state or event and expresses a relation between the entities that are involved in the event. I will refer to these entities as event participants. In this section I discuss the notion of *event participant* and define what counts as an event participant and what does not. As my notion of *event participant* is similar to the notions of *θ-role*, *argument* and *LCS-variable* (but not exactly the same, as I will point out shortly), the enterprise of defining the notion *event participant* follows up on the methodological questions with respect to lexical primitives in section 4.4.2.

4.5.1 A definition of the notion *event participant*

I take the notion *event participant* as a lexical primitive. It is a semantic concept that must be associated with verbs and other predicates (prepositions, adjectives and certain nouns) that denote an event of a certain type (state, process or transition). Predicates establish properties of or relations between one or more event participants that are involved in a state or event, or, in the case of a complex event, in one of the subevents. In traditional terminology, one would call event participants the semantic arguments of a predicate. I will use the term *event participant*, because I focus on the event-semantic status and function of the arguments in an event. Moreover, the term *event participant* replaces the confounded term *argument* which sometimes refers to lexical-semantic variables of a predicate, sometimes to the elements in an argument structure and sometimes to grammatical relations (subject, object) or positions in a syntactic configuration.

Notice that the semantic notion *event participant* and the syntactic notion *argument* (i.e., phrases in subject and object position) are fundamentally distinct (see section 4.4.3). Event participants of verbal predicates are typically mapped onto subject and object positions, but they may also appear in adjunct positions. Event participants of a prepositional predicate appear as complement of the preposition and as "subject" of the PP (which may turn out to be the subject or object in the verbal projection of which the PP is a part). Participants of nominal predicates can appear in *of-* and *by*-phrases, as possessives and as adjectives in event nominalizations (e.g., *the destruction of Sarajevo by the Serbs, the Serb's destruction of Sarajevo, the Serbian destruction of Sarajevo*). Participants of adjectives appear as "subject" of the AP and as complement of the adjective (e.g., *faithful to somebody*). Event participants can even appear inside complex words, as in compounds (e.g., *taart-eten* 'pie-eating'). Furthermore, event participants are not always mapped onto syntax; they can remain implicit. This partial discrepancy between the semantic and syntactic notions of argument has given rise to new terms (e.g., Zubizarreta's 1987 notion *adjunct-argument*; Grimshaw's 1990 notion *argument-adjunct*; see subsection 4.4.3). My term *event participant* refers exclusively to the semantic notion and is oblivious of the various syntactic incarnations which include DPs in syntactic argument positions, phrases in adjunct positions and even parts of words.

Which semantic entities fall under the notion *event participant*? In answering this question I assume a semantic approach, following Dowty (1982, 1991). Dowty defines arguments from a semantic point of view, i.e., as referents " . . . whose relationship to the event is defined by the verb's meaning itself" (Dowty 1991: fn. 19). Other phrases, i.e., PPs and adverbs such as goal, location and instrument phrases, are adjuncts semantically; they modify the event. Semantically, they are functors that take the verb or VP as their argument; their " . . . relationship to an event is the semantically compositional result of applying that phrase's meaning to the meaning of any verb or VP" (Dowty 1991: fn. 19). So, phrases that appear in subject and objects positions are clearly associated with a verb as its event participants, while most PPs and adjuncts are not.

4.5.2 Are PPs event participants?

Given that PPs can have different syntactic and semantic functions in the clause, the issue whether or not PPs are event participants needs more detailed discussion. The most straightforward kind are adjunct PPs. Since an adjunct PP is not selected by the verb in any sense, I assume the PP is not an event participant of the verb, nor that the complement of the preposition is a participant of the verb. This is not so easily determined for other kinds of PPs; in particular, what about complement PPs? Typically, complement PPs are lexically listed as an argument of the verb and are assumed to be selected by the verb. For example, they receive a "goal" or "source" θ-role (e.g., Gruber 1965), they are listed as an indirect internal argument (e.g., Marantz 1984) or they are associated with a "Path" or "Place" LCS-variable (e.g., Jackendoff 1990).

In an event-semantic approach to lexical specification in which a verb lists its event participants, one must ask whether or not the complement PP is an event participant, and, if not, whether or not the NP inside the complement PP is an event participant. First, is the PP complement a participant of the verb? Semantically, the PP is a functor that takes V or VP as its argument, rather than the other way around. So, the PP is not an argument of the verb; the verb is an argument of the PP. Adhering to an isomorphy between syntax and semantics with respect to functor-argument relations, I assume that a PP itself is not an event participant of the verb.

What about the complement of the preposition: is the DP inside a complement PP an event participant of the verb? This depends on the kind of complement PP. Consider first what is traditionally called a *prepositional complement*: a PP headed by a semantically empty preposition which is idiosyncratically selected by a verb (e.g., *vertrouwen op* 'trust on', *wachten op* 'wait for', *antwoorden op* 'answer to'; *vragen naar* 'ask for'; *kijken naar* 'look at', *houden van* 'love', *verlangen naar* 'long for'; *rekenen op* 'rely on'). The preposition does not contribute compositionally to the semantics of the clause; it is semantically empty. Hence, a prepositional complement falls under the semantic definition of *argument* given above. Therefore, I assume that the NP complement of a prepositional complement is an event participant of the verb.[7]

The other kind of complement PPs include locational and directional phrases; they are *subcategorized prepositional adjuncts* in van Riemsdijk's (1978) terminology (e.g., *blijven* 'remain' takes a locational phrase; *lopen* 'walk' can take a directional phrase). These PPs are headed by a contentful preposition; the PP is a modifier of the event denoted by the verb. I take the NP complement in a subcategorized prepositional adjunct as an event participant of the preposition itself, rather than as a participant of the verb.[8] Hence, neither these complement PPs nor their NP complements are in any sense lexically selected by the verb.

This view on the latter kind of complement PPs has the following consequences. Verbs that are typically seen as triadic predicates and appear in an oblique transitive frame have only two participants (e.g., *zetten* 'put'). Similarly, verbs that are typically seen as dyadic predicates and appear in an oblique unaccusative frame have only one participant (e.g., *naar het strand lopen* 'walk to the beach'). Déchaine (1993) assumes a similar position with respect to the question of whether or not complement PPs are arguments of the verb. She advocates a single complement hypothesis stated as: " . . . a lexical head has a single (internal) argument" (Déchaine 1993:123). Under this hypothesis double complement constructions of superficially triadic verbs (e.g., *give*, *buy*, *receive*) are analyzed as bivalent projections in which V assigns a semantic role to the direct object, P assigns a semantic role to its complement and the PP is predicated of the direct object (via Déchaine's Π-relation). "Consequently, what are standardly analyzed as P' 'complements' are adjunct predicates" (Déchaine 1993:178). She concludes that PP complements are not selected by the verb.[9]

In terms of functor-argument relations, locational and directional complement PPs are similar to adjunct PPs: these PPs modify a verb or predicate; they are not arguments of the verb or predicate. Still, in an event-semantic view, a complement PP of verbs like *zetten* 'put' (e.g., *iets in de kast zetten* 'put something in the closet') and *lopen* 'walk' (e.g., *naar het strand lopen* 'walk to the beach') differs from an adjunct PP, even though both kinds are event modifiers. The event types of the verb and of the preposition of a complement PP combine to form one compositional event type (cf. Davidson 1967; van Hout 1990; Pustejovsky 1991; Verkuyl 1993). Complement PPs participate in the composition of the event type of the VP predicate. Adjunct PPs merely modify the event or part of the event; they are not involved in constructing the event type (see section 4.7.1 on event type composition). For example, the compositional event type for both *zetten* 'put' and *lopen* 'walk' is a transition in which the PP specifies the resulting state (e.g., afterwards, something is in the closet or somebody is at the beach).

Often, complement PPs are obligatory. This requirement cannot be part of a verb's lexical specification: a complement PP is not an event participant of the verb; hence, it is not lexically selected by it. In order to account for the obligatoriness of certain complement PPs, I assume a PP is obligatory when it is needed to specify the resulting state of a transition, i.e., when the verb itself only specifies the process leading up to this final state. In this, I follow a proposal by Grimshaw & Vikner (1993) who argue that an event needs to be properly identified: their concept of *event identification*. In the case of obligatory complement PPs, the transition event type is not properly identified unless there is a PP present to identify the final state (see subsections 4.6.1, 4.7.1 and 4.8.1 on event identification). Since locational and directional complement PPs are not event participants, but, rather, event type builders, they are not lexically selected by the verb. They appear in order to identify a (sub)event.

Obligatoriness is not restricted to complement PPs: sometimes it also holds for adjunct PPs. While adjunct PPs are almost always optional, Grimshaw & Vikner (1993) present some constructions in which adjuncts are in fact obligatory (e.g., *the house was built *(in ten days)*; *the dress was designed *(by a famous designer)*). They explain this in terms of event identification, claiming that the adjunct PP is necessary to identify a subevent.

Later in this chapter, I will come back to different kinds of complement PPs. I will discuss in detail "goal" complements, analyzing them as providers of the end state of an event (see subsection 4.7.1). Other complement PPs contain an event participant of the verb, i.e., one that is mapped onto an oblique position, for example in the case of conative complement PPs (e.g., *eten van* 'eat of'; *bouwen aan* 'build on'; see subsection 4.8.2). First, I finish the discussion about event participants by positioning my definition of the concept among davidsonian and neo-davidsonian definitions.

4.5.3 Event participants in davidsonian and neo-davidsonian views

My notion of event participant is more restricted than the neo-davidsonian one. Staying close to the original proposal in Davidson (1967), I distinguish at the most two event participants. Parsons (1990), a main proponent of the neo-davidsonian approach, associates all phrases in the sentence as event participants to the verb. In his view, the verb itself contains only one variable, i.e., the event variable; its arguments and all other phrases are associated with the event variable as various kinds of event participants. Parsons would analyze Davidson's (1967) famous example, (5), as in (6).

(5) Jones buttered the toast in the bathroom with a knife at midnight.

(6) There is an event e, for e holds:
BUTTERING (e) & SUBJECT (e, *Jones*) & OBJECT (e, *toast*) &
INSTRUMENT (e, *knife*) & PLACE (e, *in the bathroom*) &
TIME (e, *at midnight*)

In (6) the SUBJECT and OBJECT participants are analyzed in the same way as location or instrument "participants". From this perspective then, all phrases are semantically equal, in that they all bear a thematic relation to the event. It is not clear whether certain relations "weigh" differently than others, i.e., are lexically specified for or not. Hence, the semantic distinction between arguments and adjuncts is abandoned.

Dowty (1991) points out that in the original approach in Davidson (1967) "agents" and "themes" are different lexical-semantic entities from the rest. Davidson analyzes verbs as predicates containing an extra event variable alongside with its arguments variables; modifying phrases are predicated of this event variable. Davidson proposes an analysis such as (7).

(7) There is an event e, for e holds:
BUTTERED (*Jones, toast*, e) & IN (*the bathroom*, e) & WITH (*knife*, e) & AT (*midnight*, e) (Davidson 1967)

The event variable and two arguments together are the three variables of the verbal predicate. The modifying phrases are conjuncts to the main predication; the preposition relates its argument to the verb's variable. Hence, in Davidson's analysis, *Jones* and *the toast* are the verb's event participants; the adverbs and PPs are not event participants, but event modifiers.

Parsons (1990) tries to find arguments to choose between the two approaches, but he must conclude in the end that there are none. To some extent then, they seem to be notational variants. Parsons' approach, however, relies heavily on the concept of thematic roles as a primitive notion. Although Parsons argues against objections to the use of thematic relations and raises arguments for the utility of thematic relations (see Parsons 1990, sections 5.5 and 5.7), I do not find that he solves the thematic role problems in a convincing way. Therefore, given the problems with thematic roles as laid out in section 4.4, I have adopted the original Davidsonian approach.

Having defined what counts as an event participant and having excluded "goal" PP complements from this definition, I continue the discussion of event participants as lexical primitive. How does the concept of event participant play a role as lexical primitive?

4.6 Event participants are a lexical primitive

All mapping theories that have been discussed or mentioned so far assume that a verb has some form of lexical specification that indicates the number of event participants (θ-roles, arguments, LCS-variables). A stronger hypothesis, however, would be to claim that a verb does not need to specify this information, but, rather, that it is derived from other semantic information. In fact, this hypothesis has been put forward by several people, including myself, in claiming that event participants are a secondary notion derived from aspectual specification (cf. van Hout 1991a,b, 1992a,b, 1994; Davis & Demirdache 1995). However, I have since become convinced of the contrary: one cannot get away with not lexically listing some information about event participants; specifically, the number of event participants must be specified for each verb. In this section I will argue why.

First, I will discuss whether or not one can derive the set of event participants from the event structure specification of a verb, concluding that one cannot do so. Independent of their (basic) event types, verbs differ from each other in the number of event participants they select. Hence, this must be a lexical feature. The number of event participants a verb selects varies from zero to two (subsection 4.6.1). Next, I discuss whether or not event participants must be semantically differentiated, either relative to each other or against some standard semantic notions. In particular, I will deconstruct their agentivity properties (subsection 4.6.2). I conclude that agentivity does not need to be lexically specified, but, rather, is an interpretational effect determined by a conglomerate of factors, including aspectual, syntactic and morphological properties, as well as extra-grammatical effects (subsection 4.6.3).

4.6.1 Can event participants be derived from event structure?

Looking closely at the elements of lexical information that are specified in Jackendoff's (1990) LCS's and in Grimshaw's (1990) combined argument and event structures, one can observe that there is a certain conceptual redundancy. If a verb denotes a state or a process, then it must also take at least one event participant that is involved in this state or process; if it denotes a transition, it needs an event participant that is changing state or location. Ideally, one should not need to specify both kinds of elements in the lexical primitives, i.e., event type and event participants. However, the formats of LCS's or combined argument and event structures force one to such a double specification with aspectual meta-predicates plus variable positions, or with a list of event participants in the argument structure plus a separate event structure.

Noticing this redundancy of lexical specification, one should ask: is there one basic kind of lexical information and can the other be derived from it? In my earlier work (van Hout 1991a,b, 1992a,b, 1994), I take a strong position and argue that event structure is more basic, and argument structure must be derived from it, proposing that event structure is the trigger for the projection of argument positions in syntax. The proposal runs along the following lines. Pursuing an idea of Grimshaw (1990) and Grimshaw & Vikner (1993), I claim that an event needs to be "identified" in syntax. In a complex event structure, each of the subevents contained in it must be "identified". Arguments in syntactic argument positions function as event identifiers by being interpreted as participants in the event. Hence, simple event structures like state and process require (at least) one argument to be properly identified; complex event structures like transitions with two subevents require two arguments to be identified, one for each subevent. In this proposal, the projection of argument positions is not read off of a list of event participants, θ-roles, arguments or LCS-variables, but is determined exclusively by event structure (cf. Pustejovsky 1991). Event participant specification is not a lexical primitive listed with each verb; only event type is. Different event types map onto different verb frames because they have different event identification requirements. Mapping rules must be defined on different types of event structure and determine for each its verb frame.[10]

Following up on this approach, Davis & Demirdache (1995) present a more precise proposal to the effect that all event participant information is derived from event structure (see also Davis 1997, in press; Demirdache 1997). They claim that every (sub)event takes exactly one participant and that each participant is associated with exactly one (sub)event. In order to account for the various kinds of "agent" participants there are (some are volitional agents, others are non-volitional agents), they deconstruct the thematic relation "agent" and reconstruct the semantic property of agentivity in completely aspectual terms (i.e., it is read off of the event structure, in particular, the relation between two subevents). Supporting their claims, they present evidence from Lillooet Salish, a language with transparent verbal morphology. In Lillooet Salish verb roots denote either a state or a transition between two states; they take exactly one argument. Transitivizing suffixes change the verb root's meaning; the suffix compositionally event type-shifts the original event type by adding a subevent which takes its own participant. Subsequently, intransitivizing suffixes may delete one of the subevents and thereby also one of the participants. Integrating these event type changes and their effects on the number of participants, Davis & Demirdache conclude that event participant (or argument) is not a primitive lexical notion. Instead, they claim it can be derived from event structure (see also subsection 4.6.3).

Can a verb's set of event participants really be determined exclusively on the basis of its basic event type features plus the effects of event type-shifting? Clearly, an affirmative answer to this question is preferred, since it reduces the amount of lexical specification per predicate. Unfortunately, however, I do not see a way to do so, at least not for Dutch. In the rest of this subsection I will discuss why.[11]

The main piece of the argumentation is the fact that different verbs with the same basic event type features select different numbers of event participants. The event type itself does not determine the choice of a particular number. Moreover, it does not determine the particular verb frame a verb with a certain event type will map onto. Consider some examples of verbs that express an atelic process. Some take one participant which they map onto an unergative frame, (8a); others take two participants which they map onto an oblique unergative or a transitive frame, (8b) and (8c). The phrases in italics are event participants of the verb.

(8) Verbs that denote an atelic process have one or two participants and map onto various verb frames:

a. *John* niest / slaapt / lacht / loopt.
'*J.* is sneezing / sleeping / laughing / walking.'

b. *Jos* praat over / kijkt naar / werkt aan / schrijft aan *een scenario.*
'*J.* is talking about / looking at / working on / writing at *a scenario.*'

c. *Mech* duwt / sleept / rijdt / zoekt *haar Eend.*
'*M.* is pushing / dragging / driving / looking for *her car.*'

Next, consider some verbs that denote a transition. Some verbs take one participant and map onto an unaccusative or an oblique unaccusative frame, (9a) and (9b). Others take two participants and map them onto a transitive frame, (9c).

(9) Verbs that denote a transition have one or two participants and map onto various verb frames:

a. *John* is gevallen / verdwenen / aangekomen / weggelopen.
J. is fallen / disappeared / arrived / away-walked
'*J.* fell / disappeared / arrived / walked away.'

b. *Jos* is naar huis gelopen / gerend / gereden / gefietst.
J. is to home walked / ran / drove / biked
'*J.* walked / ran / drove / biked home.'

c. *Mech* heeft *haar Eend* uitgezocht / gevonden / opgeknapt / weggedaan.
M. has *her car* selected / found / patched up / thrown away
'*M.* selected / found / patched up / threw away *her car.*'

Hence, the aspectual structure cannot derive the number of event participants of a verb that denotes a certain event type. Notice that some of the transition verbs in (9) denote a transition between two states (e.g., *verdwijnen* 'disappear', *aankomen* 'arrive', *vinden* 'find'); others denote a transition between a process and a state (e.g., *weglopen* 'walk away', *naar huis fietsen* 'bike home', *uitzoeken* 'select', *opknappen* 'patch up'). The number of event participants involved in a transition does not depend this distinction either, since both changes-of-state and transitions from a process to a state can involve one or two participants.

The conclusion is that the event type does not determine unambiguously the number of event participants: processes and transitions take either one or two. Moreover, the event type does not by itself determine the verb frame a verb maps onto; each event type can be associated with various different verb frames. So, unless one could distinguish more aspectual structure within the event types of process and transition in some way or another, the number of event participants cannot be derived from event type specification. Hence, it must be considered part of the lexical specification of a verb.

Another way to see the same point is with a new hypothetical Dutch verb, e.g., *flimpen* 'flimp'. Suppose *flimpen* denotes an atelic process, how many event participants does it select? Given only these event type features, *flimpen* may take either one or two participants and map onto one of the following frames, (10a)-(10c).

(10) a. *David* flimpt.
'*D.* is flimping.'
b. *David* flimpt over *zijn fiets*.
'*D.* is flimping about *his bike*.'
c. *David* flimpt *zijn fiets*.
'*D.* is flimping *his bike*.'

In an unergative frame (10a), *flimpen* takes one participant; it may mean something like *slapen* 'sleep'. In an oblique unergative frame (10b) and in a transitive frame (10c), *flimpen* takes two participants; it may mean something like *praten* 'talk' or *duwen* 'push', respectively.

Suppose it is also given that *flimpen* can event type-shift to a telic event, e.g., a transition from a process to an end state. Then, the verb may take either one or two participants in the telic alternant and appear in one of the following frame alternations, (11)-(13):

(11) a. *David* heeft geflimpt.
'*D.* flimped.'
b. *David* is weggeflimpt.
'*D.* flimped away.'

(12) a. *David* flimpt.
'*D.* is flimping.'
b. *David* flimpt *zijn fiets.*
'*D.* is flimping *his bike.*'

(13) a. *David* flimpt aan *zijn fiets.*
'*D.* is flimping on *his bike.*'
b. *David* flimpt *zijn fiets* in de auto.
'*D.* is flimping *his bike* into the car.'

In the unergative-unaccusative alternation, (11), *flimpen* may refer to something like *fietsen* 'bike'. In the intransitive-transitive pair, (12), it may refer to something like *poetsen* 'clean'. In the oblique intransitive-ditransitive alternation, (13), it may refer to something like *trekken* 'pull'. So, even though in each case a subevent has been added as a final state, *flimpen* can, but need not take an extra participant, see (11b).

The examples in (8)-(13) clearly show that event type features by themselves do not provide conclusive lexical information for deriving the number of event participants.

An additional piece of evidence is the following. One can notice item-particular differences in a verb's adicity (the number of open places lexically associated with a predicate) by comparing for each verb all its potential frames and determining the maximal number of argument positions it can project. Some verbs appear with two event participants, whereas others can appear with maximally one (and yet a few others with none). Independent of how many event participants a verb maps onto syntax in a particular frame, that is, independent of the potential discrepancy between lexical arguments and syntactic argument positions, every verb seems to have a certain number of potential event participants.[12] In order to see how verbs differ from each other with respect to the number of event participants they take, one must compare them in their "maximal" frames, i.e., the frame(s) in which they project all their event participants.

Surveying a small set of verbs that differ maximally from each other with respect to their numbers of event participants, one can distinguish the following subsets of verbs. Whereas *regenen* 'rain' and other weather verbs do not take any event participant at all, all others verbs select at least one participant. The members of one set of verbs take only one participant; for example, *slapen* 'sleep', *niezen* 'sneeze' and *rinkelen* 'clink' never map onto a frame with two argument positions. The members of another always imply a second participant, even when they map only one, e.g., *praten* 'talk', *martelen* 'torture', *eten* 'eat' and *duwen* 'push', whereas the members of yet another set always need to map their two participants, e.g., *geven* 'give' and *zetten* 'put'. Finally, some verbs basically take one participant, but take an additional one when the event is causativized, e.g., *smelten* 'melt', *breken* 'break' and *rollen* 'roll'.

This brief survey of different sets of verbs also leads to the conclusion that verbs differ from each other on an item-particular basis with respect to the number of event participants they are associated with. Naturally, this number affects the choice of frames a verb can map onto, since it sets a maximum for the number of argument positions the verb potentially projects. Unless the theory of event types is further developed into a much finer-grained analysis of events and subevents, the obvious conclusion is that the question how many participants are involved in a particular event is lexically determined for each verb.

Having seen that event type does not predict the number of event participants, and concluding that one must lexically specify this number for each verb, the next most reductionist approach is to say that only the number of event participants matters, and nothing else. This will be discussed next.

4.6.2 Deconstructing event participant features: agentivity

θ-Role and LCS (but not argument structure) theories crucially assume that one must specify verbs for the kinds of event participants they are associated with. Consider the event participants for the verbs just mentioned and compare how they are semantically different from each other. *Praten* 'talk', *martelen* 'torture', *eten* 'eat', *lopen* 'walk', *duwen* 'push', *geven* 'give' and *zetten* 'put' typically imply the participation of an agentive participant, as do transitive *smelten* 'melt', *breken* 'break' and *rollen* 'roll'. On the other hand however, *rinkelen* 'clink' and intransitive *smelten* 'melt', *breken* 'break' and *rollen* 'roll' imply non-agentivity of their single participant. For *slapen* 'sleep' and *niezen* 'sneeze' it is not so clear whether their single participant is agentive or not. Furthermore, as for verbs that take two participants, one of the two is always more agentive than the other. This holds for: *praten* 'talk', *eten* 'eat', *duwen* 'push, *geven* 'give' and *zetten* 'put', causative *smelten* 'melt', *breken* 'break' and *rollen* 'roll'.

I concluded above that surveying this set of verbs and their verb frame possibilities suggests that lexical specification in terms of the number of event participants is relevant for mapping. Minimally, the mapping system needs to "see" this number. The next question is, how much of the semantic content of event participants does the mapping system need to "see"? In other words, which semantic properties of event participants are lexical-syntactic features, if any? The strongest hypothesis is to say that only the number of event participants matters. This hypothesis, however, seems to clash with the semantic differences among the participants of the verbs just mentioned. Moreover, there are a number of further indications that the event participants are semantically differentiated from each other. The question is whether these semantic differences must be lexically encoded, or whether they can be derived from something else. Consider first how fine-grained the semantic differentiation of event participants actually is.

In principle, for an event with two participants, if nothing else mattered, either one could map onto subject position and the other one onto object or oblique position. Empirically however, this is not the case:

the subject position always contains the more agentive of the two participants in an event (if there are two).[13,14] This is a first indication that the relative agentivity properties of the event participants correlate with subject versus non-subject positions.

Agentivity features of event participants show up in another domain as well: passivization. Passivization is to some extent sensitive to whether or not the event has an agentive participant. This was first pointed out for English by Jackendoff (1972). Consider *touch* (in what became a famous example), (14).

(14) a. The lamp was touching the bookcase.
b. ??The bookcase was being touched by the lamp.
c. The bookcase was being touched.
(Jackendoff 1972)

Apparently, a lamp touching a bookcase is not agentive enough to allow passivization, (14b). The passive in (14c) must be interpreted as agentive *touch*, i.e., the bookcase was touched by somebody.[15]

In Dutch, passivization is even more restricted: only eventive verbs with a sufficiently agentive event participant can passivize. Van Voorst (1988) points out that stative verbs such as *kennen* 'know' and *weten* 'know' do not passivize.[16] As in English, Dutch verbs with non-agentive participants cannot passivize, as was first pointed out by Pollman (1970, 1975) (and further discussed by Kirsner 1973; van Voorst 1988; Zaenen 1993). As in English, verbs that are ambiguous between an agentive and a non-agentive reading become unambiguous in the passive, (15).

(15) a. Piet / De ketel floot.
'P. / the kettle whistled.'
b. Er werd gefloten.
there was whistling
'Somebody whistled.' (Pollman 1970)

The single participant verb *fluiten* 'whistle' can take either an agentive or a non-agentive participant, (15a). The passive of *fluiten* 'whistle', (15b), however, only refers to an agentive event, i.e., the whistling must come from Piet; it cannot come from the kettle. This example also shows that agentivity features are not only needed to compare two participants in an event to determine which is most agentive and appears in subject position; they also play a role if a verb takes only one participant, as impersonal passivization in (15b) demonstrates. Apparently, agentivity of an event and passivization are crucially correlated.

The conclusion is that event participants differ semantically, both relatively among each other if a verb takes more than one (i.e., the most agentive one is in subject position) as well as according to some absolute standard (i.e., the agentivity restriction on passivization). The question is, should one encode this semantic property as a lexical feature on the event participants of the verb, or can it be derived from something else?

4.6.3 Deriving the agentivity of event participants

I will argue that agentivity is not a lexical property of verbs, i.e., a feature on one of the event participants. Instead, in the lexical specification, event participants are semantically equal and non-distinct. There are a few indications that suggest that agentivity should not be lexically encoded.

Dowty (1991) meticulously points out that there are various semantic notions that contribute to agentivity; similarly, there are various semantic notions that contribute to patienthood. The role types "agent" and "patient" are not discrete categories at all. Hence, arguments may have different "degrees of membership" in a certain role type. He lists several properties that are usually associated with subject and object position respectively. The properties associated with subject position are all properties of agenthood, (16), hence his term *proto-agent* properties; those associated with object position are all properties of patienthood, (17), hence his term *proto-patient* properties. They constitute what he refers to as proto-agent and proto-patient *role types*. They must be seen as lists of possible verbal entailments about the argument in question.

(16) Contributing properties for the Agent proto-role (Dowty 1991:572):
- a. volitional involvement in the event or state;
- b. sentience (and/or perception);
- c. causing an event or change of state in another participant;
- d. movement (relative to the position of another participant);
- (e. exists independently of the event named by the verb).

(17) Contributing properties for the Patient proto-role (Dowty 1991:572):
- a. undergoes change of state;
- b. incremental theme;
- c. causally affected by another participant;
- d. stationary (relative to movement of another participant);
- (e. does not exist independently of the event, or not at all).

Dowty formulates the Argument Selection Principle to constrain what kind of lexical predicates may exist in a natural language, out of many imaginable ones: "In predicates with grammatical subject and object, the argument for which the predicate entails the greatest number of Proto-Agent properties will be lexicalized as the subject of the predicate; the argument with the greatest number of Proto-Patient entailments will be lexicalized as the direct object" (Dowty 1991:576).

The proto-agent properties all contribute to the agentivity of the subject. Hence, more and less agentive event participants all appear in subject position, irrespective of how agentive they are exactly. The same holds for the patient properties of the participant that appears in object position. The crucial question is: do these degrees of agentivity and patienthood come from the verb itself? Does it lexically specify its event participants in terms of: ± volitional, ± sentient, ± perceiving, ± causing a change of state (= ± causally affected), ± moving (= ± stationary), ± existing (= ± not yet existing), ± being incremental theme and ± undergoing a change?

I think this is very unlikely.[17] Although certain verbs can be scored plus or minus on each of these properties without any further context, many other verbs are unclear or even ambiguous in this respect. For example, *slapen* 'sleep' and *niezen* 'sneeze' were already mentioned as not clearly agentive nor non-agentive; it is just not clear how to score them on some of the proto-agent properties, e.g., volitional, sentient, perceiving. Moreover, *fluiten* 'whistle' would need to be specified ambiguously, since it can take either an agentive or a non-agentive participant (see (15)). Furthermore, agentivity seems to depend very much on the semantic properties of the subject itself. Compare *lopen* 'walk' with five different subjects, (18).[18]

(18) a. John loopt.
'J. walks.'
b. De Waal loopt dwars door Nijmegen.
'The Waal runs right through Nijmegen.'
c. De kraan loopt.
'The tab runs.'
d. De emmer loopt leeg.
the bucket walks empty
'The bucket is emptying.'
e. De grens met België loopt net ten zuiden van Tilburg.
the border with Belgium walks just to south of Tilburg
'The Belgium border runs just south of Tilburg.'

If one can order them at all, agentivity decreases from (18a) through (18e). Clearly, the agentivity of *lopen* 'walk, run' depends on the properties of the subject it combines with. The subjects by themselves are more or less agentive; the agentivity of the event depends on them or must even be equated with the independent agentivity of the subject. Either way, it cannot be considered as a lexical property of *lopen* 'walk'.

In the remainder of this section I focus on the agentivity differences between event participants (their proto-agent role properties). Circumventing the problems just mentioned with lexically specifying each verb for its agentivity properties, I claim that they can be derived to a large extent, and, hence, do not need to be lexically specified.

Along with the contribution of the independent semantics of the argument noun phrases themselves, there are three different structural sources that play a role in defining the agentivity of event participants. One kind of effect can be defined on the event structure, i.e., the ways the participants are associated with the event. A next interpretational effect involves the syntactic configuration, in particular, the relative semantics attached to subject and object position. Finally, morphological affixes bear their own semantics which is added to the verb they attach to. The latter two are strong and obligatory effects; they may even overrule the independent semantic properties of the argument noun phrases.

First, consider event structure. Following Grimshaw (1990), Pustejovsky (1991), Davis & Demirdache (1995), Davis (1997, in press) and Demirdache (1997), I assume that some form of aspectual prominence distinguishes the event participants. In Grimshaw's formulation: " . . . an argument which participates in the first sub-event of an event structure [i.e., a transition, AvH] is more prominent than an argument which participates in the second sub-event. A cause is always part of the first sub-event. Hence, it is always more prominent than the argument corresponding to the element whose state is changed" (Grimshaw 1990:26-27). Grimshaw furthermore relates the fact that "agents" always "behave well" by mapping onto subject position to aspectual prominence: " . . . the behavior of Agents is just a special case of the general behavior of causes: they are always subjects. Since Agents are always maximally prominent on the aspectual dimension, the two dimensions [i.e., the thematic and the aspectual, AvH] always coincide for Agents, and their subject status is assured" (Grimshaw 1990:33). Extending, and thereby deviating from Grimshaw's proposal, Davis & Demirdache (1995) claim that the thematic properties of event participants can be entirely reconstructed in aspectual terms (see also Davis 1997, in press; Demirdache 1997). In particular, they formulate the reconstruction of the semantic properties of an external argument from event structure in terms of entailments. The external argument entails the property of " . . . *agency* iff there is a temporal interval which defines the beginning of the event and *causation* iff there is a change of state or a resulting state" (Davis & Demirdache 1995:1).

Grimshaw thus derives the relative agentivity of two participants in an event from their positions in the event structure. According to Grimshaw, a participant in a first subevent is more agentive than one in the second subevent. Davis & Demirdache's definition adds a statement about the semantics of event participants in an absolute sense: a participant involved in a particular configuration of subevents is an "agent" and one in another configuration is a "causer". I add a further absolute interpretational principle defined on the event type of the subevent: a participant involved in a (sub)event that is a state is less agentive than one involved in a (sub)event that is a process.

This suffices to semantically differentiate the participants of verbs that denote a transition and take two participants. Participation in either of the subevents determines which of the two is the most agentive. This view of agentivity yields an interesting conclusion: one can now derive the ordering in a thematic hierarchy in which an "agent" is ordered higher than a "theme" in terms of aspectual prominence; one does not need to posit this as a primitive.

Another kind of interpretational effect can be defined on syntactic structure. Consider again the subject-object difference. In line with recent proposals by Emonds (1991a), Borer (1994), Gleitman (1995), Goldberg (1995) and Kako (1997, 1998) and also, to a lesser extent, claims by Hoekstra & Mulder (1990) and Mulder (1992), I assume that "thematic" interpretation is defined on the syntactic configuration itself: the subject and object positions themselves have semantic properties.[19] Hence, the interpretation of a simple transitive configuration (e.g., *Mien eats a sandwich*) is such that the subject is more agentive and the object less agentive. *Mien* is interpreted as the eater and the *sandwich* gets eaten, by virtue of the fact that the former participant is in subject position and the latter in object position. So, rather than saying that *eat* takes an "agent" and a "theme" and adding that the "agent" maps onto subject position and the "theme" onto object position, I simply assume that *eat* takes two event participants. The fact that the one that ends up in subject position is interpreted as the agentive participant in the eating event (i.e., the eater), and the one in object position as the less agentive participant (i.e., the thing eaten) is a *post hoc* interpretational effect, driven by semantic properties associated with subject and object position, respectively.

Notice that mapping the two arguments in the reverse order (e.g., *The sandwich eats Mien*) is not ungrammatical. It merely does not make any semantic sense, given what we know about the typical semantic properties of sandwiches and people (see Borer 1994, fn. 14). In a fairytale context, however, sandwiches and people may have atypical properties. One could imagine, in such a context, that sandwiches could just as well eat people. In fact, the fact that the reverse mapping pattern overrules the typical semantic properties of sandwiches and people (if one can make sense of it at all), is a strong piece of evidence that subject and object positions have particular semantic properties associated with them.

Work from various people argues for this structures-have-meaning idea. Emonds' (1991a) interpretative principles for "agent", "figure" and "ground" constitute an interpretational approach to the semantic differentiation of event participants.[20] The interpretation rules are defined on syntactic configurations plus a predicate's specification for the lexical feature *location*.[21] They are applicable to both non-stative and stative predicate and generate a semantic differentiation of the arguments off of syntactic structure.

The structures-have-meanings idea crucially underlies the framework of Construction Grammar. Goldberg (1995) in particular argues that constructional meanings exist independently of verb meaning. "The set of basic clause types of a language are used to encode general event types such as those denoting that someone did something to someone, something moved, someone caused something to change state, someone experienced something, someone possessed something, and so forth" (Goldberg 1995:66). For example, the semantics associated with the ditransitive construction is CAUSE-RECEIVE. Verbs with their individual participant roles are integrated into constructions whereby the grammatical roles of constructions are fused with verbal participant roles. The degree to which construction meanings and verb meanings are compatible determines whether or not particular combinations are felicitous.

Kako (1997, 1998) presents experimental evidence that supports the structures-have-meanings idea. Kako gave English-speaking adults nonsense verbs in one of six different frames (e.g., *The bilp fridded to the aggit*) and asked them with respect to a series of semantic properties whether or not the verb might have that property (e.g., *Does fridding involve someone or something moving?*). Subjects are indeed able to define the meanings of subcategorization frames in this way agreeing with each other to a large extent. When asked to judge the naturalness of (existing) verb-frame parings, varying the semantic overlap between the two, Kako finds a moderately strong relationship.

Note that the event-structural and syntactic effects reinforce each other in assigning an interpretation to the two participants of verbs denoting a transition. For verbs that denote a non-branching event type (i.e., a state or process), only the syntactic interpretational effect differentiates the two participants.

Even though subject and object position assign different semantics to the arguments in these positions, one cannot simply claim that subject position entails agentivity and object position non-agentivity, given that there are verbs that do not have an "agent"-"theme" interpretation on their subjects and objects (e.g., psychological verbs). Instead, one must assume that the properties of subject and object positions are semantically underspecified, but differ from each other in a relative way: if there are two arguments, the one in subject position is more "agentive" than the one in object position. Agentivity must be taken as an underspecified notion, or, rather, as a gradient notion, in the sense of Dowty's proto-agent properties. The semantics of the verb, in particular, whether its event type is stative or non-stative, fills it in more specifically. Hence, if a verb denotes a non-stative event (i.e., a process or transition), the subject's "agentivity" may involve volitional, sentient and/or moving participation in the event, possibly causing some change in another participant. If a verb denotes a psychological event, the subject's "agentivity" may involve volitional, sentient and perceiving participation in the event, possibly causing some change in another participant. On the other hand, if a verb denotes a (psychological) state, the subject's "agentivity" may merely involve sentience and perception.[22]

A final kind of interpretational effect is given by morphology. In similar ways, certain morphological affixes have their own semantics which they attribute to (or sometimes impose onto) the verb they attach to. This determines the semantic properties of the verb's participants. Various interpretational effects are associated with various morphemes.

For passivization, I assume that passive morphology in Dutch requires, as a kind of selection restriction, an agentive verb. Therefore, one cannot passivize non-agentive verbs. Moreover, this analysis predicts that a passive construction can never be construed as ambiguous between an agentive and non-agentive interpretation (hence, the obligatorily agentive interpretation (15)).

The requirement that passivization selects only agentive predicates must be formulated more precisely. Certain verbs are typically non-agentive, i.e., they are typically used in non-agentive contexts. However, if one passivizes such a verb, the effect is not ungrammatical, but, rather, the non-agentivity disappears. Consider *vallen* 'fall'. A falling event is typically non-agentive. Thus, *vallen* 'fall' should not be able to passivize. However, as Perlmutter (1978) illustrates, in special contexts, it can appear in an (impersonal) passive, (19).

(19) In het tweede bedrijf werd er door de nieuwe akteur op het juiste ogenblik gevallen.
in the second act was there by the new actor at the right moment fallen
'In the second act, the new actor fell on cue.'
(Perlmutter 1978:172)

In a context of theater play rehearsals and actors having to fall at a certain moment in a scene, (19) is perfectly intelligible. Apparently, a verb's typical interpretation can be overruled by the morpho-syntactic configuration it appears in, here, passive morphology (cf. Hoekstra & Mulder 1990; Zaenen 1993). In these cases, agentivity is coerced onto the event and its participant; the actor in (19) is ascribed volitional control over his act of falling. Even though the participant in a falling event is typically non-agentive, agentivity can be construed when needed (here, as required by the presence of passive morphology).[23]

The problem with the passive in a non-agentive situation such as (14b) is not that it is ungrammatical. Rather, since a lamp is typically non-agentive, it is hard to come up with an intelligible interpretation. Similarly, the passive morphology fixes *touch* and *fluiten* 'whistle' in (14c) and (15b) on an agentive interpretation, so that the potential ambiguity (or underspecification) of these verbs does not even arise in a passive construction. Hence, the restriction that only agentive verbs passivize must be taken the other way round. Passive morphology imposes agentivity on the verb it attaches to. The same holds for the *by*-phrase in a passive construction: *by* itself attributes agentivity to its participant.

Supporting evidence of a different kind for the semantic requirement of agentivity and the sensitivity of passivization to it can be derived from Kratzer's (1995) semantic account of passivization. Pursuing the semantic identification of the implicit external argument in passive constructions, Kratzer claims that passives have an external argument that is syntactically realized as a non-overt impersonal pronoun (an impersonal small pro). She supports her claim by showing that the implicit argument in passives and impersonal pronouns (i.e., German *man* 'they, we') have the same semantic properties. Assuming that an impersonal pronoun is, by its own semantics, agentive, one can derive the restriction that passive only applies to agentive verbs (or, alternatively, attributes agentive properties to the event) from the interpretation of the implicit participant in a passive as an impersonal pronoun.

Notice that accounts of passivization in terms of suppressing or blocking the external argument cannot deal with the kind of interpretational flexibility in (19). *Vallen* 'fall' is an unaccusative verb; it does not have an external argument and thus cannot passivize. The fact that it can passivize in certain contexts could only be resolved by assuming that *vallen* 'fall' has, in fact, two different argument structures, one with a single internal argument and one with a single external argument. Moreover, the systematic meaning shift between non-volitional versus volitional falling is lost, since there is no reference to the semantic content of the arguments in the argument structure.

Effects of agentivity construal can also be found with other morphological affixes and in certain constructions. They seem to be sensitive to the agentivity of one of the event participants. If a verb does not typically involve agentive participation, agentivity is imposed. Jackendoff (1990) presents an example where agentivity is required or else imposed in the construction in (20). While *belch* typically denotes an involuntarily event, it must be interpreted as a volitional act when it is embedded in a progressive *by*-phrase.

(20) Bill got out of the restaurant by belching.
(Jackendoff 1990:216)

If (20) is interpretable at all, the sentence means that Bill was belching on purpose, employing it as a trick to get out of the restaurant. The single participant of belching is thus attributed agentive properties in this construction.

In a similar way, English suffix *-er* derives a noun that denotes an agentive participant in an event (cf. van Hout & Roeper 1998). Like passive morphology, *-er* requires an agentive event, or else attributes agentivity to the event.[24] The difference between "requiring agentivity" and "attributing agentivity" cannot be noticed for verbs that are typically agentive by themselves (e.g., *runner*, *dancer*, *swimmer*). It can be detected, however, with ambiguous verbs and with typically non-agentive ones. For example, *roll* is ambiguous between active and passive rolling. The *-er* suffix on *roll* requires (or attributes) agentivity. Hence, a *roller* is unambiguously someone who is actively involved in a rolling event; it cannot refer to a non-agentive participant, such as a ball. Similarly, typical non-agentive verbs do not easily combine with *-er* (e.g., ??*faller*, ??*melter*, ??*breaker*). If such nouns can get an interpretation at all, it is one in which their typical non-agentivity is overruled in favor of an agentive one.

This concludes the discussion about the semantics of event participants and whether or not this must be encoded as a lexical-syntactic feature. I have claimed that agentivity is not a lexical-syntactic feature of verbs and that the event participants are semantically equal in a verb's lexical specification. I have argued that their semantics can to a large extent be derived. Along with the contribution of the independent semantic properties of the arguments themselves, there are (at least) three kinds of structural sources that determine the agentivity of and among event participants. One is the way the participants are associated with the event, i.e., their position in the event structure. A second source for interpretational effect is defined by the semantic properties of syntactic configurations. Morphological affixes determine a third kind of effect. These effects may even overrule the typical agentivity properties of verbs and their participants. While I have only discussed the semantic effects of relative aspectual prominence of participants, subject versus object position, passive morphology and *-er* suffixation, the approach advocated in this subsection suggest that there are probably many more syntactic and morphological factors that co-determine the semantics of event participants.

4.6.4 Consequences of deriving the agentivity of event participants

In the previous and present sections, I have discussed the first lexical primitive, *event participants*, and raised methodological questions with respect to its status as lexical primitive. After showing that one cannot derive the number of event participants from the event structure, I have concluded that a verb must list this number in the lexicon. Verbs differ from each other in how many participants are associated with the event they denote; a verb takes one or two (or no) participants (subsection 4.6.1). I have further pointed out that agentivity is a core semantic property that differentiates the participants among each other, and also characterizes the single participant of one-participant verbs (subsection 4.6.2). Rather than lexically annotating this semantic property as a feature on the event participant(s) of the verb, I have advocated an approach in which agentivity and, hence, semantic differentiation of event participants are derivative concepts (subsection 4.6.3). This approach differs crucially from θ-role or LCS-style approaches which lexically differentiate the participants in terms of different θ-role or labels of LCS-variables.

The important advantage of the present approach is that one does not need to lexically specify a verb for its agentivity properties, and, hence, it reduces the lexical burden: the lexicon becomes more parsimonious. The lexical-syntactic feature *event participants* lists a number, not the semantic kinds. Furthermore, one avoids ambiguous or arbitrary lexical specification for verbs that can take both agentive and non-agentive participants or verbs that are not really specific about the agentivity of their event participants.

I have proposed several factors that play a role as interpretational principles. Together they contribute to the derivation of the notion *agentivity* and, hence, to a semantic differentiation of event participants. Firstly, the event structure: a participant involved in the first subevent of a transition is more agentive than one involved in the second subevent (cf. Grimshaw 1990; Pustejovsky 1991; Davis & Demirdache 1995; Davis 1997, in press; Demirdache 1997). Secondly, the semantics of the syntactic positions themselves: if there are two arguments, the argument in subject position is interpreted as more agentive than one in object position (cf. Emonds 1991a; Borer 1994; Gleitman 1995; Goldberg 1995; Kako 1997, 1998). Thirdly, the semantics of morphological affixes: passive morphology and the nominalizing *-er* suffix attribute agentivity to a verb. Also, *by* in the *by*-phrase of a passive attributes agentivity to the participant in its complement position and *by* taking a progressive verb as its complement attributes agentivity to it. Finally, of course, the semantics of the noun phrases in argument positions determine their further interpretation.

In the case of verbs that are typically thought of as non-agentive, passive morphology and the *-er* suffix can overrule this typical interpretation by imposing agentivity to the verb and thereby shifting its meaning from typical to atypical (if there is any interpretation at all). Similarly, reversing the participants in subject and object positions has the effect that the interpretation (which is the agentive and which the non-agentive participant) reverses as well. These effects were taken as unambiguous indications that interpretation comes off of the syntactic and morphological structure, rather than vice versa, the verb's lexical-semantics feeding the mapping onto syntactic and morphologic structure.

I have loosely used the terms *typically agentive* and *non-typically agentive* throughout this section. They seem to create a paradox, i.e., a re-introduction of an item-particular semantic notion of agentivity in the lexicon, whereas I have been claiming at the same time that one does not need any reference to the semantics of the participants in the lexicon. Although a verb's typical agentivity properties are probably listed in the lexicon, I have argued that the mapping system does not need to "see" them. Rather, they represent encyclopedic knowledge, or knowledge of the world. They are generalizations over all contexts a particular verb has been used in; these generalizations constitute the verb's typical, or default, interpretation. They are not relevant for the mapping system, however.

The latter claim is almost intestable: what belongs to lexical-syntactic knowledge and what to knowledge of the world? Alternatively, why does one's intuition say that, for example, *fall* is typically less agentive than *bike*? The relevant question is: does this intuition need to be part of the grammatical system as a semantic property that is a lexical-syntactic feature, or not? What matters here is that certain syntactic positions and constructions and certain morphological affixes fixate a verb onto a certain interpretation and can even induce systematic shifts of interpretation. These effects are definitely part of the grammar. The effect that meaning shifts occur in the first place and that they happen to typically non-agentive verbs suggests that *typical agentivity* and *typical non-agentivity* are relative notions and, hence, can best be considered as extra-grammatical notions.[25]

Having concluded that the lexical entry of a verb includes the number of its event participants, the next question is: does this suffice as a lexical primitive? Clearly, just a number by itself does not determine how the event participants are mapped. So, next comes the issue of mapping: what determines which event participants are mapped onto syntax, if they are mapped at all, and onto which positions they are mapped?

4.7 Event type features are a lexical primitive

Chapter 3 has shown that how the mapping of event participants onto syntax, including the choice of syntactic position they are mapped onto, depends on the particular event type of or focus on the event. Generalizing over the many different forms of lexical-syntactic flexibility in Dutch, frame alternations fall into three event-semantic classes. One set of alternations is characterized by an atelic-telic event type-shift, a second set is characterized by causativization of the event, and for a final set of alternations, the two alternants denote the same event type, but present different foci on the same event.

What are the implications of the fact that frame alternations can be analyzed in terms of taking different views of the same event, more specifically, in terms of event type-shifting? First, it means that the lexical-syntactic features of a verb must also specify its basic event type properties. Likewise, mapping rules must be defined in terms of event type or event focus features. Furthermore, it means that a verb's basic event type can be altered by event type-shifting operations. Hence, the mapping algorithm must be closely connected with the event type-shifting calculus, since the final event type determines the outcome of mapping. Finally, it means that different foci on one and the same event are associated with different mapping outcomes.

Which are the relevant event type or event focus features and how do they relate to particular verb frames? The discussion in Chapter 3 showed that there are two mapping generalizations: a telic event type requires the presence of an event participant in direct object position; a causative event type requires the presence of two event participants, one in subject and one in direct object position. This means that a verb's lexical event type specification must include the properties telic/atelic and causative/non-causative. Likewise, mapping rules must refer to telicity and causativity features and associate them with appropriate frames.

In this section I examine the event type features of various verbs, showing how they vary and how they determine how a particular verb is involved in event type-shifting. I will extensively discuss atelic-telic event-type shifting. Different syntactic manifestations of the atelic-telic shift show which kind of lexical properties play a role in this event type-shift and which must thus be considered as lexical-syntactic features. First, I discuss atelic-telic event type-shifts that are brought about by the composition of the event types of a verb and a preposition, postposition, particle, prefix or resultative predicate (subsection 4.7.1). Next, I discuss the role of the lexical property *temporal scale* in this event type-shift (subsection 4.7.2). I briefly discuss causativization (subsection 4.7.3). Finally, I illustrate how different verbs can or cannot undergo atelic-telic event type-shifting and causativization by listing some one- and two-participant verbs with their different lexical-syntactic features (subsection 4.7.4).

As I have mainly concentrated on event type features, the issue of event focus is beyond the scope of this thesis. I leave an integration of the effects of taking different foci on an event for further research.

4.7.1 Deconstructing atelic-telic event type-shifting: event type composition

Recall my basic assumptions about event semantics that were introduced in Chapter 3, section 3.3. Processes and states are atelic event types; accomplishments and achievements are telic event types. In a Pustejovskian formalization of event types, a telic event type is characterized as a transition which branches into two subevents; the subevents may be states, processes or transitions, (21). Atelic-telic event type-shifting is pictured in (22).[26]

(21) Telic event type:

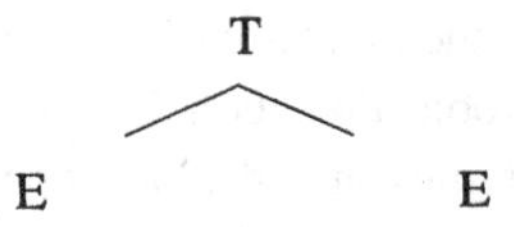

E ranges over {S, P, T}

(22) Atelic-telic event type-shifting:

P or S type-shifts into

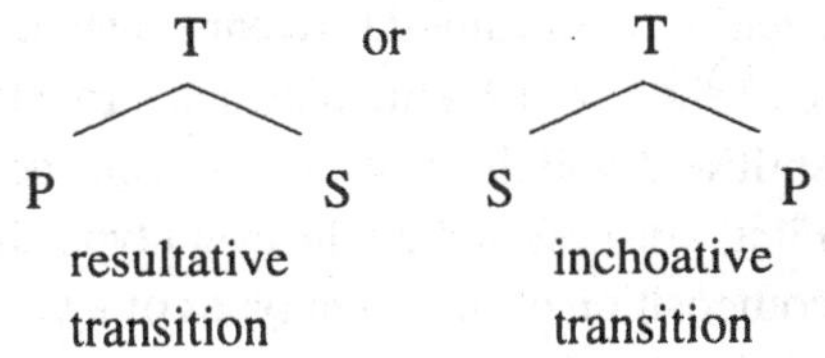

Recall also I use the term *telic* in a broad sense, referring to events of the transition type, including both resultative and inchoative events.

As discussed in section 3.3, the event type of a sentence is determined by a conglomerate of different elements and effects. One needs to distinguish between inner aspect, as determined by the lexical-aspectual properties of the verb, the aspectual properties of other predicates in the VP and the quantificational properties of the arguments, and outer aspect, as determined by tense and temporal adverbs and adverbial phrases.[27] Only inner aspect factors influence which event participants get mapped onto syntax, and which positions they are mapped onto; outer aspect operators do not. As Verkuyl (1993) puts it, " . . . inner aspect concerns the relationship between a verb and its arguments" (Verkuyl 1993:14). Since I am concerned with mapping effects, i.e., the ways arguments appear in syntax, I concentrate on inner event type-shifting.

Verbs differ from each other with respect to their event types. Some verbs denote a state (e.g., *houden van* 'love', *weten* 'know', *kennen* 'know'); others denote a process (e.g., *slapen* 'sleep', *rinkelen* 'ring', *rennen* 'run', *lopen* 'walk', *eten* 'eat', *duwen* 'push', *martelen* 'torture'); a third set denotes a transition (e.g., *breken* 'break', *smelten* 'melt', *geven* 'give', *zetten* 'put'). These event types are lexical event types; they contribute to the determination of inner aspect. An atelic-telic event type-shift may occur. There are different event-semantic ways for atelic-telic event type-shifting to come about. Not all verbs can undergo it in each of these ways. In this subsection, I first deconstruct the properties of atelic-telic event type shifting brought about by event type composition.

Event type composition is an operation which composes the event types of the verb and another predicate. Sometimes, composing two event types triggers the creation of additional event structure in which both original events are subevents. For example, a verb that denotes a process combines with a predicate that denotes a state, yielding a transition between the process and the state. At other times, composing two event types does not create a new event structure; instead, there is event structure merging of the two event types. For example, a process denoted by the verb merges with an (unspecified) subevent of a transition expressed by another predicate, or, vice versa, a state expressed by the predicate merges with one of the subevents in the transition expressed by a verb. I consider event structure merging to be a subcase of event type composition. In earlier work, I introduced the operation Event Type Composition (van Hout 1990, 1991b, 1992a,b, 1994). For very similar ideas on event type composition, see Pustejovsky (1991); Schipper

(1994); Davis & Demirdache (1995); Davis (1997, in press); Demirdache (1997).

Event type composition accounts for atelic-telic event type-shifts in complex predicates, particle and prefixed verbs and resultative formation. First, I discuss complex predicates.

Complex predicate formation: "goal" phrases

Consider *lopen* 'walk', *rollen* 'roll' and *duwen* 'push' in an atelic-telic event type-shift, (23)-(25).

(23) a. John heeft de hele nacht gelopen.
J. has the whole night walked
'J. walked all night.'

b. John is na 5 minuten weggelopen.
J. is after 5 minutes away-walked
'J. walked away after 5 minutes.'

(24) a. De tennisbal heeft nog even gerold.
the tennis-ball has still while rolled
'The tennis ball rolled for a while.'

b. De tennisbal is de baan op gerold.
the tennis-ball is the court onto rolled
'The tennis ball rolled onto the court.'

(25) a. Paola heeft urenlang de auto geduwd.
P. has hours-long the car pushed
'P. pushed the car for hours.'

b. Paola heeft de auto in 5 minuten naar de kant geduwd.
P. has the car in 5 minutes to the side pushed
'P. pushed the car to the side in 5 minutes.'

The basic event types of these three verbs are processes of walking, rolling and pushing, respectively, (23a)-(25a). The derived telic event type is an accomplishment: the processes culminate in a resulting state, (23b)-(25b). This event type-shift from a process to a transition is due to the presence of a "goal" particle in (23b) and a "goal" PP in (24b) and (25b).

I assume that prepositions, postpositions and particles have event structure (of a particular event type) and take their own event participants, following up on van Hout (1990) where I first worked out this idea with respect to prepositions and van Hout (1991b, 1992a,b, 1994) where I develop it for particles. Semantically, verbs, but also prepositions, postpositions and particles, are predicates that take arguments, i.e., they are functors (see subsection 4.5.2 on the functor status of PP complements). Event-semantically, these categories denote a state or an event in which their own event participants are involved. Other implementations of the functor status of prepositions are presented by Williams (1989) who proposes that prepositions have an internal and an external argument and Jackendoff (1990) who analyzes prepositions with their own LCS. If one views a verb as specifying the "content" of the event, PPs and particles are similar, as they specify the "content" of a state or a transition. More specifically, I assume that a locative preposition or particle denotes a state, e.g., *weg* 'away' in (23b) and directional prepositions or postpositions denote a transition, e.g., *op* 'onto' in (24b) and *naar* 'to' in (25b).

I further assume that in the case of complex predicates containing a verb and a "goal" phrase, event type composition applies; it composes the event types of the verb on the one hand and particle, preposition or postposition on the other, yielding a compositionally derived transition (cf. Pustejovsky 1991; Verkuyl & Zwarts 1992; Verkuyl 1993). In some cases, the composition of the two event types triggers the creation of a transition in which both original events are subevents, (26). In other cases, the event type of the verb merges with the unspecified subevent of the transition expressed by the other predicate, (27) and (28). In the case of complex predicates, event type composition also involves merging one of the event participants of each predicate. Some applications of event type composition are illustrated for *lopen* 'walk' in (26), *rollen* 'roll' in (27), and *duwen* 'push' in (28).

(26) Event type composition applied to *lopen* 'walk' and particle *weg* 'away':

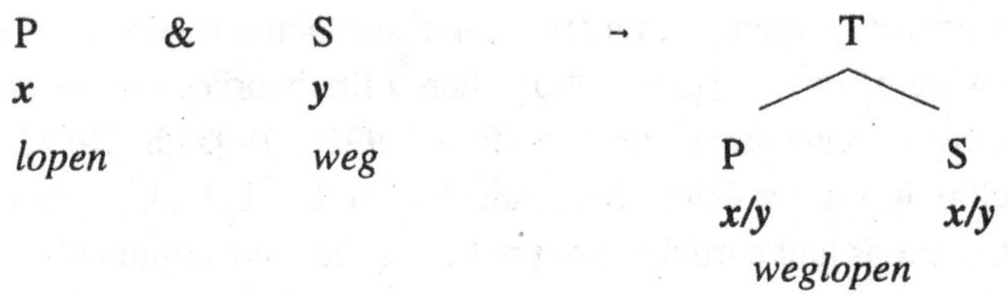

(27) Event type composition applied to *rollen* 'roll' and postposition *op* 'onto':

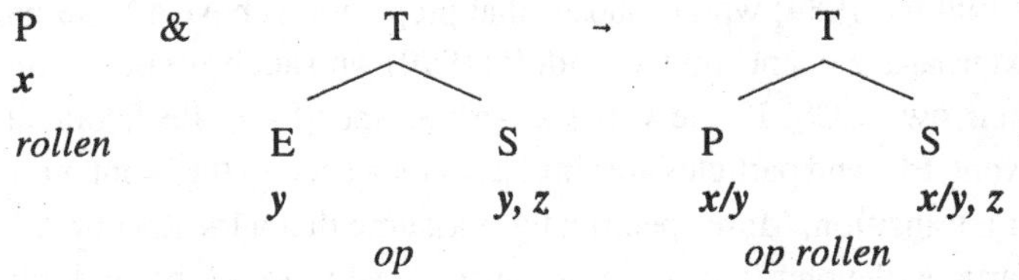

(28) Event type composition applied to *duwen* 'push' and preposition *naar* 'to':

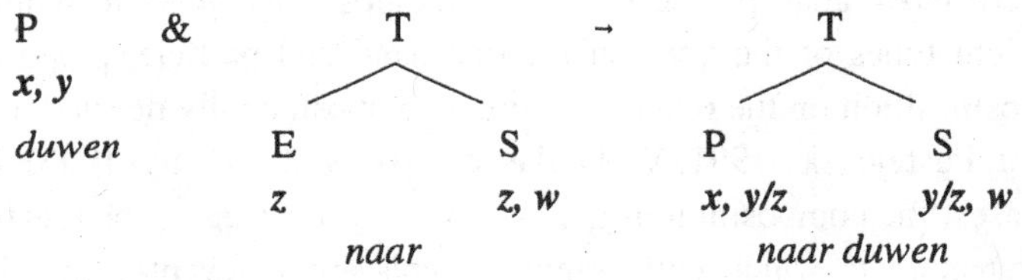

The particle *weg* 'away' in (26) denotes a state (i.e., the state of being away) and takes one participant who is in that state. *Lopen* 'walk' denotes a one-participant process. Composing a process and a state into a complex event yields a transition between the two, whereby the event participant who does the walking merges with the one who ends up in a certain state (variable merging is indicated with a slash between the two original variables: *x/y*). In (26), *John* is the walker; he ends up being *away*. Postposition *op* 'onto' in (27) denotes a transition with an unspecified first subevent and a final state.[28] It expresses a locational change of state relation between two participants (a "theme" and a "goal" in θ-role terminology); the final subevent is the state in which one participant is on top of the other, *y* and *z* in (27). In this case, event type composition involves merging the rolling process and the first subevent of the transition whereby the event participant that is involved in rolling merges with the one that ends up in the final state, *x/y*; in (27), *x/y* is the rolling ball which ends up on the court, *z*. Similarly, preposition *naar* 'to' in (28) denotes a transition and expresses a directional relation between two participants. When it merges with a two-participant verb, one participant of *naar* 'to' and one of *duwen* 'push' merge. The resulting transition in (28) denotes a pushing event in which *y/z* (the car) ends up at the side, *w*.

The merging of two event participants is a similar process to Higginbotham's (1985) θ-Identification. Higginbotham applies θ-identification to account for the predicate-argument properties in adjectival modification (e.g., *a big butterfly*). The external arguments of adjective and noun merge in θ-identification (so that, for example, a *big butterfly* is: an x such that BUTTERFLY(x) & BIG(x)). Hollebrandse (1993) uses Higginbotham's θ-identification to analyze light verb constructions, merging the underspecified θ-roles of the light verb with those of the light verb complement (e.g., in *een kus geven* 'give a kiss' the internal and external roles of the noun *kus* 'kiss' merge with the underspecified internal and external roles of light *geven* 'give'). The same mechanism has also been applied for predicate-argument relations in complex predicates. θ-identification is employed in a system for the percolation of θ-roles which sometimes involves merging them by Neeleman & Schipper (1992) to account for *ver*-prefixation and by Neeleman & Weerman (1993) to account for particles and resultative constructions. Neeleman (1994) uses the percolation mechanism to account for the θ-relations in (certain) complex predicate structures, amalgamating the θ-roles of the verb and those of the predicate (e.g., the θ-roles of *groen* 'green' [THEME_j] and *verven* 'paint' [AGENT_i, THEME_j] percolate up to derive the complex predicate *groen verven* 'paint green' [AGENT_i, THEME_j]). Hoekstra (1992) uses θ-identification to analyze the thematic relations in (intransitive) resultative predicates. The common idea in these merging operations across different kinds of constructions is that the semantic functor-argument relations are preserved in the θ-relations, or, alternatively, in present terminology, in the relations between event participants and the (sub)events they are involved in.

Event type composition applies in those cases where the particle or PP complement contributes essentially to the building of the inner aspectual event type of the VP. Hence, the verb and the "goal" phrase are aspectually connected. Adjunct PPs are not connected to the verb, as they do not contribute to the inner aspect. This event-semantic analysis of the relation between the verb and particles or PP complements parallels syntactic observations on the relation between a verb and a "goal" phrase. Alluding to an intuitive notion of being "connected" to the verb, van Riemsdijk (1978) argues that PP complements (which he calls *subcategorized PP adjuncts*) are more closely connected to the verb than PP adjuncts which are not connected at all. The degree of connectedness correlates with the possibility of extraction out of the PP: the more closely a PP is connected with the verb, the easier it is to extract elements from it.

The close connection between PP complements and verbs is found as well in various proposals for the syntactic configuration in which they are projected. One type of analysis is the so-called *complex predicate approach* in which the verb and the "goal" PP syntactically form a complex predicate. While it dates back to Chomsky (1955), there are various recent implementations of this approach. Larson (1988) argues that a PP complement is a sister of V; it syntactically reconstructs with V to become a complex transitive verb which then assigns the "theme" role to the direct object. Larson assumes that the PP is a lexically selected complement of V and is assigned a θ-role by it. As he adheres to strictly local θ-assignment, PP must be a sister of V. In order to also accommodate θ-assignment to the direct object, Larson proposes a doubly-layered VP projection with a lower and a higher VP-shell. Neeleman (1994) also assumes that PP complements form a syntactically complex predicate with the verb. Moreover, he analyzes particle verbs such as *weglopen* 'walk away' as morphologically complex predicates. The external θ-role of the PP or particle percolates up in the complex predicate to unify with the θ-roles of the V and is assigned by the complex predicate to the direct object. Koster (1993) postulates a special functional projection, the predicate phrase (PredP), into the specifier position of which a PP complement moves (or, rather, any element that is part of the predicate). The verb and the PP complement thus form a complex predicate in the PredP.

Alternatively, there is the *small clause (SC) approach* to accounting for the connection between verbs and PP complements. In SC-analyses, the PP complement is an SC predicate selected by the verb in which the direct object is a "subject" of the PP (see Stowell 1981; Kayne 1984; Hoekstra 1984; Hoekstra & Mulder 1990). In a similar approach, den Dikken (1992) proposes an SC-analysis for particle verbs in which the particle heads an SC and the direct object is a "subject" of the particle. Hoekstra & Mulder (1990) furthermore discuss several syntactic tests that distinguish between adjunct and complement PPs in Dutch, which they then account for in a SC analysis (including optionality of the PP, postverbal position of the PP, PP-adverb-verb order, independent stress on the verb).

Event type composition is a purely semantic operation and is defined independently of the morpho-syntactic configuration in which a verb and PP or particle appear. On conceptual grounds, however, it seems to combine better with a complex predicate approach, given the isomorphy between semantic and syntactic structures (see also Verkuyl 1993 who draws a similar conclusion).

Notice that from an event-semantic perspective, "goal" particles and PPs have the same function: they describe the transition and/or end state of an event. So, it follows as a natural consequence that both particles and PPs can form a complex predicate with the verb. Hence, the particle-PP alternation (see Chapter 2) is a natural kind of alternation. This parallel between "goal" complements and particles cannot be easily drawn, let alone explained, if one analyzes PP complements as arguments of the verb, lexically selected as a "goal" θ-role, as an indirect internal argument, or as a PATH LCS-variable. Particles are never considered an argument of or lexically selected by the verb. The similarity between particles and PPs lies in their contribution to the aspectual make-up of the sentence, hence, argument-centered mapping theories cannot account for it.

Clearly, not every verb that denotes a process can combine with a "goal" phrase and become a complex predicate. Consider the small set of verbs that were compared above for their event participant properties. Some verbs can combine with an additional "goal" and some cannot: *lopen* 'walk', *rollen* 'roll', *duwen* 'push', *geven* 'give' and *zetten* 'put' can; however, *regenen* 'rain', *slapen* 'sleep', *martelen* 'torture', *praten* 'talk' and *eten* 'eat' cannot. In fact, *geven* 'give' and *zetten* 'put' need to combine with a "goal". The fact that certain verbs can take a "goal" phrase whereas others cannot points toward a semantic difference between them, i.e., whether or not the verb expresses (abstract) motion. The semantic property motion functions as a selection restriction with respect to event type composition with a "goal" phrase: adding an abstract or concrete "goal" to a process event requires that the event can express "moving" toward a goal in the first place. If it is violated, it leads to semantic anomaly, not to ungrammaticality.

As for motion verbs, the fact that some verbs take a "goal" phrase optionally, whereas others take it obligatorily, needs to be accounted for by the mapping system. In the event-semantic approach advocated here, PP complements are not lexically selected by the verb (at least, not in the sense that a PP complement is an argument of the verb). Still, some verbs (e.g., *geven* 'give' and *zetten* 'put') select an obligatory PP complement. I assume that the basic event type of verbs with an obligatory "goal" is a transition. Whereas the verb itself describes the process and/or transition part of the transition, another predicate is needed to describe the final state. Hence, these verbs must combine with a PP complement or a particle. On the other hand, manner of motion verbs (e.g., *lopen* 'walk', *rollen* 'roll', *duwen* 'push') denote a process as their basic event type. Only when they event type-shift to a telic event do they need to combine with a "goal" which then describes the end state. Hence, in an event-semantic approach, the effect that certain verbs obligatorily select a PP is not a primitive, as it is in argument-centered approaches; rather, it is derived from the need to fully specify the event (see also subsections 4.6.1 and 4.8.1 on event identification).

Complex word formation: particle and prefixed verbs

The operation of event type composition has a wide array of applications. It also applies to prefixed and particle verbs. The data in Chapters 2 and 3 show that lexical-syntactic flexibility in Dutch is often accompanied by morphological effects. Often, the difference between a base verb and its prefixed and particle variants is a difference in event type. By assuming that particles and prefixes also have event structure, the event type properties of complex verbs can be transparently derived from those of the simplex verb and the prefix or particle. Hence, event type composition also accounts for the complex event type of particle and prefixed verbs.

Combining a verb that denotes a process with a particle that denotes a state derives a complex verb in which the event type has been composed to form a transition from a process to a final state (e.g., *opeten* 'eat up'), or, vice versa, from a beginning state to a process (e.g., *afreizen* 'start traveling'). The former kind of event type composition is illustrated for *opeten* 'eat up' in (29).

(29) Event type composition applied to *eten* 'eat' and particle *op* 'up':

P	&	S	→	T	
x, y		*z*			
eten		*op*		P	S
				x, y/z	*x, y/z*
				opeten	

Some other two-participant particle verbs that involve a similar form of event type composition include: *afduwen* 'push off'; *opschrijven* 'write up'; *afschrijven* 'finish writing'; *uitschrijven* 'write out'; *afknippen* 'cut off'; *afluisteren* 'listen in'; *opgraven* 'dig up'; *afgraven* 'dig off'; *uitgraven* 'dig out'; *uitpraten* 'settle by talking'; *uitlezen* 'read to the end (lit. read out)'; *uitrekenen* 'calculate'; *opsplitsen* 'split up'; *uitsplitsen* 'split out'; *uitwassen* 'wash out'; *oproken* 'smoke up'; *uitroken* 'smoke out'; *instuderen* 'learn'; *natekenen* 'copy'; *afrollen* 'roll off'; *oprollen* 'roll up'. Some one-participant particle verbs include: *inslapen* 'fall asleep', *opgroeien* 'grow up'; *opdrogen* 'dry up'; *opbloeien* 'revive'; *uitbranden* 'burn out'; *overkoken* 'boil over'; *inkoken* 'become less by boiling'.

Whether or not there is an event type-shift between root and particle verb, depends on the aspectual meaning of the particle. Some particles denote a process. In this case, combining a verb and a particle that both denote a process, event type composition reduces to event type merging. It creates a complex verb in which both processes have merged. *Door* 'on' and *mee* 'along' are productive process particles; they combine with any process verb (e.g., *doorschrijven* 'write on'; *meeschrijven* 'write along'; *dooreten* 'eat on'; *meeëten* 'eat along'; *doorpraten* 'talk continuously'; *meepraten* 'talk along'). Other particles sometimes have a similar effect; they do not change the event type: the root verb as well as the particle verb are atelic (e.g., *uitslapen* 'sleep late' and *aanduwen* 'push (to get something running)'). Event structure merging is illustrated for *meeëten* 'eat along' in (30).

(30) Event type composition applied to *eten* 'eat' and particle *mee* 'along':

P	&	P	→	P
x, y				***x, y***
eten		*mee*		*meeëten*

Notice that *mee* 'along' does not take an event participant; the same holds for other process particles. They cannot be predicated of an event participant themselves, but need to combine with a verb. So, they select another process predicate to compose with.

Atelic particles cannot combine with verbs that inherently denote a transition (e.g., **doordoden* '*kill on'; **meedoden* '*kill along'; **doorvinden* '*find on'; **meevinden* '*find along'; **meebreken* '*break along'). This has a natural explanation in the present proposal: there is no way for event type composition, including event structure merging, to combine a transition and a process.

There is no event type-shift either for the following set of particle verbs. Combining a verb that already denotes a transition and a particle that denotes a state yields a complex verb in which the latter state merges with the final state of the transition. This is illustrated in (31) for *doorbreken* 'break through'.

(31) Event type composition applied to *breken* 'break' and particle *door* 'through':

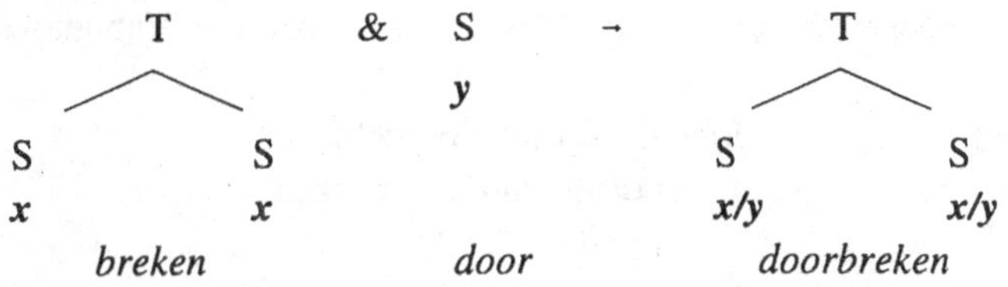

While *breken* 'break' by itself already specifies its resulting state (i.e., being broken), the state denoted by the particle further specifies it (i.e., being broken into two). In this sense, the particle functions semantically as a modifier of the verb. Some other examples with one- and two-participant verbs include: *uitbreken* 'break out'; *afbreken* 'break off'; *doorsmelten* 'melt through'; *uitvallen* 'fall out'; *omvallen* 'fall down'; *invallen* 'collapse'; *uitgeven* 'spend'; *doorgeven* 'pass on'; *aanzetten* 'put on'; *uitzetten* 'put off'.

Different particles have different aspectual effects on a verb, depending on their meaning. Consider the variants of *slapen* 'sleep'. *Slapen* 'sleep' by itself is atelic, (32a); *inslapen* 'fall asleep' denotes an inchoative transition between a state and a process of sleeping, (32b); *uitslapen* 'sleep in' denotes a process of sleeping long, (32c).

(32) a. Winnie heeft dagenlang geslapen.
W. has days-long slept
'W. slept for days.'

b. Winnie was binnen 5 minuten ingeslapen.
W. was within 5 minutes in-slept
'W. fell asleep within 5 minutes.'

c. Winnie heeft urenlang uitgeslapen.
W. has hours-long out-slept
'W. slept in for hours.'

Confusingly, some particles are ambiguous. In combination with some verbs, the particle adds a telic aspect, whereas in combination with others it focuses the atelic aspect (e.g., telic *doorbreken* 'break through' versus atelic *doorschrijven* 'write on'). Even in combination with one and the same verb, it may have either effect. Consider *door* 'on, through' as it combines with *lopen* 'walk'; *doorlopen* 'walk on' is ambiguous, (33).

(33) a. John heeft flink doorgelopen.
J. has firmly through-walked
'J. walked on firmly.'
b. John is meteen weer doorgelopen.
J. is immediately again through-walked
'J. immediately continued to walk again.'

As the glosses in (33) indicate, *doorlopen* 'walk on' is ambiguous between a telic and an atelic interpretation: the particle either denotes a process and merges with the process denoted by the verb yielding atelic *walk on*, (33a), or, it denotes a transition and the process denoted by the verb merges into it as its second subevent yielding telic *continue to walk*, (33b). Notice also the different auxiliary choices: HAVE in atelic (33a) and BE in telic (33b).

In similar ways, Dutch prefixes *ver-*, *be-* and *ont-* often add a telic aspect to the verb they attach to. I assume that in these cases, the prefix denotes a transition; event type composition composes the event types of verb and prefix, deriving the complex event type of the prefixed verb (see Schipper 1994 who works out the same idea for *ont-*). Event type composition proceeds in the same way as with particle verbs. Consider prefix *ver-* attached to process verb *branden* 'burn' which gives telic *verbranden* 'burn', (34).

(34) Event type composition applied to *branden* 'burn' and prefix *ver-*:

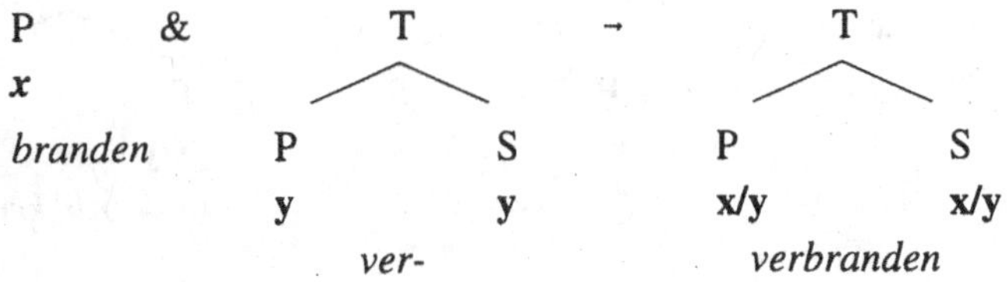

Some more examples of telic prefixed variants of atelic root verbs with one participant include: *zich verslapen* 'oversleep'; *verlopen* 'expire'; *vervliegen* 'evaporate'; *verslijten* 'wear out'; *verdrogen* 'dry out'; *verrotten* 'rot away'; *verhongeren* 'starve'; *verdwalen* 'get lost'; *verdampen* 'evaporate'; *verspringen* 'jump (to another spot)'; *verregenen* 'get spoiled by rain'; *ontbranden* 'ignite'; *ontbloeien* 'start to bloom'; *ontspringen* 'spring from'; *ontslapen* 'pass away'; *ontkiemen* 'germinate'; *ontwaken* 'wake up'. Some examples of telic prefixed verbs with two participants include: *verwerken* 'work into'; *verzorgen* 'take care of'; *verbinden* 'connect'; *vervlechten* 'interweave'; *verjagen* 'chase away'; *ontcijferen* 'decipher'; *beschrijven* 'describe'; *beschilderen* 'paint'; *besmeren* 'smear onto'; *beluisteren* 'listen to'; *bespreken* 'discuss'; *verschuiven* 'shift'.

Ver- is a productive prefix for deriving de-adjectival verbs, e.g., *vergelen* 'become yellow'; *vergrijzen* 'become gray'; *verbleken* 'lose color'; *verkleuren* 'change color'; *verarmen* 'become impoverished'; *verdikken* 'thicken'; *vervetten* 'become fat'; *verdrogen* 'dry out'. Many *ver*+adjective verbs denote a transition between a process and a state in which the state is specified by the adjective. For example, for *verdikken* 'thicken', the end state is being thick. Assuming that adjectives denote a state (at least, that stage level adjectives do, following Kratzer 1989), one can derive these de-adjectival *ver*-verbs via event type composition. Consider *verdikken* 'thicken', (35).

(35) Event type composition applied to *dik* 'thick' and prefix *ver-*:

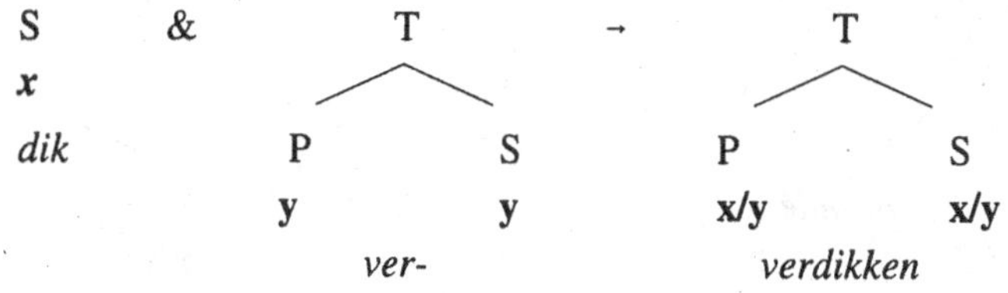

Prefixes do not always lead to an event type-shift. If the prefix combines with a verb that inherently denotes a transition, the two transitions (of verb and prefix) merge, e.g., *versmelten* 'melt together'; *vervallen* 'expire'; *verbreken* 'break up'; *verzetten* 'move'; *verleggen* 'displace'. Consider this event structure merging for *versmelten* 'melt together', (36).

(36) Event type composition applied to *smelten* 'melt' and prefix *ver-*:

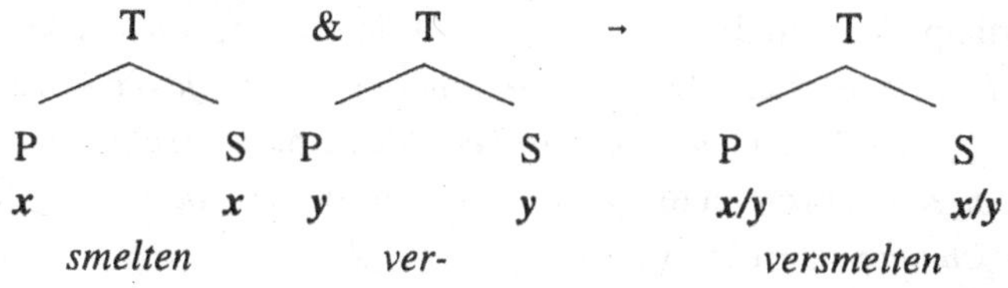

The semantic contribution of *ver-* in these cases in which two transitions merge is to further specify the final state: *versmelten* 'melt together' is melting to the effect that two things get together. Similarly, *verbreken* 'separate (lit. PFX-break)' is a breaking event with the effect that two things get separated.

Notice that the root verbs *zetten* 'put' and *leggen* 'lay' take an obligatory "goal" phrase to identify the final state of the transition. Their *ver*-variants *verzetten* 'displace' and *verleggen* 'displace', however, do not take a "goal" phrase. Prefix *ver-* sufficiently specifies the final state, adding "to another location" to the meaning of the root verb.

Prefixes *be-*, *ver-* and *ont-* not always trigger an event type-shift when they combine with a process verb. Sometimes, they only change the focus on the event (see Chapter 3, section 3.6 for some discussion of different kinds of foci). Some examples of atelic prefixed verbs are: *belopen* 'walk on'; *beslapen* 'sleep on'; *berijden* 'ride on'; *bevaren* 'sail on'; *bekijken* 'examine'; *bewerken* 'edit'; *beschieten* 'shoot at'; *bedreigen* 'threaten'; *besproeien* 'spray'; *begieten* 'water'; *bespuiten* 'spray'; *verzwijgen* 'conceal'; *verbergen* 'hide'; *ontlopen* 'outrun'. In these cases, I assume the prefix does not denote a transition, but, rather, a process. Hence, I conclude that the prefixes *be-*, *ver-* and *ont-*, like particles, are ambiguous: sometimes they denote a process and sometimes a transition.

Notice that for some of these verbs, the prefix adds an event participant: the prefixed verb has two participants whereas the root verb only takes one. For example: *lopen-belopen* 'walk-walk on something'; *slapen-beslapen* 'sleep-sleep on something'; *rijden-berijden* 'ride-ride something'; *varen-bevaren* 'sail-sail on something'; *lopen-ontlopen* 'walk-outrun'. This has been analyzed in other approaches as an effect of (lexically or syntactically) incorporating a preposition into the verb, whereby the internal argument of the preposition becomes an argument of the complex verb. See, for instance, Hoekstra (1992) and Mulder (1992) for a syntactic incorporation analysis of Dutch causative *be-* and *ver-*verbs and Wunderlich (1987) and Brinkmann (1995) for a lexical P-incorporation analysis of German *be-*verbs. Van Hout & Haverkort (1995) present an analysis of Dutch *be-*verbs in terms of the present event-semantic framework, comparing them to applicative constructions in Bantu languages.

While complex predicate formation is semantically completely transparent and fully productive, this is not always the case in the domain of complex word formation, i.e., particle and prefixed verbs. It is much less transparent, as a certain particle in combination with different verbs acquires different meanings; compare, for example, *uitlezen* 'read to the end (lit. read out)', *uitvallen* 'fall out' and *uitroken* 'get out by smoking'. It is also much less productive in that one cannot combine just any verb with just any particle or prefix. Many particle-verb and prefix-verb combinations are lexically fixed. Moreover, they often have idiosyncratic selection restrictions which differ from those of the root verb (see also section 4.9 below). Still, in almost all cases, the combination of a verb with a particle or prefix is aspectually transparent; it can be accounted for in terms of event type composition.

Several people have recently employed the operation of event type composition for particle and prefixed verbs in various languages. Van Hout (1991b, 1992a,b, 1994) shows that event type composition takes place in the formation of Dutch particle verbs and Russian and Hungarian prefixed verbs. Schipper (1994) analyzes *ont*-prefixation in Dutch as an operation of event type composition in which *ont*- adds an inchoative aspect. Davis & Demirdache (1995) propose that transitivizing and detransitivizing affixes in Lillooet Salish specify their own event types which compose with that of the verb (see also Davis 1997, in press; Demirdache 1997). Similar aspectual approaches to analyzing particle and prefixed verbs have been proposed by Tenny (1987, 1994) and Verkuyl (1993). Furthermore, other kinds of analyses express ideas similar to the idea that the particle or prefix has its own lexical specification (e.g., its own θ-grid, argument structure or LCS) which merges with that of the verb. Some have been formalized in LCS terminology, e.g., Booij (1992); Lieber & Baayen (1993); others have been formalized in terms of θ-roles, e.g., Neeleman & Schipper (1992); Neeleman & Weerman (1993); Neeleman (1994).

In conclusion, assuming that particles and prefixes are listed with their own event type specification explains the regular pattern of verb pairs that exhibit an atelic-telic event type-shift. Hence, event type composition is a general mechanism that also extends into the morphological domain. The discussion of event type composition and prefixes above is only a rough sketch. The issue of prefixation is much more complex. I have mentioned, but not discussed, the effect of focusing on particular properties of the event. Furthermore, prefixation also involves de-nominal and de-adjectival verbs which I have not touched upon at all here. I leave the aspectual exploration of the morphological domain for further research (see e.g., van Hout & Haverkort 1995).

Resultative formation

A third case in which event type composition accounts for an atelic-telic event type-shift is resultative formation (for similar aspectual accounts, see Tenny 1987, 1994; Pustejovsky 1991; Hoekstra 1992). Resultative formation is an operation that combines a verb that denotes a process with another predicate that denotes a state, yielding a transition between the process and the state. The process can be expressed by a one- or two-participant verb. The state can be expressed by an adjective or a PP which takes its own participant(s). In the case of resultative formation, event type composition results in the addition of some kind of temporal scale to the process denoted by the verb; the resultative predicate specifies the kind of scale. In the same way, a "goal" phrase adds a directional scale to a motion verb in complex predicate formation above. The event evolves along this scale, until the end state is reached. The basic analysis of resultative formation is alluded to in Chapter 3, section 3.4.2. I will review it here and discuss it with more details, in order to show that it fits into the larger picture of event type composition.

Consider first transitive resultative formation: a two-participant process verb, *martelen* 'torture', (37a), combines with a stative adjective, *dood* 'dead' to derive *doodmartelen* 'torture to death', (37b). The event type-shift is depicted in (38).

(37) a. De diktator heeft de gevangene urenlang gemarteld.
the dictator has the prisoner hours-long tortured
'The dictator tortured the prisoner for hours.'

b. De diktator heeft de gevangene binnen een uur doodgemarteld.
the dictator has the prisoner within an hour dead-tortured
'The dictator tortured the prisoner to death in an hour.'

(38) Event type composition applied to *martelen* 'torture' and *dood* 'dead':

P & S → T
x, y *z*
martelen *dood*

T
P S
x, y/z *x, y/z*
doodmartelen

Notice that event type composition in transitive resultative formation as in (38) is identical to event type composition in complex predicate formation with a two-participant process verb and a "goal" phrase, e.g., *naar de kant duwen* 'push to the side' in (28). In both cases, a process verb type-shifts to a transition and two event participants merge.

Unlike complex predicate formation, resultative formation does not always involve an accompanying merging of an event participant of the verb with one of the resultative predicate. This is the case when it applies to a one-participant verb in intransitive resultative formation: the two subevents remain independent. Consider the one-participant process verb *zwemmen* 'swim' in resultative formation, (39). The event type-shift is depicted in (40).

(39) a. Claartje heeft de hele zomer in zee gezwommen.
C. has the whole summer in sea swam
'C. swam in the sea during the whole summer.'

b. Claartje heeft haar badpak al in één zomer aan flarden gezwommen.
C. has her swimsuit already within one summer to tatters swam
'C. swam her swimsuit to tatters within just one summer.'

(40) Event type composition applied to *zwemmen* 'swim' and *aan flarden* 'to tatters':

P	&	S	→	T
x		*y*		P S
zwemmen		*aan flarden*		*x* *y*
				aan flarden zwemmen

The composed predicate *aan flarden zwemmen* 'swim to tatters' takes two participants. They are completely independent of each other, as each participant is only involved in its own subevent (i.e., the *Claartje* is the swimmer and *the swimming suit* goes to tatters in (39b)). The relation between the two events is accidental; one can relate them by infering, on the basis of one's knowledge about swimming (which is often done in a swimming suit) and swimming suits (they wear out when exposed to seawater a lot).

So, for one-participant verbs, event type composition in intransitive resultative formation as in (40) and complex predicate formation (e.g., *weglopen* 'walk away' in (26) and *de baan op rollen* 'roll onto the court' in (27)) are similar, but not quite the same: both involve a one-participant process verb and an additional final state. The difference lies in whether or not the event participants of the subevents merge: in complex predicate formation, (26) and (27), they do, but in intransitive resultative formation, (40), they do not. Hence, the resultative predicate ends up with two event participants and maps onto a transitive frame, whereas the complex predicate ends up with one (merged) participant and maps onto an unaccusative frame.

The participants in the subevents of an intransitive resultative predicate can accidentally be the same. Consider resultative formation with *zwemmen* 'swim' in (41).

(41) De gevangene heeft zich binnen 5 maanden uit de gevangenis gezwommen.
the prisoner has himself within 5 months out the prison swam
'The prisoner swam himself out of prison within 5 months.' (adapted from Seibert 1993)

The swimmer and the one leaving prison are the same person in (41). However, the relation between the two is accidental: it is a co-reference relation, rather than a merging of event participants, as the subevents still remain independent of each other.

One can construct a resultative event with two independent subevents out of a two-participant process verb as well, but only by not projecting one of these two participants, (42). The two-participant process verb *martelen* 'torture' only projects the torturer participant; the resultative predicate in (42a) projects its own participant, i.e., *zijn vingers* 'his fingers'. There is no way to project both participants of the verb and an independent participant of the resulting state, (42b).

(42) a. De diktator martelde zijn vingers stuk.
'The dictator tortured his fingers broken.'
b. *De diktator martelde de gevangene zijn vingers stuk.[29]
The dictator tortured the prisoner his fingers broken

There is no event-semantic reason to exclude event type composition of a two-participant process and an independent resulting state; it is semantically conceivable to torture a prisoner to such an extent that one's fingers break. Hence, there must be another reason for the impossibility of (42b). I assume that the ungrammaticality of (42b) lies in the mapping system: there are not enough argument positions to map the participants onto. Hoekstra (1988) explains this fact within an SC-approach: a verb can project only one complement, either an object or an SC. Carrier & Randall (1992) propose an account in terms of Case: (42b) is out, because there is only one accusative Case available; one cannot have two direct objects.[30]

Notice that in the case of one-participant verbs, a similar mapping (or Case) problem does not arise: the single participant either merges with that of the resultative predicate (which leads to complex predicate formation as in (26) and (27)) or it does not merge (which leads to resultative formation as in (40) and (41)). In either case, two argument positions suffice to map the event participants onto.

Carrier & Randall (1992) further point out that the verb exerts selection restrictions over the object only in the case of transitive resultative formation. In intransitive resultative formation the choice of the object is only restricted by selection restrictions of the resultative predicate (and pragmatic considerations, whether or not it makes sense to connect a particular process to a particular state). Carrier & Randall account for this by analyzing the direct object of a transitive resultative predicate as an argument of the verb as well as the resultative predicate. The direct object of an intransitive resultative predicate, on the other hand, is an argument of the predicate only. This explanation carries over in an event type composition perspective in a natural way: as the event participants merge, the selection restrictions of both verb and resultative predicate fuse, as well, and together they restrict the choice of object. Merging only applies in transitive resultative formation, hence the verb can only exert its influence on the participant that appears in object position in transitive resultative formation.

Finally, consider intransitive and transitive *breken* 'break' in the following "resultative" constructions, (43) and (44).

(43) a. Het ei brak.
'The egg broke.'
b. Het ei brak kapot.
'The egg broke to pieces.'

(44) a. Inge brak het ei.
'I. broke the egg.'
b. Inge brak het ei kapot.
'I. broke the egg to pieces.'

There is no event type-shifting between the a- and b-sentences in (43) and (44): the verb denotes a transition in all instances. Therefore, they do not belong to the class of resultative formation, even though these constructions look very similar to the ones discussed above. Yet, they involve event structure merging. *Breken* 'break' (both the one- and the two-participant variant) denotes a transition. Event structure merging merges the final state of the transition with the state denoted by the adjective *kapot* 'to pieces', in the same way as the merging of event types for particle verb *doorbreken* 'break through' in (31). One event participant of the verb and that of the adjective merge, as well. Hence, after event structure merging, the final state of the breaking event is specified more precisely. In this sense, *kapot* 'to pieces' is a modifier of the final state (for a similar analysis of this construction, see Jackendoff 1990; Pustejovsky 1991; Levin & Rappaport Hovav 1995).

Summary of event type composition

To conclude, verbs differ from each other with respect to their lexical event types. Event type-shifting can change a verb's lexical event type, for example in an atelic-telic event type-shift. I have introduced the operation of event type composition. Event type composition is a general mechanism that accounts for atelic-telic event type shifts that characterize syntactically complex predicates as well as morphologically ones. I have derived the fact that some verbs can combine with a "goal" phrase from their ability to event type-shift to a transition; a particle or PP complement is then needed to specify the resulting or inchoative state in the transition. Verbs that take an obligatory "goal" phrase inherently denote a transition and need a PP or particle (or prefix *ver-*) to specify the final state. Furthermore, I have shown how event type composition can account for the complex event types of particle and prefixed verbs. Finally, I have discussed event type composition in resultative formation; in a resultative predicate, the event types of the verb and the resultative predicate form one complex event type. Like inherently telic verbs, all telic verbs and predicates that are derived via event type composition take an argument in object position. Notice that Simpson's (1983) generalization over the different forms of resultative formation (that the argument in object position has to be the "subject" of the resultative predicate) can now be subsumed under the more general generalization that all telic events need to map the participant involved in the final state of a transition to object position.

Next, I discuss another kind of atelic-telic event type-shifting based on the lexical property some verbs have: an inherent temporal scale.

4.7.2 Deconstructing atelic-telic event type-shifting: a temporal scale

The instances of atelic-telic event type shifting in the previous subsection involve a verb that denotes a process and combines with another predicate that supplies the transition or final state; the derived complex predicate, complex word or resultative predicate denotes a telic event. Another kind of atelic-telic event type-shift occurs without event type composition. A verb such as *eten* 'eat' can denote a telic event by itself. Consider *eten* 'eat' in some of its atelic and telic occurrences, (45).

(45) a. Maribel heeft dagenlang niet gegeten.
M. has days-long not eaten
'M. did not eat for days.'

b. Maribel heeft dagenlang van de appeltaart gegeten.
M has days-long of the apple-pie eten
'M. ate from the apple pie for days.'

c. Maribel heeft in 10 minuten een hele appeltaart gegeten.
M. has in 10 minutes a whole apple-pie eaten
'M. ate a whole apple pie in 10 minutes.'

In an intransitive, (45a), and in an oblique intransitive frame, (45b), *eten* 'eat' denotes an atelic eating event; in the transitive frame, (45c), *eten* 'eat' denotes an accomplishment. The verb does not need an external phrase to specify what the end state of a telic eating event involves; the telic event evolves along a certain temporal scale which is inherently part of its meaning. For *eten* 'eat', this scale involves the incremental eating away at whatever is eaten (in (45), an apple pie). The endpoint is reached when the food is gone.

Notice importantly that the event is telic only if the "food" participant is mapped onto object position, as in (45c). When it is not projected at all, (45a), or when it appears in an oblique position, (45b), the event is atelic. Apparently, the verb's capability to measure out the event is strictly associated with the presence of a participant in object position. Hence, the event type-shifting outcome for a verb with an inherent temporal scale depends crucially on the syntactic configuration it appears in, i.e., whether or not there is a participant in object position.

On top of this syntactic requirement, there is also a semantic requirement: the quantificational properties of the object determine whether or not the event is telic. Consider the event type differences in (46) ((46a) = (45c)).

(46) a. Maribel heeft in 10 minuten een hele appeltaart gegeten.
M. has in 10 minutes a whole apple-pie eaten
'M. ate a whole apple pie in 10 minutes.'

b. Maribel heeft urenlang appeltaart gegeten.
M has hours-long apple-pie eaten
'M. ate apple pie for hours.'

Even though there is an object in both cases, only (46a) denotes a telic event while (46b) denotes an atelic event. Verkuyl (1972) points out that this difference must be traceable to the semantic properties of the object: only quantized NPs induce a telic event type-shift (e.g., *een hele appeltaart* 'a whole apple pie' in (46a)); bare nouns do not (e.g., *appeltaart* 'apple pie' in (46b)). In section 4.8.2, I will review these effects of the semantic properties of the object. In order to integrate them into the mapping system, I will associate these semantic properties with syntactic properties, in particular, Case, along the lines of de Hoop (1992).

Many verbs imply similar temporal scales along which the event evolves. For example, *schrijven* 'write' involves some text coming into existence as it is incrementally getting written, *bouwen* 'build' involves some building coming into existence and *roken* 'smoke' involves something smokable being smoked out of existence. However, contrary to *eten* 'eat' and similar verbs, other verbs do not have such a temporal scale, for example, *duwen* 'push' and *martelen* 'torture' do not. Compare the latter two verbs in transitive frames, (47). ((47a) and (47b) are repeated from (25a) and (37a) above.)

(47) a. Paola heeft urenlang de auto geduwd.
P. has hours-long the car pushed
'P. pushed the car for hours.'
b. De diktator heeft de gevangene urenlang gemarteld.
the dictator has the prisoner hours-long tortured
'The dictator tortured the prisoner for hours.'

Even though *duwen* 'push' and *martelen* 'torture' in (47) map their two participants onto a transitive frame and have quantized objects, they denote atelic events. The two verbs are similar to *eten* 'eat' in that they basically denote a process that takes two event participants; however, they cannot event type-shift to a telic event in the same way as *eten* 'eat' can. Apparently, *eten* 'eat' and similar verbs intrinsically involve a temporal scale which becomes activated when there is a quantized NP in object position; *duwen* 'push', *martelen* 'torture' and their counterparts lack this property. Given that these verbs are similar in all other respects, it must be considered a lexical property that divides process verbs into two kinds: certain verbs intrinsically have a temporal scale; others do not. As it influences mapping, or, rather, the aspectual interpretation of syntactic configurations, it belongs to a verb's lexical-syntactic features. I will refer to it as a verb's *temporal scale*.

While *duwen* 'push' and *martelen* 'torture' do not have an inherent temporal scale, the events can be measured out if an external scale is provided. Hence, when pushing evolves toward a certain goal, (48a), or when torturing is done to a certain, explicitly stated extent, (48b), the events become telic. In other words, they undergo atelic-telic event type-shifting when there is event type composition. ((48a) and (48b) are repeated from (25b) and (37b), respectively.)

(48) a. Paola duwde de auto in 5 minuten naar de kant.
P. pushed the car in 5 minutes to the side
'P. pushed the car to the side in 5 minutes.'

b. De diktator heeft de gevangene binnen een uur doodgemarteld.
the dictator has the prisoner within an hour dead-tortured
'The dictator tortured the prisoner to death in an hour.'

Hence, the difference between the *eten* 'eat'-class and the *duwen* 'push'-class is how the telicity of the event comes about: for the *eten* 'eat'-class, the temporal scale and its endpoint are provided by the inherent semantics of the verb; for the *duwen* 'push'-class, it is externally determined by a PP complement, particle, prefix or resultative complement. In both kinds of telic events, the semantic function of the participant in object position is the same: it is the participant that identifies the final state.

In the aspectual literature, the property of inherent temporal scale has received various names. Dowty (1979) characterizes verbs that denote a telic event when they appear in a transitive frame as verbs that select an incremental theme. The "theme" of *eten* 'eat' is an incremental theme, but those of *duwen* 'push' and *martelen* 'torture' are not. In Tenny's (1987, 1994) terminology, a verb measures out the event when it develops along a certain scale. The internal argument of *eten* 'eat' measures out the event, but those of *duwen* 'push' and *martelen* 'torture' do not. Verkuyl (1993) presents the nicest term for these verbs, characterizing them as verbs with an inherent odometer. The odometer property refers to whether or not the event denoted by the verb somehow develops along a certain path or toward a certain goal or culmination point. *Eten* 'eat' is positively specified for this odometer feature; *martelen* 'torture' and *duwen* 'push' are not.[31] The basic notion behind these different terms is the notion of a temporal scale along which the "theme" participant is involved in the event. Dowty, Tenny and Verkuyl share the idea that this notion is inherent in the meaning of the verb.

As for other two-participant verbs, *praten* 'talk' is in the *duwen* 'push'-class and has no temporal scale; *geven* 'give' and *zetten* 'put' are in the *eten* 'eat'-class and have a temporal scale. In the same way, one can classify one-participant verbs. Verbs such as *lopen* 'walk', *rollen* 'roll', *slapen* 'sleep', *rinkelen* 'ring' and *regenen* 'rain' do not have a temporal scale. On the other hand, verbs such as *smelten* 'melt', *vallen* 'fall' and *breken* 'break' do. Notice that all inherent transition verbs also have a temporal scale. By event-semantic definition, the event type of transition involves a temporal scale with a certain endpoint along which the event evolves. Hence, temporal scale is a lexical property that divides process verbs into two sets.[32]

Event type-shifting to a telic event type is limited to non-stative verbs. By event-semantic definition, one cannot impose a temporal scale onto a state, since a state is not dynamic. Hence, stative verbs are inherently atelic; they cannot type-shift to a transitional type (e.g., *liefhebben* 'love', *haten* 'hate', *vertrouwen* 'trust', *verwachten* 'expect', *kennen* 'know', *weten* 'know', *geloven,* 'believe', *veronderstellen* 'suppose ', *aannemen* 'assume', *onthouden* 'remember').

This concludes the discussion of the different ways of atelic-telic event type-shifting. Next, I will deconstruct the event type properties of causativization.

4.7.3 Deconstructing causativization

In Chapter 3, section 3.5, I discussed the event-semantic properties of causativization. After reviewing these analyses, I will briefly address the issue of which verbs can and which cannot undergo causativization.

There are two kinds of causativization patterns: those with and those without an event type-shift. The subeventual make-up of the resulting causative event determines which of these two patterns is followed. I have argued that there are two different kinds of causative events: integrated and bi-eventual causative events. An integrated causative event denotes a transition which is one integrated event, (49);[33] a bi-eventual causative event denotes a transition that is separable into two independent subevents: the causing and the caused event, (50).

(49) Causativization to an integrated causative event:

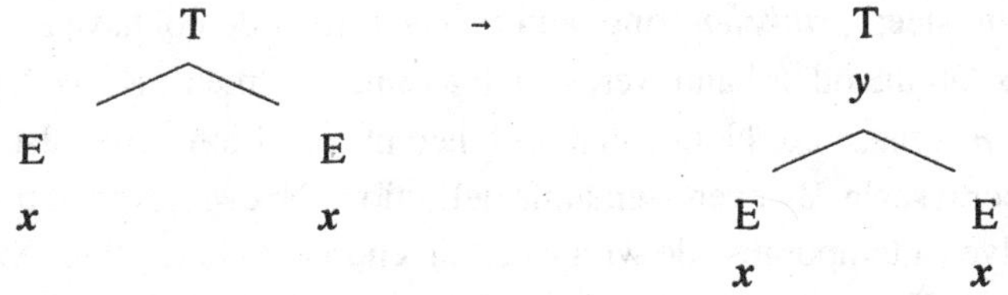

(50) Causativization to a bi-eventual causative event:

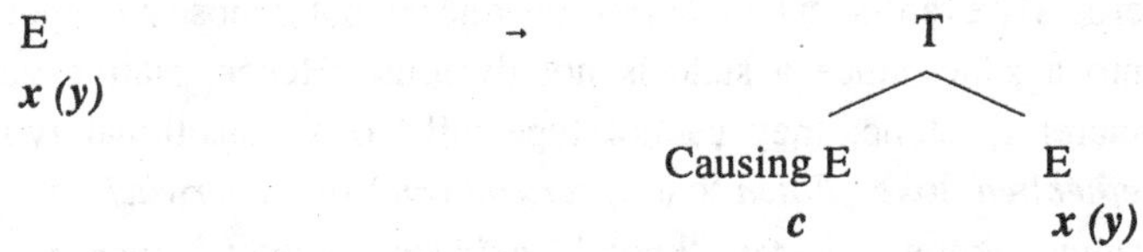

Causativization to a bi-eventual causative event type always involves an event type-shift: the addition of the causing subevent, causing *E* in (50). Causativization to an integrated causative event does not trigger an event type-shift, only the addition of a participant, *y*.[34] Integrated causatives in Dutch are expressed by a lexical causative (which is possibly morphologically marked, see below). The additional participant maps onto subject position and the other participant onto object position. Bi-eventual causatives are expressed in a periphrastic causative construction. The additional participant maps onto subject position; the original event participants appear in the embedded clause of the periphrastic causative. Consider *breken* 'break' in both kinds of causativization, (51).

(51) a. Het ei breekt.
'The egg breaks.'
b. Inge breekt het ei.
'I. breaks the egg.'
c. Dave liet het ei breken.
'D. made the egg break.'
d. Dave liet Inge het ei breken.
'D. made I. break the egg.'

Breken 'break' in the intransitive-transitive alternation in (51a) and (51b) is an instance of causativization without an event type-shift: both alternants denote a transition between two states. In (51a), the transition takes one participant, whereas the lexical causative in (51b) takes two. The pairs in (51a) and (51c) on the one hand and (51b) and (51d) on the other are causativizations with an event type-shift; the causatives in (51c) and (51d) are expressed in a periphrastic causative construction, *laten breken* 'make break' (lit. 'let break'). The causer does (or does not do) something; this event then causes another event to take place. In Chapter 3, section 3.5, I have extensively illustrated these two kinds of causativization as they apply to verbs with different event types.

Causativization always involves the addition of an event participant. In an integrated causative event, the additional participant *y* in (49) is involved in the event together with the original participant, *x*. In a bi-eventual causative event on the other hand, the additional participant, *c* in (50), is only involved in the causing subevent; the caused event has its own participants, *x* (and *y*) in (50). In an integrated event, the "causer" participant, *y*, is directly involved with the other participant, *x*. In bi-eventual events, the "causer" participant, *c*, is involved in the causing subevent; he is not directly involved with the participants in the caused event, *x* (and *y*). Hence, the difference between so-called *direct* and *indirect causation* can be read off of the associations of the event participants with particular subevents in the event structure.

I want to stress that in this proposal, a lexical causative only involves an additional participant; there is no further effect on the event structure. As I pointed out in section 3.5.1, this view is rather uncommon among analyses of (lexical) causativization: almost all proposals incorporate the idea that the non-causative event is extended in some way or another with a causative predicate which adds the extra argument; they typically use some version of the formula '*y* CAUSES *x* to BECOME *P*' (see, among others, Lakoff 1971; McCawley 1971; Dowty 1979; Hale & Keyser 1986; Pinker 1989; Jackendoff 1990; Parsons 1990; Brousseau & Ritter 1991; Levin & Rappaport Hovav 1994, 1995; Davis & Demirdache 1995; Davis 1997, in press; Demirdache 1997).

I do not see any event-structural reason for claiming that the two event types of, for example, intransitive and transitive *breken* 'break' are different from each other. There is no way to tease apart a causing and a caused subevent in (49). Intransitive *breken* 'break' denotes a transition which is identified by one participant changing state. Transitive *breken* 'break' denotes the same transition, only now with two participants; the resulting state is identified by the same participant as in intransitive *breken* 'break'. Hence, the entailment relation between the two (the one-participant *breken* 'break' event is entailed by the two-participant event) can be read off of the two event structures; the only "extension" between the two events is the additional event participant. In these respects, I follow Pustejovsky (1991), Hoekstra (1992), Ritter & Rosen (1993a,b) and van Voorst (1993) who also claim that a lexical causative does not involve additional event structure (see Chapter 3, section 3.5.1 for their motivations).

Notice that in this analysis, an integrated causative event is aspectually not different from other two-participant events. Compare, for example, transitive-causative *breken* 'break' and transitive *bereiken* 'reach': both verbs denote a transition between two states with two event participants. Similarly, both transitive-causative *smelten* 'melt' and transitive *eten* 'eat' denote transitions between a process and a state; transitive-causative *koken* 'boil' as well as transitive *duwen* 'push' denote a process. Still, there must be a difference between regular transitives and causative-transitive verbs. Regular transitive verbs such as *bereiken* 'reach', *eten* 'eat' and *duwen* 'push' do not have a non-causative intransitive variant in the same ways that causative transitives do (e.g., **de top bereikt* '*the top reaches'; **de appeltaart eet* '*the apple pie eats'; **de auto duwt* '*the car pushes'). In fact, the number of verbs with paired non-causative/causative meanings is relatively small: lexical causativization is very limited in Dutch. Periphrastic causativization on the other hand, is very productive.

Apparently, one cannot just add a participant to a certain event in causativization or delete one from it in decausativization. The reasons cannot be purely aspectual: from an event-semantic perspective, nothing would prevent it, as long as the event structure is sufficiently identified.

A number of studies discuss the productivity of causativization. Pinker (1989) describes two factors that play a role. One involves the ways one can conceive of an event. In order to be able to lexically causativize, an event must not be inherently non-causable directly by an external agent (such as English verbs of physical emission, e.g., *glow*). Conversely, in order to decausativize, the non-causative event must be be able to occur without an external cause (unlike, for example, being cut or being amused, which require an agent or instrument). Furthermore, even when a certain event can be conceived of in both ways, they may still not share the same root verb; the latter effect is a matter of lexicalization, i.e., whether or not the lexicon "decided" to treat the events as exemplars of the same kind.

In a similar kind of approach, Levin & Rappaport Hovav (1992, 1994, 1995) introduce the notions of *internally* and *externally controlled eventuality* to restrict causativizing, or, rather, in their view, decausativizing alternations: only a two-participant verb that denotes an externally controlled eventuality can decausativize. Van Voorst (1993) points out the relevance of how an additional participant is involved in the event. He claims that in Dutch and French only a participant that is the "energy source of the action chain" can be an additional participant in lexical causativization. In English, also a "responsible entity for the coming about of the event" can be the additional participant. Moreover, it matters how the other event participant is involved: only if the event unfolds on its own once it is set into action, can the verb decausativize. In any case, event-semantic notions can describe causativization, but they do not suffice to restrict the operation of causativization. Other semantic factors play a role here.

Sometimes, lexical causativization is morphologically marked: certain lexical causatives are prefixed or particle variants of non-causative root verbs. In the following pairs of verbs, the root verb takes one participant and the prefixed or particle variant takes two: *rollen-ontrollen, oprollen, afrollen, inrollen* 'roll-unroll, roll up, roll off, roll in'; *smelten-omsmelten, versmelten* 'melt-change by melting, melt together'; *breken-verbreken* 'break-break up'. Furthermore, there are many de-adjectival causative verbs that are prefixed with *ver-*, e.g., *groot-vergroten* 'large-enlarge'; *klein-verkleinen* 'small-reduce'; *kort-verkorten* 'short-shorten'; *lang-verlengen* 'long-lengthen'; *rijk-verrijken* 'rich-enrich'; *dun-verdunnen* 'thin-to thin'.

For these complex verbs, one can consider the prefix or particle as a causativizing morpheme. In a similar way as with atelic-telic event type-shifting (section 4.7.1), causativization involves event type composition of the event types of verb and prefix or particle. The additional participant is brought in by the prefix or particle. Consider *vergroten* 'enlarge', (52).

(52) Event type composition applied to *groot* 'large' and prefix *ver-*:

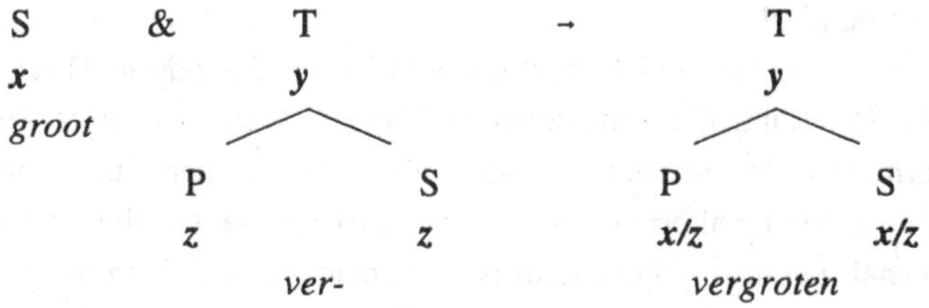

Notice that causative *ver-* in (52) and telic-inchoative *ver-* in *verdikken* 'thicken' in (35) are very similar: both denote a transition. The only difference is the number of event participants introduced by *ver-*: one in the case of telic-inchoative *ver-*, but two in the case of causative *ver-*. Hence, I conclude that there are two kinds of *ver-* (cf. Mulder 1992 and Lieber & Baayen 1993 for a similar conclusion in different frameworks).

In the discussion of event type composition with respect to complex verbs and atelic-telic event type-shifting (in section 4.7.1), I already mentioned that complex word formation is not completely productive. The same holds for causativization: one cannot causativize just any verb by combining it with the right prefix. So, not only lexical causatives but also morphologically marked causatives are very limited.

This concludes the deconstruction of the event type properties of *causativization*. Whereas periphrastic causativization is very productive, lexical causativization is very limited. I have pointed out that although event semantics can properly describe the event-semantic changes and effects in causativization, it cannot sufficiently restrict the operation; this holds in particular for lexical causatives. The restrictions are not of an aspectual nature, but involve other semantic factors. As my goal was the deconstruction of the event structure properties of causativization, it would lead too far afield to go deeper into the productivity issue here. I will leave it for further research.

4.7.4 An illustration with some verbs and their event type features

Summarizing the discussion on event types as a lexical primitive, I have shown in this section that event type is the determining factor in mapping. Verbs differ from each other with respect to their basic event types; this has direct consequences on how they map their participants. In particular, a verb that denotes a transition must map one participant onto object position and a verb that denotes a causative event must map participants onto subject and object position. Hence, an important lexical-syntactic feature is a verb's basic event type. Furthermore, the mapping system must incorporate the effects of event type-shifting, since the ultimate (inner) event type determines the mapping. I have discussed atelic-telic and causative event type-shifts. By deconstructing the properties of the event type-shifting mechanisms, I have determined which are relevant lexical-syntactic features that co-determine how a verb maps its participants onto syntax.

A non-stative atelic verb can event type-shift to become a telic event. I have presented two kinds of atelic-telic event type-shifts: via event type composition or via an inherent temporal scale. In analyzing event type composition, I have assumed that not only verbs, but also prepositions, postpositions, particles, prefixes and adjectives have a certain event structure and take their own event participants. Event type composition composes the event types of the verb and another predicate to derive a compositional event type, either by creating a new event type on top of the input event structures, or by merging one event structure into the other one. Event type composition applies in complex predicate formation when the verb combines with a "goal" phrase, in complex word formation in the derivation of particle and prefixed verbs and in resultative formation. Another form of atelic-telic event type shifting is triggered by the lexical property of temporal scale that some verbs have. A verb with a temporal scale denotes a telic event when it maps a participant onto object position (as a quantized noun phrase). So, the property of temporal scale must also be considered a lexical-syntactic feature; some verbs have it, whereas others do not. Event type-shifting involves either a temporal scale that is externally provided by another predicate or an inherent scale which is based on the meaning of the verb.

A verb can undergo causativization either via the addition of an event participant or via the addition of a causing subevent, including an additional event participant, on top of the original event structure. Hence, from an event-semantic perspective, one can distinguish two kinds of causative events: integrated and bi-eventual ones. Only causativization toward a bi-eventual causative event yields an event type-shift: a causing event is added onto the original event structure; this also adds a "causer" participant. On the other hand, causativization toward an integrated causative event only involves the addition of an event participant, but no event type-shift. A bi-eventual causative event is expressed with a periphrastic causative construction in Dutch; an integrated causative event is expressed with a lexical causative which may be morphologically marked with a causative prefix or particle. Event type composition accounts for the event type properties of these complex words.

I summarize the verbs that have been discussed in this section by listing their lexical-syntactic features: event type and temporal scale. One-participant verbs are listed in (53) and two-participant verbs in (54). A few verbs appear in both sets: the two-participant variants are the lexical causatives of the one-participant verbs.

(53) Event type features of one-participant verbs

	Basic event type:	Temporal scale:
a. *regenen* 'rain'	P	no
b. *rinkelen* 'ring'	P_x	no
c. *slapen* 'sleep'	P_x	no
d. *lopen* 'walk'	P_x	no
e. *rollen* 'roll'	P_x	no
f. *breken* 'break'	T [S_x, S_x]	yes
g. *smelten* 'melt'	T [P_x, S_x]	yes

(54) Event type features of two-participant verbs

	Basic event type:	Temporal scale:
a. *praten* 'talk'	$P_{x,y}$	no
b. *martelen* 'torture'	$P_{x,y}$	no
c. *duwen* 'push'	$P_{x,y}$	no
d. *eten* 'eat'	$P_{x,y}$	yes
e. *geven* 'give'	$T\,[P_{x,y}, S_y]$	yes
f. *zetten* 'put'	$T\,[P_{x,y}, S_y]$	yes
g. *rollen* 'roll'	$P_{x,y}$	no
h. *breken* 'break'	$T_x\,[S_y, S_y]$	yes
i. *smelten* 'melt'	$T_x\,[P_y, S_y]$	yes

By event-semantic definition, verbs that inherently denote a transition also have a temporal scale along which the event evolves. Hence, the property of temporal scale distinguishes two different subsets only within the process verbs.

Consider also the particle and prefixed variants of the verbs in this survey. The complex one-participant verbs in (55) and two-participant verbs in (56) are telic or atelic, depending on the meaning of the particle or prefix. Their causative particle and prefixed variants are listed in (57). (Notice that these lists do not contain all particle and prefix verbs that have been discussed, but only the variants of the verbs in (53) and (54)).

(55) Telic and atelic particle and prefixed variants of verbs with one participant:

a. atelic *binnenregenen*
'rain in'

b. telic *inslapen, zich verslapen, ontslapen*
'fall asleep, oversleep, pass away'
atelic *uitslapen, doorslapen*
'sleep in, sleep on'

c. telic *doorlopen, verlopen, uitlopen, aflopen*
'continue to walk, expire, sprout, go off'
atelic *doorlopen*
'walk firmly'

d. telic *afrollen*
'roll off'

e. telic *uitbreken, aanbreken, doorbreken, afbreken*
'break out, begin, break in two, break off'

f. telic *versmelten, doorsmelten, samensmelten*
'melt away, melt through, melt together'

(56) Telic and atelic particle and prefixed variants of verbs with two participants:

a. telic *bepraten, uitpraten, doorpraten*
'discuss, settle by talking, talk through'
atelic *doorpraten*
'talk continuously'

b. telic *uitgeven, opgeven, doorgeven, aangeven*
'spend, give up, pass on, hand'

c. telic *opzetten, aan/uitzetten, verzetten, inzetten*
'put on, put on/off, move, stake'

d. telic *induwen, aanduwen, afduwen*
'press, push (to get going), push off'

e. telic *opeten, afeten*
'eat up, finish eating'
atelic *dooreten, meeëten*
'eat on, eat along'

(57) Causative particle and prefixed variants:

a. *verbreken, afbreken, doorbreken*
'break up, break off, break in two'

b. *versmelten, omsmelten*
'melt together, melt down'

c. *ontrollen, oprollen, afrollen, inrollen*
'unroll, roll up, roll off, roll in'

This summarizes the discussion of a verb's event type as a second lexical primitive. By deconstructing the properties of atelic-telic and causative event type-shifting, I have concluded that a verb's lexical event type and the property of temporal scale are also lexical-syntactic features.

To conclude Part II, the number of event participants and the basic event type are the lexical primitives a verb must be listed with in the lexicon and which function as the lexical-syntactic features in the lexicon-syntax interface, (58).

(58) The lexical primitives in the lexicon-syntax interface:
- the number of event participants;
- the basic event type, including the feature of temporal scale.

Having determined what the lexical primitives are and discussed the nature of lexical-syntactic features involved in the lexicon-syntax interface, I now turn to the nature of the mapping system. Seeing the lexical-syntactic features that must be listed for each verb in (58), notice as well what does not need to be specified. Comparing the features in (58) with the kinds of lexical specification in argument-centered mapping theories, the important elements that are absent here is a "syntactic" annotation of the event participants (as in subcategorization frames or argument structures) and a "semantic" annotation (as in θ-grids or LCS's). Given that verbs map a certain participant onto a variety of syntactic positions, one should disconnect the specification of the event participants (i.e., the "arguments") from a mapping specification (i.e., the argument "structure"). Combining both kinds of specification in one format leads to massive redundancy in the lexicon, as one would need to include all syntactic position possibilities for each participant.

Knowing the lexical semantics of a verb gives one a set of event participants, but knowing the set of event participants does not tell one onto which positions they are mapped. The mapping of a verb onto a certain frame does not directly depend on its set of event participants, but, rather, on how these event participants play a role in the event. Hence, the projection of argument positions should not be read off of the set of event participants, nor be determined by what semantic kinds of participants they are. Instead, it depends on event type. Variability with respect to the event type of the VP to which the verb contributes creates flexibility as to which verb frame the verb appears in. In the next part, I will develop a new approach toward mapping that incorporates these ideas.

Part III: The nature of the lexicon-syntax interface

What is the nature of the mapping system that maps a verb onto syntax based on its lexical-syntactic features? In this last part of the chapter, I will present a model of the lexicon-syntax interface. It will be defined on event participant and event type features that have emerged as the relevant lexical-syntactic features in Part II. The approach that I will advocate is to view mapping as checking off a verb's lexical-syntactic features in the syntactic configuration it appears in. On this view, the mapping system does not consist of a set of linking rules that, for every argument of the verb, compute a certain syntactic position to map it onto. Rather, checking the event-semantic structure of a predicate determines whether or not a verb projecting a particular syntactic configuration is licensed, and if so, what the event-semantic interpretation of the verb is in this configuration.

The model of the lexicon-syntax interface that I will develop in this part is based on ideas presented in my own work (see van Hout 1991a,b, 1992a,b, 1994). The ideas have been influenced by joint work with several co-authors (see van Hout, Randall & Weissenborn 1993; Randall, van Hout, Weissenborn & Baayen 1994; van Hout, Randall, Weissenborn & Baayen in progress; Hollebrandse & van Hout 1995, 1996, 1998).

First, I will discuss the nature of the mapping system by showing how properties of the event structure interact with those of the syntactic configuration in linking syntactic argument positions and event participants (section 4.8). I advocate an approach to mapping that involves *ch*ecking *e*vent-*s*emantic *s*tructure which I will call the CHESS model. After having concentrated throughout the chapter on the systematic properties of the lexicon, I briefly discuss the idiosyncratic lexicon by discussing some effects that remain unsystematic and idiosyncratic in an event-semantic approach to mapping; these must be listed as item-particular properties (section 4.9). Finally, in section 4.10, I will position the CHESS model among other approaches to mapping by reviewing what has become of some standard notions in the present approach. I conclude the chapter with a summary of the advantages of viewing mapping as checking event-semantic structure.

4.8 A new approach: mapping is checking event-semantic structure

The event-semantic analysis of the phenomenon of lexical-syntactic flexibility presented in the present and previous chapters suggests that in the interface between lexicon and syntax, event type-shifting operations conspire with event-structural mapping requirements to create lexical-syntactic flexibility.

In order to implement this insight in a model of the lexicon-syntax interface, I will first introduce the notion *event identification* that will be the crucial concept of the theory (subsection 4.8.1). Next, working out in detail what event identification involves syntactically, I will associate event type features with structural Case assignment. Specifically, telicity involves strong Case assignment in the specifier position of AgrO (subsection 4.8.2). I will then generalize this proposal more generally to event structure features and define the CHESS (*Ch*ecking *E*vent-*S*emantic *S*tructure) mapping system (subsection 4.8.3). A summary of this approach to mapping concludes this section (subsection 4.8.4).

4.8.1 The identification of an event

Semantically, a verb describes a kind of event; the event is associated with a certain number of event participants. Grimshaw (1990) and Grimshaw & Vikner (1993) argue for a view on the relation between lexical-semantics and syntax in terms of *event identification*. The relation between a verb's semantics and its appearance in syntax involves the identification of the event. As phrases in syntactic argument positions refer to a verb's event participants, and as event participants play a certain aspectual role in the event or in a subevent (cf. Tenny's 1994 aspectual roles), the phrases in argument positions are the syntactic "identifiers" of the event. In mapping onto syntax, the verb projects a number of argument positions in which its event participants can appear. This view of the relation between a verb's lexical specification and its projection in syntax is formulated in (59).

(59) Event identification:
Mapping requires that a verb's event structure, including every subevent, be syntactically identified. A phrase in a syntactic argument position identifies (a part of) the event, because it is associated with an event participant.

Assuming that mapping involves the identification of event structure, the generalization that event type-shifting and lexical-syntactic flexibility are correlated follows automatically: lexical-syntactic flexibility is a side-effect of event type-shifting. Event type-shifting modifies the event structure; it affects the outcome of mapping as the event identification requirements change, as well. More specifically, in an atelic-telic event type-shift, the derived telic event structure is more complex than the original atelic event structure. In order to identify a telic transition, both subevents need to be identified; an atelic event has only one part to be identified, as it is a simplex event structure. Similarly, in causativization, the causative event has an additional event participant, plus, sometimes, an extra piece of event structure. Hence, a causative event has more event-semantic elements to be identified than a non-causative event.

With respect to the mapping system, the question is: what does it syntactically involve to identify a verb's event structure? I will claim that particular positions in a syntactic configuration are associated with particular event features. In order to identify a particular event feature, there must be an NP in the associated syntactic position. Hence, via the requirement to identify event structure, mapping comes down to checking event-semantic features.

4.8.2 Telicity features and the Case of the object

What exactly does checking event-semantic features, and, hence, identifying event structure, involve? In this subsection I will show that it must be associated with Case assignment. In particular, I will claim that telicity features are checked via strong Case assignment to the object, and, consequently, that an object bearing strong Case identifies a transition.

At various points, I have pointed out the correlation between telic events and the presence of a participant in object position. Inherently telic or derived telic verbs obligatorily take an object. This implies that a telic two-participant verb must appear in a transitive frame and a telic one-participant verb must appear in an unaccusative frame (which has an underlying object). Consider telic *opeten* 'eat up', (60), and *breken* 'break', (61).

(60) a. Maribel heeft de appeltaart opgegeten.
M. has the apple-pie up-eaten
'M. ate up the apple pie.'
b. *Maribel heeft opgegeten.
M. has eaten up

(61) a. Het ei is gebroken.
the egg is broken
'The egg break.'
b. *Het ei heeft gebroken.
the egg has broken

Opeten 'eat up' in an intransitive frame, (60b), and *breken* 'break' in an unergative frame, (61b), are ungrammatical (auxiliary selection HAVE in (61b) suggests an unergative frame). Hence, in the present terminology, identifying a telic event requires the presence of an argument in object position that refers to the participant involved in the transition.

Recall that the presence of an argument that refers to the event participant involved in the transition by itself does not suffice to identify telicity features. Compare another variant of *eten* 'eat' which maps both event participants onto syntax, (62). ((62) is repeated from (45b).)

(62) Maribel heeft dagenlang van de appeltaart gegeten.
M has days-long of the apple-pie eten
'M. ate from the apple pie for days.'

The argument that refers to the identifier of the transition must be mapped onto object position; in oblique position, it does not measure out the event.

Recall further Verkuyl's (1972) observation that only quantized objects induce telicity; bare noun objects do not. Consider *eten* 'eat, (63). ((63) is repeated from (46).)

(63) a. Maribel heeft in 10 minuten een hele appeltaart gegeten.
M. has in 10 minutes a whole apple-pie eaten
'M. ate a whole apple pie in 10 minutes.'
b. Maribel heeft urenlang appeltaart gegeten.
M. has hours-long apple-pie eaten
'M. ate apple pie for hours.'

The quantized object in (63a) is a "proper" identifier of telicity: it measures out the eating event as the pie gets eaten little by little until it is finished; it provides the temporal scale of *eten* 'eat' with a specific amount of apple pie. Hence, the event is a telic transition. The bare object in (63b), however, is not a proper telicity identifier: it does not activate a temporal scale, nor does it identify a final state, even though it refers to a participant in the eating process. Hence, the event is atelic. In event-semantic respect, the bare object is merely an event modifier: (63b) is not about eating events involving any kind of food, but about a subset of them: the apple-pie-eatings.[35]

So, a quantized object syntactically identifies a verb's telicity feature. How can one implement this three-way relation between a verb's event type features, a particular argument position, and the semantics of the NP in that position? I propose that this relation becomes manifest through Case assignment. In order to integrate the syntactic and semantic effects, I follow de Hoop's (1992) proposal that the semantic strength of an NP is related to Case.[36]

Starting from a different point of departure, i.e., the effects of syntax on the semantic interpretation of NPs, De Hoop arrives at similar conclusions with respect to the status of the two objects in (63). She claims that the quantized object in (63a) is a "real" argument, whereas the bare object in (63b) is a predicate modifier. De Hoop presents data from a number of languages, including Finnish, Turkish and West-Greenlandic, where bare objects differ morpho-syntactically from definite and indefinite objects; the difference concerns the object's Case. In Finnish, for example, the semantic difference is morpho-syntactically expressed as partitive versus accusative Case. Consider Finnish *tapaa* 'meet', (64).

(64) a. Anne tapaa vieraat.
A. meets $guests_{ACC}$
'A. meets the guests.'
b. Anne tapaa vieraita.
A. meets $guests_{PART}$
'A. meets some guests.' (de Hoop 1992:63)

In order to unify the association between an object's Case and its semantic interpretation across languages, De Hoop claims that an object can be marked with one of two different structural object Cases: weak or strong Case. These different structural object Cases are associated with different semantic interpretations: whereas an object with weak Case has a semantically weak interpretation, (63b) and (64b), an object with strong Case has a strong interpretation, (63a) and (64a). The Case difference is visible in some languages, but not in all; it is visible in Finnish, (64), but not in Dutch, (63).

De Hoops's theory on Case and the interpretation of NPs is embedded in the framework of model-theoretic semantic which makes a distinction between strong and weak NPs. Strong NPs function semantically as generalized quantifiers; the exact semantic status of weak NPs is presently the subject of much debate. Typically, a strong NP is a generalized quantifier and acquires a strong reading, whereas a weak NP does not have a strong reading as it is not quantized. Observing, however, that weak NPs in specific syntactic contexts also have a strong reading, De Hoop develops a proposal for how syntax plays a role in determining strong readings in NPs. She assumes there are two types of structural object Cases: weak Case is a structural default Case licensed in a certain D-structure configuration; strong Case is a structural Case licensed at S-structure. Defining an object with strong Case as an NP with a strong reading and an object with weak Case as an NP with a weak reading, she can explain why a weak NP can also get a strong reading, i.e., if it is assigned strong Case. De Hoop defines the relation between syntactic Case assignment and semantic interpretation as follows: "An object is interpreted as generalized quantifier if and only if it bears strong Case. An object that bears weak Case is interpreted as part of the predicate" (de Hoop 1992:99). In this definition, a "real" argument is an argument that denotes a generalized quantifier. Hence, only an object with strong Case is a real argument, e.g., (63a) and (64a); an object with weak case is a predicate modifier, e.g., (63b) and (64b).

De Hoop generalizes her proposal to Dutch and English by showing that an object with weak Case behaves syntactically different from an object with strong Case. She relates this to the same Case distinction (which remains abstract in these languages). In particular, she accounts for the restrictions on object scrambling in Dutch in terms of weak and strong Case. Consider the positions of the objects in (65) and (66).

(65) a. dat de politie gisteren de taalkundigen opgepakt heeft.
that the police yesterday the linguists arrested has
'that the police arrested the linguists yesterday.'
b. dat de politie de taalkundigen gisteren opgepakt heeft.
that the police the linguists yesterday arrested has
'that the police arrested the linguists yesterday.'
(de Hoop 1992:138)

(66) a. dat de politie gisteren taalkundigen opgepakt heeft.
that the police yesterday linguists arrested has
'that the police arrested linguists yesterday.'
b. *dat de politie taalkundigen gisteren opgepakt heeft.
that the police linguists yesterday arrested has
(de Hoop 1992:138)

The referential, definite object in (65) can both precede and follow the adverb *gisteren* 'yesterday'; the bare plural object in (66), however, can only be in the position following the adverb. De Hoop assumes the latter position is the original D-structure position, whereas the objects in (65b) and (66b) are in scrambled position where only strong Case is licensed. As strong Case correlates with a strong reading and the only strong reading for bare plurals is a generic interpretation (which is impossible in (66b) because of the adverb *gisteren* 'yesterday'), (66b) is ungrammatical.[37] Attributing the possibility of scrambling and the different readings of an object to the different types of Case that are licensed in different structural positions (at different levels of representation), De Hoop accounts for the fact that in Dutch, only NPs with a strong reading (and, hence, strong Case) can scramble.

Since strong/weak Case is a syntactic formalization of semantically different kinds of objects, it can also serve to formalize the identification of a telic event type. Following up on De Hoop's proposals, I assume that an object with strong Case (De Hoop's "real" argument) is a proper event identifier of a transition, (67).

(67) Identification of a telic event (preliminary version): An argument with strong object Case can identify an event participant that is involved in both subevents of a transition.

An object with weak Case is an event modifier; it cannot identify a (sub)event, even though it is associated with an event participant in the event structure. Similarly, an oblique argument cannot identify a (sub)event, even though it refers to an event participant; a strong NP with oblique Case is an event modifier. Hence, case assignment establishes the crucial relation between telic event type features, the object argument position, and the semantic strength of the NP in that position.

De Hoop does not specify in which S-structure configuration strong object Case is licensed. In order to integrate the Case proposal on the identification of event structure with a mapping system, I assume a model of grammar in which lexical features are checked in syntactic positions related to functional projections (cf. Chomsky 1993, 1995). Following my proposal in van Hout (1994), I interpret the connections between a verb's event structure features and the syntactic argument positions it projects as a form of feature checking. As feature checking is operative in a functional rather than a lexical domain of projection and since telicity is crucially associated with the object, I assume that the relevant checking domain for telicity is AgrOP. Hence, I propose that De Hoop's S-structure configuration, in which strong Case is licensed, is a functional projection, specifically AgrOP. Taking feature checking as a specifier-head agreement relation, an NP must move into Spec, AgrO in order to check the verb's telicity features, (68).[38]

(68) Identification of a telic event (final version): An argument with strong object Case can identify an event participant that is involved in both subevents of a transition. Strong Case assignment involves a specifier-head relation between the specifier and the head of AgrO.

An argument with strong Case in object position identifies a transition as it is interpreted as the participant that is involved in the final state of the event. As a verb's telicity features need to be checked off in AgrOP, the generalization that a telic predicate requires the presence of an object is accounted for (see (60) and (61)).

Many people have noted the correlation between telicity and objects (cf. Tenny 1987, 1994; van Voorst 1988; Van Valin 1990; Dowty 1991; Pustejovsky 1991; Levin & Rappaport Hovav 1992, 1995; McClure 1993; Ramchand 1993; Borer 1994; den Dikken 1994; Schmitt 1995). The proposal defined in (68) implements this relation as checking off event type features by an argument in the specifier position of AgrO. McClure (1993), Ramchand (1993) Borer (1994), den Dikken (1994) and Schmitt (1995) have proposed very similar implementations of this relation, i.e., by locating telicity in a functional head and positing a specifier-head relation between an argument and a functional head (Asp for McClure, Ramchand and Borer; AgrO for Den Dikken and Schmitt).

Notice how the mapping condition in (68) defines which objects are not good telicity identifiers. It implies that the argument that refers to the participant that identifies a transition must be assigned structural object Case, rather than an oblique object Case (hence, the atelic interpretation of the conative frame in (62)). In this way, the mapping condition accounts for the atelic-telic shift in the oblique intransitive-transitive alternation (e.g., *praten over-bepraten, uitpraten* 'talk about-discuss, talk out'): when an object has an oblique Case the interpretation is atelic, whereas when it has a structural object Case the interpretation is telic.

Reviewing the event-semantic effects of quantized versus bare objects in this proposal, a bare object has weak Case (e.g., in (63b)); hence, it is part of the predicate and modifies the event. A quantized object has strong Case (e.g., the definite object in (63a)); hence, it is an event identifier and identifies the final event of the transition. Thus, as telic event type feature checking is associated with strong Case features, it derives the obligatory presence of an object with telic verbs (and the ungrammaticality of (60b) and (61b) follows automatically).

Since telicity features are associated with strong object Case assignment, this analysis makes a strong prediction for telic predicates: a telic predicate cannot take a bare object. This prediction is indeed borne out: bare objects are impossible with telic verbs. This is because a bare object does not move to Spec, AgrO and, hence, cannot check off the predicate's telicity feature. Consider telic *opeten* 'eat up' with a bare object, (69).

(69) *Maribel at appeltaart op.
M. ate apple pie up

I have noted the impossibility of bare objects for telic particle verbs in Dutch in van Hout (1991b, 1992a,b, 1994).[39] The same impossibility has been observed for English telic particle verbs by de Hoop (1992) and for Hungarian perfectively prefixed verbs by Hopper & Thompson (1980).

Strong Case assignment to the object is a necessary, but not sufficient condition for a telic interpretation. There is interaction between the syntactic configuration (the presence or absence of an object with strong Case in Spec, AgrO) and the event type features of the verb. The verb's event type features determine whether or not the interpretation is ultimately telic. An object with strong Case only yields a telic interpretation of the sentence if the verb has an (inherent or derived) telic event type. Stative verbs that are inherently atelic never trigger a telic interpretation, independent of whether or not they have an object with strong Case. As for process verbs with a temporal scale (e.g., *eten* 'eat'), the syntactic implementation of an object's semantic strength via Case implies that the scale is only activated when an object appears with strong Case. As for process verbs without a temporal scale (e.g., *duwen* 'push', *lopen* 'walk'), this event type feature triggers an atelic interpretation, even when the verb has a strongly case-marked object. For the latter verbs, only if the verb undergoes event type composition and becomes part of a telic predicate (a complex predicate with a "goal" phrase, a complex word or a resultative predicate), is an object with strong Case an identifier of the transition.

The fact that a transitive frame can yield various aspectual interpretations implies that the event-semantic interpretation of a sentence is arrived at in an interactive way. Interpretation is fed by the event type features of the predicate and the syntactic configuration, i.e., the presence of an object with strong Case. If aspectual interpretation is construed purely on the syntactic configuration (for such constructionist approaches, see Hoekstra & Mulder 1990, Mulder 1992; Borer 1994), one cannot account for the atelic interpretation of transitive sentences with process verbs without a temporal scale (i.e., the *duwen* 'push' class) or with stative verbs.[40]

This concludes the first part of the discussion of how event features are syntactically checked. I have shown how telicity is associated with object arguments that are semantically strong. I have linked this to strong Case assignment, following de Hoop (1992). Syntactically implementing the relation between telic event type features, the object position, and the semantic interpretation of the NP in that position as strong Case assignment to the object in Spec, AgrO, I have laid the foundation for a new approach to mapping. Extending this proposal, I will now fully develop the mapping system in terms of checking event-semantic structure.

4.8.3 The CHESS mapping system: checking event-semantic structure

Having proposed how a verb's telicity features can be checked off via strong Case assignment in AgrOP, I will now generalize this proposal in two ways. First, after reviewing that mapping needs to "see" the event structure of the predicate, rather than that of the verb itself, I will argue that mapping cannot be taken as an algorithm that links a verb's lexical arguments onto syntactic argument positions. The alternative is a checking algorithm. Developing a checking approach to mapping, I will expand the telicity checking proposal to include all kinds of event structures (telic or atelic, with one or two participants). I will call this approach to mapping: CHESS, *Ch*ecking *E*vent-*S*emantic *S*tructure.[41]

As I have shown in section 4.7.1, the telicity of a predicate is determined by the event type features of the verb in combination with those of other predicates in the VP (prepositions, postpositions, particles, resultative predicates). The features that are relevant for mapping are not just the lexical event type features of the verb, but, rather, those of the whole VP predicate. Telic simplex verbs, complex verbs and syntactically complex predicates all require an argument in object position. I take this generalization to imply the following with respect to the nature of the mapping rules: mapping conditions must be defined on the lexical-syntactic features of predicates, rather than verbs.

This conclusion initiates an important departure from standard views on mapping which are designed in such a way that the item-particular specification of a verb fully determines the way it maps onto syntax. Instead, the mapping generalization across telic predicates suggests that the mapping system should not be set up so that it is exclusively driven by item-particular lexical information of verbs; it must also take into account the information of other elements in the predicate.

Consider again the multiple mapping possibilities for a one-participant verb of motion, *zwemmen* 'swim', (70). ((70a) and (70c) are repeated from (39) above.)

(70) a. Claartje heeft de hele zomer in zee gezwommen.
C. has the whole summer in sea swam
'C. swam in the sea during the whole summer.'

b. Claartje is in 2 minuten naar de overkant gezwommen.
C. is in 2 minutes to the across-side swam
'C. swam in 2 minutes to the other side.'

c. Claartje heeft haar badpak al in een zomer aan flarden gezwommen.
C. has her swimsuit already within one summer to tatters swam
'C. already swam her swimsuit to tatters within one summer.'

When the verb is part of an atelic predicate, it maps its single participant onto subject position in an unergative frame, (70a). When it forms a complex predicate with a "goal" phrase, it maps its single participant onto object position in an (oblique) unaccusative frame, (70b). When it forms a resultative predicate with a stative PP, it maps its single participant onto subject position in a transitive frame, (70c). Hence, the single participant of the process verb *zwemmen* 'swim' appears either in subject or object position depending on the event features of other predicates in the VP. Consequently, the verb projects an unergative, oblique unaccusative, or transitive frame.

In standard approaches to the lexicon-syntax interface, there is an algorithm that maps lexical-semantic arguments onto syntactic positions, either by way of argument-indexing in mapping systems defined on argument structures and LCS-variables, or via the involvement of the θ-hierarchy when mapping is defined on θ-roles (see Dowty 1991 for this classification of mapping systems). Suppose one tries to incorporate the event type generalizations in such approaches. If mapping is determined by purely item-particular features, a verb cannot "leave" the lexicon with only its basic event type feature; *zwemmen* 'swim', for example, would only map onto an unergative frame, since it denotes an atelic process with one-participant. In order to derive the three different mappings, the verb must "leave" the lexicon in three different forms: as an atelic one-participant verb, as a telic one-participant verb and, finally, as a telic two-participant verb. Each form then leads to a different mapping.

Of course, in such an approach, the lexical event structure features must be checked at a syntactic level to see if they match with those of the rest of the predicate. Specifically, if the verb is inserted with a telic event type, it must combine with a PP complement or resultative predicate. If it had been inserted with an atelic event type, a derivation with a PP complement or resultative predicate would need to be ruled out as the event types do not match.

On this view of mapping, the lexicon would become redundantly large as every verb must be listed with multiple specifications. Alternatively, one might derive multiple lexical specifications from one basic one by applying event-shifting operations at a lexical level. However, as these lexical event type-shifts must then be matched at a syntactic level with the results of event type composition, one would in fact be doing the same event type-shifting operations twice, first at a lexical and then at a syntactic level.

In order to avoid these problems, I advocate an alternative view of mapping. I interpret the event-semantic mapping requirements to involve feature checking, rather than as a linking system that associates lexical variables to syntactic positions. Mapping requirements are checked on the syntactic configuration a verb projects; they naturally take into account the event structure features of the whole VP, since other predicates are part of the configuration.

In the case of the unergative-unaccusative-transitive alternation in (70), if the verb combines with a PP complement or resultative complement, the event type of the predicate is telic; hence, there must be an argument in object position. Therefore, only a projection of an unaccusative or a transitive frame "survives". If the VP has atelic event type features, the projection of an unergative frame "survives".

Having concluded that the event type features of the predicate direct mapping, I can now expand the first set of proposals in subsection 4.8.2. I propose that mapping is defined as the syntactic identification of the event structure of a predicate as given by its event type and event participants. Expanding the assumptions that event structure must be syntactically identified and that an argument in Spec, AgrOP is a proper event identifier of a telic event, I now define the CHESS model as in (71).

(71) The CHESS mapping conditions: *ch*ecking *e*vent-*s*emantic *s*tructure:

1. Mapping requires that the event structure of a predicate be identified.
2. There are two structural argument positions: the specifier positions of Agr,S and Agr,O. An argument in either of these specifier positions identifies an event or subevent by referring to an event participant that is involved in that (sub)event.
3. Telic event type features must be checked in AgrOP. The argument in Spec, AgrO is associated with the event participant that ends in the final state.

Independent of event identification requirements, every syntactic projection seems to need a subject position (cf. Chomsky's 1981 Extended Projection Principle and various implementations of the same idea). Incorporating this generalization, I assume that every verb projects at least an AgrSP; the specifier of AgrS is the subject position. I will refer to this as the *subject requirement.* Whether or not the verb also projects AgrOP depends on the event structure: for both one- and two-participant verbs, the verb must project AgrOP if the predicate is telic, because AgrOP is the locus of telic feature checking.

The CHESS mapping conditions laid out in (71) account for the following mappings. First, consider the mappings of telic predicates. A telic one-participant predicate, T_x, maps onto an unaccusative frame. The single argument must first satisfy the telicity requirement in Spec, AgrO, before it moves on to Spec, AgrS to satisfy the subject requirement. The derivation in (72) shows an unaccusative mapping configuration. The tree in (72) and the others below only show the essentials of a particular mapping configuration, specifying just the relevant functional projections and no particulars of the structure within VP.[42] The indexed NPs are associated with participants in the event structure. Here, NP_i is associated with participant x of transition T_x.

(72) Telic one-participant predicates -- unaccusative mapping:

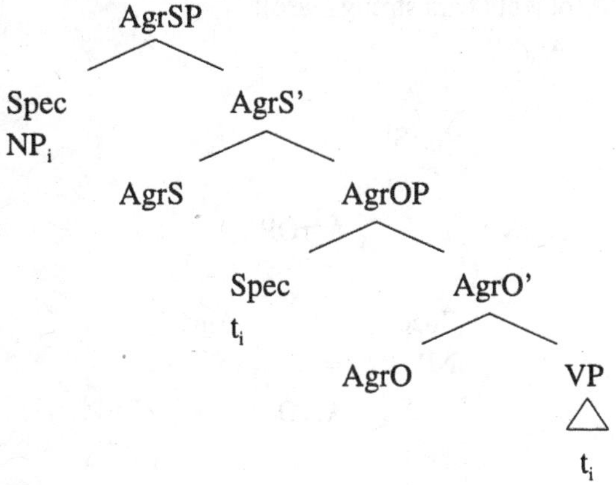

This mapping is derived for, among others: *breken* 'break'; *smelten* 'melt'; *weglopen* 'walk away'; *de baan op rollen* 'roll onto the court'; *afrollen* 'roll off'; *verbranden* 'burn'.

A telic two-participant predicate, $T_{x, y}$, maps onto a transitive frame. The argument in Spec, AgrO satisfies the telicity requirement; it is interpreted as the participant that is involved in both subevents of the transition (hence, undergoing some kind of change). The other argument, in Spec, AgrS, satisfies the subject requirement; it is interpreted as the other participant in the transition. This mapping is pictured in (73). It is derived for, among others: *eten* 'eat'; *opeten* 'eat up'; *breken* 'break'; *naar de kant duwen* 'push to the side'; *doodmartelen* 'torture to death'.

(73) Telic two-participant predicates -- transitive mapping with an AgrOP (object bears strong Case):

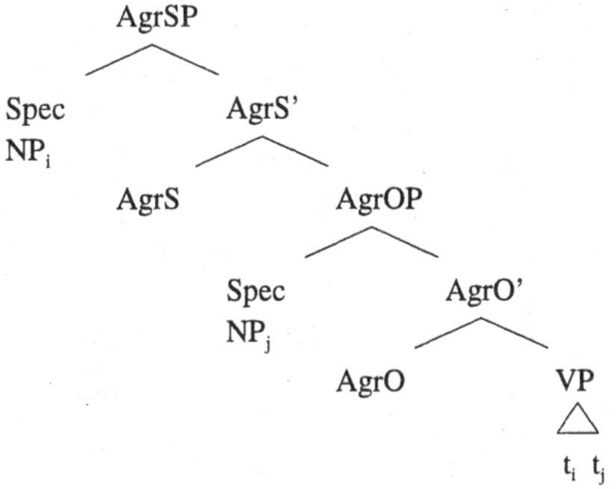

Next, consider the mappings of atelic predicates. An atelic one-participant predicate, P_x, maps onto an unergative frame. The single argument in Spec, AgrS satisfies the subject requirement, (74). There is no need for projecting AgrOP. This mapping is derived for, among others: *slapen* 'sleep'; *rinkelen* 'ring'; *lopen,* 'walk'; *rollen* 'roll'.

(74) Atelic one-participant predicates -- unergative mapping:

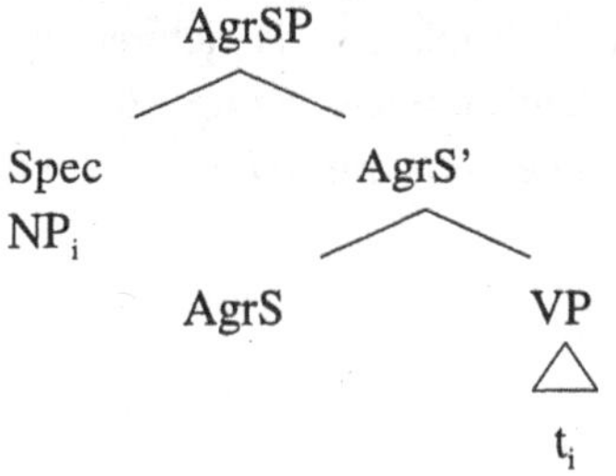

An atelic two-participant predicate, $P_{x, y}$, represents the most complex case, as mapping depends on the verb's property of temporal scale. If the verb has a temporal scale, it cannot map onto a transitive frame with an AgrOP, as this would activate the temporal scale and, hence, trigger telicity. Instead, the verb maps onto an oblique intransitive frame, with the argument in Spec, AgrS satisfying the subject requirement and the oblique argument identifying the second event participant (e.g., *van de taart eten* 'eat from the pie'). See (75).

(75) Atelic two-participant predicates -- oblique intransitive mapping:

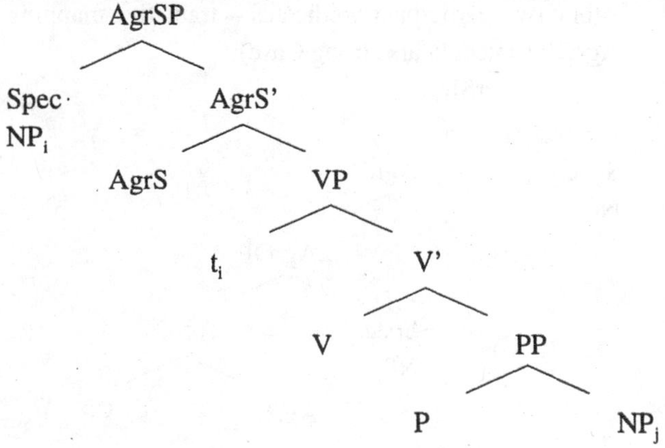

Alternatively, the object remains in the VP; it identifies the second event participant, but does not yield telicity since it does not move to AgrOP (e.g., *taart eten* 'eat pie'). This derivation is given in (76).

(76) Atelic two-participant predicates -- transitive mapping with no AgrOP (object bears weak Case):

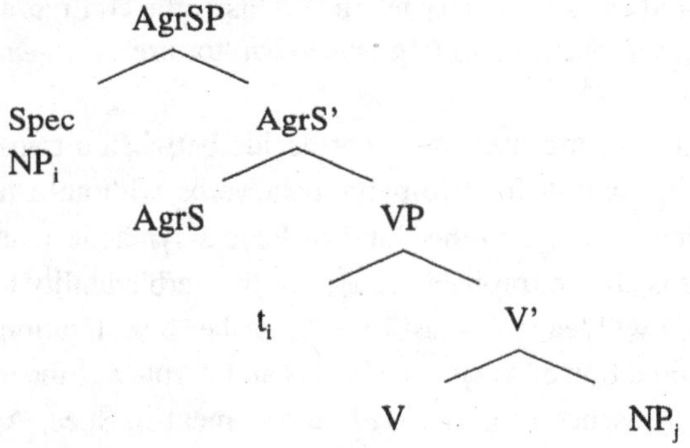

If the verb does not have a temporal scale, it can either map onto an oblique intransitive frame as in (75) (e.g., *duwen tegen* 'push against'; *eten van* 'eat of'; *praten over* 'talk about') or onto a transitive frame as represented in (77).

(77) Atelic two-participant predicates -- transitive mapping with an AgrOP (object bears strong Case):

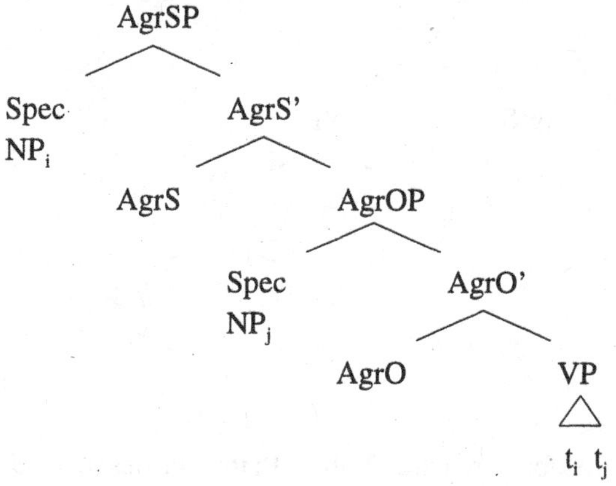

Note that in this latter derivation, the verb projects AgrOP in order to create a position for a quantized NP, so that its second event participant can be identified. However, this configuration will not yield telicity, because the verb does not specify an inherent temporal scale (and there are no other predicates to specify telicity). This is the configuration for the class of *duwen* 'push' verbs (e.g., *martelen* 'torture'; *dragen* 'carry'; *trekken* 'pull').

The event structure itself does not decide between a transitive or oblique mapping option for two-participant verbs without a temporal scale. There must be some other kind of lexical-syntactic feature that accounts for this choice (probably related to the verb's ability to assign oblique Case). I will leave this last issue to further investigation.

The interpretation of a sentence is thus an interplay of the syntactic configuration (presence or absence of an argument in Spec, AgrS and Spec, AgrO) and the predicate's event structure; it cannot be completely construed on the syntactic configuration alone (*contra* claims by Hoekstra

& Mulder 1990; Mulder 1992; Borer 1994). Whether or not a certain interpretation is indeed activated depends on the predicate's event structure features. If a predicate has a telic event type or if the verb has a temporal scale, then the argument in Spec, AgrO must be interpreted as the participant that is involved in both subevents of the transition. In addition, if an event has two participants, then the argument in Spec, AgrS must be interpreted as the more agentive of the two.

Finally, notice that on this view of mapping, the D-structure positions of the arguments do not really matter. Instead, the event type features that are composed at the VP level determine the position of arguments in the functional projection of the verb. Hence, the terms *transitive, unergative* and *unaccusative*, in fact, refer to S-structure configurations of arguments, i.e., the filling of the specifier positions of AgrOP and AgrSP. Transitive mapping refers to a configuration in which two arguments move into Spec, AgrS and Spec, AgrO as in (73) and (77); unergative mapping involves a configuration in which a single argument moves to Spec, AgrS as in (74); unaccusative mapping involves a configuration in which a single argument moves to Spec, AgrS via Spec, AgrO as in (72). (For further discussion of unaccusative mapping in the CHESS model, see Chapter 6, section 6.3).

Borer (1994) arrives at the same conclusion in her approach to mapping, which is in various respects similar to the one advocated here. In fact, Borer takes the conclusion one step further step and argues that one cannot really distinguish subject and object positions at D-structure: the internal and external arguments are hierarchically unordered in the VP.[43] She defines mapping in terms of a set of aspectual realization conditions for various functional specifier positions. Different aspectual interpretations trigger movement to the specifier positions of different functional projections (her Asp_{EM} and Asp_{OR}).[44] She assumes that a telic interpretation is necessarily related to the movement of an argument to an aspectual functional projection above VP, i.e., $AspP_{EM}$; bare objects remain in VP and incorporate semantically. Moreover, aspectual considerations determine unaccusativity: the atelic-telic difference triggers the movement of an argument to either one of these two functional projections. Note that Borer's definition of unaccusative mapping differs from the one in the CHESS model where the single argument moves though both functional projections. Also, her apporach is fully constructional (i.e., the syntactic configuration determines interpretation), whereas I assume that the event type of the verb also plays a role.

The aim of developing a new mapping system was to be able to account for the phenomenon of lexical-syntactic flexibility in an insightful way. Generalizing over different forms of frame alternations, I have concluded in Chapter 3 that they fall in three event-semantic classes. Event type-shifting is the crucial relation between the alternants of a frame alternation; I have distinguished atelic-telic and causativizing event type-shifts. As event structure is the basis of the CHESS model, and as different event structures have different mapping requirements, the phenomenon of lexical-syntactic flexibility comes as no surprise, since events can be perceived from different event-semantic perspectives. Furthermore, the CHESS mapping conditions naturally account for the various forms of lexical-syntactic flexibility. In explaining lexical-syntactic flexibility in terms of event structure differences, the CHESS model aligns with various other proposals that draw this relation, including Tenny (1987, 1994); van Voorst (1988); Hoekstra & Mulder (1990); Hoekstra (1992); Hale & Keyser (1992, 1993); McClure (1993); Borer (1994); Davis & Demirdache (1995); Davis (1997, in press); Demirdache (1997).

4.8.4 Summary: a checking approach to mapping

In this section I have developed a model of the interface between lexicon and syntax based on the event-semantic primitives number of event participants and event type. Following Grimshaw (1990) and Grimshaw & Vikner (1993), I have introduced the notion *event identification* as the crucial concept in the interface: the mapping system requires that a predicate's event structure, including every subevent, is syntactically identified. I have assumed that the presence of a phrase in an argument position identifies (a part of) the event as it is interpreted as an event participant in the event or part of the event (subsection 4.8.1).

Working out in detail which are the syntactic argument positions that are relevant for event identification in two steps, I have first claimed that telicity features must be associated with strong Case assignment in the sense of de Hoop (1992) (subsection 4.8.2). I have formalized the relation between event type features (telicity), argument position (object position) and semantic strength of an NP (a strong reading) in terms of strong Case assignment in Spec, AgrO which is required to check off the telicity feature of the predicate. This explains the following facts: the obligatory objects of telic predicates, the impossibility of weak objects with telic predicates, the effects of the semantics of the object on the aspectual interpretation of the sentence (first observed by Verkuyl 1972) and the aspectual differences between object Case versus oblique Case.

The next step was to generalize this proposal for the identification of event structure to all kinds of event structures (subsection 4.8.3). This led to the definition of the CHESS model: *Ch*ecking *E*vent-*S*emantic *S*tructure. Showing that the event structure properties of the predicate, rather than those of the verb alone determine the outcome of mapping (cf. Borer 1994), I have argued that mapping is a feature checking system rather than an algorithm that associates a verb's arguments to syntactic positions. Assuming that Case assignment is the formal link between event structure features and the projection of syntactic argument positions, I have claimed that there are two structural argument positions: the specifier positions of the functional heads Agr,S and Agr,O. Assuming further that arguments in these specifier positions can identify an event or part of an event (as they are interpreted as an event participant involved in the (sub)event), I have accounted for the different outcomes of mapping similar predicates with different event structures.

Assuming that event structure needs to be identified, the phenomenon of lexical-syntactic flexibility is accounted for as a side-effect of event type-shifting (cf. Davis & Demirdache 1995; Davis 1997, in press; Demirdache 1997). This explains why while there are many different forms of frame alternations, they can be reduced to only three event-semantic kinds. Moreover, the event-semantic generalizations across the different forms within each kind of frame alternations receive a natural foundation. To conclude, I have shown how event type-shifting operations conspire with event-structural mapping conditions to create lexical-syntactic flexibility.

4.9 Tension between a systematic and an idiosyncratic lexicon

Finally, I return to the lexicon. Although the lexicon is often called a reservoir of unpredictable exceptions and idiosyncracies (Williams 1994b refers to this view as the *Bloomfieldian lexicon*), I have shown throughout this chapter that once one knows a verb's lexical primitives, much of its further lexical-syntactic behavior can be derived. Lexical properties are to a large extent systematic, rather than unpredictable. Still, there remain exceptions to rules, idiosyncratic meaning effects, item-particular selection restrictions and unpredictable mapping outcomes. Taking the point of view of the CHESS interface model, I will pull apart the systematic verbal lexicon and the "dictionary" of verbs which lexically lists them with their unsystematic and unpredictable lexical features. I will discuss some of these lexical issues, including the productivity of complex verb formation and event type composition (subsection 4.9.1), systematic versus idiosyncratic meaning effects in complex word formation (subsection 4.9.2) and the productivity of lexical-syntactic flexibility, i.e., the predictability of which verbs appear in certain frame alternations and which do not (subsection 4.9.3).

4.9.1 Possible versus actual complex verbs

Event type composition derives the event structure of the complex verb in a compositional way (as discussed in subsection 4.7.1). As far as event type composition is concerned, complex word formation of a root verb combining with a particle or prefix is in principle unrestricted as long as it obeys the well-formedness principles of event structure. The combinatorial possibilities are large, i.e., the set of potential particle and prefixed verbs. However, not all of these potential verbs actually exist; there is a discrepancy between potential and actual complex verbs (see also subsections 4.7.1 and 4.7.3). More generally, there is a severe tension between the productivity of lexical rules and the actual list of verbs in the "dictionary" of a language. There are many gaps: verbs that might exist but happen not to. I believe the grammatical system has nothing to say about this part of lexicalization, i.e., which meanings become words of the language.[45]

Observing the tension between possible and actual words in the domains of phonology and morphology, Halle (1973) proposes an interface model between lexicon, phonology and syntax that can deal with the regularities as well as the idiosyncracies in phonological and morphological word formation and morphology. His interface model is pictured in (78).

(78) Lexicon-Morphology-Syntax model of Halle (1973):

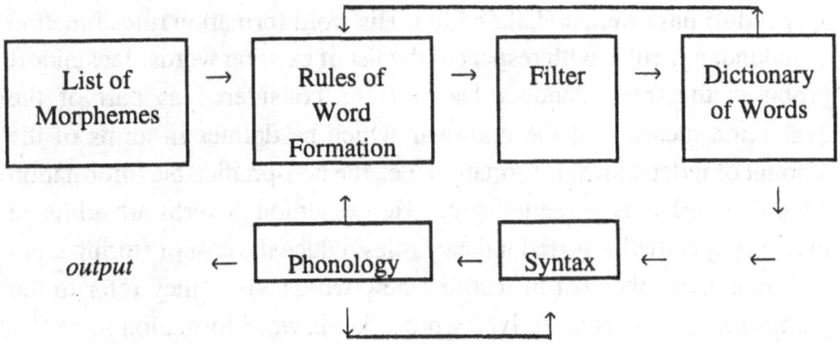

The lexicon consists of a list of morphemes, a rule-based component, a filter and a dictionary. The rule based component is a set of word formation rules that take the elements from the list of morphemes as their input; it defines the set of potential words of a language. The filter gives additional information about idiosyncratic properties of complex words formed by the word formation rules, i.e., idiomatic properties that are not predictable by rule; furthermore, it crucially marks them with either one of the features [-Lexical Insertion] or [+Lexical Insertion]. Only words that get the feature [+Lexical Insertion] pass the filter and belong to the dictionary of the language; they can be inserted into syntax. Hence, the set of actual words is defined by the set of potential words plus the filter.

Following up on Halle's (1973) view on word formation in a generative lexicon, Jackendoff (1975) has an alternative proposal for dealing with the tension between possible and actual words. He claims that the lexicon consists of two parts, (79): a set of word formation rules and a list of the existing words of a language fully specified for their phonological, morphological, syntactic and semantic properties, the dictionary.

(79) Lexicon model of Jackendoff (1975):

Lexicon	
Word Formation Rules	Dictionary

Jackendoff has omitted Halle's filter. His word formation rules function as redundancy rules with respect to the list of existing words. Jackendoff proposes that redundancy rules must be considered as part of the evaluation measure of the grammar which he defines in terms of the amount of independent information, i.e., the non-predictable information which a word adds to the lexicon.[46] Hence, although verbs are all listed in a fully specified way, redundancy rules reduce the cost of storing them and, moreover, the cost of learning new words, since they refer to the predictable elements of derived words via the word formation rules.

Booij (1977) integrates Halle's and Jackendoff's approaches in his model of the lexicon, (80), which he works out in detail for Dutch morphology. Basically following Jackendoff's conception of the lexicon by also omitting the filter but elaborating the word formation component, Booij adds conditions on morpheme structure and distinguishes productive versus non-productive word formation rules.

(80) Lexicon model of Booij (1977):

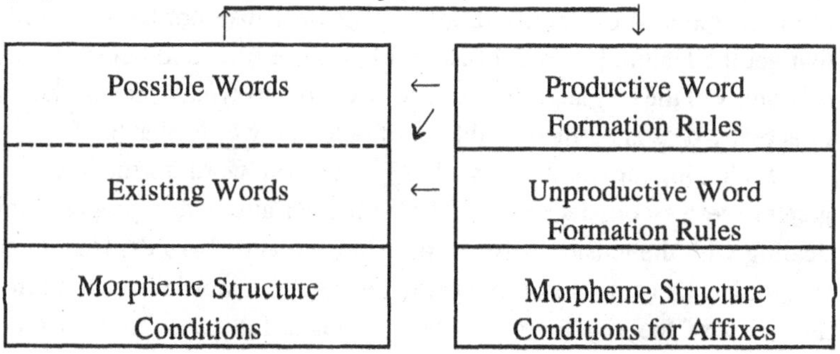

For further discussion and comparison of the differences and consequences of these three models, see Booij (1977).

In a similar vein, while referring to Di Sciullo and Williams (1987), Williams (1994b) claims more recently that "... both the word formation and the syntactic system are 'clean' streamlined systems, independent of the lexicon. The lexicon is the repository of forms about which something special must be learned. This certainly includes, for example, all the monomorphemic words, but it also includes composed units of both syntax and word formation, composed units whose properties do not all follow from the rules which compose them. This would include a great deal of words, but also a great deal of phrases." (Williams 1994b:7-8).

Note that each of the proposals discussed above deals with the discrepancy between possible and actual words by way of listing all actual words in a dictionary. With respect to the issue of possible versus actual complex verbs, I follow these authors: the existence of some form of a dictionary seems inevitable in dealing with the discrepancy.

4.9.2 Systematic versus idiosyncratic meaning effects in complex verbs

On top of the unpredictability of lexicalization with respect to complex verb formation, there are other unpredictable effects. There may occur changes in the selection restrictions in the derivation of a complex verb: a root verb sometimes has different selection restrictions than its particle and prefixed variants. Compare the selection restrictions of some pairs of verbs. For the pair *branden-afbranden* 'burn-burn down', the root verb *branden* 'burn' puts less restrictions on the kind of subject it can combine with than particle verb *afbranden* 'burn down'. Compare the subjects in (81) versus (82).

(81) a. Het huis brandt.
'The house is burning.'
b. Het huis brandt af.
'The house is burning down.'

(82) a. Het boek brandt.
'The book is burning.'
b. *Het boek brandt af.
The book is burning down

Similarly, in the pair *smelten-versmelten* 'melt-melt together', the derived prefix verb is more restricted than the root verb: whereas *smelten* 'melt' can apply to many things, (83a) and (84a), *versmelten* 'melt together' requires a plural subject. Compare (83b) versus (84b).

(83) a. Het goud smelt.
'The gold is melting.'
b. *Het goud versmelt.
the gold PFX-melts

(84) a. De gouden ringen smelten.
'The golden rings are melting.'
b. De gouden ringen versmelten.
'The golden rings are melting together.'

Consider a third pair *schrijven-opschrijven* 'write-write down'. The root verb and the particle variant have different selection restrictions on their object: whereas the object of *schrijven* 'write' must be something that does not yet exist but comes into existence through writing (compare (85a) versus (86a)), one can only *opschrijven* 'write down' something that already exists (compare (85b) versus (86b)).

(85) a. Ik schrijf een proefschrift.
'I am writing a dissertation.'
b. *Ik schrijf een proefschrift op.
I write a dissertation down

(86) a. *Ik schrijf een idee.
I write an idea

b. Ik schrijf een idee op.
'I am writing down an idea.'

All of these additional selection restrictions of derived complex verbs must be referred to the unpredictable part of the lexicon; they are listed along in the dictionary and must be learned for every single item.

Next, consider the meanings of the derived verbs. Whereas some particle and prefixed verbs have a more or less transparent meaning, compositionally based on the meanings of the root verb and the particle or prefix, many complex verbs have a completely uncompositional and therefore unpredictable meaning. Consider for example the meaning effects of particle *op* 'up' which by itself means 'finished'. It retains this meaning in *opbranden* 'burn up, *opeten* 'eat up', *opdrinken* 'drink up'; *oproken* 'smoke up', *opmaken* 'finish'. Along with this meaning, *op* 'up' in another set of particle verbs has a locational meaning which is derived from the locational preposition or directional postposition *op* 'on(to)'. This locational meaning figures in particle verbs such as: *opschrijven* 'write down'; *opladen* 'load'; *opspuiten* 'decorate'; *opzetten* 'put on'; *opkijken* 'look up'; *opstapelen* 'heap up'; *opspelden* 'pin on'; *opstaan* 'stand up'; *opstappen* 'board'. However, there is no similarly transparent meaning for many other *op*-verbs, including: *opdraaien* 'turn up'; *opgeven* 'give up'; *opzoeken* 'look up'; *opsporen* 'track down'; *opstarten* 'start up'; *opsparen* 'save up'; *opspannen* 'stretch'.

A similar case is presented by prefix *ver-*. Prefix *ver-* has a productive meaning effect on the verb it composes with: it adds a negative extent or negative outcome to the base meaning, as observed by Lieber & Baayen (1993). This holds for: *verprutsen* 'botch up'; *vergooien* 'throw away'; *verspillen* 'waste'; *verwerpen* 'reject'; *verdenken* 'suspect'; *verachten* 'despise'. It does so as well in new combinations, e.g., *ver-emailen* 'waste by emailing', which clearly shows the meaning of productive *ver-*. On the other hand, however, many *ver*-verbs do not have this negative meaning aspect, for example: *verzorgen* 'care for'; *verlichten* 'light'; *verzetten* 'move'; *verleggen* 'move'; *verdampen* 'evaporate'; *verkavelen* 'parcel out'.

All of these non-transparent meanings of complex verbs are part of the idiosyncratic lexicon; they must be listed and learned, in the same way as the additional selection restrictions of complex verbs.

Of course, alongside these complex verbs that have stronger or different selection restrictions and idiosyncratic meanings with respect to the root verbs they are derived from, the root verbs themselves must be listed in the dictionary with their item-particular selection restrictions and meanings. Furthermore, verbs that take a prepositional complement must list the idiosyncratic choice of the preposition, e.g., *vertrouwen op* 'trust on'; *wachten op* 'wait for', *antwoorden op* 'answer to'; *vragen naar* 'ask for'; *kijken naar* 'look at', *houden van* 'love', *verlangen naar* 'long for'; *rekenen op* 'rely on' (see subsection 4.5.2).

The existence of all of these unpredictable lexical facts implies that the dictionary that lists all actual verbs and their variants must also specify these verbs with their item-particular properties such as selection restrictions, idiosyncratic meanings and preposition choices.

4.9.3 The productivity of lexical-syntactic flexibility

How productive are the frame alternations that have been presented in Chapters 2 through 4? Reconsider the three kinds of lexical-syntactic flexibility I have distinguished: atelic-telic event type-shifts, causative event type-shifts and shifts of the focus on the event. Each kind of flexibility can have various manifestations (e.g., atelic-telic event type-shifts have the form of an intransitive-transitive alternation or an unergative-unaccusative alternation). The issue of the productivity of what are called argument alternations cannot be directly raised in the present framework, as frame alternations are derived from event type-shifting operations and general mapping requirements on the identification of event structure. Instead, the predictability of which verbs appear in a certain form of frame alternation and which do not is related to the following questions: which verbs can undergo atelic-telic event type-shifting, which can undergo causativization and which allow different foci on the event? The answers to these questions indirectly determine the productivity of frame alternations.

As for atelic-telic event type-shifting which has been discussed in most detail, it appears that all non-stative atelic verbs, i.e., all verbs that basically denote a process, can undergo an atelic-telic event type shift in one form or another (see subsections 4.7.1 and 4.7.2 for the various syntactic manifestations of this shift). Complex predicate formation with a "goal" phrase is restricted to verbs that express abstract or concrete motion. I have characterized this restriction as a selection restriction on the combination of verbs and "goal" phrases: adding an (abstract or physical) goal to a process event requires that the event (potentially) express motion toward a goal. For two-participant process verbs, atelic-telic event type-shifting in the form of the intransitive-transitive alternation is dependent on whether or not the verb has a temporal scale (recall the *eten* 'eat' versus the *duwen* 'push classes discussed in subsection 4.7.2). Finally, atelic-telic event type-shifting by way of resultative formation does not seem to be restricted at all except for (regular) selection restrictions of the resultative predicate on its "subject" (and for pragmatic ones: the kinds of resultative states that one may plausibly connect with the process denoted by the verb).

As for causativizing operations, causativization via the expansion of the event structure with an additional causing event and causer participant (yielding a periphrastic causative construction in Dutch) is unrestricted: any event can be causativized in this way. On the other hand, causativization which only involves the addition of a participant but no additional event structure (yielding a lexical causative) is restricted. One cannot add a participant to just any verb in order to causativize it (or delete one from it in decausativization), even though from an event-semantic perspective, nothing would prevent it. I have briefly touched upon this issue in subsection 4.7.3; I will not discuss it here in any more detail. I refer to various analyses of causative alternations that deal with the issue of productivity (e.g., Pinker 1989; Jackendoff 1990; van Voorst 1993; Levin & Rappaport Hovav 1992, 1994, 1995).

Since I have not discussed frame alternations with different event foci (other than describing some of them in Chapter 3, section 3.6), I have no comments on their productivity.

The interest in the restricted productivity of argument alternations comes not in the least place from the research domain of acquisition (e.g.,

Bowerman 1978a, 1982a,b, 1983, 1987, 1988b; Pinker 1989; Randall 1990, 1992). From the point of view of language acquisition, the fact that the productivity of argument alternations is limited is extremely relevant: how can children learn to restrict the generative power of lexical rules? Since children do not have any negative evidence at their disposal (e.g., negative feedback in the form of a correction whenever they apply a rule to a verb that it happens not to apply to), it is not trivial how they can learn about the restrictions at all. This problem is referred to as the *no negative evidence problem.*

What makes the problem particularly intriguing is the fact that children do not learn their verbs in a conservative way: it is clear from their overgeneralizations that they make use of some form of a frame relating rule system (for many different kinds of argument structure overgeneralizations, see Bowerman 1974, 1978b, 1982a,b, 1983, 1988a). In general, overgeneralizations present a learnability paradox. C. Baker (1979) was the first to point out this paradox for argument alternations. Pinker (1989) extensively discusses this paradox with respect to argument alternation patterns, focusing especially on four different patterns (the dative, locative and causative alternations and passivization) in order to find a principled way in which children can learn the restrictions on alternations in order to get rid of their overgeneralized forms. Pinker's solution is grounded in lexical-conceptual semantics in terms of which verbs are characterized and linking rules to syntax are defined. Lexical rules operate on lexical-conceptual structures; hence, indirectly, they trigger argument alternations (for an illustration, see Chapter 1, subsection 1.4.2). The lexical rules he proposes to account for the alternations under discussion are what he calls *broad-range rules*: they are very general operations that define broad patterns of selectivity in the kinds of verbs that can undergo an alternation. Restricting the application of these operations to finer patterns of selectivity, Pinker furthermore defines narrow conflation classes. While broad-range conflation classes are universal, children have to learn the much finer-grained narrow classes of verbs that actually undergo an alternation. Hence, broad-range rules provide the necessary conditions and narrow-range rules the sufficient conditions for a certain verb to alternate. While they are learning more and more details about the semantics of verbs, children are able to narrow down the application of the lexical rules and, in this way, get rid of their overgeneralizations on the basis of positive evidence only.

Studies on the productivity of argument alternation patterns show that very fine-grained semantic notions play a role. It requires further research how such notions can be incorporated into a mapping system based on checking event-semantic features.

This overview of unpredictable selection restrictions and meanings of derived verbs and the restrictions on the productivity of frame alternating patterns concludes the brief discussion of the idiosyncratic character of the lexicon.

4.10 Implications for the lexicon and the lexicon-syntax interface

Concluding this chapter, I present some final comments on the CHESS model. Positioning the model among other models of the lexicon-syntax interface, I will review some standard notions and discuss how they are incorporated in the CHESS model or can be derived from it (subsection 4.10.1). I will finish with a summary of the properties of mapping as event-semantic feature checking, pointing out the implications for the lexicon and the lexicon-syntax interface (subsection 4.10.2).

4.10.1 Positioning the CHESS model among other mapping systems

In order to compare the CHESS model with other approaches, I will point out how the lexical primitives in the event-semantic checking conditions are related to standard notions in argument-centered mapping and how they are different from them. I will furthermore discuss the nature of feature checking in the CHESS model in relation to other mapping systems.

Event participants versus θ-roles, arguments and LCS-variables

One of the central lexical primitives I have put forward in the CHESS model is that of *event participant*. At first blush, this primitive seems very similar to standard lexical primitives such as θ-role, argument and LCS-variable. Indeed, there is some overlap between event participant and standard notions to the extent that they all refer to those semantic entities that are the arguments in a functor-argument relation as expressed by the verb or another predicate. However, the notion *event participant* is more restricted than the standard notions, in that it exclusively refers to entities that are semantically arguments of the verb. θ-Roles, arguments and LCS-variables on the other hand have also been associated with "goal" or "source" phrases. Semantically however, a "goal" or "source" phrase is itself a functor, since it modifies the verb; it is not an argument of the verb. In the CHESS model, "goal" and "source" phrases are associated with the verb, forming a semantically complex predicate with it; they contribute to the inner aspect of the sentence via event type composition and identify the first or final subevent of a transition. Notice that particles and prefixes are associated with the verb in similar event-semantic ways. Yet, they are never viewed as arguments that can bear a θ-role in standard theories. The CHESS model treats "goal" and "source" phrases as modifiers, on a par with prefixes and particles; standard theories on the other hand analyze the former as arguments of the verb.

This definition of *event participant* has the conceptual advantage of bringing syntax and semantics closer together. The syntactic and semantic structures in a sentence are isomorphic as the notion *event participant* exclusively refers to semantic arguments and *event modifier* refers to semantic modifiers. Hence, the syntactic and semantic notions *argument* and *modifier* are not confounded. Furthermore, the similar event-semantic contributions of PPs, particles and prefixes are accounted for in a natural way.

Whereas mapping theories defined on θ-roles or LCS-variables crucially depend on the lexical-semantic differentiation of a verb's arguments, I have claimed that a verb only needs to specify the number of event participants without any further semantic labels. Verbs differ from each other as to how many participants are involved in the event: a verb takes one or two participants. Rather than lexically annotating a verb's event participants with a particular semantics, I derive the semantic differentiation of participants via various kinds of interpretational principles; these determine the relative agentivity of event participants. The event structure plays a role: a participant involved in the first subevent of a transition is more agentive than one involved in the second subevent (cf. Grimshaw 1990; Pustejovsky 1991; Davis & Demirdache

1995; Davis 1997, in press; Demirdache 1997). Moreover, the syntactic argument positions themselves are associated with a particular semantics: if there are two arguments, an argument in subject position is relatively more agentive than one in object position (cf. Emonds 1991a; Borer 1994; Gleitman 1995; Goldberg 1995; Kako 1997, 1998). Furthermore, morphological affixes contribute or even attribute a certain semantics (e.g., passive morphology attributes agentivity).

The main advantage of the present approach is that the lexicon is more parsimonious, since verbs do not need to be lexically specified for the semantics of their participants. Moreover, ambiguous or arbitrary lexical specification is avoided in the case of verbs that can take either agentive or non-agentive participants and verbs that are not specific about the agentivity of their event participants. Another advantage is that the mapping conditions are simple, as they are oblivious to the semantics of a verb's participants. There is no need for a θ-hierarchy as a theoretical primitive; its effects are derived via interpretation principles defined by the event structure and the syntactic configuration.

Checking event-semantic structure versus linking lexical arguments to syntactic positions

The nature of the CHESS mapping system is essentially different from those of standard mapping systems. Typically, the mapping function is defined as a set of linking rules that associate every argument of the verb with a particular syntactic position, possibly via an intermediary level of argument structure. I have presented a different view of mapping in the CHESS model: mapping involves checking off a verb's event-semantic features in the syntactic configuration it appears in. Checking the event-semantic structure of a predicate determines whether or not a verb is licensed in projecting a particular syntactic configuration. If it is, interpretative principles determine the event-semantic interpretation of the verb in this configuration.

Standard views on mapping are designed in such a way that the item-particular specification of a verb fully determines how it is mapped onto syntax. However, I have defined the mapping conditions on the event-semantic features of predicates, rather than verbs. The generalization that a telic predicate always requires an argument in object position holds across all kinds of telic predicates, including simplex and complex telic verbs and complex predicates, and independent of the number of event participants the verb selects. This generalization cannot be derived in verb-based mapping models. Hence, I have argued that it suggests that the mapping system is not exclusively driven by item-particular lexical information, as it must also take into account the information of other elements in the predicate.

These two properties of the CHESS model have several consequences which make this model stand out from standard approaches. First, the CHESS model accounts for the phenomenon of lexical-syntactic flexibility in terms of event structure differences. Events can be perceived from different event-semantic perspectives. Event structure being the basis of the CHESS conditions and different event structures having different mapping requirements, lexical-syntactic flexibility follows as a natural consequence. In a standard approach, the fact that a verb can appear in multiple frames complicates the mapping system; it means that a verb has multiple lexical representations, possibly related to each other via lexical rules or operations, or, alternatively, that other frames are derived via syntactic operations. The advantage of the CHESS approach is that flexibility is incorporated in the mapping conditions as an inherent property of the system itself; there is no need for postulating lexical or syntactic operations to derive it.

Furthermore, whereas many standard mapping approaches assume different levels of representation (i.e., argument structure, D-structure), the CHESS conditions directly relate a verb's event structure features to properties of S-structure configurations. It does not refer to any intermediate levels of representation, such as argument structure or D-structure. In this sense, the CHESS system is simpler and therefore more elegant.

A final consequence of the design of the CHESS model is that the notion *argument* is more clearly defined. While the argument-adjunct distinction is a central dichotomy in argument-centered mapping approaches (formalized as whether or not a phrase bears a θ-role or is associated with an argument in the argument structure), the status of phrases that do not appear in the typical argument positions (i.e., subject and object) is often unclear. Especially with respect to PPs, theories often do not offer clear criteria that determine which are arguments and which are not. Also, when a lexical-semantic argument appears in other than syntactic argument positions (e.g., in a *by*-phrase in a passive), it is not clear whether or not it can be considered a true argument.

The CHESS model decomposes the event-structural, the semantic and the syntactic properties of the notion *argument*. Syntactically, there are two argument positions: the specifier positions of AgrS and AgrO. Phrases in these positions are associated with an event participant in the event structure. Semantically, they function as event identifiers. One may refer to these phrases as *arguments*. However, phrases in other positions than Spec, AgrS or Spec, AgrO can also refer to an event participant (e.g., bare noun objects and oblique PPs, including conative PPs). These fall between the traditional argument-adjunct dichotomy. Syntactically, they behave differently than "real" arguments in subject and object position. Semantically they are modifiers, as they reduce the set of events denoted by the verb to a subset. Still, they are associated with a participant in the event structure. Furthermore, there are phrases that participate in building up the inner aspectual event structure (e.g., "goal" and "source" phrases, resultative complements). These are involved in event type composition with the verb, but do not refer to one of its event participants. Rather, they specify a subevent and are necessary to identify the resulting state of a transition. Semantically, they are modifiers of the predicate. Finally, one may use the term *adjunct* to refer to phrases that are not in Spec, AgrS or Spec, AgrO, phrases that are not associated with an event participant and phrases that do not participate in the composition of inner aspect. Hence, the standard argument-adjunct dichotomy is a finer-grained distinction in the CHESS model: there is no strict dichotomy between arguments and non-arguments, as the notion *argument* refers to a conglomerate of properties, including event-structural as well as syntactic and semantic ones.

4.10.2 Summary: the CHESS model

The CHESS model provides a principled account of the syntactic and semantic properties of lexical-syntactic flexibility. The event-semantic analysis of lexical-syntactic flexibility provides the insight that the many different forms of verb frame alternations reduce to only three different kinds. The relation between the two alternants in an alternation can be analyzed in terms of taking different perspectives on the same event, more specifically, in terms of event type-shifting. One set of alternations involves an atelic-telic event type-shift and another involves causativization while for a third set, the alternants present different foci on the event. The central role of event type features in the CHESS model explains why there are only few kinds of alternations. Moreover, it accounts for the mapping generalizations across the various forms of alternations of a particular kind, explaining why the alternations take on the particular syntactic forms they have.

The lexicon in the CHESS model is maximally parsimonious. The phenomenon of lexical-syntactic flexibility does not involve an exhaustive listing of a verb's set of potential argument structures or lexical-conceptual meanings. Moreover, there is no need for lexical rules that relate or derive lexical specifications, since event type-shifting is a general and independent operation. It automatically derives lexical-syntactic flexibility, as the CHESS model is defined on event-semantic properties and operations. Parsimony is not only interesting for general science-theoretic reasons; it is a necessary requirement of any theory of the lexicon in view of the learnability task children are faced with: learning the syntactic and semantic properties of all the verbs in their language.

The CHESS model implements the relation between syntax and semantics in an integrated way. The mapping conditions associate lexical event-semantic features with properties of syntactic configurations via Case assignment. Hence, the model integrates the following lexical, syntactic and semantic properties: basic event type and number of event participants; event type-shifting; object versus oblique Case; weak versus strong Case and the accompanying movement of an argument out of VP to the specifier position of a functional projection (AgrS and AgrO); weak versus strong interpretation of noun phrases. Mapping is defined by the interaction between lexical event-semantic features and properties of syntactic configurations. Interpretation is defined on event-semantic properties and properties of the syntactic configuration.

Given the event-semantic properties of prefixes, particles and root verbs, the CHESS model accounts for the frame alternating effects in pairs of root verbs and their particle or prefix variants, as event type composition composes the event structures of the verb and particle or prefix. Event type composition is at play as well in combinations with a "goal" or resultative phrase; the CHESS model also accounts for the mappings of complex predicates. In this way, the mapping generalizations across simplex verbs, complex verbs and syntactically complex predicates have been integrated in one set of mapping conditions.

In the CHESS model, mapping is not conceived of as a one-to-one linking algorithm between lexical arguments and syntactic argument positions. Instead, the mapping algorithm is a feature checking system: a verb's event-semantic features are associated with particular properties of a syntactic configuration, depending on the event structure properties of the whole predicate. Different event structures involve different checking requirements, thereby creating lexical-syntactic flexibility. Since mapping conditions are defined on event-semantic properties rather than lexical arguments and define direct associatiations with syntactic configurations, there is no need for an intermediate level of argument structure between lexicon and syntax in the CHESS model. Hence, it provides a simple model of grammar.

The aim of this chapter was to identify what are the relevant lexical-syntactic features and to model the lexicon-syntax interface in such a way as to explain the phenomenon of lexical-syntactic flexibility. As mapping conditions are defined on event-semantic structure, the event-semantic generalizations that characterize the phenomenon fall out naturally as a side-effect of event type-shifting: event type-shifting and event-semantic mapping conditions conspire to derive lexical-syntactic flexibility.

Notes

1. Chomsky writes: ". . . thus reducing syntactic representations at D-structure to projections of semantic properties of lexical items" (Chomsky 1986:90). "The representations that appear at the various levels are those that can be projected from semantic properties of lexical items in such a way as to accord with various principles of UG with their parameters set" (Chomsky 1986:93).
2. To be precise, Gross (1973) mentions that some verbs of saying and some of animal sounds do have the same properties. On a total of 3000 verbs, these similarities reduce the number of different verb classes to 1800 (!).
3. In fact, Gruber (1965) himself points out that arguments can have multiple thematic relations, which he incorporates into his system of thematic relations by allowing one NP to have multiple thematic relations. Jackendoff (1972) interprets Gruber's observation differently, concluding that thematic relations themselves are not lexical primitives, but must be defined in terms of semantic subfunctions (such as CAUSE, CHANGE and BE).
4. These cases are less of a problem for LCS-based theories. In fact, Jackendoff (1990) discusses the issue of obligatory adjuncts (of verbs such as *rid*, *provide* and *present*), concluding that they must be represented in the lexical entry. He introduces some notation that lexically distinguishes arguments and adjuncts from each other.
5. The argument structure change in which an indirect internal argument becomes a direct internal one is a hypothetical analysis for the locative and the oblique intransitive-transitive alternations. In fact, Williams (1981) claims that argument structure affecting operations may only affect the external argument, not the internal arguments. He mentions the dative alternation as an example that may not be dealt with via lexical rules; he assumes instead that these verbs lexically subcategorize for both frames.
6. Borer (1994) calls these approaches *lexical-entry-driven.*
7. Some verbs with a prepositional complement appear in the oblique intransitive-transitive alternation (e.g., *vertrouwen op-vertrouwen* 'trust on-trust'; *wachten op-verwachten* 'wait for-expect'; *kijken naar-bekijken* 'look at-examine'; *antwoorden op-beantwoorden* 'answer to-answer'). If the NP complement is considered an event participant of the verb, one can analyze this alternation as a regular position-varying alternation in which an event participant alternates between indirect and direct internal argument position.
8. The idea that prepositions take their own event participants is further developed in subsection 4.7.1.

9. Notice the contrast between Dechaine (1993) and other adherents of the single complement hypothesis (e.g., Larson 1988; Neeleman 1994): while most assume that the complement PP is lexically selected by the verb and receives a θ-role from it, Dechaine concludes that there is no need to consider it an argument.
10. In van Hout (1992b), I formulate the following Linking Principle:
    A. Aspectual structure is licensed if (i) or (ii):
       (i) in the case of a simple aspectual structure, there is an argument that identifies it;
       (ii) in the case of a complex aspectual structure, each part (being an aspectual structure) must be licensed.
    B. An argument is licensed if it identifies a simple aspectual structure, or a part of a complex aspectual structure.
11. Post-hoc thanks to Henry Davis and Hamida Demirdache for grilling me for a couple of hours on this topic. That occasion lies at the foundation of this section, even though the conclusion I reached is the contrary of what they were trying to convince me of (i.e., giving up lexical reference to event participants all together).
12. Not every event participant gets mapped onto syntax in every frame, but all of them together may get mapped onto syntax in one particular frame (or frames). The ones that do not get mapped onto syntax are understood arguments. I refer to section 2.2.2 for a discussion of the term *understood argument* and its variants (*optional, suppressed, absorbed, null, zero* and *implicit argument*).
13. This regularity is the basis of the concept of thematic hierarchies; they all list "agent" as the highest on the hierarchy.
14. Actually, it only holds for eventive verbs that the subject is more agentive. The event participants of stative verbs cannot be characterized in terms of agency, since the verb describes a property of or a relation between them. Furthermore, certain psychological verbs, i.e., the *frighten*-class, seem to align the participants in reversed order with respect to their agentivity, or, rather, sentience.
15. Notice that an analysis of passivization that is phrased in terms of suppressing or blocking the external argument cannot deal with this semantic restriction on passivization (cf. among others, Williams 1981; Di Sciullo & Williams 1987; Roberts 1987; Baker 1988; Baker, Johnson & Roberts 1989).
16. Notice that this is unlike English stative verbs which do passivize (e.g., *The answer was known to everybody*).

17. For Dowty (1991), however, this does seem to be the case, given the way he defines *argument selection* (see above). It seems to me to imply that a verb determines how many proto-agent and how many proto-patient properties each of its arguments has.
18. Thanks to Denis Bouchard who made me realize the implications of these facts, by asking me the right kind of questions.
19. Thanks to Jacqueline Gueron for pushing this point.
20. *Figure* and *ground* are Talmy's (1985) terms. He employs *ground* for a uniform treatment of the semantic roles "goal", "source" and "location". *Figure* is his term for "theme".
21. Emonds formulates his interpretative principles as follows. "*Figure Specification*: For any lexical [X^0, +T], exactly one Figure NP, distinct from the Ground, must be present among the deep structure arguments of X^0. . . . *Ground Specification.* A direct object NP of a transitive Y^0 is a ground if and only if Y^0 is +LOCATION" (Emonds 1991a:395, 397). As for the interpretation of "agents", Emonds cites Chomsky (1972):"*Agent specification.* "Thus one rule (probably universal) will stipulate that for verbs of action, the animate subject may be interpreted as the agent, etc." (Chomsky 1972:75)", repeated in Emonds 1991a:399).
22. Clearly, the derivation of the semantic properties of participants in a state or a psychological event needs to be worked out further. I will not attempt this here, having restricted my domain of investigation to eventive verbs.
23. The idea of coercing agentivity onto an event originated in discussions with Harald Baayen; he receives credit for dubbing this interpretative phenomenon *agentivity construal.*
24. In addition to this agentive *-er*, there is another *-er* which may be interpreted as an "instrument" (e.g., *lawn mower*) or "theme" (e.g., *fryer*). See further van Hout & Roeper (1998).
25. Thanks to Martin Everaert for urging me to clear up my mind and my claims with respect to this issue.
26. In a review of this dissertation, Philip (1997) correctly points out that " . . . unlike type-shifting as it is standardly understood, no complete linguistic expression ever changes its logical type when event type-shifting "occurs". Rather, the event type of a predicate is determined once and for all by the basic expressions it is made up of" (Philip 1997:15). I indeed view event type-shifting as a compositional, bottom-up process. My use of the term is somewhat confusing given the tradition of the term *type-shifting*. In that tradition, what I have in mind here would be referred to as *event sort-shifting*: within the type of events, a verb can shift from one event sort to another (Barbara Partee, personal communication).

27. For example, an event that is bounded in its inner aspect is interpreted as an iteration of events when modified by a durative temporal modifier (e.g., *Judith at de hele dag door een botherham* 'During the whole day, J. ate a sandwich'). Moreover, an unbounded event can be given temporal boundaries by the bounding temporal modifiers (e.g., *Judith at boterhammen van 1 tot 3* 'J. ate sandwiches from 1 to 3.').
28. Alternatively, one can take the first subevent in the transition denoted by *op* 'onto' as a process in which case the postposition would only be allowed to merge with a process predicate. I have opted here for a less restricted specification, an unspecified *E*, to allow the possibility that this transition of the postposition merges with a verb (e.g., *verdwijnen* 'disappear') that denotes a transition with two states as subevent (e.g., *de berg op verdwijnen* 'disappear onto the mountain').
29. In colloquial Dutch, this sentence has an interpretation, but not the resultative one I am after here: 'The dictator tortured the prisoner's fingers until they broke'. In (42b) the string *de gevangene zijn vingers* is a complex DP, headed by *vingers* 'fingers' with *de gevangene* 'the prisoner' as a possessor.
30. Neeleman (1994) offers a semantic account in terms of θ-roles. His θ-role percolation system rules out (42b) because it forbids a complex predicate from having two the same θ-roles (here, two "themes").
31. In order to accommodate the odometer effect, Verkuyl (1993) proposes different lexical features on the θ-role for the internal argument. These different θ-roles determine how the odometer "runs".
32. Of the one-participant process verbs in this small survey, none has a temporal scale. An example of such a verb with a temporal scale is *groeien* 'grow'.
33. Not all integrated causative events are transitions, though: there are also causative processes (e.g., *aardappels koken* 'boil potatoes'). See section 3.5.1 for more details and examples.
34. In section 3.5.2, I discuss one case where a stative verb event type-shifts to an integrated causative event (i.e., stative *hangen* 'hang' event type-shifts to causative *hangen* 'hang'); in this case there is an event type-shift from state to transition, in addition to the extra participant.
35. This kind of event modifier reading of the object is similar to the modifying effect of a noun on a verb in noun-incorporations like *pianospelen* 'play the piano' and *stofzuigen* 'vacuum' (lit. 'dust-suck'). Event-semantically, there is no difference between incorporated nouns and bare objects; noun-incorporated verbs have more conventionalized (fossilized) and less compositional meanings than verbs with a bare object. See van Geenhoven (1996) on the semantics of noun incorporation and indefinites.
36. I have also presented this proposal in van Hout (1991b, 1992a,b, 1994).

37. If a generic reading is available, e.g., when the adverb changes into *altijd* 'always', scrambling of a bare plural object becomes possible: *dat de politie taalkundigen altijd opgepakt heeft* 'that the police always arrested linguists'. Similarly, if a cardinal NP is substituted for the bare plural object, scrambling is possible, yielding a strong, partitive reading: *dat de politie veel taalkundigen gisteren opgepakt heeft* 'that the police arrested many linguists yesterday'. See de Hoop (1992:138-139).
38. In van Hout (1994), I propose that the relevant functional projection for checking telicity features is the Aspect Phrase (AspP). In the present proposal, I opt for AgrOP in order to stress the fact that it must be the object that bears the telicity features.
39. (69) is ungrammatical with normal intonation. It becomes better when the object bears heavy stress (for example, when one expresses surprise at the fact that she ate apple pie). De Hoop (1992) notes that focus affects semantic interpretation as well, as it introduces contrastiveness. A bare object may get a strong reading under the influence of focus.
40. Noticing the problem with atelic transitives such as *duwen* 'push', Mulder (1992) and Borer (1994) introduce additional analyses.
41. I am obliged to Henk van Riemsdijk for suggesting this name (and its abbreviation!) to me.
42. Some of the trees below in fact suggest some structure inside the VP, in particular (75) and (76). Nothing in the CHESS mapping conditions depends on what this structure is exactly.
43. Van Riemsdijk (personal communication) points out that Borer's conclusion that there is no hierarchical structure below VP has been reached earlier from a different perspective. In fact, it is one of the main research issues of the seventies and early eighties: the issue of configurationality. Several languages have been claimed to be non-configurational, i.e., to have a flat VP structure, including German (Haider 1981), Warlpiri (Hale 1983) and Hungarian (Kiss 1987).
44. In the terms $AspP_{EM}$ and $AspP_{OR}$, EM stands for *event measure*; OR stands for *originator*. Borer formulates the following Conditions on Aspectual Realization (Borer 1994:35):
    a. If $AspP_{EM}$ is specified then AspP is [+EM];
    b. If $AspP_{EM}$ is specified it must be fully realized (i.e., it must have a filled specifier);
    c. Every proposition must have (at least) one fully specified aspectual node.

    When AspP is [+EM], the sentence gets a telic interpretation.

45. With respect to other properties of verbs, however, the grammatical system does restrict lexicalization of verbal meanings into verbs; see Dowty (1991) and Hale & Keyser (1992, 1993).
46. Jackendoff (1975) defines the information measure as follows: "Given a fully specified lexical entry W to be introduced into the lexicon, the independent information it adds to the lexicon is (a) the information that W exists in the lexicon, i.e., that W is a word of the language; plus (b) all the information in W that cannot be predicted by the existence of some redundancy rule R which permits W to be partially described in terms of information already in the lexicon; plus (c) the cost of referring to the redundancy rule R." (Jackendoff 1975:643).

CHAPTER 5

Learning Verbs: Learning Light Verbs

In the present and next chapters, I address the acquisition of verbs against background assumptions on the lexicon-syntax interface as defined by the CHESS mapping conditions in Chapter 4.[1] In this chapter I argue that if verbs are characterized in the lexicon with their event types, so-called *light verbs* are easy verbs to acquire, because they are pure event type denoters. A longitudinal study of four Dutch children supports this prediction. From early on, these children produce a great variety of light verb constructions, including also some overgeneralized ones. Analyzing their light verb constructions, I have compared instances with the same complement but with different light verbs; these pairs denote different event types of the same kind of event. Furthermore, I have evaluated the nature of their overgeneralized constructions. The results lead to the conclusion that in child Dutch, verbs are lexically characterized in terms of their event types. Child language data thus provide another source of data that point to the role of event structure in lexical specification and in the interface between lexicon and syntax.

5.1 Goals of this chapter

Having developed a theory on the lexicon and its mapping onto syntax based on data from adult Dutch in the previous chapters, I will now address the issue of acquiring the lexicon and the mapping system. A child who is learning the verbs of the language must not only learn their meanings, but also their lexical-syntactic features. Verb-learning raises two main questions: (i) how does a child come to know the semantics and the lexical-syntactic features of the new verbs she is learning? (ii) how does she come to know the mapping system between lexicon and syntax?

As a first step in seeking answers to these questions about the verb-learning process, I will focus on a subset of verbs: light verbs. A well known fact about child language, but never systematically studied, is the fact that children use a lot of light verb constructions. The question of why they do so has, at least to my knowledge, never been posed. I will argue that light verbs are relatively easy to acquire in a lexicon that is designed to specify verbs' event types, because light verbs have no more semantic content than denoting a certain event type. This explains why light verbs are popular verbs for children. A systematic case study of the acquisition of Dutch light verbs reveals which light verbs children use and how they use them in various light verb constructions. It shows that light verbs are indeed commonly used by children. I will discuss the implications of child usage of light verb constructions for an analysis of light verb constructions and, more generally, for the design of lexical specification.

First, I will discuss the lexical-syntactic properties of light verbs (section 5.2). Taking the CHESS mapping conditions as a background for developing a model of verb learning, I will discuss what is involved in acquiring verbs and how light verbs are different from other verbs in this respect (section 5.3). A longitudinal study of the light verb constructions produced by four Dutch children presents evidence for the development hypotheses that I will formulate (section 5.4). I will conclude that child language data present another source of data for evaluating theories on the lexicon and its interface to syntax. In particular, they provide evidence for the notion *event type* as a lexical-syntactic primitive by which verbs must be characterized (section 5.5).

5.2 Light verbs in Dutch

Within the large set of verbs, there is a small distinguished subset of so-called *light verbs*. Light verbs (henceforth, LVs) have less semantic content than non-light verbs; they combine with a complement that adds further semantics to the LV construction. A typical example of a Dutch and English LV is *geven* 'give' in *een kus geven* 'give a kiss'. LVs have been studied in a number of languages, among which English (e.g., Cattell 1984; Kearns 1989), Japanese (e.g., Grimshaw & Mester 1988) and Dutch (e.g., Hollebrandse 1993; Everaert & Hollebrandse 1995).

A verb is referred to as a *light verb* when it occurs in particular constructions; next to this, the verb often also has a non-light usage. Syntactically, an LV behaves more or less like its non-light counterpart (for example, both LV and non-light *geven* 'give' map onto a ditransitive frame).[2] Semantically, however, an LV is a "bleached" variant of the non-light counterpart. The meaning of LV *geven* 'give' is only remotely related to non-light *geven* 'give': the event denoted by *een kus geven* 'give a kiss' is not an actual giving event; rather, it is a kissing event.

For many (but not all) LV constructions in Dutch and English, there also exists a lexical verb that expresses more or less the same meaning (e.g., *een kus geven* 'give a kiss' - *kussen* 'kiss'). To distinguish LV constructions and their lexical counterparts, I will call the latter *full verbs* (so, *kussen* 'kiss' is the full verb variant of the LV construction *een kus geven* 'give a kiss'). The meaning of an LV construction is to some extent compositional, depending on the meanings of the LV and the LV complement (an object, a PP complement or an adjectival complement). However, LV constructions are also slightly idiomatic, precisely because the verb has an abstract rather than a literal meaning. Defining what are and what are not LV constructions, I consider all non-literal uses of verbs as LV instances. Hence, I include typical LV constructions (e.g., *een kus geven* 'give a kiss'), but also combinations of an LV with an adjective (e.g., *open maken* 'open' (lit., 'make open')), a particle (e.g., *uit doen* 'put off, extinguish' (lit., 'do off')) or a PP (e.g., *in bad gaan* 'take a bath' (lit., 'go in bath')).

Looking more closely at the semantics of LV constructions, I characterize an LV as a purely aspectual verb: it has no more semantic content than denoting a certain event type. Different LVs spell out different event types. For example, while *geven* 'give', *gaan* 'go' and *komen* 'come' denote a transition, *doen* 'do' denotes a process. Some examples of LV denoting different event types are given in (1).

(1) Different LVs spell out different event types:

a. One-participant transition:

T

S S

x *x*

in bad gaan 'take a bath' (lit., 'go in bath')
open gaan 'open' (lit., 'go open')
in beweging komen 'get moving' (lit., 'get into movement')

b. Two-participant transition:

T

P S

x, *y* *y*

in bad doen 'give a bath' (lit., 'do in bath')
open maken 'open' (lit., 'make open')
een kus geven 'give a kiss'

c. One-participant process:

P

x

in bad zitten 'bath' (lit., 'sit in bath')
lawaai maken 'make noise'
een dutje doen 'take a nap' (lit., 'do a nap')

Note that there are no LV constructions that denote a two-participant process. There are transitive LV constructions, such as two of the examples in (1c). However, the LV complement itself is one of the "participants" in these constructions; hence, the LV construction as a complex predicate takes only one participant (i.e., the subject).

The semantics of an LV construction is constructed compositionally. The LV determines the event type, but it does not specify the kind of event. This information comes from the LV complement: it determines the content of the event. This explains the combinatorial properties of LV constructions: a particular LV can combine with different LV complements. LV constructions with the same LV have the same event type, but each denotes a different kind of event; some illustrations are given in (2).

(2) LVs combine with different LV complements:

a.	*geven*	*een kus; een hand; een klap*
	'give'	a kiss; a hand; a slap
		'give a kiss; shake hands; slap'
b.	*maken*	*open; kapot; een puzzel*
	'make'	open; broken; a puzzle
		'open; break; do a puzzle'
c.	*doen*	*een dutje; boodschappen; een plas*
	'do'	a nap; shopping; a pee
		'take a nap; shop; take a pee'

Notice that in the case of LV constructions consisting of an LV and an adjective, particle or PP complement, event type composition applies: it combines the event types of the verb and the complement in the same way as in complex predicates (see Chapter 4, subsection 4.7.1). Hence, when a certain LV complement combines with different LVs, they all denote the same kind of event, but each combination expresses a different event type. Some examples are given in (3).

(3) LV complements combine with different LVs resulting in different event types:

a. *open gaan* 'open' (lit., 'go open')
   open maken 'open' (lit., 'make open')
   open doen 'open' (lit., 'do open')

b. *in bad zitten* 'bath' (lit., 'sit in bath')
   in bad gaan 'take a bath' (lit., 'go in bath')
   in bad doen 'give a bath' (lit., 'do in bath')

c. *in beweging raken* 'get moving' (lit., 'get into movement')
in beweging komen 'get moving' (lit., 'come into movement')
in beweging brengen 'get moving' (lit., 'bring into movement')

The two-participant predicates *open maken* 'open' (lit., 'make open') and *open doen* 'open' (lit., 'do open') in (3a) are both causative variants of the one-participant predicate *open gaan* 'open' (lit., 'go open') which expresses a change of state. This causative/change-of-state alternation is the same as the causative-inchoative alternation (e.g., with *breken* 'break'). The other triplets in (3b) and (3c) express similar causative-inchoative patterns.

Considering in more detail the relation between LVs and the event type they denote, each kind of event type is associated with a small set of LVs, rather than just one. For example, a causative event can be formed with one of the following LVs: *geven* 'give' (e.g., *een kus geven* 'give a kiss'); *maken* 'make' (e.g., *kapot maken* 'break' (lit., 'make broken')); *doen* 'do' (e.g., *in bad doen* 'give a bath' (lit., 'do in bath')); *nemen* 'take' (e.g., *in overweging nemen* 'take into consideration'); *brengen* 'bring' (e.g., *in beweging brengen* 'bring into movement'). Furthermore, one particular LV can spell out different event types. For example, in certain LV constructions, *doen* 'do' spells out a causative event (e.g., *in bad doen* 'give a bath'; *uit doen* 'put off, extinguish' (lit., 'do off')), whereas in other constructions, it refers to a process (e.g., *boodschappen doen* 'shop' (lit., 'do shoppings'); *een dutje doen* 'take a nap' (lit., 'do a nap')). On the one hand, the relation between event types and LVs is one-to-a-few; on the other hand, the relation between LVs and event types is one-to-two for most LVs.

The fact that there is no one-to-one relation between LVs and event types is responsible for their idiomatic character. Even though knowing the event type reduces the choice of LV to a small set, one cannot completely predict the selection of a particular LV on the basis of event type properties alone. Other factors (specifically, subcategorization properties) play a role as well (see Hollebrandse 1993). Moreover, there is also some amount of idiosyncratic selection. To a certain extent then, it must simply be learned which particular LV must be selected for a certain verbal meaning (i.e., which LV combines with which LV complement). So, whereas one can analyze complex predicates, including LV constructions, in a compositional way using event type composition, LV constructions cannot be formed as productively as other complex predicates: LV constructions must be listed in the "dictionary"; other complex predicates do not need to (see also Chapter 4, section 4.9).

Comparing LV constructions and their full verb variants, notice that there are slight meaning differences between an LV construction and a full V: each focuses on a different part of the event. Hollebrandse (1993) observes that for many pairs, there is a telic-atelic distinction between the LV construction and the associated full verb. For example, *een kus geven* 'give a kiss' denotes a telic event, whereas *kussen* 'kiss' is an atelic event. Hence, the relation between an LV construction and a full verb involves event type-shifting. Note also that not every LV construction has an associated full verb. For certain verbal meanings, there exists only an LV construction (e.g., *een hand geven* 'shake hands' (lit., 'give a hand'); there is no full verb **handen* 'hand'). For others, there is only a full verb variant (e.g., *lachen* 'laugh'; **een lach doen/maken* 'do/make a laugh' does not exist in Dutch). Lexicalization of verbal meanings in a language, i.e., whether they exist as full verbs, LV constructions, or as both, seems to be rather arbitrary: a child must learn which meanings are full verbs and/or LV constructions while learning the "dictionary" of the language.

Finally, consider briefly some crosslinguistic variation in LV constructions. Languages vary with respect to how many and which LVs manifest a certain event type and with respect to the combinations of particular LVs with particular LV complements. Even in relatively closely related languages such as Dutch, German and English there is some unpredictable variation in LV selection for the same verbal meanings.[3] Compare for example, Dutch *een plasje doen* 'do a pee', German *pipi machen* 'make a pee' and English *take a pee*. Apparently, the set of LVs spelling out a particular event type is language specific; moreover, the selection of an LV for a certain verbal meaning is item specific. Again, this shows the idiosyncratic or "dictionary" character of LV constructions.

A theory of the lexicon must deal with the systematic and regular elements in the lexicon. Discussing the event-semantic properties of LV constructions, I have pulled apart what is part of this systematic lexicon and what is not; the latter kind of lexical information must be directed to the idiosyncratic lexicon (the "dictionary"; see Chapter 4, section 4.9). The different properties of light and full verbs lead to the following conclusions about their lexical specification. For all verbs, the basic event type needs to be specified. This is all for LVs: LVs are semantically light; they function as spell-out verbs of a particular event type. For non-light verbs on the other hand, the further semantics of the verb needs to be specified (i.e., what kind of event it denotes). Finally, despite the compositional nature of LV constructions, but in view of the amount of idiosyncracy in LV constructions, the lexicon must also list the set of LV constructions of a language, along with the list of full verbs in the "dictionary".

To conclude, assuming a theory of the lexicon based on event types and an analysis of LVs as event type denoters, one reduces the selection space for choosing an LV for a particular LV complement to the few LVs with the appropriate event type. Hence, under this analysis, the amount of learning involved in acquiring the LV constructions of one's lexicon is brought down to a minimum, since their systematic and compositional nature is maximally exploited.

5.3 Light-verb learning is light verb-learning

Recall the acquisition issues raised at the outset of this chapter: (i) how does a child learn the semantics and the lexical-syntactic features of the new verbs she is learning? (ii) how does she learn the mapping system between lexicon and syntax?

Turning first to the latter issue, the Strong Continuity Hypothesis claims that the child's grammar has only properties of and is fully compatible with Universal Grammar (UG) at all stages of the acquisition process (see Pinker 1984; Whitman, Lee & Lust 1990; Weissenborn 1993; Penner & Weissenborn 1996). Applying the Strong Continuity hypothesis to the acquisition of the lexicon and the mapping system, the design of the child's lexicon should be similar to that of an adult. Furthermore, the child's mapping system will be similar to the adult's. Hence, the outline of lexical-syntactic knowledge (i.e., the kinds of features by which each verb must be lexically specified) and the mapping conditions will be present form the start.

Embedding this in a lexicon-syntax model defined by the CHESS mapping conditions (see Chapter 4, Part III), under the Strong Continuity hypothesis, the child comes equipped with knowledge of the CHESS mapping conditions and the kinds of lexical primitives they are defined on. If the mapping conditions themselves are given, the child "only" needs to learn the semantics of individual verbs and fill in their lexical-syntactic features. This means that the child knows about the importance of a verb's event structure properties from the start. Hence, she will be on the look-out to determine a new verb's event type. Furthermore, the child will know the mechanism of event type-shifting. Hence, once she knows the event types of verbs and other predicates, she will be able to form complex predicates, including LV constructions, by composing two event types into one complex one.

Consider next the issue of learning the lexical-syntactic features of new verbs. Under the Strong Continuity hypothesis, LVs are relatively easy as compared to full verbs for a number of reasons. First, LVs have very unspecific meanings; they require very little lexical specification: only their event type, but no further semantics. Moreover, it is relatively easy to determine which event type a certain LV manifests, since it is precisely its event type that is the constant factor across the different LV complements it combines with.[4] On the other hand, it is much harder to determine the basic event type of full verbs, since full verbs freely undergo event type-shifting, appearing in sentences denoting several different event types. Furthermore, LVs occur in just one or, at the most, two verb frames, whereas most full verbs can occur in a whole range of frames. Determining for each full verb what exactly is its complete set of verb frames is a rather complex task; for LVs on the other hand, it is relatively easy.

Concluding then that under the Strong Continuity hypothesis, LVs are easier to acquire than full verbs in the CHESS mapping model, one is

1 led to the following predictions with respect to the process of learning verbs, (4).

(4) Predictions on learning verbs in the CHESS model under the Strong Continuity hypothesis:
  a. LVs are early and popular verbs.
  b. No verb frame errors occur with LVs. Frame errors occur with full verbs only.

Notice that if the Strong Continuity hypothesis does not hold, i.e., if the child's mapping system possibly differs from UG conditions on mapping, the predictions for verb learning will be different or even reversed. Without specific proposals on the child's deviant mapping system, it is not clear what the exact predictions would be.

Also, a different analysis of LV constructions would lead to other predictions. Highlighting the less systematic and unpredictable properties of LV constructions, one might actually argue against the claim that LVs are relatively easy verbs. To this aim, one might stress the idiomatic character of LV constructions, rather than their compositional nature. Moreover, one might stress that the meaning differences between LV constructions and their full verb variants are arbitrary. One might focus on the fact that the LV choice in a particular LV construction is ultimately idiosyncratically determined. Furthermore, one might point to lexical accidents such as whether or not there exists an LV construction for a certain verbal meaning and whether or not there is a full verb variant for it.

On this alternative view on LVs, LV constructions are viewed as unanalyzable lexical chunks, on a par with idioms. With respect to verb learning, the predictions in (4) would be reversed: LV constructions would be hard lo learn, because children do not learn idiomatic meanings until a relatively late age (Penner & Roeper 1998 claim after age 4;5; see also Roeper in press). Hence, one would expect that LV constructions occur relatively late in the child's speech and that there appear many errors in the acquisition process. Investigation of acquisition data of LV constructions may therefore resolve the paradox as presented by a compositional versus an idiomatic analysis of the construction.

Learning the verbs of the lexicon is a continuous process of learning more and more items of the set of verbal meanings listed in the adult lexicon and learning more and more details of each item. LV constructions must be acquired along with the verbs. Learning verbs in the sense of associating words to meanings essentially involves conservative learning. As for LV constructions, analyzing them compositionally in terms of complex predicate formations and event type composition, there is another, additional way of learning: abductive learning by creatively combining an LV with various predicates. However, as pointed out in the previous section, LV constructions are not formed in a totally productive way like other complex predicates are. There is some idiomatic flavor about them: the often slightly idiosyncratic meaning of the construction, the particular pairings of LVs and LV complements, and the question of whether or not there exists a LV construction for a particular verbal meaning. Given the tension between the systematic and the idiosyncratic properties of LV constructions, the abductive learning process may lead to overgeneralizations: LV constructions that are possible LV constructions, but happen not to exist in the Dutch lexicon. In particular, the child may produce LV constructions with a "wrong" LV spell-out or she may produce completely new LV constructions.

Crucially, one expects overgeneralized LV constructions only in a view of the lexicon in which LV constructions are analyzed as compositional predicates and event type is part of the lexical specification of verbs. However, if LV constructions are not compositionally analyzed, they can only be learned in the same conservative way as verbs are. If so, one does not expect any overgeneralized forms. Hence, in this way as well, child language data may clarify the issue of whether or not LV constructions have a (partially) compositional nature.

A theory that predicts overgeneralizations must also deal with the question of retreat. As has been extensively discussed in the literature, overgeneralizations in the domain of argument structure alternations pose a difficult unlearning problem given the absence of negative evidence (for discussion of and some proposals on retreat from argument alternation overgeneralizations, see Bowerman 1974, 1978a, 1988b; Pinker 1989; Randall *1990*, 1992).[5] Acquiring argument structure alternations is typically viewed as learning the lexical rules that relate argument structures, or, alternatively, learning to restrict the application of these rules to a proper set of verbs. As rules can potentially be over-applied, the learning process also requires learning fine-grained lexical-semantic details of verbs.

The unlearning problem seems less hard to me for the case of LV constructions. Acquiring the LV constructions of one's language ultimately involves learning the list of lexical (chunks of) items in the "dictionary". If the child is to finally reach a stage in which her lexicon represents the adult one, i.e., by refraining from using overgeneralized LV constructions, she needs to follow some evaluation strategy. In order to get rid of possible, but non-existent LV constructions, the child must apply some kind of evaluation measure to the LV constructions of her own creation. Assuming that the child pays attention to the input, she can simply evaluate her "own" abductively learned words and phrases against those she hears in the input. After continuous evaluation over a period of time, the verb lexicon will end up as a stable model in which the adult LV constructions and full verbs have acquired enough "credit" to survive and the overgeneralized forms erode, because they have too little "credit" to survive. In this way, overgeneralized LV constructions of the kind discussed above can disappear.

To summarize this section, I have briefly discussed what is involved in learning verbs. The discussion centered around the different properties of LVs versus full verbs. Under an analysis of LV constructions as complex predicates with a (partially) compositional meaning based on the event type provided by the LV and the semantics of the LV complement, LVs are pure event type denoters without any further semantics. LVs should be acquired relatively easily as compared to full verbs, because the child only needs to determine their event types. Hence, one predicts that LVs are early verbs and children use them without making many errors. Furthermore, assuming a Strong Continuity hypothesis in which children know the outlines of the lexicon and the lexicon-syntax interface from the start, children know the relevance of lexical event type properties and the mechanism of event type composition. Hence, one predicts that overgeneralized LV constructions may occur. On the other hand, under an analysis of LV constructions as idiomatic constructions, one expects them to be relatively hard to learn. The predictions are reversed: LVs will be produced late and with relatively many errors. In this way, acquisition data of LV constructions present a test case: they can show which of the two kinds of analyses must be preferred.

5.4 A longitudinal study: light verbs in child Dutch

Investigating the claims about LV learning and the predictions formulated in the previous section, we have done a longitudinal study of the acquisition of Dutch LV constructions.[6] The data are drawn from four Dutch children, available on Childes (cf. MacWhinney & Snow 1990). Table (5) lists the names, corpus, age range and MLU (mean length of utterances) of the children.

(5) Longitudinal data from four Dutch children:

Name	*Corpus*	*Age range*	*MLU*
Niek	Wijnen	2;7.0 to 3;10.17	2.28[7]
Hein	Utrecht	2;4.11 to 3;1.24	2.31[8]
Thomas	Utrecht	2;3.22 to 2;11.22	2.33
Laura	van Kampen	1;9.4 to 2;10.13	1.42

Notice that Laura's data are somewhat different from those of the other three children, because they are very early data and because there were relatively few files available at the time of investigation.

In order to find all LVs constructions, all inflected forms of the following (more or less exhaustive) list of potential Dutch LVs were searched for: *geven* 'give', *krijgen* 'get', *brengen* 'bring', *zetten* 'put', *nemen* 'take', *komen* 'come', *gaan* 'go', *worden* 'become', *raken* 'get', *doen* 'do' and *maken* 'make'. Defining an LV as a verb used in a non-literal sense, the actual LV constructions that were present in these search results were then selected by hand.

The results show that children use LV constructions from early on (that is, they occur in the earliest files available). For each child, the earliest tokens of LV constructions are presented in (6).[9]

(6) Earliest tokens of LV constructions:

a.	Niek	foto maakt . picture made.	2;8.00
b.	Hein	gaan die bad . go that bath.	2;4.16[10]
c.	Thomas	Thomas #poepje doen . Thomas poop do.	2;3.22
d.	Laura	ik ga onder douche . I go under shower.	1;11.21

The earliness of these LV constructions suggests that LVs and LV constructions are easy to learn. Early LV constructions confirm a compositional analysis of LV constructions. They argue against an idiomatic analysis, if idioms are not learned until a late age (cf. Penner & Roeper 1998).

Even though the LVs found in the children's data form a subset of the adult set of LVs that was searched for, each child uses several different LVs. Many different types of LV constructions are produced, for some of which many tokens appeared. In particular, there were many constructions with the LVs *gaan* 'go', *doen* 'do' and *maken* 'make'; these verbs are combined with several different LV complements. The examples in (7) through (10) illustrate some of this variety (the sets of LV constructions in (7) are not exhaustive). Note that the examples in (7) through (10) represent types of LV constructions, not the actual tokens.

(7) Niek's LVs occurring with different LV complements:

a. foto / wakker / kapot / tekening / open / grapjes *maken*
picture / awake / broken / drawing / open / jokes *make*

b. overleg / boodschappen / plasje / in bad / pijn / poepie *doen*
consult / shoppings / pee / in bath / pain / poop *do*

c. kapot / mis / open / los / dicht / aan *gaan*
broken / wrong / open / loose / closed / on *go*

d. antwoord / hand *geven*
answer / hand *give*

(8) Hein's LVs occurring with different LV complements:

a. stuk / puzzel / lawaai / vol / troep / ruzie / muziek *maken*
broken / puzzle / noise / full / mess / row / music *make*

b. pijn / open / plasje / poep / in de was / gek / spelletje *doen*
pain / open / pee / poop / in the laundry / crazy / game *do*

c. in bad / kapot / open *gaan*
in bath / broken / open *go*

d. kusje / flesje *geven*
kiss / bottle *give*

(9) Thomas' LVs occurring with different LV complements:

a. poepje / open / au / boodschappen / plasje / dicht / eng *doen*
poop / open / ay / shoppings / pee / closed / scary *do*

b. open / muziek / dicht / kapot / los / vast *maken*
open / music / closed / broken / loose / fixed *make*

c. kusje / hand / tik / hapje / water *geven*
kiss / hand / flick / bite / water *give*

(10) Laura's LVs occurring with different LV complements:

a. bad / douche *gaan*
bath / shower *go*

b. zeer / bad / slapie / plasje *doen*
pain / bath /sleep / pee *do*

c. goed / open *maken*
good / open *make*

These examples show the variety in the children's production of LV constructions, which suggests that LVs are common verbs and LV constructions are common expressions for these children. Moreover, they show that children know the mechanisms of complex predicate formation and event type composition, as they combine a certain LV with more than one complement. The combinatorial variety suggests that LV constructions are compositionally analyzed, rather than stored as big idiom chunks.

The same conclusions can be drawn on the next set of data. Children combine particular LV complements with several LVs, as shown in (11) through (14). The asterisks in front of certain LVs below indicate "creative" LV choices; these will be repeated and discussed right below.[11]

(11) Niek's combinations of an LV complement with several LVs:

a. *in bad* doen / zitten
in bath do / sit

b. *open* maken / gaan / doen
open make / go / do

c. *een botsing* hebben / *maken / *krijgen / *zijn
a collision have / make / get / be

d. *pijn* hebben / *zijn
pain have / be

(12) Hein's combinations of an LV complement with several LVs:

a. *een puzzel* maken / *doen
a puzzle make / do

b. *een spelletje* doen / *maken
a game do / make

c. *poep* doen / *hebben
poop do / have

d. *een kusje* geven / *hebben
a kiss give / have

e. *lawaai* maken / *doen
noise make / do

f. *au* doen / hebben / *zijn
ow do / have / be[12]

(13) Thomas' combinations of an LV complement with several LVs:

a. *in bad* gaan / zitten
in bath go / sit

b. *open* maken / doen
open make / do
c. *een hapje* geven / nemen
a bite give / take

(14) Laura's combinations of an LV complement with several LVs:
in bad doen / gaan / zitten
in bath do / go / sit

The sets of LV complements combined with several LVs in (11) through (14) not only show that children know how to form complex predicates, but also that they know how to refer to different event types of the same verbal meanings, i.e., by means of choosing different LVs. This suggests that they know that LVs are spell-outs of event types. Moreover, they know which LV spells out which event type in an almost adult-like way.

The next two sets of data present some overgeneralized LV constructions. Children in effect overgeneralize LV constructions. They do so in two different ways: (i) children are creative in their selection of the LV spell-out and use a different LV than adults do; (ii) children make up completely new LV constructions. The examples in (15) through (18) present all instances of the first type of overgeneralizations (including the asterisk-marked ones above).

(15) Niek's overgeneralized LV constructions with a creative LV (plus the adult LV choice):
a. &mm moet dicht brengen [?]. 3;1.17
.. must closed bring (cf. *doen* 'do')
b. is ie dan botsing ? 3;6.21
is he then collision (cf. *hebben* 'have')
c. mamm heef een botsing gekregen. 3;8.2
mom has a collision gotten (cf. *hebben* 'have')
d. wordt mij huis es klaar . 3;8.30
get my house PRT ready (cf. *maken* 'make')
e. is ie oor van jou pijn ? 3;9.25
is that ear of you pain (cf. *doen* 'do')

(16) Hein's overgeneralized LV constructions with a creative LV (plus the adult LV choice):

a. &aai doen [//] doete lekker . 2;4.21
pet do .. do nice (cf. *geven* 'give')

b. is &6 &p # au . 2;5.19
is .. ow (cf. *doen* 'do')

c. <ik heb poep>[?] . 2;6.5
I have poop (cf. *doen* 'have')

d. &dududu [//] &di [/] doet (la)waai . 2;6.23
.. that .. does noise (cf. *maken* 'make')

e. een kusje heef hij . 2;7.27
a kiss has he (cf. *geven* 'give'; *krijgen* 'get')

f. &Caj ga doen van lang zal &6 leven . 2;7.30
go go do of long shall .. live (cf. *zingen* 'sing')

g. &6n een [!] puzzel heb Arjan gedaan . 2;10.30
.. a puzzle has Arjan done (cf. *maken* 'make')

h. een spelletje maken . 2;11.16
a game make (cf. *doen* 'do')

(17) Thomas' overgeneralized LV construction with a creative LV (plus the adult LV choice):

ik ga zachtjes dankjewel doen . 2;11.1
I go quietly thank you do (cf. *zeggen* 'say')

(18) Laura' overgeneralized LV construction with a creative LV (plus the adult LV choice):

isse au . 2;1.27
is ow (cf. *doen* 'do')

Dutch adults have no problem interpreting the creative LV constructions in (15) through (18); the LV selected by the child seems a possible LV, but happens to be the "wrong" one. These creative LV constructions suggest that children know about event type composition. Their creativity in choosing an LV shows that they play with the possibilities provided by the mechanism of event type composition. In all instances, the child does not select just an arbitrary LV as the (creative) spell-out; rather, they seem to pay attention to the event type of the verbal meaning they want to express and choose their LV accordingly. Hence, these overgeneralizations strongly suggest that LVs function indeed as spell-out verbs for particular event types. They further suggest that LV selection is indeed to some extent an idiosyncratic choice and needs to be learned on an item-by-item basis. The examples in (15)-(18) are the only "mistakes" found across all the children's LV constructions. Overall, children know and select the right LVs in their usage of LV constructions.

The second kind of overgeneralizations that were produced are creations of new LV constructions all together, i.e., combinations of an LV with an LV complement that do not exist in the adult lexicon. The verbal meanings they reflect exist, but the adult Dutch lexicon employs full verbs to express these meanings. (19) through (21) list all examples of this kind (plus the corresponding adult full verb).

(19) Niek's overgeneralized LV constructions (plus the adult full verb counterpart):

a.	overleg doen .	2;11.10
	conference do	(cf. *overleggen* 'confer')
b.	auto ging botsing maken .	3;4.1
	car went collision make	(cf. *botsen* 'crash')

(20) Hein's overgeneralized LV constructions (plus the adult full verb counterpart):

a.	<ik heb poep>[?] .	2;6.5
	I have poop	(cf. *moeten poepen* 'must poop')
b.	gieter doen .	2;10.24
	pitcher do	(cf. *gieten* 'pour')

(21) Thomas' overgeneralized LV constructions (plus the adult full verb counterpart):

a.	is veeg doen .2;7.20	
	is do wipe	(cf. *vegen* 'sweep')[13]
b.	ikke mag dweiltje doen .	2;10.15
	I can mob do	(cf. *dweilen* 'mob')

Given that Dutch speakers do not have any problem interpreting the LV constructions in (19) through (21), a first conclusion is that these overgeneralizations, like the ones in (15)-(18), show that LV constructions are analyzed by the children in a compositional way based on the semantics of the LV and LV complement which provides evidence in favor of a compositional analysis of LV constructions. Furthermore, the overgeneralizations in (15) through (21) show that children do not learn their lexicon in a conservative way; on the contrary, they are able to play with words. Finally, these overgeneralizations point out the arbitrary character of the lexicon (i.e., the "dictionary" of listed items). For example, *poep hebben* 'have poop' in (20a) points out a lexical gap: Dutch does not have a simple predicate that expresses this meaning.

This concludes the presentation of LV constructions in child Dutch. In the final section, I will discuss what these findings imply for the acquisition of verbs in the CHESS mapping model.

5.5 Discussion and conclusions

In this chapter, I have discussed verb learning, focusing especially on light verbs. Assuming a lexical theory that specifies verbal meanings in terms of their event types as required by the CHESS mapping conditions, I have analyzed an LV as a purely aspectual verb that spells out a certain event type; it needs an LV complement to express a full verbal meaning. Event type composition composes the event types of the LV and LV complement in an LV construction. Under this view and assuming the Strong Continuity hypothesis, LVs will be acquired relatively easily as compared to full verbs, because the child only needs to determine their event types. Moreover, given that the mechanism of event type composition is involved in LV constructions, overgeneralized LV constructions may occur. However, if LV constructions are considered idiomatic constructions, one expects them to be relatively hard to learn. The predictions are reversed: LVs will be produced late. Moreover, one does not expect any overgeneralized constructions.

A systematic longitudinal case study of the acquisition of Dutch light verbs by four Dutch children was set up in order to investigate these opposite predictions. The data show that they produce LV constructions from early on, using several different LVs. Each child produces a great variety of LV constructions, varying on the one hand the LV complements of a particular LV and combining on the other hand various LVs with a particular LV complement. Children also produce some overgeneralized LV constructions: they construct LV constructions with a "creative" LV and create "new" LV constructions. These results suggest that children know the mechanisms of complex predicate formation and event type composition. They apply it to form complex predicates, combining different LVs with different complements. Moreover, they seem to use LVs as spell-outs of different event types and know which LVs spell out which event types.

Children's early and productive usage of LV constructions, including overgeneralized ones, shows that a compositional analysis of LV constructions must be preferred over an idiomatic one. The results further suggest that verbs are specified for their event types in the child's lexicon, and furthermore, that they employ event type composition to form LV constructions. Hence, the child language data presented in this chapter provide another source of data for testing theories on the lexicon and the lexicon-syntax interface. Specifically, they show the relevance of specifying verbs in the lexicon for their event type.

Notes

1. The research presented in this chapter is based on joint research with Bart Hollebrandse, University of Massachusetts, Amherst, which has been published as Hollebrandse & van Hout (1995, 1996, 1998). Jacqueline Vermeul has participated in this project as a research assistant. My research has been supported by grant #WE-1236-2-2 of the Deutsche Forschungsgemeinschaft to Jürgen Weissenborn.
2. Hollebrandse (1993) discusses some differences in syntactic behavior between Dutch LV and non-light usages of these verbs.
3. Henk van Riemsdijk (personal communication) pointed out this observation (plus the accompanying examples).
4. Martin Everaert (personal communication) argues that precisely this property would make LVs hard to learn, because the child must abstract over all kinds of semantic details and compare them across many different situations. However, I believe that one does not need to doubt the child's capacity for doing abstractions and comparisons of this kind.
5. Difficult for the acquisition researcher, that is. Children seem to do just fine, as they all end up as perfect adult speakers.
6. The *we* in this section refers to Bart Hollebrandse and me.
7. According to Wijnen (1988), Niek is a "slow starter": at the age of 2.7, he has an MLU of only 1.72.
8. Hein and Thomas are both disfluent children (see Elbers & Wijnen 1990).
9. Henk van Riemsdijk (personal communication) remarks that *gaan* 'go' in (6b) and (6d) is an aspectual auxiliary, rather than an LV. Still, although *gaan* 'go' may be a borderline case of LV in these cases, I have classified them as LV constructions, because the verb does not mean *gaan* 'go' in its literal sense: the two LV constructions refer to bathing and showering events, rather than events of going.
10. Notice that the preposition *in* 'in' is lacking in Hein's first token of *in bad gaan* 'go in bath'.
11. Judging how "creative" the choice of a particular LV is depends very much on one's dialect or idiolect, given that there is a lot of variation in adult Dutch. Since there is no reliable way to find out the idiolects or dialects with respect to LV constructions in the child's input, the asterisks in (11)-(21) reflect my own judgements.
12. These expressions are typical child talk; adult Dutch uses *pijn* 'pain' here.
13. The LV construction *een veeg doen* 'do a sweep' does not exist; *een veeg geven* 'give a sweep' exists, but is very uncommon. The most natural way to express this verbal meaning in Dutch is with a full verb: *vegen* 'sweep'.

CHAPTER 6

Learning Verbs: Learning Intransitive Verbs

The seemingly homogeneous class of one-participant verbs, i.e., verbs with a single argument in subject position, splits up into two distinct subclasses when one considers their syntactic behavior more carefully.[1] This is the phenomenon of unaccusativity. Unaccusativity poses an intriguing acquisition problem: how can the child find out that there are two different subclasses when they look so similar at the surface? Moreover, how does she determine to which subclass a new one-participant verb belongs? After defining what unaccusativity involves in the CHESS model, I will discuss these acquisition questions. Approaching them from two opposite development perspectives, the Strong Continuity hypothesis and the Maturation hypothesis, I will outline two scenarios for learning unaccusativity. Different predictions follow from these two scenarios. They have been tested in an experiment that aimed at finding out whether or not two semantic factors, *telicity* and *agentivity*, determine unaccusativity in Dutch. The results from two groups of children (4 and 5 year-olds, 7 and 8 year-olds) and a group of adults show that subjects split up novel intransitive verbs in two subclasses. They do so from early on: even the youngest children make a distinction. This is evidence in favor of the Strong Continuity hypothesis. Furthermore, the split is defined by telicity alone; agentivity does not play a role. This result suggests that mapping must be defined on the event-semantic properties of verbs, as in the CHESS model; it does not support mapping theories defined on the semantic properties of the arguments (for example, in terms of θ-roles).

6.1 Goals of this chapter

This chapter presents a case study of the acquisition of intransitive verbs. Its primary goal is to discuss how children acquire unaccusativity. A secondary goal is to further develop the analysis of unaccusativity within the CHESS model (see also Chapter 4, section 4.8.3).

First, before introducing the acquisition issues that are at play in learning intransitive verbs, I will sketch the theoretical background of unaccusativity. I briefly present the phenomenon of unaccusativity, illustrating it with so-called *unaccusative diagnostics* in Dutch (section 6.2). Next, I discuss what unaccusativity involves in the CHESS model; I will develop in detail how the CHESS mapping conditions define how one-participant verbs with different event types map onto syntax in different ways (section 6.3). These two sections prepare the ground for discussing the acquisition of unaccusativity.

Approaching next the phenomenon of unaccusativity from the point of view of acquisition, the following questions arise: how does a child discover that there are two kinds of intransitive verbs and how does she go about classifying the new verbs she is learning (section 6.4)? Unaccusativity seems to pose a difficult problem for learning, since intransitive predicates do not directly show their unergative or unaccusative classification. I will discuss this acquisition problem in two opposite approaches to language development: the Strong Continuity Hypothesis and the Maturation Hypothesis. For each approach, I formulate predictions with respect to learning unaccusativity. Furthermore, in view of the fact that unaccusativity is a syntactic phenomenon that is semantically determined in the CHESS model, I will discuss the consequences of learning intransitive verbs in the semantic versus the syntactic bootstrapping approaches to verb-learning.

The predictions were tested in an experimental study that was designed to study the role of semantic factors that distinguish unergatives and unaccusatives in Dutch; the factors that are incorporated are telicity and agentivity (section 6.5). The experiment was run with two groups of children, 4 and 5 year-olds and 7 and 8 year-olds, as well as adults. One aim was to find out if telicity and/or agentivity play a role in defining unaccusativity in the adult grammar of Dutch. Another aim was to find out whether or not children distinguish two kinds of intransitive verbs, and if they do, whether they use the same semantic factors as adults do. The results show that telicity defines unaccusativity for both adults and children (section 6.6). The chapter concludes with an evaluation of the results for learning unaccusativity in the CHESS model (section 6.7).

6.2 Unaccusativity in Dutch

First, I consider the phenomenon of unaccusativity, focusing on what it involves with respect to mapping intransitive verbs onto syntax. I will briefly introduce the phenomenon (subsection 6.2.1) and then illustrate it in some detail for Dutch (subsection 6.2.2). Specifically, I will discuss the validity of the unaccusative diagnostics that have been proposed for Dutch (impersonal passivization, prenominal adjectival usage of past participles and auxiliary selection).

6.2.1 The phenomenon of unaccusativity

Essentially, the term *unaccusativity* refers to the following phenomenon: although the set of intransitive verbs seems to be a homogeneous set, because all verbs have a single argument that appears in subject position, the intransitives nevertheless split up into two distinct subsets of verbs with different syntactic behavior. The two kinds of intransitives are referred to as *unergatives* and *unaccusatives*.[2] The question is: what exactly determines the distinction between unergatives and unaccusatives? Do they differ from each other with respect to their lexical, their semantic or their syntactic properties, or is it a combination of these properties?

Perlmutter (1978) is the first to present a proposal that accounts for the fact that there are two kinds of intransitives and, moreover, that they have the particular properties ascribed to them. He introduces this proposal as the *Unaccusative Hypothesis*. The Unaccusative Hypothesis claims that there are two subclasses of intransitive verbs that are associated with different syntactic configurations in mapping: the single argument of an unergative verb is mapped onto subject position, whereas the single argument of an unaccusative is mapped onto object position after which it is "promoted" to subject position. In this way, the Unaccusative Hypothesis explains why a subject of an unaccusative has to some extent the same properties as an object of a transitive (see further, subsection 6.2.2). Perlmutter furthermore observes that the two intransitive classes also differ from each other semantically. This observation seems to hold cross-linguistically. Combining the syntactic and semantic generalizations, Perlmutter concludes that the unergative-unaccusative distinction is semantically determined and is syntactically represented as different kinds of mappings onto syntax.

Perlmutter introduces his Unaccusative Hypothesis within the framework of Relational Grammar. Burzio (1981, 1986) adopts it for the Government & Binding framework. Translating the Unaccusative Hypothesis in this framework, an unergative takes a D-structure subject and no object, whereas an unaccusative takes a D-structure object and no subject. Phrased in terms of argument structures, an unergative has a single external and an unaccusative has a single internal argument. Burzio observes that no unaccusative verb seems to assign structural object Case. The correlation between unergative versus unaccusative argument structures on the one hand and object Case assignment on the other has become known as *Burzio's generalization*: the ability to assign accusative Case is restricted to verbs that take an external argument.

Grimshaw (1987) presents an overview of different syntactic phenomena in various languages that have been put forward as distinguishing the two kinds of intransitives. Such phenomena are typically referred to as *unaccusative diagnostics*. Many of them (but not all) can be explained by the Unaccusative Hypothesis, i.e., by assuming that an unaccusative subject is underlyingly an object. Unaccusative diagnostics include varied phenomena, such as the (im)possibility of *ne*-cliticization and the absence or presence of subject-past participle agreement in Italian; restrictions on resultative formation in English; voice-marking morphology in Albanian. With respect to diagnosing a verb's unergative or unaccusative status, Levin & Rappaport Hovav (1995) point out that only phenomena that can in effect be explained by assuming different syntactic configurations are valid unaccusative diagnostics; there may be other phenomena that also divide the set of intransitives, but which are not true diagnostics in this sense.

Unaccusativity is an important phenomenon in the lexicon-syntax interface. If one assumes that a verb's lexical semantics determines how it maps onto syntax, unaccusativity must be analyzed as a semantically determined syntactic phenomenon (as is proposed in Perlmutter's 1978 original hypothesis). This view implies that all unaccusative verbs form one semantically homogeneous class and that it is one particular semantic property that determines that they map onto object position. Most often, people refer to (some form of) agentivity as the determining semantic factor (cf. Perlmutter 1978; Baker 1988 and other approaches based on UTAH; Pinker 1989): a verb with a single agentive argument (e.g., with an "agent" role or governed by an ACT predicate in the LCS) is unergative, whereas a verb with a single, but non-agentive argument (e.g., a "theme" role or governed by a GO or BE predicate in the LCS) is unaccusative. Another semantic factor that has been proposed to determine unaccusativity, sometimes in conjunction with agentivity, is telicity: a telic single argument verb is unaccusative, whereas an atelic single argument verb is unergative (cf. Tenny 1987, 1994; Van Valin 1987, 1990; Abraham 1988, 1990, 1993; Zaenen 1988, 1993; Grimshaw 1990; McClure 1990, 1993; Dowty 1991; Pustejovsky 1991; Levin & Rappaport Hovav 1992, 1995; Mulder 1992; van Hout 1993; van Hout et al. 1993; Borer 1994; Randall et al. 1994).

This view that the semantics of an intransitive verb determines its mapping onto syntax is challenged by the existence of so-called *unaccusative mismatches* (see L. Levin 1986 for the introduction of this term). Unaccusative mismatches arise on both sides of the syntax-semantics relation. C. Rosen (1984) discusses semantic unaccusative mismatches: verbs with similar semantics but different syntactic behavior with respect to unaccusativity diagnostics (e.g., of the Italian verbs that denote bodily processes, *russare* 'snore' behaves as an unergative, while *arrossire* 'blush' behaves as an unaccusative). Rosen concludes that unaccusativity must be seen a purely syntactic phenomenon without an underlying semantic basis.

The challenge from the other side comes from syntactic unaccusative mismatches. Drawing on data from Italian and Dutch, Van Valin (1990) observes that not all verbs that are classified as unaccusative with respect to one unaccusative diagnostic also come out as unaccusative with respect to another one. Van Valin concludes that unaccusativity is a purely semantic phenomenon: one-argument verbs only differ semantically. Various syntactic constructions are sensitive to different semantic properties; there is no need to postulate a syntactic distinction. In a similar vein, Jackendoff (1990) claims that one does not need to syntactically distinguish two kinds of intransitives; the distinction is present in the LCS's of single-variable verbs. His mapping system (called *Hierarchical Argument Linking*; see Chapter 1) maps the highest LCS-variable onto subject position, independent of its semantic type. Hence, if there is only one LCS-variable, it is mapped as a subject.

For further general questions, I refer to Levin & Rappaport Hovav (1995) who discuss in detail the issues related to unaccusativity as a semantic and/or a syntactic phenomenon and the different approaches that have been put forward in analyzing it. In the next subsection, I focus on unaccusativity in Dutch.

6.2.2 Unaccusative diagnostics in Dutch

For Dutch (as well as for German, for that matter), three unaccusative diagnostics have been put forward in the literature: impersonal passivization, past participles as prenominal modifiers and HAVE/BE auxiliary selection (see Perlmutter 1978; Hoekstra 1984; Everaert 1986, 1995, 1996; Zaenen 1988, 1993; Hoekstra & Mulder 1990; Van Valin 1990; van Hout 1993). I will illustrate how these three diagnostics are employed to show unaccusativity. Furthermore, I will extensively discuss the validity of auxiliary selection as a diagnostic, because auxiliary selection is the crucial element in the design of the unaccusativity experiment presented in section 6.4. As auxiliary selection differs cross-linguistically, one may doubt its status as a diagnostic. However, after presenting some theoretical and acquisitional arguments, I will conclude that BE-selection is a diagnostic for unaccusativity in Dutch.

If one analyzes passivization as the suppression of a verb's external argument, one can argue that unergative verbs can undergo impersonal passivization because they have an external argument, but unaccusatives cannot because they do not have one. Two verbs that illustrate this difference are *lachen* 'laugh', (1), and *vallen* 'fall', (2). Compare these two intransitives with a transitive verb that takes an external and an internal argument, e.g., *bakken* 'bake', (3).

(1) Er werd gelachen.
there was laughed
'People/somebody were/was laughing.'

(2) *Er werd gevallen.
there was fallen

(3) Er werd gebakken.
there was baking
'People/somebody were/was baking.'

Unergative as well as transitive verbs have an external argument that can be suppressed, but unaccusatives do not. So, if impersonal passivization works out fine for a particular one-participant verb, the verb must be unergative. Hence, *lachen* 'laugh' in (1) classifies as an unergative verb because it can passivize; *vallen* 'fall' in (2) classifies as unaccusative because it cannot.

Zaenen (1988, 1993), however, claims that impersonal passivization is not related to different argument structures or unergative versus unaccusative mapping configurations. She shows that it is an independent phenomenon, determined by a participant's (non)-agentivity rather than its status as internal or external argument or subject or object (see also Chapter 4, section 4.6.3). Hence, Zaenen concludes that impersonal passivization is not a reliable diagnostic to test unaccusativity.

Prenominal adjectival usage of past participles divides the Dutch intransitive verbs into two sets. This test shows that subjects of an unaccusative pattern with objects of a transitive verb; an unergative subject patterns with a transitive subject. Consider *lachen* 'laugh', (4), *vallen* 'fall', (5), and *bakken* 'bake', (6).

(4) a. Susan lachte.
'S. laughed.'
b. *de gelachen Susan
the laughed S.

(5) a. De vaas viel.
'The vase fell.'
b. de gevallen vaas
the fallen vase

(6) a. Maribel bakte een appeltaart.
'M. baked an apple pie.'
b. de gebakken *Maribel / appeltaart
the baked *M. / apple pie

The generalization is that a past participle can modify an (underlying) object, as in (5b) and (6b), but not a subject, as in (4b) and (6b). Hence, it provides a diagnostic for unaccusativity: since transitives and unaccusatives, but not unergatives, have an internal argument, the past participle form of a transitive or unaccusative verb can modify its internal argument.

A third syntactic property that differentiates two kinds of intransitives in Dutch is HAVE/BE auxiliary choice (in perfect tense): one class of verbs takes *hebben* 'have'; the other class takes *zijn* 'be'. Consider again *lachen* 'laugh', (7), and *vallen* 'fall', (8), and compare them with transitive and passive *bakken* 'bake', (9a) and (9b).

(7) Susan heeft gelachen.
S. has laughed
'S. laughed.'

(8) De vaas is gevallen.
the vase is fallen
'The vase fell.'

(9) a. Maribel heeft een appeltaart gebakken.
M. has an apple-pie baked
'M baked an apple pie.'
b. De appeltaart is gebakken door Maribel.
'The apple pie is baked by M.'

Lachen 'laugh' takes HAVE, but *vallen* 'fall' takes BE. Transitive *bakken* 'bake' takes HAVE, whereas passive *bakken* 'bake' takes BE. The generalization one may draw is that auxiliary selection is sensitive to the internal or external argument status of the single argument: verbs with a single external argument select HAVE (like transitives which also have an external argument), whereas verbs with a single internal argument select BE (like passives which also have one internal argument).

There is a methodological problem with auxiliary selection as an unaccusative diagnostic: it is not clear why auxiliary selection would be sensitive to external or internal single arguments or to subject or object position, i.e., it is unclear whether or not it is a valid unaccusative diagnostic. Several people have generalized the association between BE-selection and unaccusativity to also include passive constructions, but have not offered an explanation for it (see Burzio 1981, 1986; Vikner & Sprouse 1988; they formulate the generalization that both unaccusatives and passives select BE in terms of A-chains). In a recent proposal on auxiliaries and participles within the Minimalist Program, den Dikken (1994) provides an account for variable auxiliary selection.

The fact that auxiliary selection divides the intransitive verbs in many languages is striking and seems to provide some crosslinguistic support for considering auxiliary selection as an unaccusative diagnostic. Unfortunately, the intransitives of languages that have the two auxiliaries are divided along almost but not quite the same lines; auxiliary selection does not yield exactly the same HAVE and BE subsets. Looking at the set of intransitive verbs that select BE in German, Dutch, Italian and French, one notices that the number of BE-selecting verbs differs: German has more BE-selecting verbs than Dutch (for discussion and illustration, see Randall et al. 1994) and Italian has more than French (for discussion and illustration, see Sorace 1993a,b, 1995). Furthermore, Kayne (1993) discusses the variation of HAVE/BE selection within a large number of Italian dialects: across these Italian dialects, there does not seem to be a clear division into two subclasses of verbs, especially given the existence of dialects in which the same verb selects one auxiliary for 1st and 2nd person forms and the other for 3rd person forms. A final problem is raised by the fact that even within a language, some HAVE verbs have further unaccusative diagnostics. Observing this for Dutch, Mulder & Wehrmann (1989) claim that positional verbs (e.g., *hangen* 'hang'; *staan* 'stand') are unaccusative, even though they select HAVE.

So, there are also empirical problems with respect to the status of auxiliary selection as an unaccusative diagnostic. Auxiliary selection does not make exactly the same distinction across languages. Furthermore, even within a language, auxiliary selection does not make the exact same split in the intransitives as compared to other unaccusative diagnostics. One way to get around the latter problem is to assume, as propose Mulder & Wehrmann, that BE-selection is a sufficient, but not a necessary characteristic of unaccusative verbs. Hence, all BE-selecting intransitive verbs are unaccusative, but HAVE-selecting verbs are not necessarily unergative. Legendre (1989) concludes the same with respect to auxiliary selection and unaccusativity in French. More in general, this solution can also serve to solve the problem raised by crosslinguistic variation: BE-selection suffices to establish a verb's unaccusative status, but some HAVE-selecting verbs may also be unaccusative.[3]

Levin & Rappaport Hovav (1995) reach a similar conclusion following another line of argumentation. They argue that the class of unaccusative verbs does not need to be semantically homogeneous. Discussing unaccusativity in English, they show that there are three different semantic classes of verbs that are syntactically unaccusative: verbs that denote directed change, verbs that assert or deny existence and verbs whose single argument is not an immediate cause of the eventuality described by the verb. Different syntactic diagnostics may be associated with one, two or each of these classes. They argue that a semantic unaccusative classification is a necessary, but not always a sufficient condition for a verb to test positive with respect to a particular syntactic unaccusative diagnostic. They attribute this effect to the fact that there are different semantic classes of unaccusatives which may each be sensitive to different syntactic diagnostics. With respect to auxiliary selection in Dutch, they assume it is a valid diagnostic, even though not all unaccusatives select BE. Unaccusative HAVE-selecting verbs have the necessary semantic properties of (one class of) unaccusative verbs, but these are not sufficient conditions for passing this particular syntactic diagnostic.

Everaert (1995) presents further support for the association between BE-selection and syntactic configuration by showing that auxiliary selection in Dutch is (at least partially) determined by the syntactic configuration a verb appears in and not only by its semantic properties (as claimed by Van Valin 1990). In order to demonstrate his point, Everaert uses synonymous pairs that consist of a verb and an associated idiomatic or light verb construction. For example, *landen* 'land' and *een landing maken* 'make a landing' are more or less synonymous; they refer to the same kind of (telic) event. The intransitive verb *landen* 'land' selects BE, whereas the transitive light verb construction *een landing maken* 'make a landing' selects HAVE. Hence, auxiliary selection is sensitive to the syntactic configuration a verbs appears in and not exclusively to its semantics.

A last argument in favor of auxiliary selection as a valid diagnostic comes from the perspective of acquiring unaccusativity. Van Hout et al. (1993) argue that a grammar in which the split between unergatives versus unaccusatives coincides with a split between HAVE- versus BE-selecting verbs is easier to learn and, hence, to be preferred theoretically, than a grammar in which the split into two classes of intransitive verbs is completely unrelated to the split into HAVE- and the BE-selecting classes. The argument runs as follows. Suppose the unergative-unaccusative distinction of intransitive verbs is not at all related to the HAVE-BE distinction. This would mean that there are two different parts of the grammar that each divide the set of intransitive verbs; they divide them up in very similar but not quite the same ways. A learner probably comes equipped with a (universally determined) unergative-unaccusative distinction, but has to find out about a completely unrelated split for the same set of verbs that governs auxiliary selection. In this scenario, the learner needs to sort out which distributional patterns of intransitives belong to the unergative-unaccusative distinction and which do not. It is not clear what kind of criteria she can use to determine this, as superficial distributional similarities between the two splits cannot be relied upon. The alternative for the learner is to assume, at least as a first hypothesis, that the two splits are in fact the same, i.e., that auxiliary selection is a distributional characteristic of the unergative-unaccusative distinction.

Finally, notwithstanding the unclear relation between auxiliary selection and unaccusativity, many people use auxiliary selection as an unaccusative diagnostic (among others, Perlmutter 1978; Hoekstra 1984; Burzio 1981, 1986; Haider 1985, 1993; Van Valin 1987, 1990; Abraham 1988, 1990, 1993; Vikner & Sprouse 1988; Zaenen 1988, 1993; Grewendorf 1989; Legendre 1989; Mulder & Wehrmann 1989; Levin & Rappaport Hovav 1992, 1995; Mulder 1992; Sorace 1993a,b, 1995; van Hout et al. 1993; Randall et al. 1994; van Hout et al. in progress; Ackema 1995; Everaert 1995, 1996).

Despite the doubts with respect to its status as a diagnostic I have raised in this subsection, I will assume auxiliary selection is a valid diagnostic (at least, that BE-selection is an indication of unaccusativity) in light of the arguments presented above.

This concludes the overview of unaccusativity and its manifestations in Dutch. Next, I will discuss what unaccusativity means in the CHESS model.

6.3 Unaccusativity in the CHESS model

The CHESS model developed in Chapter 4 is based on data of verbs in all kinds of frames (not only intransitive verbs). It implements mapping as a feature checking system: a predicate's event structure features must be checked off in the syntactic configuration projected by the verb. The mapping relation is defined in terms of the syntactic identification of a predicate's event structure; the CHESS mapping conditions are repeated in (10).

(10) The CHESS mapping conditions: *ch*ecking *e*vent-*s*emantic *s*tructure:

1. Mapping requires that the event structure of a predicate be identified.
2. There are two structural argument positions: the specifier positions of Agr,S and Agr,O. An argument in either of these specifier positions identifies an event or subevent by referring to an event participant that is involved in that (sub)event.
3. Telic event type features must be checked in AgrOP. The argument in Spec, AgrO is associated with the event participant that ends in the final state.

Furthermore, I have assumed that every verb projects at least an AgrSP. Independent of event identification requirements, a full syntactic projection seems to need a subject position (i.e., Chomsky's 1981 Extended Projection Principle and various ways it has subsequently been implemented); I have referred to this condition as the *subject requirement*. For further motivation and discussion of the CHESS model, see Part III of Chapter 4, especially, subsection 4.8.3.

Recall that the first step in the development of the CHESS conditions was based on the properties of atelic-telic event type-shifting of two-participant verbs. This led to the association of telicity features with the object position via strong object Case assignment in Spec, AgrO (see subsection 4.8.2). Next, this association was generalized and formulated as the mapping condition that telic event type features must be checked in AgrOP, see the third clause in (10). These features are checked off if there is an argument in its specifier position (for similar views on the association between telicity features and a functional specifier position for objects above VP, see McClure 1993; Ramchand 1993; Borer 1994; den Dikken 1994; van Hout 1994; Schmitt 1995; and as discussed in Chapter 4, section 4.8).

Consider now the implications of this telicity condition for the mapping of one-participant verbs in the CHESS model. In order to satisfy the subject requirement, there must always be an argument in the subject position (Spec, AgrS) of the projection of all one-participant verbs.

Furthermore, depending on the telicity properties of the predicate, this argument must or must not first pass through Spec, AgrO. Specifically, if the verb itself or the predicate it appears in has a telic event type, its telicity features must be checked off in Spec, AgrO, i.e., an argument in Spec, AgrO must be present to identify the transition. Since the verbs under consideration have only one participant, the argument that identifies the transition moves to Spec, AgrO and, subsequently, moves on to Spec, AgrS.[4] If the predicate is atelic, the argument that refers to the single event participant moves straight to Spec, AgrS without passing through Spec, AgrO, because there is no need for it to do so.

So, in the CHESS model, a one-participant verb maps onto syntax in one of two ways: the argument that identifies the single participant ends up in the specifier position of AgrS either after first passing through the specifier position of AgrO or by moving directly to the specifier position of AgrS, by-passing that of AgrO. Hence, by referring to these two patterns of movements, one can distinguish two kinds of intransitives. Movement of an argument via the specifier position of AgrO to the specifier position of AgrS is *unaccusative mapping*; movement straight to the specifier position of AgrS is *unergative mapping*. The implementation of the Unaccusative Hypothesis in the CHESS model is thus defined by whether or not there is movement via the specifier of AgrO. Leaving out all other functional projections and the structure within VP, these two different mappings are depicted in (11).

(11) a. Unergative mapping: b. Unaccusative mapping:

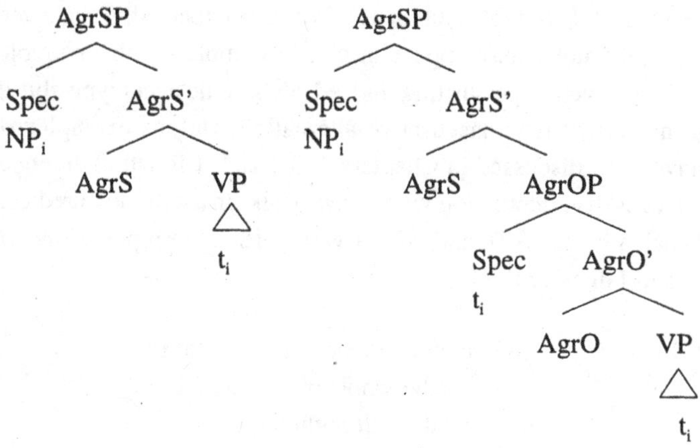

In order to check off telicity features, both one- and two-participant verbs must project an argument in Spec, AgrO. In the case of two-participant verbs, telicity features are visibly checked off via strong object Case assignment. If the argument moves on, as in the case of unaccusative mapping, there is no strong object Case assignment (at least, not visibly). Apparently, telicity features are not always checked off by way of strong object Case assignment. In unaccusative mapping, object Case is either not assigned at all or, if it is, subject Case overrules it when the argument ends up in Spec, AgrS.[5]

For another implementation of unaccusativity in terms of movement of an argument to different functional specifier positions, see Borer (1994). Borer proposes that a single argument moves to the specifier position of either one of two different aspectual functional projections; movement to one is unergative mapping and movement to the other is unaccusative mapping. Her proposal differs somewhat from the one presented here, in that she proposes that the relevant functional projections are aspectual ones whereas I assume they are AgrS and AgrO. Furthermore, she does not assume that an unaccusative single argument moves via one aspectual specifier position to another one. I have discussed her proposal in some detail in Chapter 4, subsection 4.8.3.

The CHESS conditions are defined on the event structure properties of the predicate rather than those of the verb by itself. Hence, the existence of "flexible" intransitive verbs is expected, since a verb that is basically atelic may appear in a telic complex verb or predicate and undergo event type-shifting. Indeed, atelic-telic event type-shifting leads to an unergative-unaccusative alternation, various examples of which have been discussed in Chapters 2, 3 and 4. I illustrate the unergative-unaccusative alternation with *lopen* 'walk' in a complex predicate with a "goal" phrase, (12), and with a verb/particle verb pair *slapen-inslapen* 'sleep-fall asleep', (13).

(12) a. John heeft de hele nacht gelopen.
J. has the whole night walked
'J. walked all night.'
b. John is in 5 minuten naar de bus gelopen.
J. is in 5 minutes to the bus walked
'J. walked to the bus within 5 minutes.'

(13) a. Winnie heeft dagenlang geslapen.
W. has days-long slept
'W. slept for days.'
b. Winnie was binnen 5 minuten ingeslapen.
W. was within 5 minutes in-slept
'W. fell asleep within 5 minutes.'

In this proposal, the phenomenon of unaccusativity is syntactically implemented in such a way that the semantic property of telicity plays a crucial rule. Assuming that auxiliary selection in Dutch is in some way or another sensitive to the unergative versus unaccusative mapping configuration, the CHESS model thus accounts for the correlation between auxiliary selection and telicity which has been observed by several people and for various languages. Drawing conclusions on the basis of this correlation, some people claim unaccusativity is a purely semantic phenomenon, defined by telicity (e.g., Centineo 1986; Shannon 1988; Van Valin 1987, 1990; Seibert 1993). Others present an analysis of unaccusativity as a syntactic phenomenon in which the semantic factor telicity derives a syntactic representation of unaccusativity (cf. Tenny 1987, 1994; Abraham 1988, 1990, 1993; Zaenen 1988, 1993; Grimshaw 1990; Pustejovsky 1991; Levin & Rappaport Hovav 1992, 1995; McClure 1993; Borer 1994). My proposal joins with the latter proposals.

Notice that the semantic factor agentivity does not play a role in determining unergative versus unaccusative mapping in the CHESS model; agentivity does not figure in the mapping conditions in (10). This is in contrast with various other proposals in which some notion of agentivity (at least partially) determines unaccusativity (cf. Perlmutter 1978; Baker 1988; Pinker 1989; Levin & Rappaport Hovav 1992, 1995).[6] Looking more closely at the unergative-unaccusative split in Dutch in order to see if there are any effects of agentivity, it turns out that split is determined purely in terms of telicity (without agentivity). Consider, for example, *lopen* 'walk', a verb that can take various kinds of subjects that differ in how agentively they are involved in the event. Reconsider (12) above. In both (12a) and (12b), the subject is actively involved in the walking event. Still, given the different auxiliaries, there is a split: atelic *lopen* 'walk' in (12a) involves unergative mapping and telic *lopen* 'walk' in (12b) involves unaccusative mapping. Agentivity either does not play a role at all, or it is overruled by telicity in (12b). Consider next *lopen* 'walk' with a non-agentive participant, e.g., *water* 'water' in (14).

(14) a. Het water heeft urenlang langs de muren gelopen.
the water has hours-long along the walls walked
'The water ran along the walls for hours.'

b. Het water is binnen een minuut de zee ingelopen.
the water is within a minute the sea in-walked
'The water ran into the sea within a minute.'

While the subject in both (14a) and (14b) is a non-agentive participant, there still is a difference in mapping: atelic *lopen* 'run' in (14a) is unergative (it takes HAVE) and telic *de zee in lopen* 'run into the sea' in (14b) is unaccusative (it takes BE). If agentivity mattered for mapping, one would expect unaccusative mappings for both predicates in (14). In particular, in (14a) where telicity does not play a role, an analysis in terms of agentivity would predict BE (cf. Levin & Rappaport Hovav 1992 who in fact make exactly this claim for English; see also below). Hence, how agentively a participant is involved in walking or running does not matter for mapping; what matters is whether or not the event is telic or atelic: (12a) and (14a) are atelic and are mapped as unergatives; (12b) and (14b) are telic and are mapped as unaccusatives. An analysis of unaccusativity in terms of telicity as in the CHESS model derives these mapping patterns.

Levin & Rappaport Hovav (1992, 1995) argue that along with telicity, agentivity (or rather their 1992 notion *internal control* or their 1995 notion *immediate cause*; see note 6) also matters for unaccusativity in English. They substantiate their claim by showing how verbs of manner of motion behave differently depending on whether or not the argument has internal control over the motion. They thus distinguish two classes of verbs: the internally controlled class (e.g., *run*) versus the externally controlled class (e.g., *roll*). Levin & Rappaport Hovav further claim that when a verb from either class of verbs appears in a telic predicate, it maps as an unaccusative (i.e. the telicity linking rule overrules the internal control rule).[7] However, when it appears in an atelic predicate, there is a difference between the two classes: atelic internally controlled verbs (the *run*-class) are unergative, whereas atelic externally controlled verbs (the *roll*-class) are unaccusative. Hence, *roll*-verbs are always unaccusative, independent of the (a)telicity of the predicate. However, this analysis does not carry over to Dutch: externally controlled *rollen* 'roll' is sometimes unergative and sometimes unaccusative; it only depends on the (a)telicity of the predicate, (15).

(15) a. De knikker heeft minutenlang over tafel gerold.
the marble has minutes-long over the table rolled
'The marble rolled over the table for minutes.'

b. De knikker is binnen een minuut de tafel afgerold.
the marble is within one minute the table off-rolled
'The marble rolled off the table within one minute.'

So, the comparison of one and the same verb with an agentive and a non-agentive subject, *lopen* 'walk' in (12) versus (14) and the comparison of a non-agentive verb in different contexts, *rollen* 'roll' in (15), show that only telicity, but not agentivity matters for mapping one-participant verbs in Dutch.

To conclude, consider the following interesting consequence of the implementation of unaccusativity in the CHESS model. Assuming that specifier positions can only be occupied once in a derivation, there cannot be another argument that ends up as an object in Spec, AgrO, since this position has been occupied during the derivation of an unaccusative verb. This is exactly the correlation described by Burzio's generalization (i.e., only a verb with an external argument is able to assign accusative Case), which is a correlation but not an explanation. The CHESS approach to mapping thus explains Burzio's generalization. It is derived by an interaction of three independent sets of conditions: event-semantic mapping conditions, conditions on structural object Case assignment and conditions on the filling of specifier positions.[8]

6.4 Learning intransitive verbs

Consider now the phenomenon of unaccusativity from the learner's point of view. At the surface, all intransitive verbs look alike: they all denote an event with just one participant and the verb is mapped onto a frame with one argument in subject position. So neither the number of event participants involved in the event nor the surface configuration distinguishes between the two kinds of intransitives. This poses a learnability problem: as the surface configurations of the two types of intransitives are the same, how can the learner find out that there is a distinction in the first place? Furthermore, once she knows that there is such a distinction, how can she determine the classification of a new verb into one of the two categories? I will first discuss these questions as they constitute the core issues of the learning task (subsection 6.4.1) and embed them in the debate on semantic versus syntactic bootstrapping (subsection 6.4.2). I then proceed to discuss the process of learning unaccusativity by formulating the predictions that arise in scenarios presented by the Strong Continuity and the Maturation hypotheses (subsection 6.4.3).

6.4.1 The learning task

As for the first question, I assume the child does not need to learn that there are two kinds of intransitive verbs that look similar at the surface but differ underlyingly. Since Universal Grammar allows for an option in mapping a one-participant verb onto syntax, either as an unergative or as an unaccusative, the knowledge that there is a distinction between the two kinds is given. Hence, the child starts the language acquisition process knowing that intransitives come in two kinds. Even stronger, she will be "on the look-out" for different distributional patterns across verbs in intransitive frames.

Assuming thus that the child comes equipped with the knowledge that there are two kinds of intransitive verbs, learning unaccusativity involves finding out the lexical-syntactic features for each individual one-participant verb, so that the child can use the verb appropriately in either an unergative or an unaccusative frame. Distributional differences between the two sets of intransitive verbs (e.g., in Dutch, auxiliary selection and past participle as prenominal modifier) can help determine which class a certain verb belongs to. The child may deduce the lexical-syntactic features of a new verb when it is presented in one of these patterns. However, there must be something beyond learning from these distributional patterns associated with unaccusativity, since not every verb will be presented in one of these patterns. The child cannot learn her complete verbal lexicon by being a conservative learner. Instead, she must draw generalizations across the various distributional patterns intransitives appear in, so that she can also classify other verbs that she happens to hear without a distributional clue.

Consider next what learning unaccusativity involves more specifically in the CHESS model: what must the child know (in the end) in order to be able to appropriately map one-participant verbs onto syntax? With respect to the mapping system itself, the child must know the CHESS mapping conditions. In particular, the association between telicity and AgrO is crucial, since (a)telicity determines the difference between unergative and unaccusative mapping (as discussed in section 6.3). Furthermore, the child must be able to apply event type composition, since mapping is defined on the event type properties of the predicate, rather than those of the verb by itself. As for the mapping of particular verbs onto syntax, the child must know the event structure properties of every individual verb: its number of event participants and its basic event type. Once she has accumulated all these pieces of knowledge, she will be able to derive appropriate mappings.

Must all of this be learned or is part of it given? Clearly, item-particular event structure specifications must be learned. On the other hand, however, reasoning in the same way as above, one may say that since the grammar allows for two options for mapping one-participant verbs, at least this part is given knowledge and does not need to be learned. The question then is: what exact part can be assumed to be given? Even though I have only discussed mapping and the CHESS mapping conditions with respect to Dutch, I will assume the strongest hypothesis with respect to their applicability across languages and claim that they hold universally and need not be acquired. This claim is supported by observations in other languages which show a crucial association between telicity features and object position (see Tenny 1987, 1994; Pustejovsky 1991; Levin & Rappaport Hovav 1992, 1995; McClure 1993; Ramchand 1993; Borer 1994; Schmitt 1995). This means that learning unaccusativity in the CHESS model "only" involves finding out a verb's event semantics, specifically, in the case of one-participant verbs, finding out their basic event type.

6.4.2 Unaccusativity and semantic versus syntactic bootstrapping

How can the child discover the features of a one-participant verb's lexical representation? I will position the task of acquiring unaccusativity within the debate on syntactic versus semantic bootstrapping.

Both the Syntactic and Semantic Bootstrapping hypotheses are hypotheses about verb learning, in particular, about learning the meanings of verbs.[9] In her discussion of the two approaches, Grimshaw (1994) sketches the following picture of the learning problem, (16).

(16) The learning problem for learning verbs:

SITUATION \
OBSERVER >>>>>>> WORD REPRESENTATION
SENTENCE /

(Grimshaw 1994:415)

The input for the learning child consists of a pair of elements: on the one hand, the representation of a situation, which is the learner's interpretation of a perceived event, and on the other hand, the (S-structure) sentence. In this learning situation, the child's task is to arrive at the lexical representation for the verb in the sentence. The semantic and syntactic bootstrapping hypotheses have been put forward to provide a solution for this learning problem.

Pinker (1982, 1984, 1989) proposes the Semantic Bootstrapping hypothesis which has been further developed by him and his colleagues (see Gropen et al. 1991a,b; Pinker 1994). Developing the idea that meaning plays a role in allowing the child to perform an initial syntactic analysis upon which the syntactic system of the language can then be erected, and in particular, developing the idea that the meaning of a verb can make aspects of its syntax predictable to the learner, Pinker seeks the solution to the learning problem in the child's analysis of the situation. This analysis should make it possible to determine the meaning of a verb which in turn can make it possible to determine its syntax. Landau & Gleitman (1985) and Gleitman (1990) propose what is referred to as the *Syntactic Bootstrapping* hypothesis; it has been further developed by Gleitman and her colleagues (see, among others, Naigles 1990; Fisher et al. 1991; Naigles et al. 1993; Fisher et al. 1994). Their solution to the verb learning problem is that an analysis of the sentence, along with information in the situation, makes it possible to determine (parts of) its semantics, including the lexical semantics of the verb.

Consider now the verb learning problem for the case of unergative and unaccusative verbs. In the child's input, both types of intransitive sentences look alike: the sentences have a subject and a verb. Hence, an analysis of the sentence does not distinguish between the two kinds. However, the target word representations differ. The conclusion is that the child must analyze the situations that accompany the sentences if she is to find out these different word representations. The problem is that situations are almost always multi-interpretable.

On the other hand, in certain instances, there is a difference in the sentences, e.g., some Dutch intransitive sentences in the perfect tense select HAVE, while others select BE. In these circumstances, an analysis of these distributional patterns in the sentences may indirectly help the child arrive at different word representations. That is, noticing that there is a syntactic differentiation among intransitive verbs, the child may realize that the class is not homogeneous. So, she may start looking for differences between the two subsets, differences she will ultimately find in an analysis of the situations, i.e., in terms of atelic versus telic events. In this way, auxiliary selection may be a syntactic clue for the Dutch child to "bootstrap" into the phenomenon of unaccusativity.

6.4.3 Unaccusativity and the Strong Continuity versus Maturation hypotheses

Having established the learning task with respect to unaccusativity, one must consider the acquisition process itself: how does the acquisition of unaccusativity develop? This depends on one's assumptions on the acquisition process. Under the Strong Continuity hypothesis (see Pinker 1984; Whitman, Lee & Lust 1990; Weissenborn 1993; Penner & Weissenborn 1996), the child's grammar has only properties that are allowed for by and are fully compatible with the principles of Universal Grammar at all stages of development. Hence, even though the child's grammar is a grammar of an intermediary stage in the acquisition process, it is a complete grammar. Under the Strong Continuity hypothesis then, the unergative-unaccusative distinction is present from early on.

Consider the predictions for acquiring unaccusatives in the CHESS model under the Strong Continuity hypothesis. Since event-semantic features play a determining role in the CHESS model, the Strong Continuity hypothesis predicts that the child is sensitive to these features from early on. Hence, children should be able to classify predicates in terms of a telic-atelic distinction from early on. Furthermore, with respect to one-participant verbs and unaccusativity, the Strong Continuity hypothesis predicts that they are able to distinguish unergatives and unaccusatives from early on.

Borer & Wexler (1987, 1992) propose the Maturation hypothesis in contrast to the Continuity hypothesis. They claim that certain aspects of linguistic competence develop, as certain linguistic principles have to mature. Borer & Wexler argue that there is no *a priori* reason to assume that a continuity hypothesis is the simplest hypothesis. They claim furthermore that there is no general argument from linguistic theory in favor of the continuity hypothesis. Substantiating their claims, Borer & Wexler discuss the acquisition of passivization. They explain the course of development of verbal and adjectival passives they find by assuming that A-chains have to mature. This explains why initially, children do not have verbal passives, i.e., because they cannot yet form A-chains.

Consider the acquisition of unaccusativity under the Maturation hypothesis. As the projection of an unaccusative verb involves an A-chain (at least, in the standard interpretation of unaccusativity in which the movement of an argument from D-structure object to S-structure subject position is an A-chain), the prediction is that the child cannot distinguish unergatives and unaccusatives at first, as this would require the principle of A-chains.[10] In fact, the prediction is even stronger: the child can only map unergative verbs onto syntax; she literally is not able to an unaccusative mapping, since she lacks the tools (A-chains) for doing so.

I have several objections to the latter view on learning unaccusativity: it creates methodological, acquisitional and theoretical problems. From a general methodological perspective, I prefer the Strong Continuity hypothesis to the Maturation hypothesis. Strong Continuity makes the strongest claims and predictions, hence, it is the more explanatory hypothesis of the two. The Maturation hypothesis merely describes the process of language acquisition, but does not have much explanatory value. It may turn out to be necessary, but as long as language development can be analyzed in a different way, that is preferable.

Next, consider the problem from an acquisition point of view. Suppose the child does in fact start out with only one kind of mapping for one-participant verbs; suppose she is only able to map these verbs in the unergative way and cannot yet map them in the unaccusative way (because she cannot yet construct A-chains). Does this imply that the child initially only uses unergative verbs and that she will start using verbs that require unaccusative mapping only in a later stage when the principle of A-chains has matured? Clearly, this is not desirable: children use both unergative and unaccusative verbs from the start. Looking at what kinds of verbs Dutch children in the CHILDES corpus use, one finds that they use both unergative and unaccusative verbs. Also, Jürgen Weissenborn (personal communication) tells me that the children in his German and French longitudinal corpora use both kinds of intransitive verbs. In fact, van Hout, Randall & Weissenborn (1992) present data that show that not only do French and German children use unergative and unaccusative verbs, they correctly distinguish them in their selection of auxiliaries as well.

Alternatively, one may argue that initially children map all one-participant verbs in the same, unergative way, because they have no other technical way at their disposal. In this scenario, the problem lies in the transition to the next stage. Given that the child has a perfectly adequate way for mapping one-participant verbs onto syntax, why would she ever change to another, more complex system in which there are two kinds of intransitive mappings? Furthermore, she would have to decide which of the verbs she has been mapping in the unergative way must now be mapped in another (unaccusative) way. Even when the principle of A-chains matures at a certain moment, this is not a reason for the child to change the way she has been mapping one-participant verbs. Hence, with respect to learning the unergative-unaccusative distinction, the Maturation hypothesis leads to a severe unlearning problem. Therefore, the learning process itself provides another reason to prefer the Strong Continuity hypothesis that posits that the unergative-unaccusative distinction is present from the start.

A last objection to a Maturation approach to learning unaccusativity is that it raises a theoretical problem with respect to the mapping system. Suppose, as before, the child maps all one-participant verbs in the same, unergative way. What kind of mapping system can describe this (part of the) grammar? The child's mapping conditions for one-participant verbs cannot be defined on event type properties, as the single participant of predicates that denote telic events as well as those that denote atelic events is mapped onto subject position. Nor can they be defined on the thematic properties of event participants, as every kind of argument is mapped onto subject position, independent of its θ-role. Concluding then that the mapping conditions for one-participant verbs are not defined on event type nor on thematic roles (nor can they be based on any other semantic property), the problem is: what is the child's mapping system defined on? In view of this theoretical problem of how to describe the child's mapping conditions, I think an acquisition approach in which the child starts out with only one kind of mapping for one-participant verbs cannot be maintained.

To conclude, learning unaccusativity in a Maturation approach yields many problems. These or similar problems do not arise in a Strong Continuity approach. The two hypotheses can be empirically tested. Under the Strong Continuity approach, the unergative-unaccusative distinction is present in the child's grammar from early on; hence, one predicts that the child is able to distinguish unergative and unaccusative verbs from early on. This means that once she knows the relevant event structure features of a new one-participant verb, she will map the verb in an adult-like way. Furthermore, once the child finds out which distributional patterns are associated with unaccusativity in her language, she will correctly use verbs in one of these patterns. Under a Maturation hypothesis on the other hand, at first the child is not able to correctly distinguish two classes of intransitive verbs. Hence, at first, she will not use intransitive verbs correctly in their distributional patterns. The study presented in the next section introduces an experimental design that tests these opposite predictions.

6.5 An experimental study: unaccusativity in child and adult Dutch

Since production data cannot give any insight about the child's underlying generalizations about unaccusativity, one must devise experimental ways for studying the role of semantic factors that distinguish unergatives and unaccusatives. Van Hout et al. (1992, 1993) designed an experiment to study the semantic factors that determine unaccusativity in Dutch. The results from this pilot study looked promising, so that the experiment was further developed and worked out for German as well as Dutch (see

Randall et al. 1994; van Hout et al. in progress). I will discuss this experiment and present a subset of the results, i.e., those for Dutch, from the perspective of the CHESS model.

6.5.1 Experimental design and predictions

The semantic factors that were investigated in the experiment are telicity and agentivity, which have both been claimed in the literature to (co)-determine unaccusativity. While telicity is crucial in describing the Dutch (adult) unaccusativity data, agentivity does not play a role i.e., the unergative-unaccusative distinction in Dutch is empirically characterized as an atelic-telic distinction. In the CHESS model (see section 6.3), telicity plays a crucial role in distinguishing two kinds of one-participant verbs; agentivity does not play a direct role in mapping. Hence, in an experiment that tests the roles of these factors, the CHESS model predicts a main effect of telicity and no effect of agentivity. That is, these are the predictions for the adult subjects. As discussed in the previous section, under the Strong Continuity hypothesis, one expects that children, including the youngest ones, are also sensitive to the role of telicity in mapping. Hence, one predicts that they are able to distinguish two classes of intransitive verbs and that they will do so in terms of (a)telicity.

I have pointed out at several points in the previous chapters that telicity is not a feature of the verb by itself, but, rather, of the whole predicate. Some verbs are inherently telic, some are inherently atelic and others are flexible, undergoing event type-shifting when they combine with a "goal" or resultative phrase. In order to study the effect of event type composition, the factor inherency was incorporated as well. Inherency distinguishes verbs with a lexically fixed event type from verbs that are basically atelic, but can event type-shift to a telic event type in combination with another phrase. It is a secondary factor in describing the event type properties of a predicate. The experimental design thus involves three factors which create eight different conditions; it is sketched in (17).

(17) Design of the unaccusativity experiment:

		+Agentivity	-Agentivity
+Telic	+Inherent		
	-Inherent		
-Telic	+Inherent		
	-Inherent		

The experiment was run with Dutch adults and two groups of children: four and five year-olds and seven and eight year-olds. Running the experiment with adults aimed at finding out if the semantic factors telicity and/or agentivity determine unaccusativity in the adult grammar of Dutch. Running the same experiment with children aimed at finding out if children are able to distinguish two kinds of intransitive verbs, and if they do, whether they use the same semantic factors as adults do.

As sentences with both unergative and unaccusative predicates look similar at the surface (both have one argument in subject position), one cannot check unaccusativity directly. In order to study the role of semantic factors in unergative and unaccusative mapping, one must resort to examining an intermediary effect. The experimental method uses auxiliary selection. If auxiliary selection is considered a valid unaccusative diagnostic, the choice of a particular auxiliary points to the kind of intransitive mapping: in Dutch, *hebben* 'have' suggests unergative and *zijn* 'be' suggests unaccusative mapping.

6.5.2 Method

In this subsection, I will describe the subjects, the materials of the experiment and the procedure. For more elaborate descriptions, I refer the reader to van Hout et al. (in progress).

Subjects

A total of ninety-six subjects have participated in the experiment I report of here: 52 four and five year-old children, 24 seven and eight year-old children and 20 adults.[11] All subjects were monolingual native Dutch speakers. For both children groups, the experiment was carried out at the St. Michaëlsschool in De Bilt; the adults were tested in their homes.

Materials

The experiment follows a paradigm using nonsense verbs. The materials include short videotaped movies showing puppets and objects involved in novel events and sentences describing these video clips with nonsense verbs. The "content" of the video clips varies along the three factors telicity, inherency and agentivity.[12] All video clips show one-participant events.

The three factors have been rendered in the following ways. In order to distinguish [+Agentive] and [-Agentive] events, a person or a "live" Sesame Street puppet participated in the [+Agentive] video clips, whereas the single participant of the [-Agentive] video clips was always a non-animate object. Moreover, to underline the non-agentive participation of the latter kind of participant, the [-Agentive] video clips also show an instigator that gets the participant going in the event. For example, in one of the [+Agentive] video clips, Bert from Sesame Street is doing a kind of dance on his head. In one of the [-Agentive] video clips, a top and a ball are spinning around each other after a hand gives the top a turn.

In order to distinguish [+Telic] and [-Telic] events, all [+Telic] events come to a natural stop by the end of the video clip, whereas the event in the [-Telic] video clips is still continuing at the end. In order to underline the endpoints of [+Telic] video clip, the last 3 seconds of the video clip were made into a still. Moreover, the [+Telic] video clips involve some kind of a change: the single participant is involved in either a change of state or a state of location; the single participant in the [-Telic] video clips is involved in the event in a constant way.

In order to render the factor inherency, the [-Inherent] video clips display an action that shows some new manner of motion. Motion verbs are flexible verbs: they are basically atelic, but when combined with a "goal" phrase, they denote a telic event (e.g., (12), (14) and (15)). Hence, if the kind of event is a motion event, one must pay attention as to whether the motion is directed toward some goal and comes to an end or, alternatively, whether it is not directed toward a goal and is on-going. In the [+Telic, -Inherent] video clips, the motion is directed toward a goal and comes to an end there; the participant in the video clip is involved in a change of location. For example, Ernie walks on his hands, with his arms stuck in blue tubes onto a pile of books. The sentence that describes the video clip (see procedure section below) contains an explicit "goal" phrase (i.e., a postpositional PP). In the [-Telic, -Inherent] video clips, the participant is involved in some manner of motion which might potentially be directed at a goal, but is not in this video clip. For example, Bert is head-dancing upside down on a purple box; in this video clip he is dancing around, but he could have head-danced to a certain goal (e.g., off the box).

The [+Inherent] video clips are non-motion events; they denote either inherently telic or inherently atelic events. The [+Telic, +Inherent] video clips show a participant involved in a change of state. For example, in one video clip a set of vertical blinds makes a quarter turn, changing from a pattern of white striped lines to a white closed wall. The [-Telic, +Inherent] video clips depict some ongoing event; in this respect they do not differ from the [-Telic, -Inherent] video clips. The only difference between these two kinds of atelic video clips is a difference in their potential to event type-shift: only the events depicted in the [-Telic, -Inherent] video clips can turn into telic events by the addition of a "goal" phrase; the events in the [-Telic, +Inherent] video clips cannot. For example, in one such video clip, Ernie makes continuous movements with a closed mouth, wriggling it from side to side. As this event is ongoing and does not have any transition moments, it is inherently atelic; the addition of a "goal" phrase cannot turn it into a telic event.

For each of the eight experimental conditions, two video clips were designed, leading to a total of 16 video clips. A list of all 16 video clips appears in Appendix 1. One video clip of each condition was collected in a set, the other one went into a second set. Within each set, the video clips were randomly ordered. In order to counter-balance the ordering of video clips, two different versions were created by presenting the two subsets of video clips in one order for half of the subjects and in the alternative order for the other half. A fixed block of training video clips was added before the first subset of video clips; a final block of transitive video clips was added at the end of the second subset.

The video clips were used to teach the subjects fantasy words (see procedure section below). The fantasy words are novel verbs used in an intransitive frame. They are phonologically possible, yet non-existent Dutch verbs. The verbs were randomly assigned to the video clips twice in order to counter-balance any effects of a particular form triggering a particular auxiliary. Half of the subjects heard one version of verb-video clip pairings; the other half heard the other version. A list of the novel words appears in Appendix 2.

Procedure

The experimenter introduces a child subject to a puppet assistant. The experimenter tells them she/he will teach them some new, fantasy words with which they are going to play a game. The experimenter then asks the child if she/he is willing to help the puppet play this game, because the puppet is not good with new words. The puppet is also somewhat deaf and does not always pay careful attention, so the child may also have to repeat things to him. The aim of the game is to learn a fantasy word by looking at a short videotaped movie that shows what this word is about and then use this word in describing what happened in the video clip. The puppet starts telling what he saw in the video clip, but he always gets stuck when the new word must be used. So, the child's job is to help him finish his sentence adding the new word. Adult subjects were also taught fantasy words by showing them a video clip. However, no puppet assistant participated in the adult procedure; the adult's task was to describe each video clip using the fantasy word.

All trials were self-paced. Each trial ran as follows. First, the experimenter says the new word (e.g., *morken*) which the child repeats. Then the video clip starts; it shows a 5-second still of one shot in the video clip. The experimenter introduces the elements in the scene. For example, one video clip introducing the novel verb *morken* 'mork' shows

Ernie walking onto a pile of books on his hands with his arms stuck in blue tubes. It is introduced as follows, (18).

(18) Hier is Ernie. En een geel boek. En nu komt morken.
'Here is Ernie. And a yellow book. And now comes morking.'

Subsequently, the video clip starts running; each video clip lasts 10-12 seconds. When the video clip is over, the experimenter repeats the new word again and presents an intransitive sentence in the present tense; the new word is the intransitive verb, (19).

(19) Dat was morken. Ernie morkt het boek op.
'That was morking. Ernie morks onto the book.'

The child repeats the new word and the whole intransitive sentence for the puppet assistant. In this way, the subject uses the new verb in an intransitive frame. The repetition not only familiarizes the subject with the new verb; it also indirectly tells her/him that it is an intransitive verb, rather than a transitive one. This was particularly relevant for the [-Agentive] video clips, where one could also use a new verb in a transitive frame, because there is also an external instigator shown in the video clip.

Finally, the experimenter asks the puppet assistant to tell her/him what he saw in the video clip with the use of the new word. The puppet starts a sentence, but gets stuck when he reaches the spot where he must use the new word, (20).

(20) Ik zag dat Ernie het boek op gem-, um, ge-, um, ...
'I saw that Ernie onto the book PFX-m...'

At the end of the puppet's sentence, a past participle of the fantasy word and an auxiliary are missing, prefix *ge-* suggesting the start of a missing past participle. The child then repeats the puppet's sentence and finishes it with a participle and an auxiliary, (21).

(21) Ik zag dat Ernie het boek op gemorkt heeft/is.
'I saw that Ernie onto the book PFX-morked has/is.'

The SOV order of Dutch embedded clauses thus creates a cloze task (a task in which a subject has to fill in the missing part of an incomplete sentence); the child fills in a participle and, crucially for the purposes of the experiment, an auxiliary. The structure of the trigger sentence is sketched in (22).

(22) Puppet: *Ik zag dat* [Subject PP *ge-* ...]
'I saw that [Subject PP PFX- ...]'
Child: ... *ge*-V-t HAVE/BE]

All sentences contain the same grammatical categories: an NP subject, a PP and a verb. The PP plays a role in the derivation of telicity in the [+Telic, -Inherent] conditions by providing a "goal" for the event. In order to avoid ambiguity, the "goal" PPs are all postpositional phrases.[13] In all other conditions, the PP denotes a "location"; it has the form of a prepositional phrase.[14] The trigger sentences (of one of the four versions) are listed in Appendix 2.

At the beginning of each video clip, a yellow dot appears on the screen to focus the subject's attention. In between the still and the running video clip and in between subsequent video clips, the screen goes black to indicate the transition and to allow for a pause, if necessary.

In order to make the subject familiar with the game, she/he was first given some training trials. These also served as a pre-test. The first four training trials used normal, familiar verbs: one transitive and three intransitive ones. Two of these verbs take auxiliary HAVE and the other two take BE. In order to pass the pre-test, the subject had to give the correct auxiliary for at least one of the HAVE verbs and one of the BE verbs. If the subject failed this pre-test, even after one or two additional trials with a normal verb, or if she/he could not do the task, she/he was not run in the main experiment. If the subject passed, two more training trials were presented, now with fantasy words, in order to get her/him used to using fantasy words. At the end of the experiment, there were four more trials with transitive fantasy verbs. These results have not been included in the present study. All sessions were recorded on DAT tapes.

6.5.3 Results

Six of the 4 and 5 year-old subjects failed in the pre-test and did not participate in the main experiment. Another 32 were excluded from further analysis, either because of too large a number of missing responses or because of high error rates.[15] Hence, the results involve 14 4 and 5 year-olds. Of the 7 and 8 year-olds, six were removed for similar reasons, leaving 18 for analysis. Finally, four of the 20 adult subjects were removed.[16]

The results of the experiment are presented in the form of percentages of HAVE and BE choices in each of the eight conditions in the design and for each of the three age groups in (23)-(25). The absolute numbers of auxiliary choices appear in Appendix 3.

(23) Percentages of HAVE and BE choices among the 4 and 5 year-olds (n=14):

		+Agentivity	-Agentivity
+Telic	+Inherent	.79 HAVE .21 BE	.75 HAVE .25 BE
	-Inherent	.54 HAVE .46 BE	.32 HAVE .68 BE
-Telic	+Inherent	.79 HAVE .21 BE	.68 HAVE .32 BE
	-Inherent	.75 HAVE .25 BE	.82 HAVE .18 BE

(24) Percentages of HAVE and BE choices among the 7 and 8 year-olds (n=18):

		+Agentivity	-Agentivity
+Telic	+Inherent	.67 HAVE .33 BE	.58 HAVE .42 BE
	-Inherent	.47 HAVE .53 BE	.22 HAVE .78 BE
-Telic	+Inherent	.75 HAVE .25 BE	.64 HAVE .36 BE
	-Inherent	.83 HAVE .17 BE	.69 HAVE .31 BE

(25) Percentages of HAVE and BE choices among the adults (n=16):

		+Agentivity	-Agentivity
+Telic	+Inherent	.97 HAVE .03 BE	.41 HAVE .59 BE
	-Inherent	.12 HAVE .88 BE	0 HAVE .97 BE
-Telic	+Inherent	.81 HAVE .19 BE	.88 HAVE .12 BE
	-Inherent	.91 HAVE .09 BE	.78 HAVE .22 BE

The HAVE/BE percentages in the tables in (23)-(25) present a first impression of the influence of the factors telicity, inherency and agentivity on auxiliary choice. In order to see globally which factor(s) determine(s) when HAVE is the preferred auxiliary and which determine(s) it for BE, consider in which cells HAVE is chosen more often and in which

BE is chosen more often. In each age group, the preferred auxiliary for all [-Telic] events is HAVE; BE is preferred in some of the [+Telic] cells. In order to see developmental effects, look at the percentages across the tables. Adults use BE more often than the 7 and 8 year-olds and the latter use it more often than the 4 and 5 year-olds; with age, BE comes to be the preferred auxiliary in more cells. Furthermore, one notices that the differences in the pairs of HAVE and BE percentages become larger. Hence, the choice for one of the other auxiliary becomes clearer and more stable by age.

In order to find statistical support for these trends in the data, the results (in their raw form) have been analyzed in a number of different ways (see van Hout et al. in progress). I will present here the results from analyses that use so-called *tree-based methods* (cf. Breiman et al. 1984). Van Hout et al. describe the tree-based method as follows: "Tree-based models are fitted by binary recursive partitioning whereby a data set is split into increasingly homogeneous subsets, until further splitting is statistically unattractive. Cross-validation takes the place of classical significance testing in that it guarantees that the classifications obtained are statistically reliable".

In the case of the auxiliary experiments, the tree-based method determines which factors play a role in the auxiliary choice (HAVE or BE). It not only determines which factors play a role, but also which factors interact and how they interact. The result of the analysis is a classification with various subclasses of verbs defined in terms of telicity, inherency and agentivity. This classification is represented as a tree (mathematically, a graph) with binary splits. The factor that creates the main effect is at the top node; other factors that create secondary effects are embedded on either or both sides of the split defined by the top node. Depending on how many factors play a significant role and depending on their interactions, the tree has more or less structure below its top node. The "leaves" at the bottom of the tree represent subclasses of verbs; each subclass contains one of the two auxiliaries. Hence, the resulting classification tree describes which kinds of verbs take which auxiliary. If only one factor plays a role, the tree has only one node that splits into two subclasses. The more factors play a role, the more structure the tree has and the more subclasses are distinguished.

Separate trees have been fitted for each of the three age groups. The resulting trees are depicted in (26)-(28).[17] The left branch of each split represents the video clips characterized by the minus variants of a certain factor; the right branch represents the plus variants. The auxiliaries at the leaves of the trees (HAVE or BE) represent the preferred auxiliary in that subclass; the percentage below each leaf indicates the percentage of the preferred auxiliary with respect to the other one.[18]

(26) Classification tree for HAVE and BE choices for the 4 and 5 year-olds:

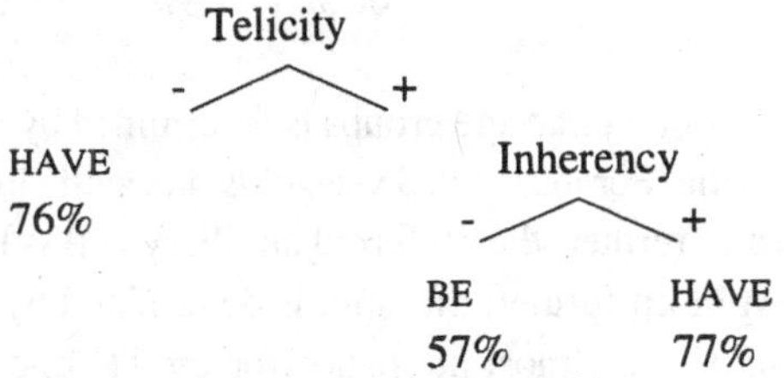

(27) Classification tree for HAVE and BE choices for the 7 and 8 year-olds:

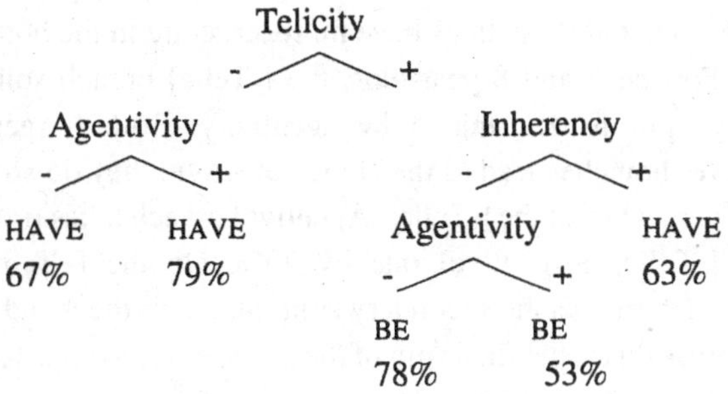

(28) Classification tree for HAVE and BE choices for the adults:

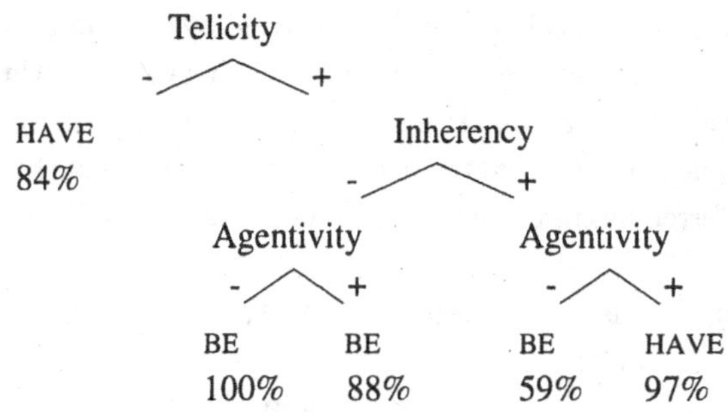

The first split for all three age groups is determined by whether or not the video clip is telic. For the 4 and 5 year-olds, the atelic branch in (26) does not split up any further; the preferred auxiliary is HAVE (76%). The telic video clips split up further; this split is determined by inherency. The 4 and 5 year-olds are almost at chance for the [+Telic, -Inherent] video clips, choosing BE by a mere 57%, whereas they prefer HAVE for the [+Telic, +Inherent] video clips (77%).

The tops of the classification trees of both the 7 and 8 year-olds in (27) and the adults in (28) have the same geometry and splits as the 4 and 5 year-old tree, but these trees have more structure in the bottom part of the tree. For the 7 and 8 year-olds, the [-Telic] branch splits up; this secondary split is determined by agentivity. Both [-Agentive] and [+Agentive] branches lead to the choice of HAVE; they do so in slightly different percentages: the [-Telic, -Agentive] branch takes HAVE by 67% and the [-Telic, +Agentive] one by 79%. On the [+Telic] branch, inherency determines the secondary split, just as in the 4 and 5 year-old tree. Whereas this is the final split of the [+Telic] video clips for the 4 and 5 year-olds, the 7 and 8 year-olds' tree splits up again for agentivity for the [+Telic, -Inherent] video clips. For both leaves, BE is the preferred auxiliary, but in different degrees: it is chosen 78% for [+Telic, -Inherent, -Agentive] video clips and only 53% for [+Telic, -Inherent, +Agentive] ones. Like the 4 and 5 year-olds, the 7 and 8 year-olds choose HAVE for the [+Telic, -Inherent] video clips (63%).

Finally, the adult classification in (28) is very similar to that of the 7 and 8-year olds. On the [-Telic] branch, there is no further splitting; HAVE is preferred (by 84%). On the [+Telic] branch, inherency determines the secondary split. Each of its branches has a further agentivity split. For the [+Telic, -Inherent] video clips, agentivity splits them up only with respect to the percentage of the preferred auxiliary which is BE for both branches: 100% for [+Telic, -Inherent, -Agentive] video clips versus 88% for the [+Telic, -Inherent, -Agentive] ones. At the [+Telic, +Inherent] branch, agentivity determines a distinction between HAVE and BE: BE is slightly preferred for the [+Telic, +Inherent, -Agentive] video clips (59%), whereas HAVE is preferred for the [+Telic, +Inherent, +Agentive] ones (97%).

With telicity as the top split in all trees, notice that the classification trees support the HAVE/BE patterns in the percentage tables in (23)-(25) that also pick up an atelic-telic distinction.

6.5.4 Discussion

In this subsection I discuss the results of the HAVE/BE experiment as represented by the classification trees. Even though classification trees look like grammar flow charts, they cannot be interpreted as such. A tree is a form of representation of the statistical analysis of the results yielded by the technique of tree-based modelling. It cannot be directly transposed into hierarchically ordered grammatical rules for auxiliary selection. Instead, the trees suggest that there are different classes of intransitive verbs and present the factors and the interactions of factors in terms of which these classes can be characterized.

A first observation that deserves attention is the fact that all age groups distinguish two kinds of intransitive verbs; there is a classification of HAVE- versus BE-selecting verbs even for the youngest children. While this result was expected for the adults given that the Dutch adult grammar makes this distinction, one of the main questions of the experiment was to find out whether children also distinguish two kinds of intransitives. The results clearly show that they do. This result was expected in a Strong Continuity approach, but not in a Maturation approach.

Looking at the trees across the three age groups, notice first the similarities. Each tree has telicity as its primary split. Moreover, the top parts of the three trees are very similar: there is a preference for HAVE at the [-Telic] branch of the primary split and there is a further split determined by Inherency at the [+Telic] branch. Furthermore, all age groups prefer BE for the [+Telic, -Inherent] video clips. The [+Telic, -Inherent] video clips are those in which the "goal" PP determines the telicity. Moreover, these video clips were presented with a postpositional phrase containing the "goal", whereas all other video clips were presented with a prepositional phrase denoting a "location". Compare for example *morken* 'mork', (29a), and *kwaren* 'quare', (29b).

(29) a. Ernie morkt *het boek op.*
'Ernie morks onto the book.'
b. Ernie kwaart *in de ring.*
'Ernie quares in the ring.'

The combination of video clip and sentence for the [+Telic, -Inherent] conditions takes away any possible doubt about their aspectual interpretation: they are telic, because the postpositional phrase can only be interpreted as a "goal" phrase. It explicitly names the endpoint of the event and, hence, functions as an event type-shifter. The fact that BE is selected in exactly these conditions across ages is a strong indication that telicity is the determining factor for BE-selection. The only variation across ages is the strength of the BE-preference as suggested by the increase of the percentage of BE's; it grows from 59% for the 4 and 5 year-olds via 65% for the 7 and 8 year-olds to an almost unanimous 94% for the adults.[19] Hence, the role of telicity for BE-selection is present in the grammars of the youngest children in the experiment; its influence stabilizes over time. Assuming that auxiliary choice reflects unaccusativity, this main effect of telicity determining auxiliary selection was expected in the CHESS model.

While telicity is crucial for BE-selection, atelicity determines HAVE-selection, as suggested by the across-the-board preference for HAVE for the [-Telic] video clips at all ages. Like the association between telicity and BE, the association between atelicity and HAVE becomes stronger over age; it grows from 76% for the 4 and 5 year-olds through a slight dip to 73% for the 7 and 8 year-olds to 84% for the adults. Hence, along with the conclusion with respect to telicity and BE-selection, there is a similar conclusion for atelicity and HAVE-selection: both associations are present in the youngest grammars and become more robust in the adult grammar.

Consider next the differences across the age groups. By looking at the geometries of the trees, one may note that both children's groups' trees deviate from the adult classification trees. Moreover, the 4 and 5 year-olds do not have the same one as the 7 and 8 year-olds. Hence, there is a development from 4 and 5 to 7 and 8 year-olds' grammars and from 7 and 8 year olds to adult grammars. Looking more closely at how the trees differ from one another, one sees that the classification becomes increasingly more complex as more factors, in particular, agentivity, play a role and determine more splits. Agentivity is not present in the classification system of the youngest children. It does appear in the 7 and 8 year old tree, but does not make any crucial distinctions there (both [-Telic] branches take HAVE and both [+Telic, -Inherent] branches take BE). Only in the adult tree does agentivity play a distinguishing role, albeit only on one lower branch: at the [+Telic, +Inherent] branch, it splits up a [+Agentive] HAVE and a [-Agentive] BE class. The increasing complexity of the classification trees suggests that while the youngest children make a distinction in two kinds of intransitives, they must further develop their classification system toward the finer-grained target classification. As the adult system has more distinctions than the child's, the child must learn about these additional semantic details. The trees show that the effects of agentivity come in relatively late, that is, later than those of telicity.

Finally, notice that the adult classification tree characterizes four distinct classes of verbs. For three of them, the choice of auxiliary is clear: adults prefer HAVE for all [-Telic] conditions (84%) and for the [+Telic, +Inherent, +Agentive] condition (97%); furthermore, they select BE in the [+Telic, -Inherent] conditions (94%). In a fourth class, however, adults are unsure which auxiliary to select: in the [+Telic, +Inherent, -Agentive] condition, there is only a slight preference for BE (59% BE versus 41% HAVE). This suggests that there are conflicting auxiliary selection rules at work in this particular condition: subjects seem at a loss which rule to follow; roughly, one (large) half decides on BE and the other (smaller) half on HAVE.

In the next section, I will interpret the results of auxiliary selection as a function of telicity and agentivity in light of the issues of unaccusativity and learning unaccusativity.

6.6 General discussion of the unaccusativity experiment

First, I will interpret the results in light of the CHESS model. Next, I will draw some conclusions about learning unaccusativity.

6.6.1 Conclusions for the CHESS model

As discussed in section 6.3, telicity has a central role in the CHESS model; it is modelled as the checking of telic event type features in AgrO. With respect to mapping one-participant predicates, telicity determines a crucial distinction: the argument that identifies the single participant in a telic event moves to Spec, AgrS via Spec, AgrO where telicity is checked off; the argument that identifies the single participant in an atelic event on the other hand moves straight to Spec, AgrS. Movement via Spec, AgrO is unaccusative mapping; movement straight to Spec, AgrS is unergative mapping. Hence, in the CHESS model, an unergative denotes an atelic event, whereas an unaccusative denotes a telic one.

The experiment has tested unaccusativity as a function of telicity and agentivity via the intermediary of auxiliary selection. If auxiliary selection reflects unaccusativity, i.e., if the choice of HAVE reflects unergative mapping and the choice of BE reflects unaccusative mapping, the results show in which ways telicity and agentivity determine unaccusativity. The CHESS model predicts a main effect for telicity and no effect of agentivity, at least in the adult system.

The results show that adults as well as children are sensitive to the semantics of nonsense verbs in choosing an appropriate auxiliary. Assuming then that auxiliary selection is a diagnostic of unaccusativity, this means that both adults and children distinguish unergative and unaccusative verbs in a productive way by means of semantic criteria. Furthermore, the results indicate a main effect of telicity: telicity is the primary split in all trees. Atelic conditions trigger HAVE; hence, unergatives are characterized as atelic. Furthermore, telic conditions roughly trigger BE; hence, unaccusatives are characterized as telic. So, these results confirm the prediction made in the CHESS model that telicity plays the major role in distinguishing unergatives and unaccusatives.

In particular, BE is selected by both groups of children and the adults in the telic conditions in which telicity is determined by a "goal" PP (i.e., the [+Telic, -Inherent] conditions). This result shows that in mapping a one-participant verb onto syntax, both adults and children are sensitive to the event type properties of the predicate, rather than those of the verb by itself. Hence, they employ the operation of event type composition to determine the event type of the clause. This provides support for a predicate-driven approach to mapping as advocated by the CHESS model and contra an individual verb-driven approach which is a central property of argument-centered mapping theories (for discussion of these different approaches, see Chapter 4, section 4.4).

Alongside telicity, agentivity plays a secondary role for the adults, showing up as a distinctive factor in the [+Telic, +Inherent] conditions. This is unexpected in the CHESS model. It is also unexpected on the basis of adult Dutch data with existing one-participant verbs which show a distributional pattern in which only telicity matters for mapping (see section 6.3). Furthermore, not all [+Telic] events trigger the selection of BE; in fact, subjects prefer BE only in the [+Telic, -Inherent] conditions. BE is only just preferred in the [+Telic, +Inherent, -Agentive] conditions and HAVE is selected in the [+Telic, +Inherent, +Agentive] conditions. I will propose an explanation that accounts for these unexpected results.

In order to interpret the role of agentivity in the [+Telic, +Inherent] conditions, recall how these conditions were rendered in the video clips and compare them with the [+Telic, -Inherent] conditions. The [+Telic, -Inherent] conditions are the ones in which the telic character of the event is beyond doubt since the postpositional phrase in the clause that accompanies these video clips can only be interpreted as a "goal" phrase: the endpoint of the event is not only visible in the video clip, but also syntactically explicit. In the [+Telic, +Inherent] conditions on the other hand, telicity can be determined only by interpreting the video clips; there are no linguistic clues that help. Hence, the two kinds of telic conditions differ as to how explicit the telic character of the event is, and, consequently, how easily telicity may be picked up (or, alternatively, how easily it may be missed). In particular, if a subject did not pay attention to the the whole video clip, she/he could miss the telic character of the [+Telic, +Inherent] conditions and would interpret the video clip as an atelic event. In this situation, the subject would select HAVE. This may account for the fact that not all [+Telic] conditions have been classified alike, i.e., with the same auxiliary.

Furthermore, before comparing the [+Inherent] versus the [-Inherent] telic conditions, note that there is another difference between inherent versus derived telic predicates for existing Dutch verbs. The set of inherently telic verbs are represented as such in the lexicon (i.e., with a transition as their basic event type). This set is relatively small as compared to the set of flexible verbs that can become telic via event type composition; the latter set sometimes takes HAVE and sometimes BE, whereas the former set always selects BE. If inherently telic BE-selecting verbs appear as a closed set in the adult Dutch lexicon, adult subjects will be very reluctant to classify novel verbs as inherently BE-selecting verbs, precisely because they are not part of this lexically closed set. In the experiment, however, they are presented with novel verbs that suggest inherent telicity and should therefore get BE. Hence, they are at a loss which auxiliary to select for the verbs in the [+Telic, +Inherent] conditions. In order to solve this problem, they must interpret the verbs that accompany these video clips in a different way, i.e., by choosing HAVE and viewing them as atelic verbs. They may do so by zooming in on an ongoing part of the video clip, rather than on the change of state (that takes place as well). So, in order to avoid adding new BE-verbs to the closed set of verbs, the subject might conceptualize the verb in the [+Telic, +Inherent] conditions as an atelic verb and choose HAVE.

These two reasons explain why both adult and child subjects do not prefer BE across the board in all [+Telic] conditions, but, instead, select BE for the [+Telic, -Inherent] video clips and HAVE for some [+Telic, +Inherent] ones. Still, it does not completely explain the adult classification. Adult subjects make a distinction within the [+Telic, +Inherent] conditions; it is exactly in this branch of the tree that agentivity shows up: whereas HAVE is strongly preferred in the [+Telic, +Inherent,

+Agentive] conditions, there is a slight preference for BE in the [+Telic, +Inherent, -Agentive] ones. For the choice of HAVE in the class of [+Telic, +Inherent, +Agentive] conditions, I assume the explanation that the lexical fixedness of the closed set of BE-selecting verbs blocks classifying a novel verb as a BE-verb and forces the subjects into choosing HAVE. However, for the [+Telic, +Inherent, -Agentive] conditions, subjects do not select the same number of HAVE's; in fact, BE is slightly preferred (59%). Hence, there must be some other effect that sits in the way of a HAVE-choice here.

The effect must be attributed to agentivity, since this is the only distinction between the two kinds of [+Telic, +Inherent] conditions. I suggest that the non-agentive participation of the subject in the [+Telic, +Inherent, -Agentive] conditions creates confusion with respect to the voice of the trigger sentence. Recall the form of the the trigger sentence which subjects had to respond to given in (22); (30) is a trigger sentence for a [+Telic, +Inherent, -Agentive] condition.

(30) Ik zag dat de witte gordijnen achter Ernie ge-bl...
'I saw that the white curtains behind Ernie PFX-bl...'

The trigger sentence in (30) is potentially ambiguous between an active and a passive voice. Instead of finishing the trigger sentence in the active perfect tense (i.e., with *hebben* 'have' or *zijn* 'be'), some subjects may have chosen to finish it as a passive sentence (i.e., with *worden* 'become' or *zijn* 'be'). The latter option is in fact a plausible one given the way non-agentivity was rendered in the video clips: by having an external instigator that gets a non-animate participant going, underlining the non-agentive involvement of this participant. The trigger sentence was intended to be used in the active voice; this was indirectly "trained" by having the subject repeat the presentation sentence with the novel verb in present tense that accompanied the video clip (e.g., (19)). However, there is no way to determine which voice a subject has chosen when repeating and finishing the trigger sentence when she/he responds with BE, since the perfect tense and (perfect) passive auxiliaries are homophonous in Dutch: *zijn* 'be'.

So, the fact that there is confusion with respect to auxiliary choice in the [+Telic, +Inherent, -Agentive] conditions may be explained by the grammatical and conceptual ambiguity in interpreting the novel verbs in these conditions: either as a HAVE-verb in the active voice (in order to avoid expanding the closed set of BE-selecting verbs) or as a BE-verb (where BE is an auxiliary of the passive voice). Note that the latter option is not available in the [+Telic, +Inherent, +Agentive] conditions: as the single participant is actively involved, it is unlikely that the subject misconstrues the trigger sentence as a passive. In this way then, the factor agentivity creates a split in the [+Telic, +Inherent] conditions. However, this split does not reflect a difference in auxiliary choice for intransitives, but, rather, a difference in the possibility of opting for a passive auxiliary which is an option for the [-Agentive] conditions, but not for the [+Agentive] ones.[20]

Notice that the claim that the trigger sentence in the [-Agentive] conditions may be construed as a passive and, hence, trigger passive BE, holds more in general for all [-Agentive] conditions. In fact, the potential ambiguity created by the indeterminacy of the voice of the trigger sentence (active or passive) may also have caused the small percentage of BE-choices in the [-Telic] conditions (16%). Hence, while agentivity indirectly plays a role in auxiliary selection, it does not determine the selection of the auxiliary of an intransitive predicate (in the active perfect tense). Rather, it sets apart those conditions in which the trigger sentence might be construed in a passive voice, i.e., the [-Agentive] conditions, and passive BE may be selected.

This interpretation of the auxiliary choices on the [+Telic, +Inherent] branch of the adult classification tree provides an explanation for the unexpected result that subjects did not select BE in all [+Telic] conditions and for the fact that agentivity determines a split in this part of the classification. Thus, the semantic factors that determine auxiliary choice for one-participant predicates and, hence, unaccusativity, are reduced to just one: telicity.

To conclude, the results from the auxiliary experiment show very clearly that both adults and children split the intransitives into two classes; the split is defined by telicity: atelic events are associated with HAVE; telic events are associated with BE. Assuming that auxiliary selection is an indication of unaccusativity, I conclude that the results support the CHESS model which naturally posits a crucial role for telicity in mapping one-participant verbs onto syntax. Furthermore, the results also show that agentivity does not play a role in determining unaccusativity; this provides counter evidence against an analysis of unaccusativity in terms of this semantic notion (cf. Perlmutter 1978; Baker 1988; Pinker 1989; Levin & Rappaport Hovav 1992, 1995).

6.6.2 Conclusions for learning unaccusativity

Turning next to the results of the two child groups in the auxiliary experiment, what do they suggest with respect to the acquisition of unaccusativity?

Given that there are classification trees for the 4 and 5-year and the 7 and 8-year olds in the first place, the first result is that both groups, including the youngest children, distinguish two kinds of intransitive verbs by way of HAVE versus BE selection. Assuming that auxiliary selection is an indication of unaccusativity, this result supports the Strong Continuity hypothesis which predicts that the unergative-unaccusative distinction is present from the start.

This result is not expected in a Maturation approach. According to the Maturation hypothesis, unaccusatives cannot yet be formed, because children cannot form A-chains (cf. Borer & Wexler 1987). Hence, the prediction is that children cannot distinguish two kinds of intransitives. However, the auxiliary experiment results show that the opposite situation obtains. The conclusion is that children are able to distinguish unergatives and unaccusatives from early on, that is, they do so at the age of four.

Looking more closely at the trees, a next result is the fact that the primary (and, as argued above, the sole) factor is telicity. This result supports a Strong Continuity approach to acquiring unaccusativity in a grammar with a mapping system based on event-semantic features. Event-semantic features are the primitives in the CHESS conditions. Furthermore, unaccusativity is determined by the event type features of one-participant predicates (the atelic-telic distinction). While the Strong Continuity hypothesis predicts that children are able to distinguish two kinds of one-participant predicates from early on, the CHESS model predicts, more specifically, that children are able to classify intransitive predicates in terms of an atelic-telic distinction from early on. Hence, the result that telicity is the primary factor provides evidence in favor of the CHESS model.

A final result is the fact that the percentages of particular auxiliary choices increase over time. Subjects become more and more determined in their preference for a particular auxiliary. This suggests that while unaccusativity is present from the start, the robustness of the grammar grows during the process of acquisition.

6.7 Summary: learning intransitive verbs in the CHESS model

In this chapter, I have discussed a case study of the acquisition of one-participant verbs in the CHESS model. After a brief introduction of the phenomenon of unaccusativity and its syntactic manifestations in Dutch (section 6.2), I presented an implementation of unaccusativity in the CHESS model. One-participant predicates are mapped onto syntax with an argument in the specifier position of AgrS. If the predicate is telic, this argument moves via the specifier position of AgrO which is the locus for checking telicity features; this is unaccusative mapping. If the predicate is atelic, it moves straight to AgrS; this is unergative mapping (section 6.3).

Next, I approached the phenomenon from the point of view of acquisition (section 6.4). How does a child discover that there are two kinds of intransitive verbs and how does she classify the new verbs she is learning? This question is particularly intriguing, since verbs do not wear their classifications on their sleeves. I have compared the scenarios for acquiring unaccusativity under two different development hypotheses: the Strong Continuity and the Maturation hypothesis. Assuming the CHESS model, I have argued in favor of learning unaccusativity under the Strong Continuity approach. This view predicts that the syntactic unergative-unaccusative distinction is present from the start and, moreover, that it is associated with an atelic-telic distinction. The Maturation approach, however, expects no initial bifurcation within the class of intransitives, as the syntactic mechanism (i.e., A-chains) for deriving unaccusative mapping is not present from the start, but, rather, has to mature (cf. Borer & Wexler 1987).

The predictions formulated for both approaches were tested in an experimental study (section 6.5). The experiment was designed to find out whether or not the semantic factors telicity and agentivity determine unaccusativity and how much the child knows about this. Since a verb does not openly show its unaccusative or unergative mapping, the experimental design made use of an intermediary: auxiliary selection. Subjects (Dutch 4 and 5 year-olds, 7 and 8 year-olds and adults) had to provide the auxiliaries for nonsense verbs that described events which they were shown in videotaped movies; the events in the video clips varied in telicity and agentivity.

Assuming that auxiliary selection reflects unaccusativity, the results from the experiment tell about the roles of telicity and agentivity for determining unaccusativity. Hence, one can evaluate the analysis of unaccusativity in the CHESS model, i.e., it is a telic-atelic distinction among one-participant verbs, versus other analyses in which agentivity plays an (additional) role. Moreover, by comparing the results from the children subjects with the scenarios for learning unaccusativity under a Strong Continuity versus a Maturation approach, one can determine which development hypothesis fares best.

The results show that all age groups distinguish two classes of intransitives; the split is defined by telicity. Essentially, subjects select HAVE for atelic predicates and BE for telic ones. Interpreting these results, I have concluded that they present evidence in favor of a mapping model in which telicity is the determining factor in mapping intransitives; they show no role for agentivity. Hence, these experimental results support the CHESS model, which is defined on event type features and equates the unergative-unaccusative distinction with an atelic-telic distinction. As for learning unaccusativity, the fact that all age groups, including the 4 and 5 year-olds distinguish between two classes of intransitives supports a Strong Continuity approach to language development.

Notes

1. The research presented in this chapter is based on joint research in a project on the acquisition of verb-argument structure at the Max-Planck Institut für Psycholinguistik, Nijmegen, I have been engaged in (1992-1995). This project, including my research in it, was supported by grant #WE-1236-2-2 of the Deutsche Forschungsgemeinschaft and the Max-Planck Forschungspreis to Jürgen Weissenborn. My colleagues in the project and co-authors on several talks and papers are Janet Randall (Northeastern University, Boston), Jürgen Weissenborn and Harald Baayen (both Max-Planck Institut during the project; Weissenborn is presently affiliated with Universität Potsdam). Many research assistants have participated as well: Berdine Bodegom, Simone Boezewinkel, Gertjan Hakkenberg, Bianca Hettlich, Bart Hollebrandse, Tamar Israël, Jeannette de Koning, Christina Lamertz, Tina Lieb, Ellis van Lieshout, Nancy Oprinsen, Suzanne Requardt and Colinda Verlinde. I want to thank the schools that cooperated in the experiments: *Pius X* in Steensel, *St. Jan Baptist* in Oerle, *St. Michaëlsschool*, De Bilt and *De Ichtus*, *Zeister Schoolvereniging* and *St. Willibrordusschool*, all three in Zeist. My ideas on unaccusativity and its acquisition have taken further shape during many intense discussions with my co-authors and research assistants and have been sharpened by them. I assume responsibility for the particular form of the proposals on unaccusativity and its acquisition as well as for the interpretation of the experimental results presented in this chapter.
2. Another pair of terms that is used to refer to the two subsets is *intransitive* versus *ergative* verbs, respectively. In this terminology however, the term *intransitive* is ambiguous, since it refers to the complete set of one-argument verbs as well as one of its subsets. Therefore, I prefer the terms *unergative* and *unaccusative* to refer to the subsets, reserving the term *intransitive* to refer to the full set of intransitive verbs.
3. This solution still cannot account for the Italian dialects (cf. Kayne 1993) in which individual verbs vary HAVE/BE-selection according to person. Nor does it account for the fact that there are BE-selecting verbs in German that have further unergative properties, e.g., *laufen* 'walk'; *springen* 'jump'; *fahren* 'drive' (cf. Seibert 1993; Randall et al. 1994).
4. For licensing purposes, it would actually suffice that the argument remains in Spec, AgrO and that an expletive fills up the subject position in Spec, AgrS. However, such a configuration is not manifested (at least, not in Dutch). I have no explanation why this is so.

5. Recall that the CHESS model is designed for mapping non-stative verbs. Hence, the unergative and unaccusative mapping configurations in (11) are only defined for non-stative one-participant verbs; stative and psychological predicates have not been investigated.
6. Different people use different terminology which I have collapsed here in the term *agentivity*. In fact, Levin & Rappaport Hovav (1992, 1995) argue for broadening the concept of agentivity to what they call *internal control* in 1992 and *immediate cause* in 1995. They claim that the latter notion rather than agentivity plays a role in determining unaccusativity, i.e., a verb with an immediate cause or an internal controller is unergative. Events with an immediate cause argument include agentive and protagonist controlled events, but also non-agentive events that are nevertheless "internally caused" (e.g., *sleep*, *snore* and *tremble*), verbs of emission (e.g., *shine*, *ring*, *stink*) and verbs of spatial configuration (e.g., *sit*, *lie*, *stand*).
7. To be precise, Levin & Rappaport Hovav (1992, 1995) broaden the concept of telicity to include all events that denote what they call *directed change*.
8. Thanks to Bart Hollebrandse, who pointed out this consequence.
9. Pinker (1994) discusses and rejects the terms *semantic* and *syntactic bootstrapping* for theories about learning word meanings. Instead, he proposes *semantic cueing of word meaning* and *syntactic cueing of word meaning*, respectively. His original term *semantic bootstrapping* refers to a theory about how a child starts out learning syntax. Pinker argues that certain contingencies between perceptual categories and syntactic categories mediated by semantic categories can help the child get syntax acquisition started (cf. Grimshaw 1981; Pinker 1982).
10. It is not really clear how to transpose the concept of A-chain into Chomsky's (1993) feature checking framework, since the distinction between two levels of representation (D- and S-structure) has disappeared.
11. Alongside this experiment, three more sets of experiments were run: one with German subjects and two others with Dutch subjects (see van Hout et al. in progress).
12. In order to check whether the movies were interpreted in the ways they were intended to, they were semantically "rated" by both adults and children. Unclear movies were adjusted according to the outcome of this rating study (for more details, see van Hout et al. in progress).
13. Many prepositional phrases in Dutch are ambiguous between a "location" and a "goal" interpretation, whereas postpositional phrases are unambiguously "goals".

14. The same experiment was run using prepositional phrases in all conditions, including the [+Telic, -Inherent] ones. Globally, it yielded the same results as the experiment I report here (see Randall et al. 1994; van Hout et al. in progress).
15. A common error pattern was that a subject responded exclusively with *hebben* 'have' or *zijn* 'be' or varied only once out of the 16 responses, after she/he had been correctly varying the auxiliaries with the normal verbs in the pre-test. It is hard to decide whether such patterns reflect the child's "true" auxiliary choices for the novel verbs she/he is confronted with or whether it reflects some kind of a strategy for playing along in the game. An indication that the latter possibility was often the case was the fact that most of these subjects only use one form (the 3rd person singular *heeft* 'has' or *is* 'is') throughout the experiment, even when the subject of the sentence is plural and requires a plural form of the auxiliary.
16. The four adults that were removed used the passive auxiliary *worden* 'become, get' more than once; this was counted as a missing value, since *worden* 'become, get' is not an auxiliary of perfect tense.
17. The trees in (26)-(28) only depict the geometry of the trees. In fact, graphs derived by tree-based modelling are more detailed, as these models not only derive a certain tree geometry but also compute the relative proportions of the reduction in deviance that is brought about by a split at any particular node. This is represented by the length of the lines in the more elaborate graphs (see van Hout et al. in progress).
18. For presentational purposes, I have left out the proportions of HAVE and BE at each intermediate split in the tree which are present in a full tree model (see van Hout et al. in progress).
19. The latter two proportions are not shown in the trees of the 7 and 8 year-olds in (27) and the adults in (28), but are drawn from the full trees in van Hout et al. (in progress) (see note 17). One can obtain them here by calculating the mean of the two BE-proportions at the [+Telic, -Inherent] leafs.
20. In fact, four of the adult subjects were not incorporated in the analyses because they used the passive auxiliary *worden* 'become' more than once. A look at the distributional pattern of *worden* in their data shows that *worden* is selected in [-Agentive] conditions most of the time (of the 33 instances that these four subjects answered with *worden*, 26 were given for a [-Agentive] condition). This confirms the suggestion offered in the text that [-Agentive] conditions allow a passive interpretation, whereas [+Agentive] ones do not (at least, not as easily).

Conclusions

This dissertation set out to review and challenge existing theories on the lexicon and the lexicon-syntax interface. Surveying the syntactic and semantic properties of Dutch verbs in Chapters 2 and 3, in particular, analyzing a verb's flexibility in occurring in several different verb frames (so-called *verb frame alternations*) and the meaning shifts associated with different frames, it turned out that verb frame alternations are determined by event type-shifting. I have argued in Chapter 4 that the lexical primitives a verb is specified for include its event type and a certain number of otherwise unspecified event participants, rather than a set of argument structures, lexical-conceptual structures or subcategorization frames. Instead of defining the interface system between lexicon and syntax in terms of mapping a verb's arguments onto positions in the syntactic configuration, I have proposed an alternative approach. I assume that an event must be syntactically identified; the presence of phrases in syntactic argument positions serves to identify the event or part of the event, as these arguments are interpreted as participants in the event (cf. Grimshaw 1990; Grimshaw & Vikner 1993).

Implementing this view within the Minimalist framework (see Chomsky 1993, 1995), I have claimed that a verb's, or, rather, a predicate's event type features must be checked. Particular features are checked in particular syntactic configurations; specifically, I propose that telic event type features are checked via a specifier-head relation in AgrOP. An argument in the specifier position of AgrO is interpreted as the participant that is involved in the transition that occurs in a telic event. In this proposal, checking the event-semantic structure of the predicate the verb is part of determines whether or not this verb is licensed in projecting a particular syntactic configuration. I have dubbed this approach to mapping *the CHESS model* (*ch*ecking *e*vent-*s*emantic *s*tructure).

Interpretative principles that are defined on event structure, syntactic configuration and morphology yield a semantic differentiation of the verb's event participants. A participant involved in the first subevent of a complex event is interpreted as more agentive than one involved in the second subevent; a participant involved in a non-stative (sub)event is more agentive than one in a state (cf. Grimshaw 1990; Pustejovsky 1991; Davis & Demirdache 1995; Davis 1997, in press; Demirdache 1997). The argument positions in a syntactic configuration, subject and object position, are associated with a particular semantics: if there are two participants in the event, the argument in subject position is interpreted as the more agentive participant than the one in object or oblique position (cf. Emonds 1991a; Borer 1994; Gleitman 1995; Goldberg 1995; Kako 1997, 1998). Furthermore, morphological affixes contribute to the interpretation of the event and its participants (e.g., passive morphology contributes agentivity to an event).

The event-semantic view of mapping as defined in the CHESS model has a number of consequences in which it deviates from standard approaches, circumventing the problems that arise in those approaches. In standard views (e.g., Gruber 1965; Chomsky 1986; Grimshaw 1990; Jackendoff 1990), a verb lexically specifies the semantics of its arguments (in terms of particular θ-roles or lexical-conceptual variables). In the CHESS model, verbs only specify a number of event participants; general interpretative principles take over the task of semantically distinguishing the event participants. Hence, a verb's item-particular information in the lexicon is less detailed and specific. This makes the learning task for the child who must acquire the verbs of her language lighter. Furthermore, defining the mapping conditions in event-semantic terms allows for a correct expression of generalizations across the many different forms of verb frame alternations which were shown to belong to one of only three kinds of alternations (atelic-telic alternations, causative alternations and alternations with alternants presenting different foci on the event). Telic event types require an argument in direct object position; causative event types require arguments in subject and object position. Standard mapping theories cannot express these mapping generalizations, as they do not make reference to event type properties. Finally, while standard models define mapping based on the properties of the verb only, the CHESS conditions are defined on the event type properties of the predicate to which the verb's properties contribute. Event type properties of the predicate, rather than those of the verb by itself, turned out to be crucial for determining the outcome of mapping for one-participant verbs in the unergative-unaccusative alternation (cf. Borer 1994). This fact is captured in the CHESS model, but cannot be accounted for in standard approaches.

Even though I have only discussed Dutch data in this dissertation, the claims I make are suggested to hold more generally across languages, representing universal properties of how Universal Grammar organizes the lexicon and the lexicon-syntax interface. Clearly, the universal nature of the CHESS model needs to be confirmed in other languages. In particular, one would like to know to what extent the telicity and causative generalizations hold in other languages. The predictions the CHESS model makes are straightforward: telic predicates map onto a verb frame with an argument in object position and causative predicates map onto a verb frame with arguments in subject and object positions.

While I have argued extensively that the mapping model does not need to "see" what kind of participants are involved in the event, the set of interpretative principles I have proposed instead needs to be further developed. In the research presented here, I have concentrated on activity verbs only, leaving out stative and psychological verbs. Assuming that there is no semantic specification of event participants in the lexicon, the interpretative principles defined on event structure, syntactic configuration and morphology need to be worked out in finer-grained terms than the rather sketchy definitions I have proposed here, if they are to be applied to all kinds of verbs and account for the interpretation of their arguments.

There is one set of verb frame alternations which I have deliberately left aside in the discussion after having pointed out their existence: alternations such as the dative and the locative alternation in which the alternants present different foci on the event, rather than expressing different event types. Since the CHESS model is defined in terms of event type features, it naturally explains the fact that verbs map onto different verb frames when they refer to different event types. However, it does not offer any explanation as to why different foci on the same event yield different mapping outcomes. The conclusion is that the CHESS conditions as formulated at the moment do not suffice; the model needs to be expanded with more primitives in order to also account for this third set of alternations.

The last two chapters discuss the acquisition of verbs viewed from the event-semantic mapping perspective developed in Chapter 4. The two Dutch case studies involve light verbs (Chapter 5) and intransitive verbs (Chapter 6). These studies represent a first step only; further research has to address other classes of verbs. As of yet, we do not know very much about the process in which children learn the verbs of their language. The little knowledge that is available essentially concerns the acquisition of English verbs; verb learning in other languages has hardly been studied from a generative perspective. One would like to know in which verb frames children use new verbs and whether they vary the choice of verb frames for the same reasons as the adults, i.e., to express different event types. Furthermore, one would like to know if their mapping system is based on the same event type checking conditions as the adult system, or, if it is not, what it is based on instead and how it develops toward the target system. Some of these questions require longitudinal research; others need experimental studies. Acquisition insights such as these are not only relevant for a better understanding of language development and for determining what part of it is universal and what is language specific. Whatever kinds of results will be found in child data, they will also have implications for the theory of the lexicon and lexicon-syntax interface.

Therefore, the ultimate conclusion at the end of this dissertation is that the conclusions that have been reached suggest a research program for both theoretical and acquisition research in which much further work can be done.

APPENDIX 1:

Video Clips in Experiment

Description of 16 video clips in auxiliary experiment (Chapter 6)

For each of the eight conditions in the experiment, two video clips have been constructed that show novel events. Each video clip is briefly described below.

[-Telic, +Inherent, +Agentive]

1. Ernie is moving his mouth and lips making grimaces while sitting on a grey book.
2. Ernie is making scissor-motions with his hands joined in a blue ring behind his back.

[-Telic, +Inherent, -Agentive]

1. A ball and top are jumping around in a saucer after a hand starts the top spinning.
2. A pitcher is dangling on a rubber band while a hand pulls the rubber band.

[-Telic, -Inherent, +Agentive]

1. A man's feet are moving back and forth on a grey floor, twisting in and out.
2. Bert is spinning and dancing upside down on his head on top of a purple box.

[-Telic, -Inherent, -Agentive]

1. A black hat is shuffling around on a book while a hand shakes the book.
2. A chocolate easter egg is spinning around on a dish after a hand gives it a push.

[+Telic, +Inherent, +Agentive]

1. Bert straightens up while turning under a picture.
2. Oscar "melts" into a fuzzy ball on a red carpet.

[+Telic, +Inherent, -Agentive]

1. White vertical blinds turn to form a closed wall next to Ernie when he pulls a cord.
2. A blue balloon empties in Bert's hands.

[+Telic, -Inherent, +Agentive]

1. Bert ends up in a paper bag by "mouthing" his way across the floor.
2. Ernie walks onto a pile of books on his hands with arms stuck in blue tubes.

[+Telic, -Inherent, -Agentive]

1. A red block jumps off of a shovel when a fist hits the handle of the shovel.
2. A yellow block rolls into a house when a ladder is lifted by a hand.

APPENDIX 2:

Nonsense Verbs and Trigger Sentences

The 16 nonsense verbs and trigger sentences in the auxiliary experiment (Chapter 6)

The Dutch nonsense verbs below were used in the experiment. Each has been paired with a particular video clip twice, yielding two different pairings of novel verbs and video clips. The video clips have been presented in two different orders which yielded four different versions in all. The trigger sentences constituted a cloze-task for the subjects (i.e., they had to fill in the missing part of an incomplete sentence); the sentences below are taken from one of the four versions.

1. [+Telic, +Inherent, +Agentive]
   rippen Ik zag dat Oscar op het kleed ger...
   I saw that Oscar on the carpet PFX-r...

2. [+Telic, -Inherent, -Agentive]
   smoeken Ik zag dat het blok het huis in gesm...
   I saw that the block the house into PFX-sm...

3. [-Telic, +Inherent, +Agentive]
   kwaren Ik zag dat Ernie in de ring gekw...
   I saw that Ernie in the ring PFX-kw...

4. [-Telic, -Inherent, +Agentive]
proenen Ik zag dat Bert op de doos gepr...
I saw that Bert on the box PFX-pr...

5. [-Telic, -Inherent, -Agentive]
truven Ik zag dat het paasei op het bord getr...
I saw that the easter egg on the plate PFX-tr...

6. [+Telic, -Inherent, +Agentive]
morken Ik zag dat Ernie het boek op gem...
I saw that Ernie the book onto PFX-m...

7. [+Telic, +Inherent, -Agentive]
flimpen Ik zag dat de ballon in Berts handen gef...
I saw that the balloon in Bert's hands PFX-f...

8. [-Telic, +Inherent, -Agentive]
domen Ik zag dat de gieter aan het elastiek ged...
I saw that the pitcher on the rubber band PFX-d...

9. [-Telic, -Inherent, +Agentive]
ropsen Ik zag dat de man op de vloer ger...
I saw that the man on the floor PFX-r...

10. [-Telic, +Inherent, +Agentive]
plurgen Ik zag dat Ernie op de boeken gepl...
I saw that Ernie on the books PFX-pl...

11. [+Telic, -Inherent, -Agentive]
giepen Ik zag dat het blok de schop af geg...
I saw that the block the shovel off PFX-g...

12. [+Telic, +Inherent, -Agentive]
bluren Ik zag dat de gordijnen achter Ernie gebl...
I saw that the curtains behind Ernie PFX-bl...

13. [+Telic, -Inherent, +Agentive]
klepen Ik zag dat Bert de zak in gekl...
I saw that Bert the bag into PFX-kl...

14. [-Telic, -Inherent, -Agentive]
jalpen Ik zag dat de hoed op het schrift gej...
I saw that the hat on the notebook PFX-j...

15. [-Telic, +Inherent, -Agentive]
melten Ik zag dat de tol en het balletje in de schaal gem...
I saw that the top and the ball in the saucer PFX-m...

16. [+Telic, +Inherent, +Agentive]
trassen Ik zag dat Bert onder het schilderij getr...
I saw that Bert under the painting PFX-tr...

APPENDIX 3:

Numbers of HAVE/BE Choices

The absolute numbers of HAVE/BE choices in the auxiliary experiment (Chapter 6)

In the tables below, the absolute numbers of HAVE and BE choices for each condition and each age group are listed. The answers for the two items of each condition have been added up.

Numbers of HAVE and BE choices of the 4 and 5 year-olds (n=14):

		+Agentivity	-Agentivity
+Telic	+Inherent	22 HAVE 6 BE	21 HAVE 7 BE
	-Inherent	15 HAVE 13 BE	9 HAVE 19 BE
-Telic	+Inherent	22 HAVE 6 BE	19 HAVE 9 BE
	-Inherent	21 HAVE 7 BE	23 HAVE 5 BE

Numbers of HAVE and BE choices of the 7 and 8 year-olds (n=18):

		+Agentivity	-Agentivity
+Telic	+Inherent	24 HAVE 12 BE	21 HAVE 15 BE
	-Inherent	17 HAVE 19 BE	8 HAVE 28 BE
-Telic	+Inherent	27 HAVE 9 BE	23 HAVE 13 BE
	-Inherent	30 HAVE 6 BE	25 HAVE 11 BE

Numbers of HAVE and BE choices of the adults (n=16):

		+Agentivity	-Agentivity
+Telic	+Inherent	31 HAVE 1 BE	13 HAVE 19 BE
	-Inherent	4 HAVE 28 BE	0 HAVE 31 BE
-Telic	+Inherent	26 HAVE 6 BE	28 HAVE 4 BE
	-Inherent	29 HAVE 3 BE	25 HAVE 7 BE

References

Abraham, Werner, 1988, 'Unaccusatives in German'. *Groninger Arbeiten zur Germanistischen Linguistik* 28.

Abraham, Werner, 1990, 'A note on the aspect-syntax interface'. In J. Mascaro & M. Nespor (eds.) *Grammar in progress: GLOW essays for Henk van Riemsdijk*, Foris Publications, Dordrecht.

Abraham, Werner, 1993, 'Ergativa sind Terminativa'. *Zeitschrift für Sprachwissenschaft* 12, 2, 157-184.

Ackema, Peter, 1995, *Syntax below zero.* Dissertation, OTS, Utrecht University.

Ackema, Peter & Maaike Schoorlemmer, 1994, 'The middle construction and the syntax-semantics interface'. *Lingua* 93, 59-90.

Ackema, Peter & Maaike Schoorlemmer, 1995, 'Middles and nonmovement'. *Linguistic Inquiry* 26, 173-197.

Anderson, Mona, 1978, 'NP preposing in noun phrases'. *Proceedings of NELS 8*, 12-21. GLSA, Amherst.

Anderson, Steven, 1971, 'On the role of deep structure in semantic interpretation'. *Foundations of Language* 7, 387-396.

Atkinson, Martin, 1992. 'Introduction'. In Roca (ed.), 1-22.

Bach, Emmon, 1986, 'The algebra of events'. *Linguistics and Philosophy* 9, 5-16.

Baker, C.L., 1979, 'Syntactic theory and the projection principle'. *Linguistic Theory* 10, 533-581.

Baker, Mark, 1988, *Incorporation: A theory of grammatical function changing.* University of Chicago Press, Chicago.

Baker, Mark, Kyle Johnson & Ian Roberts, 1989, 'Passive arguments raised'. *Linguistic Inquiry* 20, 219-252.

Belletti, Adriana & Luigi Rizzi, 1988, 'Psych-verbs and theta-theory'. *Natural Language and Linguistic Theory* 6, 291-352.

Booij, Geert, 1977, *Dutch Morphology: A study of word formation in Generative Grammar*. The Peter de Ridder Press, Lisse.

Booij, Geert, 1992, 'Morphology, semantics and argument structure'. In Roca (ed.), 47-64.

Borer, Hagit, 1994, 'The projection of arguments'. In E. Benedicto & J. Runner (eds.) *Functional projections*, University of Massachusetts Occasional Papers 17, 19-47. GLSA, Amherst.

Borer, Hagit & Kenneth Wexler, 1987, 'The maturation of syntax'. In T. Roeper & E. Williams (eds.) *Parameter Setting*, 123-172. D. Reidel Publishing Company, Dordrecht.

Borer, Hagit & Kenneth Wexler, 1992, 'Bi-unique relations and the maturation of grammatical principles'. *Natural Language and Linguistic Theory* 10, 147-189.

Bowerman, Melissa, 1974, 'Learning the structure of causative verbs: A study in the relationship of cognitive, semantic and syntactic development'. *Papers and reports on child language development* 8, 142-178. Stanford University Department of Linguistics, Stanford.

Bowerman, Melissa, 1978a, 'Systematizing semantic knowledge: Changes over time in the child's organization of word meaning'. *Child Development* 49, 977-987.

Bowerman, Melissa, 1978b, 'Words and sentences: Uniformity, individual variation and shifts over time in patterns of acquisition'. In F. Minifie & L. Loyd (eds.) *Communicative and cognitive abilities: Early behavioral assessment*, 349-396. University Park Press, Baltimore.

Bowerman, Melissa, 1982a, 'Reorganizational processes in lexical and syntactic development'. In E. Wanner & L. Gleitman (eds.) *Language acquisition: The state of the art.* Cambridge University Press, Cambridge.

Bowerman, Melissa, 1982b, 'Starting to talk worse: clues to language acquisition from children's late speech errors'. In S. Strauss (ed.) *U-Shaped Behavioral Growth*, 101-145. Academic Press, New York.

Bowerman, Melissa, 1983, 'How do children avoid an overly general grammar in the absence of feedback about what is not a sentence?'. *Papers and reports on child language development* 22, 23-35. Stanford University Department of Linguistics, Stanford.

Bowerman, Melissa, 1988a, 'Inducing the latent structure of language'. In F. Kessel (ed.) *The development of language researchers: Essays in honor of Roger Brown*, 23-51. Lawrence Erlbaum Associates, Hillsdale NJ.

Bowerman, Melissa, 1988b, 'The 'no negative evidence' problem: How do children avoid constructing an overly general grammar?'. In J. Hawkins (ed.) *Explaining language universals.* Basil Blackwell, New York.

Breiman, Leo, Jerome Friedman, Richard Olshen & Charles Stone 1984, *Classification and regression trees.* Wadsworth International Group, Belmont.

Bresnan, Joan & Jonni Kanerva, 1989, 'Locative inversion in Chichewa: A case study of factorization of grammar'. *Linguistic Inquiry* 20, 1-50.

Brinkmann, Ursula, 1995, *The locative alternation: Its structure and acquisition.* Dissertation, Nijmegen University.

Brousseau, Anne-Marie & Elizabeth Ritter, 1991, 'A non-unified analysis of agentive verbs'. *Proceedings of WCCFL 10,* 53-64. CSLI Publications, Stanford University, Stanford.

Burzio, Luigi, 1981, *Intransitive verbs and Italian auxiliaries.* Dissertation, MIT.

Burzio, Luigi, 1986, *Italian Syntax.* D. Reidel Publishing Company, Dordrecht.

Carrier-Duncan, Jill, 1985, 'Linking of thematic roles in derivational word formation'. *Linguistic Inquiry* 16, 1-34.

Carrier, Jill & Janet Randall, 1992, 'The argument structure and syntactic structure of resultatives'. *Linguistic Inquiry* 23, 173-234.

Carrier, Jill & Janet Randall, 1993, 'Lexical mapping'. In Reuland & Abraham (eds.), 119-142.

Cattell, Ray, 1984, *Composite predicates in English.* Academic Press Australia, North Ryde.

Centineo, Guilia, 1986, 'A lexical theory of auxiliary selection in Italian'. *Davis Working Papers in Linguistics* 1, 1-35. Linguistics Program, University of California, Davis.

Chomsky, Noam, 1955, *The logical structure of linguistic theory.* Ms. MIT. Published by Plenum Press, New York, 1975.

Chomsky, Noam, 1965, *Aspects of the theory of syntax.* MIT Press, Cambridge.

Chomsky, Noam, 1970, 'Remarks on nominalization'. In R. Jacobs & P. Rosenbaum (eds.) *Readings in English transformational grammar,* 184-221. Ginn & Company, Waltham.

Chomsky, Noam, 1972, 'Deep structure, surface structure and semantic interpretation'. *Studies on semantics in Generative Grammar,* 62-119. Mouton, The Hague.

Chomsky, Noam, 1981, *Lectures on Government and Binding.* Foris Publications, Dordrecht.

Chomsky, Noam, 1986, *Knowledge of language, its nature, origin and use.* Praeger, New York.

Chomsky, Noam, 1993, 'A minimalist program for linguistic theory'. In Hale & Keyser (eds.), 1-52.

Chomsky, Noam, 1995, *The minimalist program.* MIT Press, Cambridge.

Clark, Eve, 1993, *The lexicon in acquisition.* Cambridge University Press, Cambridge.

Comrie, Bernard, 1976, *Aspect.* Cambridge University Press, Cambridge.

Coopmans, Peter, Martin Everaert & Jane Grimshaw (eds.), in press, *Lexical specification and lexical insertion.* Lawrence Erlbaum Associates, Hillsdale.

Davidson, Donald, 1967, 'The logical form of action sentences'. In N. Rescher (ed.) *The logic of decision and action.* University of Pittsburgh Press. Republished in D. Davidson (ed.), 1980, *Essays on actions and events*, 105-122. Clarendon Press, Oxford.

Davis, Henry, 1997, 'Deep unaccusativity and zero syntax in St'át'imcets'. In Mendikoetxea & Uribe-Etxebarria (eds.).

Davis, Henry, in press, 'Salish evidence on the causative-inchoative alternation'. In W. Dressler, O. Pfeiffer, M. Pöchtrager & J. Rennison (eds.) *Morphologika 96.* Holland Academic Graphics, The Hague.

Davis, Henry & Hamida Demirdache, 1995, 'Agents and events'. Talk presented at *GLOW 18*, University of Tromso, Norway.

Déchaine, Rose-Marie, 1993, *Predicates across categories.* Dissertation, University of Massachusetts. GLSA, Amherst.

Demirdache, Hamida, 1997, 'Out of control in St'át'imcets Salish and event (de)composition'. In Mendikoetxea & Uribe-Etxebarria (eds.), 355-401.

den Dikken, Marcel, 1992, *Particles.* Dissertation, HIL, Leiden University. Published in 1995. Oxford University Press, New York.

den Dikken, Marcel, 1994, 'Auxiliaries and participles'. Proceedings of *NELS 24*, 65-79. GLSA, Amherst.

Di Sciullo, Anna Maria & Edwin Williams, 1987, *On the definition of word.* MIT Press, Cambridge.

Dittmar, Norbert & Zvi Penner (eds.), 1998, *Issues in first and second language acquisition. Studies in honor of Jürgen Weissenborn.* Peter Lang Verlag, Berlin.

Dowty, David, 1979, *Word Meaning and Montague Grammar: The semantics of verbs and times in Generative Semantics and in Montague's PTQ.* D. Reidel Publishers, Dordrecht.

Dowty, David, 1982, 'Grammatical relations and Montague grammar'. In P. Jacobson & G. Pullum (eds.) *The nature of syntactic representation*, 79-130. D. Reidel Publishing Company, Dordrecht.

Dowty, David, 1989, 'On the semantic content of the notion of 'thematic role''. In G. Chierchia, B. Partee & R. Turner (eds.) *Properties, types and meaning*, Vol. II, 69-129. Kluwer Academic Publishers, Dordrecht.

Dowty, David, 1991, 'Thematic proto-roles and argument selection'. *Language* 67, 547-619.

Elbers, Loeki and Frank Wijnen, 1990, 'Effort, production skill and language learning'. In C. Ferguson, L. Menn & C. Stoel-Gammon (eds.) *Phonological development: Models, research, implications.* York Press, Monkton.

Emonds, Joseph, 1976, *A transformational approach to English syntax.* Academic Press, New York.

Emonds, Joseph, 1985, *A unified theory of syntactic categories.* Foris Publications, Dordrecht.

Emonds, Joseph, 1987, 'The invisible category'. *Linguistic Inquiry* 19, 613-633.

Emonds, Joseph, 1991a, 'Subcategorization and syntax-based theta-role assignment'. *Natural Language and Linguistic Theory* 9, 369-429.

Emonds, Joseph, 1991b, 'The autonomy of the (syntactic) lexicon and syntax: Insertion conditions for derivational and inflectional morphemes'. In C. Georgopoulos & R. Ishihara (eds.) *Interdisciplinary approaches to language: Essays in honor of S.-Y. Kuroda*, 119-148. Kluwer Academic Publishers, Dordrecht.

Emonds, Joseph, 1992, 'Complement selection and the syntactic lexicon: rereading *Syntactic Structures*'. In Tasmowski & Zribi-Hertz (eds.), 215-228.

Everaert, Martin, 1986, *The syntax of reflexivization.* Foris Publications, Dordrecht.

Everaert, Martin, 1995, 'Auxiliary selection in idiomatic constructions'. In L. Nash & G. Tsoulas (eds.) *Actes du premier colloque Langues et Grammaire.* University Paris-8, Paris.

Everaert, Martin, 1996, 'The encoding of the lexical semantic structure of verbs: The case of auxiliary selection in idoms'. In E. Weigand & F. Hundsnurscher (eds.) *Lexical structures and language use*, 27-37. Max Niemeyer Verlag, Tübingen.

Everaert, Martin & Bart Hollebrandse, 1995, 'The lexical representation of light verb constructions'. *Proceedings of BLS 21*, 94-104. University of California, Berkeley.

Fillmore, Charles, 1968, 'The case for case'. In E. Bach & R. Harms (eds.) *Universals in linguistic theory*, 1-88. Holt, Rinehart and Winston, New York.

Fisher, Cynthia, Henry Gleitman & Lila Gleitman, 1991, 'On the semantic content of subcategorization frames'. *Cognitive Psychology* 23, 331-392.

Fisher, Cynthia, Geoffrey Hall, Susan Rakowitz & Lila Gleitman, 1994, 'When it is better to receive than to give: Syntactic and conceptual constraints on vocabulary growth'. *Lingua* 92, 333-375. Reprinted in Gleitman & Landau (eds.).

Fodor, Jerry, 1970, 'Three reasons for not deriving 'kill' from 'cause to die''. *Linguistic Inquiry* 1, 429-438.

van Geenhoven, Veerle, 1996, *Semantic incorporation and indefinite descriptions: Semantic and syntactic aspects of West Greenlandic noun incorporation.* Dissertation, Tübingen University.

Gleitman, Lila, 1990, 'Structural sources of verb meanings'. *Language Acquisition* 1, 3-55.

Gleitman, Lila, 1995, 'When prophecy fails: How do we discard our theories of learning?'. Keynote address at *20th Annual Boston University Conference on Language Development.*

Gleitman, Lila & Barbara Landau (eds.), 1994, The acquisition of the lexicon. MIT Press, Cambridge.

Goldberg, Adele, 1995, *Constructions: A Construction Grammar approach to argument structure.* University of Chicago Press, Chicago.

Grewendorf, Günther, 1989, *Ergativity in German.* Foris Publications, Dordrecht.

Grimshaw, Jane, 1979, 'Complement selection and the lexicon'. *Linguistic Inquiry* 10, 279-326.

Grimshaw, Jane, 1981, 'Form, function and the language acquisition device'. In C. Baker & J. McCarthy (eds.) *The logical problem of language acquisition.* MIT Press, Cambridge.

Grimshaw, Jane, 1987, 'Unaccusatives - an overview'. *Proceedings of NELS 17*, 244-259.

Grimshaw, Jane, 1990, *Argument structure.* MIT Press, Cambridge.

Grimshaw, Jane, 1994, 'Lexical reconciliation'. *Lingua* 92, 411-430. Reprinted in Gleitman & Landau (eds.).

Grimshaw, Jane & Armin Mester, 1988, 'Light verbs and θ-marking'. *Linguistic Inquiry* 19, 205-232.

Grimshaw, Jane & Sten Vikner, 1993, 'Obligatory adjuncts and the structure of events'. In Reuland & Abraham (eds.), 143-155.

Gropen, Jess, Steven Pinker, Michelle Hollander, Richard Goldberg & Ronald Wilson, 1989, 'The learnability and acquisition of the dative alternation in English'. *Language* 65, 203-257.

Gropen, Jess, Steven Pinker, Michelle Hollander & Richard Goldberg, 1991a, 'Syntax and semantics in the acquisition of locative verbs'. *Journal of Child Language* 18, 115-151.

Gropen, Jess, Steven Pinker, Michelle Hollander & Richard Goldberg, 1991b, 'Affectedness and direct objects: The role of lexical semantics in the acquisition of verb argument structure'. *Cognition* 41, 153-195.

Gross, Maurice, 1973, 'Méthodologie de la grammaire générative transformationelle'. In M. Gross, M. Halle & M.-P. Schüttenberger (eds.) *The formal analysis of natural languages.* Mouton, The Hague.

Gruber, Jeffrey, 1965, *Studies in lexical relations.* Dissertation, MIT. Republished in J. Gruber, 1976, *Lexical structures in syntax and semantics.* North-Holland, Amsterdam.

Haider, Hubert, 1981, 'Dependenzen und Konfigurationen'. *Groninger Arbeiten zur Germanistischen Linguistik* 21, 1-59.

Haider, Hubert, 1985, 'Über *sein* oder nicht *sein*: Zur Grammatik des Pronomens *sich*'. In W. Abraham (ed.) *Erklärende Syntax des Deutschen*, 223-254. Gunter Narr Verlag, Tübingen.

Haider, Hubert, 1993, *Deutsche Syntax Generativ.* Gunter Narr Verlag, Tübingen.

Hale, Kenneth, 1983, 'Warlpiri and the grammar of non-configurational languages'. *Natural Language and Linguistic Theory* 1, 5-47.

Hale, Kenneth & Samuel Jay Keyser, 1986, 'Some transitivity alternations in English'. *Lexicon Project Working Papers 7.* Center for Cognitive Science, MIT, Cambridge.

Hale, Kenneth & Samuel Jay Keyser, 1987, 'A view from the middle'. *Lexicon Project Working Papers 10.* Center for Cognitive Science, MIT, Cambridge.

Hale, Kenneth & Samuel Jay Keyser, 1992, 'The syntactic character of thematic structure'. In Roca (ed.), 107-143.

Hale, Kenneth & Samuel Jay Keyser, 1993, 'On argument structure and the lexical expression of syntactic relations'. In Hale & Keyser (eds.), 53-109.

Hale, Kenneth & Samuel Jay Keyser (eds.), 1993, *The view from Building 20: Essays in linguistics in honor of Sylvain Bromberger.* MIT Press, Cambridge.

Halle, Morris, 1973, 'Prolegomena to a theory of word formation.' *Linguistic Inquiry* 4, 3-16.

Higginbotham, James, 1985, 'On semantics'. *Linguistic Inquiry* 16, 547-593.

Hoekstra, Teun, 1984, *Transitivity. Grammatical relations in Government-Binding theory.* Foris Publications, Dordrecht.

Hoekstra, Teun, 1988, 'Small clause results'. *Lingua* 74, 101-139.

Hoekstra, Teun, 1992, 'Aspect and theta theory'. In Roca (ed.), 145-174.

Hoekstra, Teun & René Mulder, 1990, 'Unergatives as copular verbs: Locational and existential predication'. *The Linguistic Review* 7, 1-79.

Hoekstra, Teun & Ian Roberts, 1993, 'Middle constructions in Dutch and English'. In Reuland & Abraham (eds.), 183-220.

Hollebrandse, Bart, 1993, *Dutch light verb constructions*. MA thesis, Tilburg University.

Hollebrandse, Bart & Angeliek van Hout, 1995, 'Light verb learning in Dutch'. In M. Verrips & F. Wijnen (eds.), *Papers from the Dutch-German Colloquium on Language Acquisition*, Amsterdam Series in Child Language Development 3, 65-89. University of Amsterdam.

Hollebrandse, Bart & Angeliek van Hout, 1996, 'Light-verb learning is light verb-learning'. In M. Dickey & S. Tunstall (eds.), *Experimental linguistics*, University of Massachusetts Occasional Papers 19, 261-288. GLSA, Amherst.

Hollebrandse, Bart & Angeliek van Hout, 1998 'Learning light verbs: aspectual bootstrapping'. In Dittmar & Penner (eds.).

de Hoop, Helen, 1992, *Case configuration and noun phrase interpretation*. Dissertation, Groningen University. Published in 1996. Garland Publishing, New York.

Hopper, Paul & Sandra Thompson, 1980, 'Transitivity in grammar and discourse'. *Language* 56, 251-299.

Hornstein, Norbert & Amy Weinberg, 1981, 'Case theory and preposition stranding'. *Linguistic Inquiry* 12, 55-91.

van Hout, Angeliek, 1990, 'PPs and Theta theory'. *Proceedings of the Leiden Conference for Junior Linguists 1*, 49-62. Leiden University.

van Hout, Angeliek, 1991a, 'Deverbal nominalization, object versus event denoting nominals, implications for argument and event structure'. In F. Drijkoningen & A. van Kemenade (eds.) *Linguistics in the Netherlands 1991*, 71-80. John Benjamins Publishing Company, Amsterdam.

van Hout, Angeliek, 1991b, 'How lexical is argument structure? The case of activity verbs'. Talk presented at *Workshop on Lexical Insertion and Lexical Specification*, OTS, Utrecht University.

van Hout, Angeliek, 1992a, 'On the role of aspect in the lexicon: linking activity verbs'. In P. St. Dizier & E. Viegas (eds.) *Proceedings of the 2nd Workshop on the Computational Lexicon*, 132-144. IRIT, Université Paul Sabatier, Toulouse.

van Hout, Angeliek, 1992b, 'Linking and projection based on event structure'. Ms. Tilburg University & Max Planck Institute.

van Hout, Angeliek, 1993, 'On unaccusativity: the relation between argument structure and aspect'. Talk presented at Tilburg University; *GISSL* 2, Girona University; University of Amsterdam; Arbeitsgruppe Strukturelle Grammatik, Berlin; Köln University. Ms. Max Planck Institute.

van Hout, Angeliek, 1994, 'Projection based on event structure'. Ms. Max Planck Institute. In press. In Coopmans, Everaert & Grimshaw (eds.).

van Hout, Angeliek, 1996, *Event semantics of verb frame alternations: A case study of Dutch and its acquisition.* Dissertation, Tilburg University.

van Hout, Angeliek & Marco Haverkort, 1995, 'Bantu applicatives and their Germanic counterparts: A first reconnaissance'. Presented at *Applicative architectures: the 8th Niger-Congo syntax and semantics workshop*, Boston University. Ms. University of Massachusetts & Boston University.

van Hout, Angeliek, Janet Randall & Jürgen Weissenborn, 1992, 'On the acquisition of unaccusatives'. Talk presented at *17th Boston University Conference on Language Development*, Boston.

van Hout, Angeliek, Janet Randall & Jürgen Weissenborn, 1993, 'Acquiring the unergative-unaccusative distinction'. In M. Verrips & F. Wijnen (eds.) *The Acquisition of Dutch*, Amsterdam Series in Child Language Development 1, 79-120. University of Amsterdam.

van Hout, Angeliek, Janet Randall, Jürgen Weissenborn & Harald Baayen, in progress, 'Learning linking? Unaccusativity in Dutch and German'. Ms. Max Planck Institute & Northeastern University.

van Hout, Angeliek & Thomas Roeper, 1998, 'Events and aspectual structure in derivational morphology'. In H. Harley (ed.), *Papers from the UPenn/MIT roundtable on argument structure and aspect.* MIT Working Papers in Linguistics 32, 175-200. MIT, Cambridge.

Jackendoff, Ray, 1972, *Semantic interpretation in Generative Grammar.* MIT Press, Cambridge.

Jackendoff, Ray, 1975, 'Morphological and semantic regularities in the lexicon'. *Language* 51, 639-671.

Jackendoff, Ray, 1983, *Semantic and cognition.* MIT Press, Cambridge.

Jackendoff, Ray, 1987, 'The status of thematic relations in linguistic theory'. *Linguistic Inquiry* 18, 369-411.

Jackendoff, Ray, 1990, *Semantic structures.* MIT Press, Cambridge.

Jackendoff, Ray, 1993, 'On the role of conceptual structure in argument selection: a reply to Emonds'. *Natural Language and Linguistic Theory* 11, 279-312.

Jaeggli, Osvaldo, 1986, 'Passive'. *Linguistic Inquiry* 17, 587-622.

Kako, Edward, 1997, 'Subcategorization semantics and the naturalness of verb-frame pairings'. *University of Pennsylvania Working Papers in Linguistics* 4.2, 155-167.

Kako, Edward, 1998, *Event-related properties in syntax.* Dissertation, University of Pennsylvania.

Kayne, Richard, 1984, *Connectedness and binary branching*. Foris Publications, Dordrecht.

Kayne, Richard, 1985, 'Principles of particle constructions'. In J. Guéron, H.-G. Obenauer & J.-Y. Pollock (eds.) *Grammatical representations*, 101-140. Foris Publications, Dordrecht.

Kayne, Richard, 1993, 'Toward a modular theory of auxiliary selection', *Studia Linguistica* 47, 3-31.

Kearns, Kate, 1989, 'Predicate nominals in complex predicates'. In I. Laka & A. Mahajan (eds.) *Functional heads and clause structure*, MIT Working Papers 10, 123-134. MIT Press, Cambridge.

Keenan, Edward & Bernard Comrie, 1977, 'Noun phrase accessibility and Universal Grammar'. *Linguistic Inquiry* 8.1, 63-98.

Keyser, Samuel Jay, & Thomas Roeper, 1984, 'On the middle and ergative constructions in English'. *Linguistic Inquiry* 15, 381-416.

Kimenyi, Alexandre, 1980, *A Relational Grammar of Kinyarwanda*. University of California Press, Berkeley.

Kirsner, Robert, 1973, 'Natural focus and agentive interpretation: On the semantics of Dutch expletive *er*', 101-114. *Stanford Occasional Papers in Linguistics 3*, Stanford University, Stanford.

Kiss, Katalin É., 1987, *Configurationality in Hungarian*. D. Reidel Publishing Company, Dordrecht.

Koopman, Hilda & Dominique Sportiche, 1988, 'Subjects'. Ms. UCLA.

Kornfilt, Jaklin & Nelson Correa, 1993, 'Conceptual structure and its relation to the structures of lexical entries'. In Reuland & Abraham (eds.), 79-118.

Koster, Jan, 1993, 'Predicate incorporation and the word order of Dutch'. Ms., Groningen University.

Kratzer, Angelika, 1989, 'Stage-level and individual-level predicates'. Ms. University of Massachusetts, Amherst.

Kratzer, Angelika, 1995, *The event argument and the semantics of voice*. Ms. University of Massachusetts, Amherst. In preparation for MIT Press, Cambridge.

Krifka, Manfred, 1989a, *Nominalreferenz und Zeitkonstitution: Zur Semantik von Massentermen, Pluraltermen und Aspektklassen*. Wilhelm Fink Verlag, Munich. (Revised 1986 PhD thesis, University of Munich).

Krifka, Manfred, 1989b, 'Nominal reference, temporal constitution and quantification in event semantics'. In R. Bartsch, J. van Benthem & P. van Emde Boas (eds.) *Semantics and contextual expressions*, 75-115. Foris Publications, Dordrecht.

Krifka, Manfred, 1992, 'Thematic relations as links between nominal reference and temporal constitution'. In Sag & Szabolcsi (eds.), 29-53.

Lakoff, George, 1971, *On syntactic irregularity*. Holt, Rinehart and Winston, New York.

Landau, Barbara & Lila Gleitman, 1985, *Language and Experience*. Harvard University Press, Cambridge.

Larson, Richard, 1988, 'On the double object construction'. *Linguistic Inquiry* 19, 353-391.

Legendre, Géraldine, 1989, 'Unaccusativity in French'. *Lingua* 79, 95-164.

Levin, Beth, 1993, *English verb classes and alternations: a preliminary investigation*. University of Chicago Press, Chicago.

Levin, Beth & Malka Rappaport Hovav, 1992, 'The lexical semantics of verbs of motion: The perspective from unaccusativity'. In Roca (ed.), 247-269.

Levin, Beth & Malka Rappaport Hovav, 1994, 'A preliminary analysis of causative verbs in English'. *Lingua* 92 35-77. Reprinted in Gleitman & Landau (eds.).

Levin, Beth & Malka Rappaport Hovav, 1995, *Unaccusativity: At the syntax-lexical semantics interface*. MIT Press, Cambridge.

Levin, Lori, 1986, *Operations on lexical forms: Unaccusative rules in Germanic languages*. Dissertation, MIT.

Lieber, Rochelle & Harald Baayen, 1993, 'Verbal prefixes in Dutch: a study in lexical-conceptual structure'. In G. Booij & J. van Marle (eds.) *Yearbook of morphology 1993*, 51-78. Kluwer Academic Publishers, Dordrecht.

Link, Godehard, 1987, 'Algebraic semantics for event structure'. *Proceedings of the 6th Amsterdam Colloquium*, 243-262. Institute for Language, Logic and Information, University of Amsterdam.

Macfarland, Talke, 1994, 'Argument and event structure of cognate objects'. *ConSole 1 Proceedings*, 165-182. Holland Academic Graphics, The Hague.

Macfarland, Talke, 1995, *Cognate objects and the argument/adjunct distinction in English*. Dissertation, Northwestern University.

MacWhinney, Brian & Catherine Snow, 1990, 'The Child Language Data Exchange System: An update'. *Journal of Child Language* 17, 457-472.

Manowsky, Jürgen, 1995, 'German middles: a syntactic account'. Ms. University of Massachusetts, Amherst.

Marantz, Alec, 1984, *On the nature of grammatical relations*. MIT Press, Cambridge.

McCawley, James, 1971, 'Prelexical syntax'. In R. O'Brien (ed.) *Monograph series on languages and linguistics: 22nd annual round table*, 19-33. Georgetown University.

McClure, William, 1990, 'A lexical semantic explanation for unaccusative mismatches'. In K. Dziwirek, P. Farrell & E. Mejías-Bikandi (eds.) *Grammatical relations: A cross-theoretical perspective*, 305-318. CSLI, Stanford University.

McClure, William, 1993, 'Unaccusativity and 'inner' aspect'. *Proceedings of WCCFL 11*, 313-325.

McConnell-Ginet, Sally, 1982, 'Adverbs and logical form: A linguistically realistic theory'. *Language* 58, 144-184.

Mendikoetxea, Amaya & Myriam Uribe-Etxebarria (eds.), 1997, *Theoretical issues at the morphology syntax interface, Supplements of the International Journal of Basque Linguistics and Philology*, Vol. XL. Donostia (Spain).

Mulder, René, 1992, *The aspectual nature of syntactic complementation.* Dissertation, HIL, Leiden University.

Mulder, René, & Pim Wehrmann, 1989, 'Locational verbs as unaccusatives'. In H. Bennis & A. van Kemenade (eds.) *Linguistics in the Netherlands 1989*, 111-122. Foris Publications, Dordrecht.

Naigles, Letty, 1990, 'Children use syntax to learn verb meanings'. *Journal of Child Language* 17, 357-374.

Naigles, Letty, Henry Gleitman & Lila Gleitman, 1993, 'Children acquire word meaning components from syntactic evidence'. In E. Dromi (ed.) *Language and development*, 104-140. Ablex, Norwood.

Neeleman, Ad, 1994, *Complex predicates*. Dissertation, OTS, Utrecht University.

Neeleman, Ad & Joleen Schipper, 1992, 'Verbal prefixation in Dutch: Thematic evidence for conversion'. In G. Booij & J. van Marle (eds.) *Yearbook of Morphology 1992*, 57-92. Kluwer Academic Publishers, Dordrecht.

Neeleman, Ad & Fred Weerman, 1993, 'The balance between syntax and morphology: Complex predicates in Dutch'. *Natural Language and Linguistic Theory* 11, 433-475.

Oehrle, Richard, 1976, *The grammatical status of the English dative alternation.* Dissertation, MIT.

Oversteegen, Eleonore, 1989, *Tracking time: A proposal for the representation of temporal expressions in Dutch.* Dissertation, Utrecht University.

Parsons, Terence, 1990, *Events in the semantics of English.* MIT Press, Cambridge.

Penner, Zvi & Thomas Roeper, 1998, 'Trigger theory and the acquisition of complement idioms'. In Dittmar & Penner (eds.).

Penner, Zvi & Jürgen Weissenborn, 1996, 'Strong Continuity, parameter setting and the trigger hierarchy: On the acquisition of the DP in Bernese Swiss and

High German'. In H. Clahsen (ed.) *Generative perspectives on language acquisition*, 161-200. John Benjamins Publishing Company, Amsterdam.

Perlmutter, David, 1978, 'Impersonal passives and the Unaccusative Hypothesis'. *Proceedings of BLS 4*, 157-189. University of California, Berkeley.

Perlmutter, David & Paul Postal, 1984, 'The 1-advancement exclusiveness law'. In D. Perlmutter & C. Rosen (eds.) *Studies in Relational Grammar* 2, 81-125. University of Chicago Press, Chicago.

Pesetsky, David, 1982, *Paths and categories*. Dissertation, MIT.

Philip, William, 1997, 'Review of 'Event semantics of verb frame alternations: A case study of Dutch and its acquisition''. *GLOT International* 2;7, 14-16.

Pinker, Steven, 1982, 'A theory of the acquisition of lexical interpretive grammars'. In J. Bresnan (ed.) *The mental representation of grammatical relations*. MIT Press, Cambridge.

Pinker, Steven, 1984, *Language learnability and language development*. Harvard University Press, Cambridge.

Pinker, Steven, 1989, *Learnability and cognition: The acquisition of argument structure*. MIT Press, Cambridge.

Pinker, Steven, 1994, 'How could a child use verb syntax to learn verb semantics?'. *Lingua* 92, 377-410. Reprinted in Gleitman & Landau (eds.).

Pollman, Thijs, 1970, 'Passieve zinnen en het geïmpliceerd logisch subject'. *Studia Neerlandica* 2, 34-51.

Pollman, Thijs, 1975, *Oorzaak en handelende persoon*. Dissertation, Nijmegen University.

Pustejovsky, James, 1988, 'The geometry of events'. In C. Tenny (ed.) *Studies in generative approaches to aspect*, Lexicon Project Working Papers 24. Center for Cognitive Science, MIT, Cambridge.

Pustejovsky, James, 1991, 'The syntax of event structure'. *Cognition* 41, 47-81. Reprinted in B. Levin & S. Pinker (eds.), 1992, *Lexical and conceptual semantics*. Blackwell Publishers, Cambridge.

Pustejovsky, James, 1995, *The generative lexicon*. MIT Press, Cambridge.

Ramchand, Gillian, 1993, *Aspect and argument structure in Modern Scottish Gaelic*. Dissertation, Stanford University.

Randall, Janet, 1990, 'Catapults and pendulums: The mechanics of language acquisition'. *Linguistics* 28, 1381-1406.

Randall, Janet, 1992, 'The catapult hypothesis: An approach to unlearning'. In J. Weissenborn, H. Goodluck & T. Roeper (eds.) *Theoretical issues in language acquisition*, 93-138. Lawrence Erlbaum Associates, Hillsdale.

Randall, Janet, Angeliek van Hout, Jürgen Weissenborn & Harald Baayen, 1994, 'Approaching linking'. Talk presented at *18th Boston University Conference on Language Development*, Boston; *Langues et Grammaire 1*, Université Paris-8. Ms. Max Planck Institute & Northeastern University.

Rappaport, Malka & Beth Levin, 1988, 'What to do with θ-roles'. In Wilkins (ed.), 7-36.

Reuland, Eric & Werner Abraham (eds.), 1993, *Knowledge and Language*, Vol. II. Kluwer Academic Publishers, Dordrecht.

van Riemsdijk, Henk, 1978, *A case study in syntactic markedness: The binding nature of prepositional phrases.* Foris Publications, Dordrecht.

van Riemsdijk, Henk, 1992, 'Complements, adjuncts and adjacency in phrase structure'. In Tasmowski & Zribi-Hertz (eds.), 498-512.

Ritter, Elizabeth & Sara Rosen, 1993a, 'The independence of external arguments'. *Proceedings of WCCFL 12*, 591-605. CSLI, Stanford University, Stanford.

Ritter, Elizabeth & Sara Rosen, 1993b, 'The status of causer arguments'. *Proceedings of 1993 annual conference of the Canadian Linguistic Association.* Toronto Working Papers in Linguistics, Department of Linguistics, University of Toronto.

Roberts, Ian, 1987, *The representation of implicit and dethematized subjects.* Foris Publications, Dordrecht.

Roca, Iggy (ed.), 1992, *Thematic structure: Its role in grammar.* Foris Publications, Berlin.

Roeper, Thomas, 1987, 'Implicit arguments and the head-complement relation'. *Linguistic Inquiry* 18.2, 267-310.

Roeper, Thomas, in press, 'Inherent binding and the distinction between DP/NP and N''. In Coopmans, Everaert & Grimshaw (eds.).

Rosen, Carol, 1984, 'The interface between semantic roles and initial grammatical relations'. In D. Perlmutter & C. Rosen (eds.) *Studies in Relational Grammar 2*, 38-77. University of Chicago Press, Chicago.

Rothstein, Susan, 1983, *The syntactic forms of predication.* Dissertation, MIT.

Rozwadowska, Bozena, 1988, 'Thematic restrictions on derived nominals'. In Wilkins (ed.), 147-165.

Sag, Ivan & Anna Szabolcsi (eds.) *Lexical matters.* CSLI, Stanford University, Stanford.

Schipper, Joleen, 1994, '*Ont*-prefixation in Dutch: Linking aspect and argument structure'. Talk presented at workshop *Argumentdiathese und Argumenterweiterung: Zur Argumentstruktur komplexer Verben*, Stuttgart University. Ms. OTS, Utrecht University.

Schmitt, Cristina, 1995, *Aspect and the syntax of noun phrases.* Dissertation, University of Maryland.

Seibert, Anja, 1993, 'Intransitive constructions in German and the Ergative Hypothesis'. *Working Papers in Linguistics 14.* University of Trondheim.

Shannon, Thomas, 1988, 'Perfect auxiliary variation as a function of Aktionsart and transitivity'. *Proceedings of WECOL 1988*, Vol. I, 254-266. Department of Linguistics, California State University, Fresno.

Shibatani, Masayoshi (ed.), 1976, *The grammar of causative constructions*, Syntax and Semantics 6. Academic Press, New York.

Simpson, Jane, 1983, 'Resultatives'. In L. Levin, M. Rappaport & A. Zaenen (eds.) *Papers in Lexical-Functional Grammar.* Indiana University Linguistics Club, Bloomington.

Smith, Carlota, 1991, *The parameter of aspect.* Kluwer Academic Press, Dordrecht.

Sorace, Antonella, 1993a, 'Unaccusativity and auxiliary choice in non-native grammars of Italian and French: asymmetries and predictable indeterminacy' *French Language Studies* 3, 71-93.

Sorace, Antonella, 1993b, 'Incomplete vs. divergent representations of unaccusativity in non-native grammars of Italian'. *Second Language Research* 9,1, 22-47.

Sorace, Antonella, 1995, 'Contraintes sémantiques sur la syntaxe: l'acquisition de l'inaccusativité en italien L2'. *Acquisition et Interaction en Langue Etrangère* 5, 79-113.

Speas, Margareth, 1990, *Phrase structure in natural language.* Kluwer Academic Publishers, Dordrecht.

Stowell, Tim, 1981, *Origins of phrase structure.* Dissertation, MIT.

Stowell, Tim, 1992, 'The role of the lexicon in syntactic theory'. In T. Stowell & E. Wehrli (eds.) *Syntax and the lexicon*, Syntax and Semantics 26, 9-20. Academic Press, New York.

Talmy, Leonard, 1985, 'Lexicalization patterns: Semantic structure in lexical forms'. In T. Shopen (ed.) *Language typology and syntactic description 3: Grammatical categories and the lexicon*, 57-149. Cambridge University Press, Cambridge.

Tasmowski, Liliane & Anne Zribi-Hertz (eds.) *De la musique à la patalinguistique: Hommages à Nicolas Ruwet.* Communication and Cognition, Ghent.

Tenny, Carol, 1987, *Grammaticalizing aspect and affectedness.* Dissertation, MIT.

Tenny, Carol, 1989, 'The aspectual interface hypothesis'. *Lexicon Project Working Papers 31.* Center for Cognitive Science, MIT, Cambridge.

Tenny, Carol, 1992, 'The aspectual interface hypothesis'. In Sag & Szabolcsi (eds.), 1-27.

Tenny, Carol, 1994, *Aspectual roles and the syntax-semantics interface*. Kluwer Academic Publishers, Dordrecht.

Van Valin, Robert, 1987, 'The unaccusative hypothesis vs. lexical semantics: syntactic vs. semantic approaches to verb classification'. *Proceedings of NELS 17*, 641-661. GLSA, Amherst.

Van Valin, Robert, 1990, 'Semantic parameters of split intransitivity'. *Language* 66, 221-260.

Vendler, Zeno, 1957, 'Verbs and times'. *Philosophical review* 66, 143-160.

Verkuyl, Henk, 1972, *On the compositional nature of the aspects*. D. Reidel Publishing Company, Dordrecht.

Verkuyl, Henk, 1987, 'Aspect, quantification and negation'. *Proceedings of the 6th Amsterdam Colloquium*, 353-372. Institute for Language, Logic and Information, University of Amsterdam, Amsterdam.

Verkuyl, Henk, 1989, 'Aspectual classes and composition'. *Linguistics and Philosophy* 12, 39-94.

Verkuyl, Henk, 1993, *A theory of aspectuality*. Cambridge University Press, Cambridge.

Verkuyl, Henk, & Joost Zwarts, 1992, 'Time and space in conceptual and logical semantics: The notion of path'. *Linguistics* 30, 483-511.

Vikner, Sten & Rex Sprouse, (1988) 'HAVE/BE selection as an A-chain membership requirement'. *Working Papers in Scandinavian Syntax* 38.

van Voorst, Jan, 1988, *Event structure*. John Benjamins Publishing Company, Amsterdam.

van Voorst, Jan, 1993, 'Against a composite analysis of certain causative constructions'. *Belgian Journal of Linguistics 8*, 145-165.

van Voorst, Jan, 1994, 'De la correspondance en sémantique'. *Folia Linguistica* XXV/3-4, 395-419.

van Voorst, Jan, 1995, 'The semantic structure of causative constructions'. *Studies in Language* 19:2, 489-523.

Wasow, Tom, 1977, 'Transformations and the lexicon'. In P. Culicover, T. Wasow & A. Akmajian (eds.) *Formal syntax*, 327-360. Academic Press, New York.

Weissenborn, Jürgen, 1993, 'Matrix infinitives and economy in language development: Comments on Wexler'. Talk presented at the OTS 5th anniversary conference *The robustness of the language faculty*, Utrecht University.

Whitman, John, Kwee-Ock Lee & Barbara Lust, 1990, 'Continuity of the principles of Universal Grammar in 1st language acquisition: The issue of functional categories'. *Proceedings of NELS 21*, 383-397. GLSA, Amherst.

Wijnen, Frank, 1988, 'Spontaneous Word Fragmentation in Children: evidence for the syllable as a unit in speech production'. *Journal of Phonetics* 16, 187-202.

Wilkins, Wendy (ed.), 1988, *Thematic relations*, Syntax and Semantics 21. Academic Press, San Diego.

Williams, Edwin, 1981, 'Argument structure and morphology'. *The Linguistic Review* 1, 81-114.

Williams, Edwin, 1989, 'The anaphoric nature of θ-roles'. *Linguistic Inquiry* 20, 425-456.

Williams, Edwin, 1994a, *Thematic structure in syntax.* MIT Press, Cambridge.

Williams, Edwin, 1994b 'Remarks on lexical knowledge'. *Lingua* 92, 7-34. Reprinted in Gleitman & Landau (eds.).

Woolford, Ellen, 1993, 'Symmetric and asymmetric passives'. *Natural Language and Linguistic Theory* 11, 679-728.

Wunderlich, Dieter, 1987, 'An investigation of lexical composition: The case of German *be*-verbs'. *Linguistics* 25, 283-331.

Zaenen, Annie, 1988, *Unaccusatives in Dutch and the syntax-semantics interface.* CSLI Report 123, Stanford University, Stanford.

Zaenen, Annie, 1993, 'Unaccusativity in Dutch: integrating syntax and lexical semantics'. In J. Pustejovsky (ed.) *Semantics and the Lexicon*, 129-161. Kluwer Academic Publishers, Dordrecht.

Zubizarreta, Maria Luisa, 1987, *Levels of representation in the lexicon and in the syntax.* Foris Publications, Dordrecht.

Index